AUTO BODY REPAIR

CHILTONS CHILTONS

CEO	Rick Van Dalen
President	Dean F. Morgantini, S.A.E.
Vice President–Finance	Barry L. Beck
Vice President–Sales	Glenn D. Potere
Executive Editor	Kevin M. G. Maher, A.S.E.
Manager–Consumer Automotive	Richard Schwartz, A.S.E.
Manager–Professional Automotive	Richard J. Rivele
Manager–Marine/Recreation	James R. Marotta, A.S.E.
Manager–Electronic Fulfillment	Will Kessler, A.S.E., S.A.E.
Production Specialists	Brian Hollingsworth, Melinda Possinger
Project Managers	Thomas A. Mellon, A.S.E., S.A.E., Christine L. Sheeky, S.A.E., Todd W. Stidham, A.S.E., Ron Webb
Schematics Editors	Christopher G. Ritchie, A.S.E., S.A.E., S.T.S., Stephanie A. Spunt

CHILTON Automotive Books

PUBLISHED BY **W. G. NICHOLS, INC.**

Manufactured in USA
© 1990 W. G. Nichols, Inc.
1020 Andrew Drive
West Chester, PA 19380
ISBN 0-8019-7898-X
0123456789 9876543210

SAFETY NOTICE

Proper service and repair procedures are vital to the safe, reliable operation of all motor vehicles, as well as the personal safety of those performing repairs. This manual outlines procedures for servicing and repairing vehicles using safe, effective methods. The procedures contain many NOTES, CAUTIONS and WARNINGS which should be followed, along with standard procedures to eliminate the possibility of personal injury or improper service which could damage the vehicle or compromise its safety.

It is important to note that repair procedures and techniques, tools and parts for servicing motor vehicles, as well as the skill and experience of the individual performing the work vary widely. It is not possible to anticipate all of the conceivable ways or conditions under which vehicles may be serviced, or to provide cautions as to all possible hazards that may result. Standard and accepted safety precautions and equipment should be used when handling toxic or flammable fluids, and safety goggles or other protection should be used during cutting, grinding, chiseling, prying, or any other process that can cause material removal or projectiles.

Some procedures require the use of tools specially designed for a specific purpose. Before substituting another tool or procedure, you must be completely satisfied that neither your personal safety, nor the performance of the vehicle will be endangered.

Although information in this manual is based on industry sources and is complete as possible at the time of publication, the possibility exists that some car manufacturers made later changes which could not be included here. While striving for total accuracy, Nichols Publishing cannot assume responsibility for any errors, changes or omissions that may occur in the compilation of this data.

PART NUMBERS

Part numbers listed in this reference are not recommendations by Nichols Publishing for any product brand name. They are references that can be used with interchange manuals and aftermarket supplier catalogs to locate each brand supplier's discrete part number.

CONTENTS

ACKNOWLEDGMENTS

Nichols Publishing wishes to express its sincere appreciation to J. P. S. Licari for his contributions in the creation of the Auto Detailing section.

Nichols Publishing wishes to express its sincere appreciation to Marson Corporation, Chelsea, Massachusetts 02150; The Oatey Company, Cleveland, Ohio 44135; PPG Industries, Ditzler Automotive Finishes, Southfield, Michigan 48037; Repair-It Industries, 436-440 Hopocan Avenue, Barberton, Ohio; Larry Speer; Ritt Jones Collision, Prospect Park, Pennsylvania; Silvatrim Corporation of America, South Plainfield, New Jersey 07080 who gave their assistance and expertise in the preparation of the Minor Body Repair section. Original photography by Lillian Harman and Kerry A. Freeman.

Nichols Publishing wishes to express its sincere appreciation to Robert L. Sargent for his contributions in the preparation of the Sheet Metal Repair section. Sincere and grateful acknowledgment is made to the following organizations that supplied copyrighted illustrations and information used in this book or whose material has been re-used from previous editions: Air Reduction Sales Co.; Albertson & Co., Inc.; Applied Power, Inc., Automotive Division; Controlled Systems (Windsor), Ltd.; Fairmount Tool & Forging, Inc.; General Motors Corporation, Fisher Body Division; Guy Chart; Hougen Manufacturing, Inc.; Hobart Brothers Co.; Lenco, Inc.; Marquette Manufacturing Co.; H. K. Porter, Inc.

Sincere thanks to the following firms for their cooperation in furnishing information and material on request: Lenco, Inc.; Guy Chart; Air Reduction Sales Co.; Controlled Systems (Windsor), Ltd.; Fairmount Tool & Forging, Inc.; Applied Power, Automotive Division; General Motors Corporation, Fisher Body Division; Hougen Manufacturing, Inc.; Hobart Brothers Co.; Albertson & Co., Inc.; H. K. Porter, Inc.

Within General Motors Corporation, the help of the following subsidiaries and divisions is acknowledged and appreciated: General Motors Institute, Motors Insurance Corporation, Chevrolet Motor Division, and Fisher Body Division.

We greatly appreciate the contributions of E. D. Hougen, M. B. Nelson, H. O. Swanson, John C. Pursell, E. E. Smith, Uriel Hoskins, Keith Willoughby, Morris D. Thomas, Neil Lucey, Willard Duddles, Morley Wiederhold, and R. J. Kakuska, Warren Bok, Douglas Hammond, Guy Chartier, E. R. Maynerick, David Fleming, Wilson Burry, Frank Flynn, Robert Hamlyn, Edward Vatcher, and Dermont Linegar, who have been very helpful in the preparation of this edition.

Auto Detailing

WASHING THE VEHICLE

The importance, to the detailer, of properly washing the vehicle before attempting "cosmetic restoration" cannot be over emphasized. For some, it will require a relearning of what you assumed was a basic task. Washing the car is more than just slopping soap all over it and squirting it clean with a hose. It's hard work and, done properly, result in an efficient first step to a great detail.

A great deal of time can be saved in this aspect of detailing. For instance, if you do not adequately remove road tar from the car prior to buffing you will end up smearing the tar into the paint during the buffing process. It will then be much more difficult to remove and waste time and compound. Further, it will be a source of irritation which will put you in the wrong frame of mind to work on that valuable car. Irritation and frustration over minor mistakes has a way of snowballing. Performing each task at the right time with the right chemicals will avoid these problems.

This plan of action should be a guide. Adapt it as you see fit, so that it fits the way you work best. The important thing is to have a plan.

Steps in Washing the Vehicle

NOTE: *On specialty vehicles, like trucks and vans, or motorcycles you will need to adapt this list to include the peculiarities that relate to these vehicles. If the vehicle you are detailing does not have a vinyl top, for instance, then you can obviously omit this from your list.*

1. **REMOVE ALL GREASE AND ROAD TAR FROM EXTERIOR SURFACES:** as explained, in the example above, you can save a good deal of time and material by doing this step correctly. In the "Products" section you will find what works best and how to use the best and least expensive materials to remove road tar. Read this section before you start. If you do not remove tar first you will probably pick some up on your car wash sponge and smear it all over the car. Further, when you do soap the car, you will remove small specs of tar and any residue from the tar remover.

2. **APPLY ENGINE DEGREASER AND ALLOW TO PENETRATE:** at this point you should spray engine degreaser on the engine, which should be slightly warm, and give it a few minutes to work. This is not the time to take a coffee break though. You don't want the degreaser to stay on too long as it will evaporate. You have just

enough time to clean the wheels, tires, and vinyl top before you power-hose the engine degreaser from the engine compartment.

3. **CLEAN WIRE WHEELS, MAGS OR HUB CAPS:** there are special products available from local parts retailers for whichever type of wheel you are working on. Most of these work best sprayed on dry surfaces. So apply your chemicals to the wheels and wait to hose them off until after you have cleaned the tires.

4. **CLEAN TIRES (WHITEWALLS OR BLACKWALLS):** whether your car has blackwalls or whitewalls makes no difference since, both must be cleaned and you can use the same products. Usually tire cleaners work best on dry tires so that the cleaner is not diluted by the water on the tire. Clean the whole tire from the rim up to the tread. After you have cleaned the whole tire, power-hose the rubber part and whatever you have applied to the wheels (rims or hub caps).

5. **SCRUB VINYL TOP:** use the right chemicals diluted as the manufacturer suggests, and the right scrubber or brush recommended by the manufacturer. Confine your cleaners to the vinyl surface and do not get any cleaner on the painted surfaces since, it may stain. Next, power hose the top until all of the cleaner has been washed off.

6. **WET THE WHOLE VEHICLE:** you want to make certain that the car is wet before you power-hose the engine compartment. The reason for this is that some degreaser may splash out of the engine compartment, while power hosing, and permeate the paint on the fenders leaving a permanent stain.

7. **REMOVE ENGINE DEGREASER WITH A POWER HOSE:** a power hose, one that combines both water and air under pressure, works best here but, you can also use your garden hose if you adjust it for a stiff spray and use a brush to loosen what the hose misses. Make sure you again hose off the fenders and anywhere else stray engine degreaser may have landed. If you don't, you will smear engine degreaser all over the car when you sponge it with car soap.

8. **SOAP THE VEHICLE:** mix your car wash soap as directed and spread it all over the car. Soap the wheels, tires, doorjambs, trunk and hood jambs, vinyl top, headlights and taillights, and chrome. This will insure that any residue left from previously used cleaning agents will be completely removed. Remember that car wash soap will remove any wax from the painted surfaces so you will have to wax the car after you use a detergent to wash it.

9. **RINSE THE VEHICLE COMPLETELY:** do not allow the soap to dry on the windows or painted areas of the car. Rinse well, including the fender wells, until clear water is all that remains on the vehicle.

10. **CHAMOIS DRY INCLUDING WINDOWS AND CHROME:** Do not leave any water spots as these are difficult to remove when they dry. Dry the windows, chrome, hood, trunk and door jambs with a chamois cloth.

11. **APPLY TOUCH-UP PAINT:** now that the car is clean you can see all of the defects that need your attention. Refer to the section on "Touch-Up Paint" or to the sections on painting in other sections of the manual. Touching up now will give the paint a chance to dry before you run a buffer over the repaired area.

INTERIOR

Most detailers hate to do interiors. It's a lot like getting on your knees, in the kitchen, to scrub the floor. But, you might as well get used to it because, if you don't do it, you'll realize that you have made a mistake because, after the exterior has been detailed the interior looks worse by contrast.

Here again, the "ZONAL" approach to detailing works best. Get one section done, close it up and go on to another section. Avoid areas that have been detailed so that you avoid duplication of effort.

Steps in Cleaning the Interior

1. **VACUUM TRUNK, WIPE ALL SURFACES AND SHAMPOO CARPET:** let's get the trunk out of the way so we can forget it. Clean the spare by removing it from the car and use tire cleaner as you would a tire mounted on the car. Wipe all inside surfaces with a damp then dry cloth. Shampoo the inside surfaces with a damp then dry cloth. Shampoo the carpets and, if need be, spray the carpet with carpet dye or semi-flat paint. Dress the spare with rubber dressing and return it to the trunk. Organize whatever you keep in the trunk into boxes or plastic bags. Wipe the trunk jamb after you have dressed the trunk weatherstrip with rubber dressing. Close the trunk and forget it (until your final inspection).

2. **VACUUM SEATING AREA CARPET, ASHTRAYS, HEADLINER AND DOOR PANELS:** be thorough on this one. Vacuum under the seats as you move the front seats forward and back on their tracks. Vacuum ashtrays and remove them from the car to be washed. Vacuum sun visors and map pockets too. If equipped, vacuum the rear shelf (the area behind the rear seat and up to the rear window). It is best to vacuum before you shampoo so that you don't create mud when you shampoo over dirt that may be in the carpets. You should re-vacuum after you shampoo the seats.

3. **APPLY SPOT REMOVER TO UPHOLSTERY STAINS:** after you have vacuumed, you will be in a better position to see any subtle stains on the seats and carpets. Apply the spot remover now so that it will have time to work before you shampoo the seats and carpet.

Check the section on "Stain Removal" before you do anything with stains.

4. **SCRUB VINYL SURFACES:** use the chemicals and scrubbers recommended in the "Products" section and clean all vinyl including seats, armrests, door panels, visors, dashboards, and trim. Wipe with a clean dry cloth. Do this now, so that the vinyl dressing we apply will have time to dry.

5. **DRESS VINYL TOP:** while you have the vinyl dressing rag or sponge in your hand do the vinyl top. This will keep you from getting dressing on your hands twice (some of it is difficult to remove). Further, wax and compound splattered on the vinyl top during buffing will be easier to remove if the top has been dressed.

6. **CLEAN WINDOWS AND MIRRORS:** first, scrape off any unwanted window stickers with a window scraper. The remaining glue can be removed with a chemical intended for this purpose, or with an all-purpose, non-abrasive cleaner or alcohol. To clean windows and mirrors I suggest you use newspapers (as opposed to paper towels) as they cut through nicotine better and leave a gloss on the windows.

7. **SHAMPOO CARPETS, SEATS, HEADLINER AND DOOR PANELS:** be careful not to scrub any vinyl trim or you will remove the dressing that you applied earlier. Start with the headliner then do the seats. Next scrub the carpets and, finally, the door panels. Do not oversoak when shampooing as it will take hours before the seats are dry enough to sit on them. This is one of the reasons why you do the interior before the exterior. After shampooing vacuum the seats and carpets again. Wipe any stray shampoo from the vinyl surfaces and glass. Use the shampoo to again clean the door jambs. Wipe them dry with a clean cloth. You can also use the shampoo to wash the ashtrays (remember to wipe them dry) and floormats. Do not put floormats on top of damp carpets or you will get a musty smell.

8. **CLEAN INTERIOR METAL TRIM AND DASHBOARD PLASTIC:** use window cleaner on the lenses that cover the instrument panel (gauges) and chrome cleaner on real metal parts like the shift lever, turn signal indicator, door handles and window riser handles. Wipe any remaining residue from the previous operations.

9. **DEODORIZE:** you can use commercial products that are sprayed on the carpets. Shampooing removes a large amount of foul odors but, you want something that lasts. A bar of soap works well. First, cut the paper off the tip side of your favorite body soap then place it under the front seat. It lasts a long time.

EXTERIOR

Now that the drudgery of the interior is over we can finally get to the fun part of the detail. After scrubbing carpets, you can now get to the part that makes the exterior look great. In keeping with the "ZONAL" approach, the trunk, hood and interior should all be completed. Make sure you have rolled up the windows.

Steps in Completing the Exterior

1. **APPLY CHROME CLEANER TO BUMPERS AND ALL BRIGHTWORK:** do this now, so that you can get the tedious work out of your way. Another reason is that some chrome cleaners take some time to dry completely. If it's not completely dry it is hard to remove. Apply chrome cleaner to bumpers, grills, window moldings, wheel lip moldings, door handles and anything else made of chrome. You can also use chrome cleaner on stainless steel (like the roof of a Cadillac Eldorado Biaritz) but, a can of cleaner intended especially for stainless steel will work better.

2. **BUFF PAINTED SURFACES:** first read the section on "Using the Buffer". Also see Step 9, "Dressing the Engine Compartment" to see which you want to do first. On some vehicles you may have to buff as many as three or four times. Caution is the name of the game. One burn mark can ruin the whole job. Some chrome cleaner will be removed as you buff. That's OK it will save you from removing it by hand.

3. **WIPE ALL BUFFING RESIDUE:** the section on "Using the Buffer" advises not to try to remove all of the compound or wax with the buffer and that some residue be left in corners and around moldings. This would be best removed by hand. Now is that time. Use a very soft, clean rag and avoid removing the chrome cleaner until you have removed all of the wax from the painted surfaces. Use a separate rag to remove chrome cleaner because, some chrome cleaners contain an abrasive that will scratch painted surfaces.

4. **USE A DETAIL BRUSH AROUND MOLDINGS AND CREVICES:** a detail brush is the only way to remove wax from tight areas like emblems and moldings. If you don't do this step, the final detail will look unprofessional. Keep a rag in your other hand to wipe up areas that have been smeared by the detail brush.

5. **WIPE HOOD, TRUNK AND DOOR JAMBS ONE MORE TIME:** the buffer will splatter residue into these jambs and they must be wiped clean one last time. On the hood area make sure you wipe the sides of the hood and the inside (engine compartment side) of the fenders.

6. **REMOVE CHROME CLEANER:** this part is saved for last partly because it is so tedious. Use a different rag than you did when you wiped the painted surfaces down and keep your detail brush handy.

7. **DRESS TIRES AND ALL BODY RUBBER:** do this now so that the product will have time to dry before you drive the car out. After spraying on tires make sure you wipe the wheels clean. Apply it to body side moldings by spraying onto a rag or sponge first. Then wipe on the molding. If equipped, apply to bumper rub strips. You can also wipe on all door weatherstripping for a super appearance. This also keeps the rubber pliable. Most rubber looks best dressed twice.

8. **CLEAN OUTSIDE WINDOWS AND MIRRORS:** as recommended, for inside windows, use newspapers since the ink, from the newsprint, leaves a nice sheen on the glass. Doing it now will also remove any splashed wax or compound on the glass. Also do the headlights and taillights again.

9. **DRESS ENGINE COMPARTMENT:** this puts the finishing touch under the hood. Be careful not to get overspray on the fenders. This can be done prior to buffing so that, if you get overspray on the fenders, you can buff it off. Usually the engine takes a long time to dry since water from the power-hosing procedure forms puddles. You can speed this up by drying up the puddles with compressed air, if you have a compressor, or with rags if you don't have a compressor. It's up to you whether you dress before or after buffing.

You're not done yet! Read on.

REVIEW

CRITICALLY INSPECT THE VEHICLE: have your detail brush and a rag handy. Use the "Summary Plan of Action" as a checklist to make sure everything has been done and, done right. Spend some time with your review. Even the slightest missed item is magnified many times by comparison to the rest of your clean car. Detailing also includes protection. That is, coating all surfaces with wax or dressing to prolong life.

A properly detailed car glows. Does your car glow?

EQUIPMENT

It is vital that you use the right equipment. It is more than a matter of saving time, it's also important to insure quality work. Not everyone has an unlimited budget that they can spend on all of the equipment recommended. Use some judgement and try to prioritize within your budget. For instance, do without a compressor and power hose but, do not avoid buying a buffer. If you can find a substitute, that's cheaper and you're on a tight budget, then buy it. You can use your garden hose, instead of the power hose. You may take more time and work a little harder but, you can get by. But you cannot do a quality detail job without a buffer. Do not rely on your ¼ in. drill equipped with a buffing attachment. This will make more of a mess than you can correct.

Beware of miracle products and equipment. Scrubbing an interior, by hand, with a scrub brush often works better and is more efficient than a steam cleaning upholstery machine.

So, avoid the simple solutions, especially if they cost a lot of money. In the beginning, when funds are low, all you can do is swap labor for your lack of money. If you can do the job by hand, don't buy a machine.

Recommended Equipment

You might expect that you need to purchase most of your equipment from specialty suppliers. Quite the contrary is true. While you need to buy a few things from detail supply houses, most of your needs can be filled at local automotive retailers.

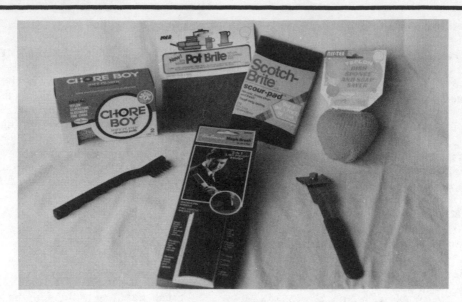

Detail supplies

Here's what you'll need:

PLASTIC SCRUBBERS: these are marketed under brand names. They are strips of nylon spun together to look like a birds nest. They work well for removing grease and tar from auto exteriors. Even though stiff, they do not scratch the paint noticeably unless you stay in one spot too long or rub too hard. What small scratches do appear are easily removed when buffing.

STEEL WOOL: this product has many uses for the detailer. Use them to remove scuff marks on whitewalls, chrome cleaning, window cleaning and for removing paint overspray. There are many grades of steel wool but, "0000" and "00" grits are the best. Use the coarser "00" when you don't have to be concerned with scratching.

SCOURING PADS: Get pads that are not to coarse. The best applications for these are to scrub vinyl seats, dashboards and tops. Never use them dry as the will scratch the vinyl. They can be washed out and reused many times.

SPONGES: several are required to do the job properly. Buy a large natural sponge for car washing. Synthetics are OK but, they don't last as long. Buy synthetics for applying vinyl dressing and rubber dressing because they are cheaper and will need to be discarded after a few washings. Always wash immediately after use. You can also use a sponge to apply hand waxes. Cut them to size.

LINT BRUSH: nothing looks worse than dog hair and lint on velour seats. No matter how clean you get the seats, from shampooing, if you have lint all over them they look terrible.

BRUSHES: good brushes are the essence of a good detail job. For whitewalls, a stiff brass bristle brush is best. These can be purchased in the auto parts stores. To break up caked-on grease in the engine compartment, use a long handle, stiff bristled brush with a small head so that it can fit in tight spots. For vinyl tops that have a coarse grain a scouring pad may not clean completely.

Use a stiff nylon bristle brush. To remove wax residue from around moldings, emblems, cracks and crevices buy a good "detail" brush. Some people use old tooth brushes but, they are just too soft to do a good job and they wear out quickly. To scrub carpets and seats you will need a stiff brush that fits comfortably in the palm of your hand. You can buy inexpensive kitchen floor scrubbing brushes at the hardware store but, you are much better off buying a good contoured brush that will eliminate hand fatigue. Buy some cheap artists paint brushes for touch up work. Don't bother trying to clean them as they will disintegrate in your hands. An old house paint brush works well to apply paste compound prior to buffing.

CHAMOIS: for wiping windows, paint and chrome, after washing, you can't beat a natural skin chamois. There are a lot of synthetics on the market that all claim to be more absorbent than a natural chamois, but a natural skin chamois is best. Follow the manufactures instructions for care and it will last a long time. Dropping a chamois on the ground or using it to wipe grease will ruin it.

RAGS: you will need tons of these. Soft cotton rags are the best for all around use. Wash them several times before using it for the first time. This breaks down the fibres and makes them softer, like pre-washed jeans.

WET/DRY VACUUM: you can't do the job without one. There are may types on the market. Buy one that is wet/dry and that you can use either way without having to remove a filter. Smaller than a 5–7 gallon size is best because, when full, they are lighter. Another reason is that with larger sizes the hoses are more rigid and harder to maneuver. Make sure you have the crevice nozzle, as this is especially good for ashtrays and between seats.

SPRAY BOTTLES: finding good ones is a chore. Some of the chemicals like, wire wheel acid, devours the plastic pumps on some bottles so, shop around for good ones. You will need several. Use one for whitewall tire cleaners, wire wheel cleaner, engine degreaser, window cleaner, vinyl cleaner, and deodorizer. Some products

Detail brush

like, vinyl and rubber dressing are easy to apply from a spray bottle but, since these products harden when they dry, they clog the sprayers.

SQUIRT BOTTLES: you can buy the cheap ketchup and mustard bottles at your supermarket or you can use anything like, shampoo or conditioner bottles, that you may find around your hose. Use them to hold spot removers, waxes, compounds, vinyl and rubber dressings and anything else that does not perform well in a spray bottle.

RAZOR BLADES AND SCRAPERS: single edge razor blades are useful for removing window stickers, glue, tree sap from windows and many other uses. You should get several different types of scrapers. Short handle scrapers have their uses and can be picked up in hardware stores. Get the retractable type since, they are safer. Long handle scrapers can be obtained from a detail supply house and are especially useful for getting at hard to reach window stickers.

RECHARGEABLE SCRUBBERS: while they are not absolutely required they will make your life easier. I find that they work well on cloth headliners and on rough grained vinyls (seats and tops). They leave swirl marks which gives the interior a just scrubbed look.

PLASTIC PAILS: you will need at least two, preferably the five gallon size. One is for car wash soap and the other is for interior shampoo. It would help if you had a few more for carpet dye and other uses. If you buy chemicals, in bulk, you will accumulate many of these—at no charge.

BUFFERS: To perform professional quality details you need one. As stated previously, don't think you can get by using your ¼ in. drill with a buffing attachment. It just won't work. Price should not be the determining factor in your selection. Visit several auto parts stores. Ask the salesman for his recommendations. Whatever style you choose the most important factor is durability. If you buy a cheap one and the motor burns out with the first use, you have wasted your money. From an rpm

standpoint, the ideal buffer rotates at 1750 rpm—no load speed. Faster buffers will burn the paint. Slower ones will not do a good job of cleaning the paint.

There are three types of buffers in general use; rotary, orbital and dual pad orbital. They each have their benefits and drawbacks.

1. **Rotary:** this is the best choice for all around use. With a 9 in. pad it is the best set up for compounding and polishing. You can cover large areas in a short time and pads are easier to get and less expensive than other types. Not handled properly however, you will experience swirl marks and burns.

2. **Orbital:** these are easy to use and it is difficult to burn with this type of buffer. The reason is that they move slowly, which is also a big disadvantage since it takes longer to buff a car as with the rotary. Pads are easy to clean, but expensive to buy. This type is also good for getting rid of swirl marks on some cars.

Rotary buffer

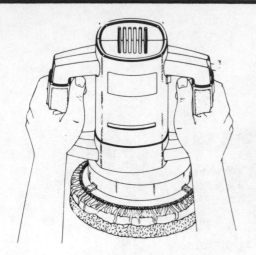

Orbital buffer

3. **Dual Pad Orbital:** These are easier on your body, because they are light and small but, they are not heavy enough to adequately clean the paint. Their main advantage is that they do not leave swirl marks. The main disadvantages are that it is so slow and pads are a unique size. As such, they are difficult to locate and expensive.

Dual pad orbital buffer

NOTE: *whichever type of machine you buy make sure you perform the periodic maintenance suggested by the manufacturer. Buffing pads give off a good deal of "fuzz" which clogs the machines, brushes, and switches. These must be cleaned often to prolong the life of the machine.*

HAND TOOLS: keep that screwdriver handy. You should have a slotted and a phillips head screwdriver nearby to tighten trim screws around the vehicle. A droopy sun visor can detract from an otherwise great appearance. A putty knife is handy for scraping off globs of tar and for removing old body side molding. A utility knife is important for trimming new body side molding, trimming shredded carpet and many other uses.

ROLLING CART OR TRAY: It is advantageous to have all of your supplies, equipment and tools organized near the car you are detailing. There are two methods I have used: plastic tray and roll-about cart. The plastic tray can be purchased at automotive or hardware stores and resembles a tool tote tray. Usually they are made of a tough plastic and can carry most of your detailing needs. The cart is also a nice way to go because you can fit alot of things on it, including your buffer, and you don't have to lift it. Just wheel it around to where it is needed. A strong carboard box or an old milk crate makes a good substitute.

POWER HOSE OR JET GUN: these go under many names but, the idea is the same, water under pressure. Generally they require a compressor of from one to two horsepower. An air line is attached to the compressor and joined at the power hose with a water line. These are especially good to break up the grease build-up in an engine compartment and for cleaning wheel wells. The cost of the power hose is well worth it. An alternative is to drive the car over to a coin operated car wash to spray the engine clean. Bring your own engine degreaser and just use the power hose for the pressured water. There are other, less expensive, power hoses that work without a compressor, and should also be given consideration. Shop around.

WATER HOSE: buy the more expensive rubber hose. They stay flexible, even in cold weather, and seem to never wear out.

EXTENSION CORDS: these are a must for the buffer and any other electrical tools you may use. Buy a good quality, three-wire grounded cord in suitable lingth.

EQUIPMENT CHECKLIST

Quality will vary depending on how often you detail your own vehicle, and how mush money you want to save by buying in larger quantities.

2   Plastic Scrubbers
2   Scouring Pads
2   Sleeves Steel Wool — 0000
2   Sleeves Steel Wool — 00
1   Car Wash Sponge
1   Sponge for Vinyl Dressing
1   Sponge for Rubber Dressing
2   Extra Sponges
1   Lint Brush
1   Whitewall Tire Brush
1   Engine Cleaner Brush
1   Vinyl Top Brush
1   Detail Brush
1   Carpet and Upholstery Brush
    Artists' Paint Brushes
1   Chamois
    Cotton Rags

1 Wet/Dry Vacuum
   Spray Bottles (1 qt size)
   Squirt Bottles.
   Single Edge Razor Blades
1 Retractable Scraper
1 Long Handle Scraper
1 Rechargeable Scrubber (Optional)
2 Five Gallon Plastic Pails
1 Buffer
   Buffing Pads
   Hand Tools
1 Rolling Cart or Tray (Optional)
1 Power Hose or "Jet Gun"
1 Compressor for above (Optional)
1 Rubber Water Hose

PRODUCT INFORMATION

Use products designed to do a specific job. Most automotive stores carry the products you'll need, although you can also buy commercial versions (labeled *for professional use only*) in bulk at a lower price than retail products. The reason that the manufacturer lists *for professional use only* on his product, is that he means to imply that a certain amount of knowledge (and caution) is a prerequisite for proper use. You can ruin a project by not handling these products properly, so try them out first in areas where they will do no harm.

Like most rules there are exceptions. You may find that substitute products do an incredible job.

The real truth in the quality of a product comes after you have tried it. Don't confuse things by having, for instance, four vinyl cleaners. If one works well, stick with it. Don't litter your garage with partially full bottles of products that don't work.

Price alone should not be the deciding factor in your choice of one product over another. Remember that detailing is a quality oriented business, and a few cents more for a product that works well, is a few cents well spent. Further, the expensive product may save you time, and time is money.

Products that are available as a concentrate, should be preferred over pre-mixed products for two reasons. Usually, concentrates are less expensive. But, the most important reason is that, by mixing it yourself, you can control the strength and match it to your requirements.

Most of the products you'll need are available at the local auto parts store, if not, look in the Business to Business edition of the Yellow Pages under "Car Wash Supplies".

In this section, we will cover products for interiors and exteriors, cleaners and protective coatings, hybrid products and some tricks of the trade. Supplement these procedures with your own tricks that you have found to work.

Learn too, from the way non-auto surfaces are cleaned or protected. For example, some great techniques that work around your home can be applied to your detail work.

Products are grouped into two generic categories: Cleaners and Protective Coatings. There are products that do both, for example a "One Step" cleaner and polish used to buff the car, and you will be able to determine which they are by the descriptions included.

CLEANERS: cleaning agents that are inherent to the detail trade, do not differ greatly from those used in the home. It makes no difference, if you are cleaning vinyl covered kitchen chairs, or the vinyl seats in your car. The techniques are also generally the same.

PROTECTIVE COATINGS: just about every surface that has been thoroughly cleaned, should be coated with some sort of protection. Even cloth seats or carpets, should be sprayed with Scotchgard®, to keep dirt from penetrating the fibers. Painted surfaces should be waxed to make it difficult for dirt and airborne particles (like acid rain) to destroy the finish. In some cases, cleaning alone can speed up the destructive forces. For instance, when paint is cleaned by buffing, the open pores are like magnets pulling in dirt and other impurities.

At the risk of belaboring a point, do not limit yourself to over the counter products. Until now, you may only be familiar with heavily advertised retail products, or whatever has been your favorite product over the years. These products are good but, there are many specialized products that are better.

Cleaners and protective coatings are treated in the order of our "Summary Plan of Action" which was included in the PROCEDURES section. You may want to refer to that section, while you are reading this segment. It would also be helpful for you to cross reference to the EQUIPMENT section, to familiarize yourself with the tools used to apply these products.

CLEANING AGENTS

GREASE AND ROAD TAR: There are many products available for this purpose. Kerosene works well, and is relatively inexpensive. Apply it by spraying with a fine mist. Allow a few minutes for the product to loosen the grease or tar. If the spot is difficult to remove, try using a scrubber. Pot scrubbers work well. It is made of plastic, and resembles a birds nest. These are available in most supermarkets but, the nicest thing about them, is they do not scratch the paint. For really stubborn spots, you may need to use a razor blade scraper, or a single edge razor blade, laid as flat as possible, so as not to dig into the paint. NEVER use paint thinner.

ENGINE DEGREASER: kerosene also works well under the hood but, it can be dangerous since heat from the motor could cause a fire. You should give preference to water based cleaners, since they will be less harmful to painted surfaces, and are usually cheaper. Aerosols and retail products work well, but are much to expensive. Where necessary, help your degreaser along by using a stiff brush to loosen heavily caked on grease. If possible, power-hose with hot water and avoid overly wetting the distributor. Cover the carburetor or other moisture sensitive parts with a plastic bag.

WHEEL CLEANERS: since most wheels have difficult to clean surfaces, for example, the spokes on a wire wheel hub cap, you should spray your cleaner on. Painted wheels and hub caps are easily cleaned with car wash soap. Wire wheel hub caps should be cleaned with an acid based product. Caution should be exercised, since acid based products are very strong and should not be left on for more than a minute or two. Apply to a dry wheel so as not to dilute the product. You can also use an acid product on aluminum or mag wheels. Check with your suppliers, and read label cautions, before application of any acid based product. Rinse completely to insure that no trace of the acid remains. You want to get those hard to clean wire wheel hub caps clean, take them off the car and place them in your dishwasher. The dishwasher will not remove surface rust, like the acid cleaners, but they will come out very clean.

TIRE CLEANERS: remember that you must clean blackwalls as well as whitewalls. The same product will work on both. Clean wheels are critical to a good detail. Obtain a bleach based product that is inexpensive, because the secret to clean tires, especially whitewalls, is the scrubber you use. Obtain a stiff brass-bristled wire brush. Spray the cleaner on a dry tire and scrub with a brush. If the whitewalls don't come out spotless, try steel wool or a scouring pad. Rinse well and redo if necessary.

VINYL CLEANER: there are some very fine liquid vinyl cleaners available through detail suppliers. It doesn't matter if you're cleaning a vinyl top or a vinyl interior - use the same product. Vinyl cleans up very nicely, if you use the right cleaner and scrubber. Don't scrub too hard, or you will break through the protective coating, which is present on all vinyls. Give preference to concentrated cleaners since you can control the strength of the mixture, and they are usually cheaper. Wet surrounding painted areas prior to applying vinyl cleaner, so as not to stain the paint. Some suppliers carry a paste like cleaner, that has a grit to it. This works well on vinyl tops, but cannot be used on vinyl seats, because you need to hose it off. Apply this type of cleaner with a stiff brush.

CAR SOAP: you can use dishwashing liquid if you're not planning to do a lot of cars. If you plan to do a number of cars, buy a concentrate. Bulk buying, will save you money. Test several types and make certain that the one you select does not leave a filmy residue. Apply with a sponge and hose off before it dries.

SPOT REMOVAL: see the section that covers all types of stains and spots.

CARPET AND SEAT SHAMPOO: there are quite a few different products in this category from retail products to commercial products simply known as interior shampoos. If you are doing just one car, buy a retail product. If you plan to do several cars, seek a good commercial product that is a concentrate. There are drycleaning-type cleaners, which are expensive but have their benefits in that, if you need to drive the car right away and you don't want to wait for the seats to dry, this is the type to use. However, if you use the shampoo type (mixed with water) properly, you can also drive the car in a short while. The secret is to whip up the shampoo, with your brush, and apply only the foam to the seats and carpets. Use a stiff nylon bristled

brush and scrub. Vacuum to remove lifted dirt and moisture. If you are faced with severely dirty seats or carpets, try mixing a little whitewall cleaner in with the interior shampoo.

VINYL INTERIORS: follow the instructions for vinyl tops but, do not use the paste type cleaner described. After scrubbing it with a nylon mesh scrubber, wipe off the dirt with a clean, dry cloth. Then use a rag dampened with water to wipe the surface again. This will remove any final residue. Wipe again with a clean, dry cloth.

GLASS CLEANERS: there are literally hundreds of glass and mirror cleaners on the market. Find a good concentrate that contains ammonia. Ammonia content products, cut through dirt and nicotine nicely. They also deodorize at the same time. Apply with a fine spray and wipe with newspaper until dry. Abuse of a concentrate will, with a little experimentation, helps to eliminate streaking. Keep trying mixtures until you solve the streaking problem. Newspaper leaves the windows with a glossy sheen. Whatever the reason, newspaper works well, and is very inexpensive. You can also use glass cleaner on dashboard plastic and the lenses that cover dash gauges. Glass cleaner is also good for removing fingerprints and smudges from chrome. Avoid expensive aerosols.

CHROME CLEANER: there are a number of products available to clean and remove rust from chrome. They also smell like they contain ammonia. You can use light duty compound or any car wax applied with steel wool (0000 grit), but be sure the material is actually chrome, and not plastic. Steel wool will remove surface rust, for heavier rust try naval jelly. Make sure you let chrome cleaner dry completely and never use the same rag to wipe painted surfaces since the grit in chrome cleaner will scratch the paint. Aluminum foil will also remove rust from chrome. Takes a sheet of foil, wrinkle it into a ball, unfold it and rub it on the chrome. It works!

PAINT CLEANERS: commonly known as compounds, these products are sold in varying grits, like sandpaper. The grit seems to follow a color scale such as, the darker the color the stronger the grit. If you're new to buffing, stick with the light duty—usually white or beige compound - and avoid the heavy duty stuff, so that you don't burn through. It is preferable, even to an accomplished detailer, to apply several light coats of compound to one heavy duty application. There is no sense to removing more paint than you need to. It takes a little more time to use light duty compounds, but it can save you from repainting the car. As you gain buffing experience, you will develop a sixth sense which will tell you which grade of compound matches which application. To assist you, the following section has been compiled. Read this section, and the section on "Using the Buffer", before using the buffer.

PRIMER ON COMPOUNDS:

Take a close look at the paint after the car has been washed. Is the color bright with no visible clouding? Are there fine car wash scratches present? Is the paint dull and non-reflective? Has it faded to the point where it seems that the color has changed? Compare the color of the hood with the underside of the trunk lid. Try to determine how far the paint has deteriorated.

Color resembles the underside of the trunk: use the finest compound you have. This would be a white or very light shade of beige. There are also "One Step" cleaners which contain wax, that will do the job. Try the product first in an inconspicuous area to make certain there is enough abrasive in the cleaner.

Car wash scratches: you should use a slightly more abrasive product than for the example above. Try one or more of the darker beige or light gray compounds. You may also need to apply two or three applications to remove all of the scratches and restore the color.

Dull paint: depending on how dull it is, continue to use stronger compounds. First test them in out-of-the-way areas. If you can't see your reflection in the paint, you can forget "cleaners", you must use a compound. Some manufacturers make a superlight compound, which works well on dulled paint. Do a small section. If it cleans close to what you want, use a lighter compound for the second buffing.

Color seems to have changed: experienced detailers will go right to a heavy compound, which is called "mud", that is very dark gray or even black. If you're an inexperienced buffer, stay away from this stuff. Before proceeding with subsequent applications of compound, look closely at the paint to make certain that you are not removing too much paint. If you start to see traces of primer, you have gone too far.

Study the section on "Using the Buffer" before attempting any compound work. Remember to move the buffer slowly but, not to spend too much time in one place. Compounds should be applied to small sections. Compounds should never be applied to large sections by hand. The buffer creates heat which lifts the dirt from the paint. It is impossible to build up that much heat by hand, and hand applications tend to streak.

PROTECTIVE COATINGS

You should have two types of vinyl dressing—a high gloss and a semi-gloss. You should use the semi-gloss on the dashboard to minimize the suns reflection. The high gloss is good on the seats and vinyl top.

You can use the same dressings on the vinyl top as you use on the seats, but make sure it is long lasting and can handle the effects of the weather. Although it is expensive, high quality floor wax can be used for a high gloss and it seems to last forever.

Do not get water on vinyl that has been dressed until the vinyl dressing is totally dry (about 1 hour after application). If you do, the dressing will streak and may turn yellow. Apply with a sponge and wash your hands and the sponge, in hot water, immediately after use. If you don't, it will be very difficult getting the dressing off your hands and you will never be able to use the sponge again - except as a paperweight.

RUBBER DRESSING: regardless of what you hear, to the contrary, vinyl dressings do not work well on rubber. Plan on using two types as you did for vinyl - semi-gloss and high gloss. Some car dealers want their tires to look like patent leather. That is, they want a very high gloss, so that the tires will look like they are not worn. Others want a clean natural rubber look so, use the semi-gloss. Rubber dressing should be sprayed on tires and wiped into the rubber with a sponge or rag. Rubber should be dressed twice and, if you want the highest gloss, do not wipe the second coat. Make sure the rubber is completely dry, before applying any rubber dressing, and do not allow water to touch a dressed surface for at least 1 hour after it has been applied. Dress body side moldings and bumper rub strips by spraying the dressing on a rag first, then wiping (two coats) on the moldings. You can use rubber dressing on weatherstripping, mud guards, hoses in the engine compartment and, of course, on full rubber bumpers. Make sure the type dressing you select stays flexible, so that you don't have

Apply heavy compound with a paint brush

unsightly cracks to contend with. Some rubber dressings will yellow whitewalls, if you have not completely removed whitewall cleaner or wheel cleaners by rinsing with water.

CLEAR PAINT: you can use clear lacquer or fast drying enamel to "dress" under the hood. Make sure there are no puddles left from the power-hosing operation. If there are, either blow them away with compressed air, or wipe them dry with rags. Spray the clear laquer being careful not to get any overspray on the fenders or header panel. This procedure has two benefits; it makes the engine look great and, it seals the wires and electrical connections from moisture and corrosion. Buy the cheaper generic spray paint that is often on sale at automotive and hardware stores.

BLACK PAINT: this is excellent for spraying wheel wells and covering up overspray that the bodyman may have left on the frame and exhaust system. You can also touch up rusted areas (after repairing the rust), under the hood, with flat black paint.

CHROME: most chrome cleaners also contain wax, if not, use any non-abrasive wax. Some detailers believe in spraying chrome with clear paint, but when it ages it will turn yellow and start to flake off. It is also very difficult to remove when you need to redo it.

STAINLESS: this type of metal needs no protection but, its a good idea to apply a coat of wax which makes it easier to clean between details.

SEATS AND CARPETS: the best protection is Scotchgard®. Scotchgard® is available in bulk (gallons) or for single applications, purchase several aerosol cans and apply liberally to carpets and cloth seats. Detail suppliers or auto parts stores may carry other brands that may be less expensive. Seats and carpets should be resprayed after each shampooing. After you apply this type of product leave the car outside with the windows open for at least an hour. The fumes in products of this type can be hazardous if not used with adequate ventilation.

LEATHER DRESSING: vinyl dressing will give leather a nice appearance, but it will do nothing to soften the leather or give it that natural feel. Generally, you will not have a choice between high gloss and semi-gloss. Leather is a natural product, which should be returned to it's natural sheen by the detailer. Leather should not have a high gloss unless you want it to look like vinyl. You can use saddle soap to clean and soften leather but, it's hard to work with in large areas. Leather cream can be wiped on and off with a clean cloth. Beware of miracle products that claim to remove all cracks and renew leather.

PAINT COATINGS: the previous section explained how to clean paint with compounds. Once that paint is clean you must seal the open pores with a wax type product. There are so many different products that do what we have come to believe a wax does. Protective coatings for paint, are known by many names including waxes, glazes, one-steps, poly-products and polishes.

To simplify this, these products are referred to as either waxes or polishes. The distinction between waxes and polishes, will simply be that waxes are applied to older paint and polishes to freshly painted (newer than 90 day) surfaces.

1. **POLISHES:** these are available as liquids and as a paste. They contain no wax or silicon and are perfectly safe for freshly painted surfaces. They are also fine for older paint but, generally, do not last as long as a wax.

Once the paint has been cleaned with a compound or cleaner, you can apply either liquid or paste with a buffer. Work the product into the paint until all traces are gone. After buffing, wipe any remaining residue from corners and around moldings with a soft cloth. Get into tight areas with your detail brush.

Apply one coat with a buffer and a second coat by hand. For the second coat, use a product that was designed to eliminate swirl marks caused by the buffer.

2. **WAXES:** like polishes, waxes are also available in liquid and paste form. With a paste you spread some on the body of the car with a small applicator (a sponge works well) and remove by buffing, either by hand or with a power buffer. With liquids you squirt some on the car and spread with the buffer. Work into the paint until all of the product disappears. As with polishes, only apply waxes to painted surfaces that were previously cleaned with a compound or cleaner. Waxes should not be used on freshly painted sections because they seal so well that they do not allow the paint to fully dry. Cracking of the paint will result if you attempt to wax freshly painted areas.

Waxes are made from natural products like carnuba and synthetics, like silicon and poly-products. Carnuba waxes are best for longevity and ease of application. Make sure you seal containers well, or the wax will dry up.

Try different wax product and test how long the wax lasts, and the gloss. You should also be concerned with speed and ease of application.

Regular, periodic applications of wax are better than several coats applied at one time. Another misconception is that, if you leave the haze, which comes about when wax dries, on the car, in hidden areas like the door jambs, that you will get more protection.

Remember, every time you go through a car wash or use detergents on your car, you are removing some of the wax. Between waxings, wash you car with cold water only.

USING A BUFFER

There is no other single operation in auto detailing that produces a more dramatic change, nor one which causes more fear for the novice detailer, than buffing. When you use the right products and handle the buffer properly, you can literally save a paint job with a buffer. When you mishandle a buffer (this includes using the wrong products), you can expect to pay for a paint job.

There is a law of diminishing returns that takes over when you begin using a buffer. You want to get as much shine out of the painted surface as you can before you remove too much good paint and "burn through". It takes experience, in most cases, to be able to gauge the thickness of paint by looking at it. An experienced detailer knows which grade (coarseness) of compound to use on the first application that will produce the desired results. Inexperienced detailers should make several passes with light duty compound to avoid burns.

How do Burns Occur?

As the buffing pad is applied to the painted surface, the friction of the buffing pad creates heat, which opens the pores of the paint and allows the dirt within the paint to be drawn into the buffing pad. The amount of heat is a factor of the speed of the buffing pad, and the movement of the pad across the surface. The ideal buffer rotates at 1750 rpm. Some detailers make the mistake of using a machine that is intended as a grinder (for bodywork). These generate speeds up to 5000 rpm which, if not used with extreme care, will most certainly produce a burn. Further, even if you use a machine rated at 1750 rpm you can cause burns by moving the machine too slowly across the surface, that is, buffing in one spot too long.

The most common burns occur on sharp fender edges and creases in the hood or trunk. For example, check the front fender edges on 1979-84 Toronados and Eldorados. Even if you move quickly over them with a buffer they have a funny way of disappearing. Try to come within ½ in. of sharp edges and do the edge itself by hand. It takes a little longer, but is much safer.

You can also burn through on flat surfaces, by spending too much time in one spot or by applying too much downward pressure on the buffer. Keep the buffer moving and let the weight of the machine do the work.

Another way to burn on a flat surface, is to use a compound that is too coarse for the application. The only way to avoid this, is to know your products and their capabilities.

Swirl marks

Swirl marks are another malady of a mishandled buffer. Swirl marks occur when the buffing angle is too large. The correct buffing angle is 10–15 degrees. That is, if you lay the buffing pad flat on the paint then lift up on the handle 10–15 degrees you have achieved the correct angle. When you increase this angle you increase the possibility of leaving swirl marks. and will increase the probability of burning through.

Normally swirl marks are removed by rebuffing with a product especially formulated for the removal of swirl marks. However, there are also hand applied liquids that work very well.

Proper Buffing Method

Stand with your feet spread shoulder width apart. Lay the buffing pad flat on the painted surface. Raise up on the handle so that your comb (laid flat) will fit under the raised end of the (without touching the fibres). This is

approximately 10–15 degrees. Keep this angle as you buff the car. Remember to remove your comb before you start buffing.

Never buff a surface unless you have compound or wax on it. Buffing a dry surface increases the possibility of swirl marks and burns. Apply waxes and compounds either with a small cloth, sponge or directly with the buffing pad. Try to get used to applying products with the buffing pad as this will save a step. To do this first squirt some product on the area to buffed. Next, with the buffer off, smear the product, around the area to be buffed, with buffing pad. This technique will partially wet the pads fibres and help to eliminate swirl marks. Now, spread the product with the buffer intermittently hitting the buffers trigger (on/off switch) so as not to build up to top speed. This will spread the product more evenly and reduce splatter. Once you have spread the product work it into the paint by buffing at full speed (approximately 1750 rpm). When buffing, move the buffer from left to right. Some of the product will begin to disappear or may start to haze if are using a wax. Now lightly buff in a front to back pattern (perpendicular to the left to right application) until almost all of the is absorbed. Finish the buffing operation with a final left to right pass buffing to a high luster. Do not attempt to remove 100% of the product with the buffer. Some residue will remain in corners and around moldings which are easier removed by hand when you do the final wipe down.

When compounding you should buff small sections say, one foot by one foot. The reason for this is that compounds dry very quickly and may dry before you complete a large area. With waxes you can expand the area to maybe half of the hood or a whole fender or door since, waxes dry slower than compounds. With some cleaners and 'one step' products you can even do as much as one half of the car. The best way to find out how far you can go, with a product, is to completely test your products to get used to the results you can expect. If the product ever drys before you remove it all you should be able to remove it with a wet rag. Then start over again.

Buffing Cautions

Be especially careful in areas where the spinning buffing pad can get hung-up or jammed. You can be injured by an antennae that gets caught up in a buffing pad. On some late model cars it is a simple matter to unscrew the antennae mast from the base. In this manner it will be completely out of you way and you can avoid injury to yourself or the car. On those cars where you cannot easily remove the antennae it is best to do around the base by hand.

Windshield wipers present a similar problem. Some wipers can be lifted out of the way. On vehicles where this is not possible do the area by hand.

A large percentage of cars are made with flush mount door handles these days. The painted area, under the door handles, becomes scratched by fingernails and should be buffed. With a little practice you can do this

Correct position for buffing sides

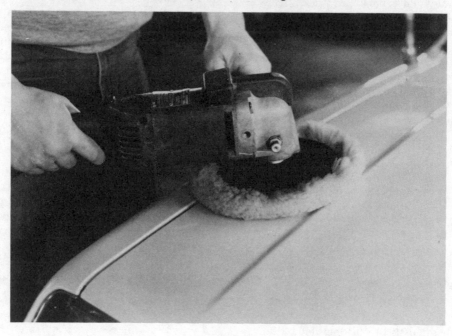

Correct buffing angle

with the buffer by cutting the speed down to less than half. Be careful since, this is an easy area to burn. Once again, if you feel that you lack competence in this area, do it by hand.

Buffing cars with rust areas or holes requires extreme caution and common sense. The buffing pad could loosen some of the rust and hurl it into your eyes. Wear protective glasses if insist on buffing these areas or do them by hand. Make sure you have recently had a tetanus shot.

Some cars, for example the 1984 Mustang GT, have sections of the body panels painted with a flat black paint. Never buff flat paints, if you buff these areas they will look spotty. Usually a good washing is enough to make these areas look good. If you feel that some protection is in order use a wax applied by hand.

Buffing pads

There are as many different kinds of buffing pads on the market as there are waxes. Use 100% wool pads over the synthetic since the wool fibres are softer and are less prone to leaving swirl marks. Your best buy, for general purpose use, is the type with a hefty rolled edge (usually molded) and a nice thick pile of approximately 1½–2 in.

Care of Your Buffing Pads

Buffing pads should be cleaned several times during the buffing of a car by using a "spur" or other pointed object such as a phillips head screwdriver. Make sure that the tool is allow to go with the rotation of the pad so that it doesn't kick back.

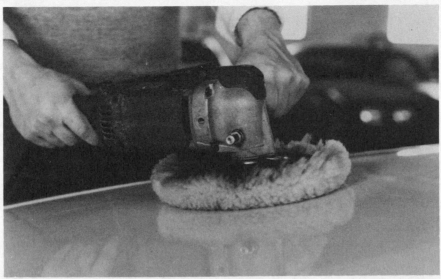

Correct buffing angle

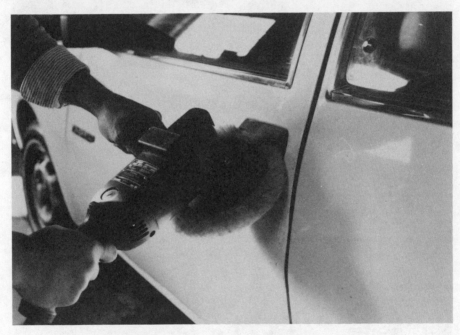

Buffing area under flush mount door handles

You can reuse a buffing pad 5–6 times (that is on 5 or 6 cars) before it needs to washed. To wash your pads, in your washing machine, use the following formula:

    10 ounces of interior shampoo (or liquid detergent)
    4 ounces of liquid bleach
    2 ounces of liquid fabric softener

Wash in warm water (not hot) and use the full cycle. DO NOT PLACE PADS IN A DRYER. Allow to dry (out in the sun is OK). IF you place pads in a dryer they will shrink to the size of drink glass coasters.

Special Note

From time to time you may encounter very heavy oxidation where it will appear that no matter what product you use you just keep making a mess with the buffing pad. The way around this is to use more compound than you would ordinarily, work the compound into the paint, then clean the compound off with a rag, apply a second coat of compound and rebuff. As the pad becomes saturated place it on the side and us a new pad.

PAINT TOUCH-UP

There are many ways to touch up scratches and minor rust damage. See the section on repairing the apprpriate type(s) of damage. If you can resist the tendency to just brush paint on, straight from the bottle, and spend a little more time to do it right the results will amaze you.

The right time to apply touch up paint is immediately after you have washed the car. That way sufficient time will have elapsed, allowing the paint to dry, before you buff the touch up paint.

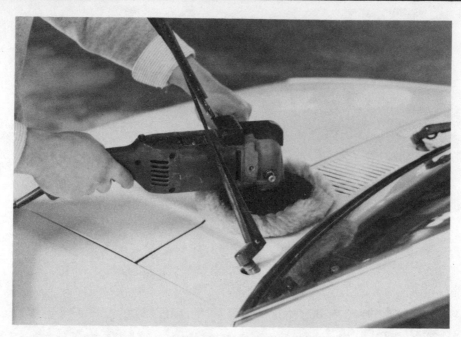

Lift wipers out of your way

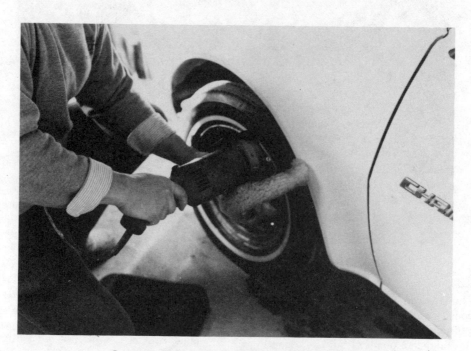

Sure way to burn through! Too close to an edge

NOTE: *touch up paint is no substitute for completely repainting a panel but, it is a simple and inexpensive way to make the vehicle look better. Don't expect great results. For instance, metallic paints will be difficult to color match because it is very difficult to get uniformity in the spreading of the metallic chips from a brush or small sprayer. The same is true with cars that have clear coats or color mixed with clear coats. Spot spraying will occasionally leave a halo effect and be difficult to color match.*

Surface Preparation

Whether you are preparing to touch up a scratch or a rust spot, the method you use to prepare the are is critical to how it will look and how long the repair lasts.

Minor scratches: careful area buffing, with compound, will remove scratches that are not deeper than the color coats of paint, Concentrate on an area approximately twice the size of the scratch. Use a lot of com-

Buffing angle too large. Burns will result

pound to keep the area wet. This will minimize the chance of burning through. Cut down the buffer speed and blend the area by buffing gradually outward to a larger area in all directions from the scratch.

Major scratches: usually you will be able to see metal or rust through these scratches. With a single edge razor blade create a V-groove on both sides of the scratch being careful not to open up the scratch too much. If rust is present attempt to scrape it out with the razor blade or some other pointed object.

Rust spots: remove all flaking paint with a razor blade. Cut along the perimeter of the damage with slicing motion of the razor blade. You are trying to create a slope, like the banks of a lake, for the new paint to blend into. Sand the area to remove all rust. If pitting remains apply a rust neutralizer followed by a thin coat of spot putty. Next, finish sand and mask the area to be painted. Apply at least one coat of primer, allow to dry, then resand.

Applying Paint

There are several methods of applying touch up paint. You can use thin artists paint brushes or matches from a match book. For larger work, as in rust repair, it is best to spray the paint on. Touch up paint is available, from auto parts stores and auto dealers, in color coded spray cans and bottles or cans. First, find the color code for your car from the data plate located under the hood or inside the door jamb. Check with your owners manual if you are not sure of the location of your data plate. You will need to know the year of the car and the color code to buy the paint from a dealer, parts store or variety store.

You can also use a CO_2 sprayer to apply thinned bulk paint. If you have access to compressor you can use a detailers spray gun which is smaller version of an auto painter spray gun. Whatever method you use follow the instructions that are listed below.

Scratches: stir the paint well especially if you are using metallics. Shaking is not sufficient for auto paints you must also stir the paint. Thin with the appropriate reducer and apply several THIN coats with a brush or match. Stay within the V-groove you created and build up the area allowing each coat to dry. Build up slightly higher than the surrounding paint and allow to dry. Follow the buffing instructions given for ''Minor Scratches'' elsewhere in this section.

Rust spots: on rust spots smaller than 1 inch in diameter you can brush the paint on as you would for a scratch. Apply several thin coats then buff. For larger areas use either spray touch up aerosol cans or bulk paint (properly thinned) sprayed from a CO_2 sprayer or detailers spray gun. Begin by masking the area slightly larger than the damaged area. Spray thin even coats (not too dry or too wet) until the area is built up slightly higher than the surrounding good paint. When completely dry, wet sand with 400 grit sandpaper, until the spot feels smooth and no ridge can be felt between the repaired area and the good paint. Finally, buff as you would for a scratch.

STAIN REMOVAL

Getting the stains out of cloth sets will increase your cars general appearance and value. It certainly beats reupholstering. Some stains will not come out no matter how hard you scrub, but with the correct materials and knowledge you can get out most stains and minimize the others.

A critical issue, in removing a stain, is that you not make it worse in your efforts to remove the stain. You can do this easily by using the wrong cleaning agent which bleaches the color out of the surrounding fabric, Therefore, always test your cleaning agents in an inconspicuous area like, a swatch of material from under the seats or where the backrest meets the seat cushion, to insure color fastness.

Another way to avoid ruining the area, around the spot, is to dilute your cleaner so that you are applying several light applications instead of one strong application. Most cleaners can be diluted with water but, if you're in doubt, read the label directions on the package.

Retail products, as sold in supermarkets and drug stores, can be used, but are fairly expensive. Among the most expensive are those that are packaged as aerosols. Aerosols are very convenient but, when you consider the content of the can is 70–80% CO_2 and 20–30% cleaner, they are expensive. Most of the over-the-counter stain removers contain amyl acetate which can be purchased from the local drug store.

This section will consist of three subsections: Spot Removal Supplies, Techniques, and Removal of Specific Stains. Most are common to auto interiors, but exotic stains are not covered here.

Spot Removal Supplies

Most stain removal items can be found around the house or purchased, inexpensively, at any supermarket, drug store or auto parts store. Let common sense rule as far as possible substitutes. For instance, do not use an alcohol that has an added color as a substitute for denatured. Try something else like, ammonia.

ABSORBENT MATERIALS: you will need lots of clean cotton rags that have absolutely no dye (color) in them. If you use for instance, a blue towel, you run the risk of having some of the towels color bleed through onto the area you are cleaning. Now you will have two overlapping stains to remove. If you don't have the rags recommended use WHITE paper towels. You can also use sponges for blotting and absorbing excess moisture. A really absorbent synthetic sponge for instance, which is specially formulated for stain removal.

BRUSHES: this is a key ingredient to good stain removal. You should have several types. Long bristle for sensitive materials and stiff bristle for velour and other not so sensitive materials. A detail brush is goodfor small stains and a carpet scrubbing brush is good for larger stains.

SCRAPER: razor blades work well to lift the bulk of tar and chewing gum if you are careful and use an upward slicing motion. In some cases you may be able to slice gum or tar from carpets without a trace and without having to remove a stain with chemicals. Be careful, however, since carpets look bad with bald spots.

MISCELLANEOUS: You'll need plastic mixing bowls to mix chemicals in, extra sponges, a hair dryer, Q-Tips and some cotton balls.

CHEMICALS: there are so many different types available that it is not possible to list them all in a section of this book. Try to simplify your selection by using a few

types that you know work. Always test your chemicals in areas where you can do no harm and follow the safety directions packaged with the product.

Alcohol: this is a good all purpose cleaner. Use caution when using because it does fade some dyed materials. You can dilute with water and lift the stain out in stages. Buy rubbing alcohol or denatured alcohol with a 70–90% concentration. Care should be taken when using on acetate materials. Dilute with water by mixing one part alcohol with two or more parts water.

Ammonia: the best type to get is chemically pure 10% ammonia which can be obtained from most drug stores. This product, like alcohol above, can stain some dyed materials. Do not mix with any other type of cleaning agent unless you have properly tested the mixture and allowed the test swatch to dry. After application rinse the affected area with water.

Acetone: can be purchased in drug stores. A clear liquid which works very well on a great number of stains caused by paint, varnish, lacquers and some glues. Acetone is harmless to most natural fibres but, it does adversely affect some sythetics and dyes.

Amyl Acetate: To be effective it must be chemically pure. You can purchase amyl acetate at your local drugstore. Amyl acetate is made from bananna oil and will sometimes be listed as banana oil. This product should not come in contact with plastics. The majority of nail polish removers containing amyl acetate and, if you use nail polish removers as a substitute, make sure you get the NON-OILY type.

Bleach: If you have ever done the laundry at home you know that bleaches can be a mixed blessing. They clean and remove stains beautifully but, if not diluted properly they are strong enough to burn holes in fabrics. They are especially good on light colors but, unfortunately, car manufacturers are not turning out too many white cloth interiors these days. Mix in plastic containers as metal containers will speed up their action. There are several types of bleaches you should know about:

1. Chlorine bleach: available as liquids and in granular form. Liquids are easier to use since they mix quicker. Follow label directions carefully and, if anything, tend to over-dilute with water. Several applications with a weak mixture are preferred to one too strong mixture which may burn a hole in the fabric.

2. Peroxy bleaches: these are available in powder form. Follow the instructions and cautions, listed above, for chlorine bleach.

3. Other bleaches: you can also use bleaches such as hydrogen peroxide for stain removal. Some products that have a bleach content, like whitewall tire cleaner, can also be used if you know what you're doing. Remember it is one thing to get the stain out and another thing if the material corrodes two to three weeks later.

Drycleaning solvent: you can buy this in supermarkets, drug and variety stores. Follow label directions and do not wet with water after application as you would for ammonia or other stain remover.

Detergents: these favorites for stain removal because they are safe to use. The trouble is that detergents will not always do the job as well as you want it done. Use liquid dishwashing detergents. Liquid car wash soap can also be used. Generic detergents work well and are much less expensive. Dilute with water and if necessary use full strength. Flush with water and force fry (with a hair dryer) or blot dry with a sponge or rag. One note of caution—know your products' limitations before you use them. Some products may work well for their intended purpose, but have an adverse effect if accidentally applied to other surfaces.

Hand cleaner: get the type that mechanics use to clean grease and oils from their hands. Some brands work well on grease and oil related stains on seats and carpets. Apply with a stiff brush and work into the fabric. Several applications may be necessary. Flush with water after application and force dry with a hair dryer or blot dry with cotton balls or rags.

Bar soap: Get the strong soaps that are meant for cleaning really dirty hands. Drop some water on the bar of soap and work up a lather with a stiff brush. Work into the stain and flush with water. Force or blot dry.

Saddle soap: used for smooth leathers however, stain removal from leather is difficult. Try some over the counter products for leather.

Special mixtures: Always try your concoction out in an inconspicuous area. Remember, you cannot tell if a mixture really works until it is completely dry.

SPOT/STAIN REMOVAL TECHNIQUES

Spot and stain removal from automotive interiors is, in many respects, the same as removing stains from clothing. The materials are similar, the chemicals are basically the same and the techniques are almost the same. What is different is the accessibility to stains on auto interiors. You cannot readily remove the material and throw it in the washer like you would a pair of slacks. Further, you cannot always get to the stain before it dries. Sometimes you will not even be able to identify the stain.

First, try to identify the stain. For instance, if you can see a yellowish tint to the stain there is good chance that it may be mustard. Try to relate to what most people do in their cars while closely examining the spot. If you cannot identify the stain start with milder stain removers and gradually work towards stronger removers. Test each in a safe area. In the list of stains, find the remover that works best and use the technique recommended for that stain.

The following list will tell you how to remove the stain.

SPONGING: dip your sponge in the cleaning agent and lightly rub into the stain. Continue to dip and rub until the stain has disappeared. Do not overly wet. Apply fresh water in the same manner. Sponging is a good technique for sensitive materials like some velours and woven fabrics where too stiff a brush will shred the fibres. Blot or force dry after vacuuming.

FLUSHING: the use of some stain removers dictates that you flush them out of the material immediately after application. If you don't do this the spot remover will continue to work and may fade the material or re-

move the color completely. Use the sponging method described above, only soak more, then immediately vacuum the area. Reapply fresh water two or three times. Revacuum and force or blot dry.

BRUSHING: care must be taken to use the correct brush. On softer materials, like deep pile velour, you should use a softer, long bristle brush to keep from damaging the knap and to reach down all the way into the lower fibres. on tight woven fabrics, like nylon blends, you can use a stiff brush and scrub hard. Have several different brushes available. Large brushes for large areas, like carpets, and small brushes for small spots so you don't spread the stain remover over too large an area. Dip your brush into the stain remover and apply directly to the material. Scrub in all directions to attack the fibres on all side.

WIPING: on non-porous surfaces, like vinyl or plastic, use a rag dipped in the spot remover. On stubborn stains on non-porous surfaces you can use a mesh nylon pot scrubber but, do no rub too hard. If you do you can remove the plasticizer coating and, depending on the strength of your chemicals, could remover the color from the viny.

DRYING: three methods are used effectively, either singly, or in combination. The first is vacuuming with a wet/dry vac. This will remover the bulk of the moisture. The next is a blotting technique where you use a sponge or cloth to lift out the moisture by capillary action. Keep pressing the sponge or rag or cotton balls onto the moist area and the moisture will be drawn up into whatever material you are using to blot with. The third technique is to force dry with a hair dryer. Use cooler settings. IF you use a hot setting you could melt some synthetic fibres.

OTHER: if you purchase over the counter products they will have specific instructions relating to application techniques. Follow instructions carefully.

Removing Specific Stains

It will not always be easy to identify a stain. If it's your own car and the stain is just occurred then you have a good chance of getting it all out and a better chance of remembering what it is. If it was someone else's car, try to get some information from the owner to at least limit what the stain is not. After awhile you will be able to guess, with some accuracy, what kind of stain you are facing.

Listed below are stains that are common to auto interiors.

BLOOD: actually blood stains are relatively easy to remove. The fresher they are the better. Mix warm water 2:1 with liquid detergent. Sponge onto stain and brush lightly. Once stain is removed flush with cool water and vacuum. If stain persists add a small amount of bleach to your mixture (first test fabric for color fastness) repeat the sponging and brushing technique. Flush very well and dry.

CRAYON: apply liquid detergent directly to the spot (undiluted) and work into a suds with a stiff brush. Repeat as often as necessary. If necessary, apply heat with a hairdryer, to help loosen wax compound in crayon.

GREASE/TAR: you will find these on carpets, seats and door kick panels. A stiff brush works well on carpets and kick panels while a detail brush works well on seats. Scrape off as much of the bulk as can with a razor blade using an upward slicing motion. Try bleaches (whitewall tire cleaner works well) that have been diluted at least 5:1 (5 parts water, 1 part bleach) or detergents diluted 1:1. Small spots on seats can be handled with hand cleaner or bar soaps.

GUM: scrape off as much of the bulk as you can with a razor blade. Apply drycleaning solvent with a sponge. Rub until all residue is removed. You might have to pick at this stain with you fingernail to loose hardened chewing gum.

HUMAN DISCHARGE: this is a common stain to auto interiors. Use a stiff brush and ½ teaspoon detergent, 1 tablespoon ammonia and 1 quart of warm water. Rub until a foam appears. Flush with water and vacuum, then dry.

KETCHUP/MUSTARD: these are very common because so many of us use our vehicles like restaurants on wheels. If these stains are fairly recent they should not be hard to remove. The best method is to scrape all possible buildup then apply drycleaning solvent. Rub into the fabric with a sponge or stiff brush if that becomes necessary. Repeat if required.

LIPSTICK: apply detergent full strength, with a sponge, and build up a suds. Flush with water, vacuum and dry. Repeat if necessary.

NAIL POLISH/PAINT: if not too hardened this stain can be removed with nail polish remover or acetone using a combination of the sponging and brushing methods. It might also be possible to do some scraping but, use your fingernails since, most stains of this sort are found on seats where a razors use is risky.

RUST: common to trunk and seating area carpets. Us a bleach applied with a sponge and work in the fabric with a stiff brush. Flush with water, vacuum and dry. Repeat as often as necessary. Do not expect miracles. Dilute bleach with 5 parts water to one part bleach.

TRANSPARENT STAINS: sometimes a fabric will be stained but all that's visible is a darkened spot or slightly yellowish stain. Other times there will be no obvious stain but a strong odor is present. First, locate the source of the odor by smell.

Yellowed areas: mix liquid detergent (1 part) with 1 part ammonia and eight parts water. Scrub with a brush then flush with water and vacuum. Butter, soda pop, beer, liquor and urine are this category.

Smelly stains: mixture as above (for yellowed stains) but, increase ammonia to two parts. Apply as above, This will remove, instead of masking with deodorizer, odors from pet urine, perfume and other unfavorable odors.

INK STAINS: I have saved the best for last. Do not expect good results. There are three types of ink stains to know about; ballpoint, drawing ink (from a fountain pen and marking pen. There are two surfaces to be concerned with, vinyl and fabric. The best way to remove ballpoint ink from vinyl is to use warm glycerine rubbed on the stain with a sponge. Some success is possible with an ink eraser but, I do not recommend it's use because of the danger of rubbing through the plasticizer coating which could lighten the color of the vinyl and make it easier to tear. Since most of you will not run out to the drugstore to buy glycerine I substituted liquid detergent which is readily available to you, but glycerine is better!!

Ballpoint on vinyl: use vinyl cleaner or strong detergent undiluted applied with a sponge. If the stain persists use a mild pot scrubber (green mesh nylon) and avoid tendency to overscrub. You don't want to scrub through the plasticizer. Wipe dry.

Drawing ink from vinyl: use the same technique listed above for ballpoint ink.

Drawing ink from fabric: first flush with cool water. Apply liquid detergent full strength and brush. Keep stain wet and continue applications until spain is minimized. I say minimized because, it is almost impossible to remove all for this stain.

Marking pen of vinyl: try the technique listed above for ballpoint ink from vinyl.

Marking pen from fabric: sponge first with cool water. Next apply 50–50 mixture of liquid detergent and water by sponge. Brush until suds appear. IF stain remains apply a few drops of iodine on it. Again brush with detergent/water mixture, flush with cool water and vacuum.

NOTE: *some interiors become so badly stained that your only recourse is to dye the whole interior. This is not as difficult as it sounds if you follow label directions. Color coded liquid dyes that mix in with your interior shampoo are available and will do a good job of concealing (not removing) most subtle stains. You can also apply dye in isolated spots rather than doing the whole interior. If you cannot locate a line of color coded dyes, then buy some fabric dye in the supermarket. Mix with boiling water and stir well. Always test the shade before applying and dilute with more water. Apply with a sponge and wear rubber gloves so that you do not burn your hands and wind up with permanently blue fingers. Vacuum dry.*

Vinyl seats, dashboards and tops can likewise be dyed. There are two types of products for this purpose. One product is available from paint suppliers. It comes in color coded quarts and is meant to be sprayed on. The other kind is available in basic shades and can be brushed on using a special nylon paddle. Both work well but, make sure the surface to be dyed is thoroughly cleaned. Scrub with vinyl cleaner and a scrubber then wipe with a rag dampened with fresh water. Wipe dry. For the sprayed on type you may be instructed, on the can, to use a lacquer thinner as a pre-application wipe down. Always follow label directions.

Fabric and vinyl dying can be a simple solution to a major problem or it can be a major problem. As always, experiment before applying to someone's car, and obtain as much knowledge - beforehand - as you can get.

Getting Started

Most minor auto body damage can be repaired by the owner of the vehicle. Minor auto body damage falls into 5 general categories: (1) small scratches and dings in the paint that can be refinished without the use of body filler, (2) deep scratches and minor dents that require body filler but do not require pulling the dent out or hammering it out from behind, (3) dents and deep gouges that require pulling the panel back into shape and then filling with body filler, (4) rust holes and (5) lightly crumpled panels.

There are many reasons for wanting to repair your car's body yourself. Perhaps you enjoy working on or around your car or truck. Maybe you want the vehicle to look its best before you try and sell it. Some owners discover that their older model is in good mechanical condition and that doing some minor body work is far cheaper than going in hock for a new model. If you are carrying a higher collision deductible on your insurance policy, you may want to repair a minor dent yourself rather than deal with the insurance company. Or, you simply may not feel that the price the local body shop wants to fix that rust hole is worth it to you. Whatever

the reason(s), you can repair minor damage yourself, using the actual repairs in this book as a guide. Everything you need, except the materials, is here. All the work photographed in this book was done with readily available tools and materials.

All the step-by-step repairs involve basically the same steps, and you should be able to find one that approximates the repair you wish to make on your vehicle.

DECIDING WHAT TO DO

The first step is to decide what you want to tackle yourself.

It makes no difference what panel you are repairing. Hoods, doors, fenders and rear quarter panels are all the same when it comes to body repair; they are stamped into their shape in a press. When you make a dent in one, you stretch the metal. If you stretch it too far, it either requires a new panel or special equipment to repair it. The biggest mistake most do-it-yourselfers make is stretching the panel more, in trying to repair it, than it had been with the dent in it. As a result, they end up

Use common sense. If the repair is too big, don't attempt it yourself.

with a bulge instead of a dent. When you do this, you have twice the trouble you had when you had the dent, and if you don't have access to special equipment and some very special talent, you could get in big trouble.

You must use common sense. If the job is too big or if the panel is stretched badly, don't try to repair it. You could end up with a larger project than you had originally. And no body man likes to pick-up where somebody else left off, and try and undo their mistakes. It takes longer and is more costly in the end.

There are many ways of deciding what to do yourself or what would be better to have done professionally, but the answers to these questions will go a long way to making your decision for you.

1. What is the extent of the damage?
Carefully assess the damage relative to the repairs and procedures in this book. Use common sense-many repairs are not as hard as they look, but if the panel is severely misshapen, torn or mangled, don't attempt it unless you have plenty of time and the vehicle is not worth a great deal. When assessing the damage, be sure to check carefully for hidden damage that is not readily apparent.

2. How many and what kinds of tools are required to do the job?
At the beginning of each repair in this book, we've listed the tools that are necessary to make the individual repair.

3. Consider the value of your time.
How long will the car be out of service? How long will the work take? Each repair in this book is also accompanied by an estimate of the time required for a person of average mechanical ability to make the repair using commonly available tools and materials.

4. How much will it cost YOU to make the repair?
Get several estimates from body shops and compare these with the cost of do-it-yourself tools and materials. Each repair lists the materials you'll need to make the individual repair.

5. Do you plan to sell the car?
Will the repairs you make help sell the car? Will the repairs you make help get more money for the car? Remember, that if the work is done professionally, the higher cost of the repair must be deducted from your profits.

6. Do you plan to keep the car?
Will the repairs increase the value of the car? Will this repair mean that future repairs will be less likely (for instance checking the spread of rust)? Can you afford NOT to make the repair?

7. Consider the age of the car.
Is it worth spending more money to have the work done professionally, or is the market value of the car less than the cost of a professional repair job?

8. Consider your insurance policy.
Is the cost of a professional repair less than the collision deductible on your policy, so that you will wind up paying for the whole thing anyway? If so, consider saving what you can, by doing it yourself. Also consider the effect on your premiums by reporting a minor accident that may not have been your fault. You can save insur-

ance premium money over the cost of the repair by repairing minor damage yourself.

If you've considered the answers to these questions, you've probably concluded that you can save a good deal of money on minor body repairs by doing it yourself. You may already be familiar with some of the skills necessary, but even if you're not, you can easily develop these with a little practice and patience.

TOOLS AND MATERIALS

The first thing to do is to assemble the tools you will need. They are inexpensive and readily available at most auto paint supply stores, auto parts stores, discount stores, and mail order auto suppliers. You might think that for a small job on a door or fender, it would seem silly to buy any tools. Look at it this way. You probably have a claw hammer hanging in your garage or a quarter inch drill with an assortment of drill bits, etc., which you don't use every day of the week. So there is nothing wrong with having a few inexpensive body tools hanging that can pay for themselves time and again.

The basic tools for minor repair are as follows:
Body hammer
Dent puller (depending on the repair)
Sanding board
Sanding rubber block
$\frac{1}{4}$ in. drill w/drill bits
Half round plastic file
Package of plastic spreaders
Putty squeegee
Grinder attachment for drill
Paint paddles

Materials you need for your first job:

1   quart auto body plastic, with tube of hardener
1   tube of glazing putty
1   can of aerosol lacquer base primer
2   5 in. grinding discs (24-grit), used on drill
6   17 in. x $2\frac{2}{3}$ in. sanding paper (36-grit), for sanding board
6   17 in. x $2\frac{2}{3}$ in. sanding paper (80-grit), for sanding board
3   $3\frac{3}{4}$ in. x 9 in. sanding paper (36-grit), for hand use
3   $3\frac{3}{4}$ in. x 9 in. sanding paper (80-grit), for hand use
3   $3\frac{3}{4}$ in. x 9 in. sanding paper (100-grit), for blocking
1   gallon lacquer thinner, for tool clean up

CAUTION
Most of the products you will be using contain harmful chemicals, so be extremely careful. Always read the complete label before opening the containers. When you put them away for future use, be sure they are out of children's reach!

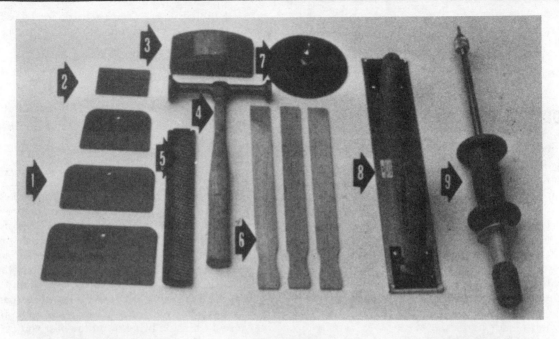

1. Three assorted spreaders
2. Glazing squeegee
3. Standing block
4. Body hammer
5. Plastic file
6. Paint paddles
7. Grinding attachment
8. Sanding board
9. Dent puller

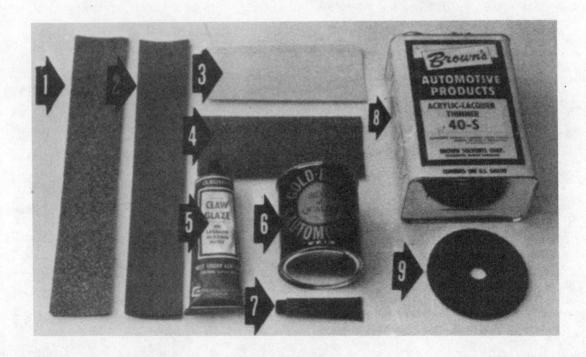

1. 17 in. x 2$\frac{2}{3}$ in. sanding paper (36-grit)
2. 17 in. x 2$\frac{2}{3}$ in. sanding paper (80-grit)
3. 3$\frac{3}{4}$ in. x 9 in. sanding paper (100-grit)
4. 3$\frac{3}{4}$ in. x 9 in. sanding paper (36 and 80-grit)
5. Glazing putty
6. Plastic filler
7. Hardener for plastic filler
8. Gallon of lacquer thinner
9. 5 in. grinding discs (24-grit)

2 MINOR BODY REPAIR

You won't use up all these materials on your first job, but they can be used at a later time. Put the lids and caps on them when you're through, and store them away for future use. Perhaps if you do a good job on your car, you'll be using them on your neighbor's car next week. Ever think of that? (Don't do it too cheaply though.)

AUTO BODY REPAIR KITS

If you are just beginning in auto body repair, you may be unsure of exactly what kinds and amounts of materials are required for a given job.

Most manufacturers of auto body repair products began, supplying materials to professionals. Their knowledge of the best, most-used products has been translated into body repair kits for the do-it-yourselfer. Kits are available from a number of manufacturers and contain the necessary materials in the required amounts for the repair identified on the package.

Kits are available for a wide variety of used, including:

    rusted out metal
    all purpose kit for dents and holes
    dents and deep scratches
    fiberglass repair kit
    epoxy kit for restyling.

Kits offer the advantage of buying what you need for the job. There is little waster and little chance of materials going bad from not being used. The same manufacturers also merchandise all of the individual products used in this book-spreaders, dent puller, fiberglass cloth, polyester resin, cream hardener, body filler, body files, sandpaper, sanding discs and holders, primer, spray paint, etc.

BASIC METHOD

Now you're ready to begin. All repairs discussed in this book involve more or less the same basic steps.

Study the Damage

Take a few minutes to study the damaged area. Try to visualize what shape or contour it had before it was damaged. If the damage is on the right fender, go around and look at the left fender. Study the lines of the panel, and then try to think the problem out. Even professional body men get into trouble on small jobs, because they start swinging a hammer before they study the damage. There is no substitute for using your head.

If there is access to the back side of the panel so you can use a hammer to bring the panel back, fine. If not, you will have to bring it out the best you can from the outside. Until now, I haven't mentioned the most important tool a body man has, and that is the palm of his hand. By laying your hand, palm down and flat, on the panel, you can determine a lot of things you can't even see.

Let's categorize the two types of repairs we will be making. The first are the door dings, stone dents, or in other words, dents that are so slight that there's no point in trying to metal finish them i.e., to bump them out. For

Auto body repair kits contain all the materials in the proper amounts for specified repairs.

Learn to identify body panels by their proper names.

dents that fall into this category, just grind the old finish back and fill them with plastic. Follow the steps at the end of the next category, beginning with, Preparing the Panel for Plastic Filler.

The second category is the one that requires the most care. This is where the novice can get into trouble. Let's assume you have a fair size dent in your front fender. As you look at the damage, try to visualize how the damage was done. You might say to yourself, "The point of impact was here and the angle of impact was about thirty degrees to the rear." Try to figure how the dent was actually made. In most cases, to repair it you follow the reverse in pulling or hammering it out. Let's assume again

that you can get to the back side of the damage with a hammer or pry bar and you begin working the metal back to its original position. Go slowly. Work a little at a time. This is where the palm of your hand is so very useful. Arrow shows good example of stress line. Pull or hammer out along this line. When the dent is close to being back to its original shape, lay your hand flat on the panel and slowly slide it back and forth. Get your body behind your hand, and as you move your hand across the panel, think where the highs and lows are. THINK STRAIGHT. Be sure your hand is flat, as you can tell nothing by feeling with your finger tips.

Arrow shows good example of stress line. Pull or hammer out along this line.

Using the Dent Puller

Quite frequently, you'll find that there is no way to get behind a damaged panel. Now the dent puller comes into use. Study the panel carefully and determine where the lowest spot is. This is usually the best part to pull out first. Quite often there are stress lines in a damaged panel. Once you learn to read these, you will be well along in learning sheet metal working. Stress lines usually run from the lowest part of the damage toward the outside.

Using a ¼ in. drill and a drill bit about half the size of the end on the dent puller, drill a series of holes along the stress lines to the lowest place in the dent. Make a few trial pulls and carefully watch what the panel does. Since no two dents are the same, you can't be told exactly where to make your pulls. If you watch what the panel is doing when you put tension on it, you can tell whether of not you are pulling in the right place. If it looks as if you should move over a few inches, drill more holes and try it. The important thing to remember is not to be in a hurry.

Later in the book, there is a series of step-by-step repairs to various panels. It may be helpful to compare one of these jobs with your own.

Working the Panel Out: Go Slowly Here

The important thing to remember, when working the panel back to its original shape, is not to push or pull it out too far. That is the reason we put so much importance on going slowly on the first couple of jobs. On a small area it is fairly easy to determine whether your damaged area is very close to its original shape by using the palm of your hand as I described before. IF the area is quite large, however, such as the whole length of the panel, a trick used by a lot of body men is to take an ordinary yardstick and lay it flat across the repair area. Yardsticks, the kind you get from the hardware stores and lumber companies, are very flexible and will curve over just about any panel-including contoured ones. Lay the yardstick flat over the area and slide it up and down the panel. Watch the edge of the yardstick that is against the metal. High and low spots may now be seen very easily.

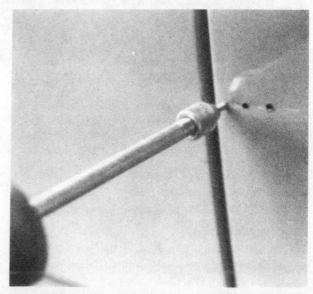

Using the dent puller. On a small dent like this, be careful not to pull the metal out too far. Just a few light taps with the puller in each hole with suffice.

Using a yardstick to find highs and lows on a large area is an old body man's trick. Use it when straightening metal and when filling in with plastic.

When you are finished bringing the panel out to its original position, low spots shouldn't be more than ¼ in. at the deepest point. There are shops that allow much more variation than that, and there are shops that insist that the panel be even closer than one quarter of an inch. If you don't get your pane close to original, the plastic filler will be much too thick. In a few months it will begin to crack and will have to be redone. I once had an old timer tell me when I first went to work for him, "I don't care if your plastic work is thick, just so it isn't deep." Keep the plastic as thin as you can. Plastic was designed to take the place of lead when it became too expensive and panels became too thin to be re-shaped with heat. It was never intended to be used for filling large low spots.

Now, compare your work with some of the photos, and when you are satisfied that you are as close as you can get, then start with the second phase.

Preparing the Panel for Plastic Filler

Insert the grinder attachment into your ¼ in. drill and put on one of the 5 in. grinder discs. You should wear safety goggles. If you don't have them, put on a pair of light shaded sun glasses. Most ¼ in. drills don't turn at a dangerously high rpm, but the chips and dust can very easily get into your eyes.

Grind the old finish off the damaged area. You will have a hard getting all the paint off in areas where you have done some pulling, especially around holes you've drilled. Do the best you can. If you have a wire brush for your drill, this sometimes does a good job around such places and in other areas that are inaccessible. If you are working around a bumper or chrome molding, it is a

good idea to put several layers of making tape over them in case you should slip during the grinding operation. This will also keep the plastic, which can be very hard to get off, from getting on them. Leave the tape on until you have completed the job.

As you grind back the old finish, be sure to go three or four inches away from the damaged area, so that there won't be any plastic on top of the old finish at the edges of your repaired area when you're finished. When you take the car to the paint shop and the painter looks at your work, there won't be any question in his mind that you know what you're doing if there's no filler on top of the paint. To explain this as simply as possible without getting into the technical end of the painting process, if your plastic filler work goes out beyond the old paint edge, the finished panel will have an ugly ring showing right where the plastic starts and ends. If the painter has to work right up to the edge of your filler, there is always the chance of his getting low spot in your repair with his air sander. All the effort you made to get a perfect job will have been for nothing and you can't blame the paint shop.

Mixing and Applying the Plastic

Now we're ready to "mud" the panel. Make a mixing board out of a piece of cardboard box. Open your package of plastic spreaders and select the size that seems to fit the situation. For larger areas, you would use a larger spreader. After you have read the label on the can of filler, open the can. Using one of the paint paddles, remove enough material to apply a medium coat to the panel and put it on the mixing board. Apply the correct amount of hardener from the tube and thoroughly mix

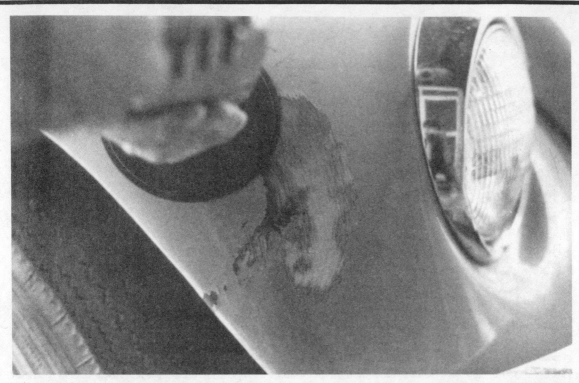

Using the ¹/₄ in. drill with a grinding attachment. Always use safety precautions such as a three prong electrical plug and glasses.

it. This is tricky. The correct amount of hardener is dependent on many factors-temperature, humidity, etc. Too much hardener will cause the filler to harden before it is applied. Too little hardener and the filler will not cure properly. When using hardener, it is better to use too little than too much. This gives you more working time and less chance of getting lumps in the mixture.

As you first apply the plastic, take small amounts on your spreader and sort of wipe it into the metal. This insures that you will obtain good adhesion and is called tinning the metal. After the area is tinned, go ahead and spread the plastic in smooth, even strokes. This is important. Spread the material on as smoothly and as quickly as you can. When you have a fairly smooth coat,

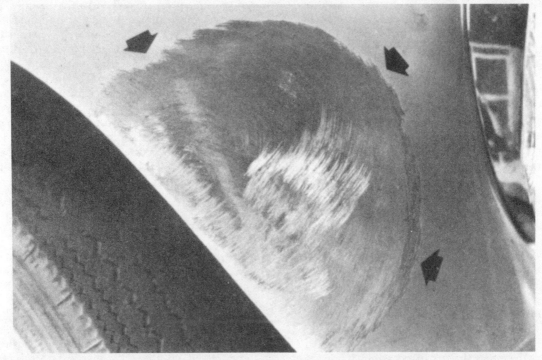

Arrows indicate how the old finish is ground back several inches from the damage. This gives you plenty of working room.

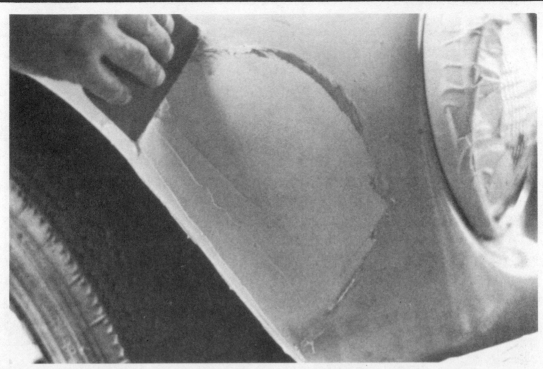

Spreading plastic is simple once you get the hang of it. Apply plastic smoothly and quickly, and then allow it to harden.

leave it to dry. As soon as the plastic turns to a solid state (about the consistency of soft rubber) take your plastic file and, very lightly, knock off any high spots. Don't file too heavily, though, as the file will dig in and puller the plastic loose from the metal. After you've done this, let it set up for about fifteen to thirty minutes, depending on the temperature and the amount of hardener you used. One word of caution here. Don't spread the plastic on and then go in to eat lunch, because when you come back, the filler will be hard as stone. If you don't work the plastic in stages as just explained, your labor will be doubles. It is ready for filing when you can barely nick the surface with your fingernail.

After the plastic has set for about half an hour, it is time to work it down with the sandpaper. If the area is very small, use the rubber block and a piece of $3\frac{3}{4}$ in. x 9 in. (36-grit). If it is large, use the sanding board and a piece of 17 in. x $3\frac{3}{4}$ in. (36-grit). Sand the plastic

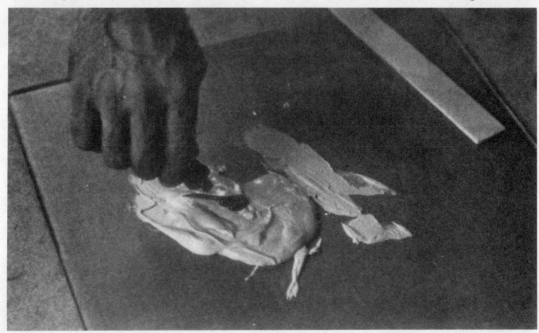

Mixing the hardener into the plastic takes practice because temperature and humidity determine how much hardener to use. Too little is better than too much.

Mix the plastic thoroughly before applying it to avoid soft spots in your work.

smooth, watching that you don't get the area too low. This is just the first coat so if you notice low spots and pin holes in the work, don't worry about it. When you first sanding on fresh plastic, you will notice that the sandpaper tends to clog. Use a small knife or similar object to flick off the specks from time to time to keep the paper from completely filling up. After you have gotten the area to about the right height, wipe the panel with a clean rag and recoat it with another application of plas-

tic. You will notice that this time the material will go on much smoother and you will have more control when spreading it. Just as before, get it smooth and then leave it alone. Repeat the procedure you used on the first coat with the file and then allow it to set up hard. Now, work the plastic down with a sanding block or sanding board to one sixteenth of an inch of the desired finished height.

Now, change your paper to the 80-grit and continue to

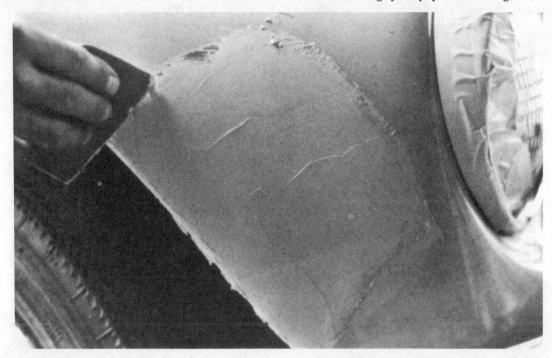

Learn to apply the plastic quickly. Once you get use to it, there is plenty of time to tin the metal with small amounts of your spreader.

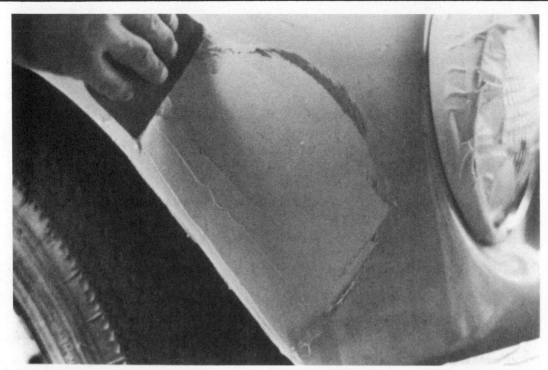

When making your final strokes, try to follow the contour of the panel. The smoother you apply the plastic, the easier the rest of your work will be.

work it down to the finished level. Knowing when to stop with the 36-grit and start with the 80-grit will come to you after a few times. The beauty of it all is that if you get too low with the 80-grit, you can always apply another coat. If you have trouble telling whether you are too low or too high by using the palm of your hand, grab the yardstick again the use it to spot the voids. It works just as well during this stage as it did when you were bumping out the panel. Usually a second or third coat on the damaged area is the standard for a good body man, but if it takes you five or six, don't worry about it. You're new at this.

THINK STRAIGHT. The important thing is to learn to read what the palm of your hand tells you as you run it

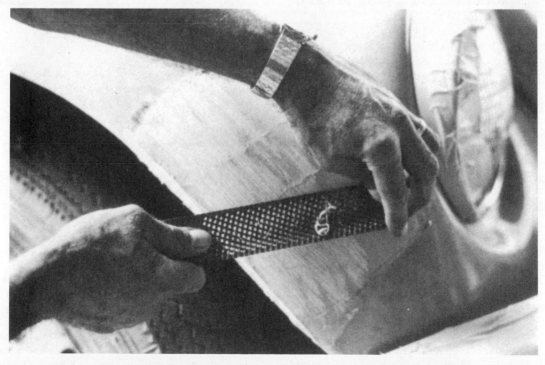

Remember to use the plastic file as soon as the plastic hardens to the consistency of rubber. If you wait too long to file, you work will be doubled.

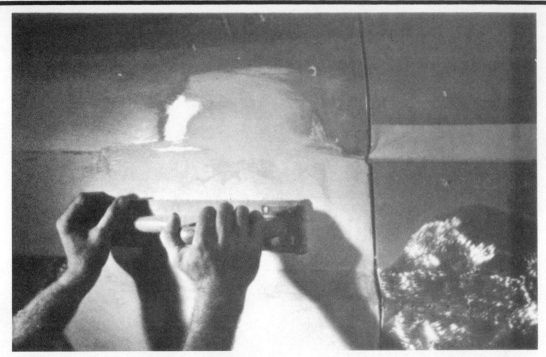

Using the sanding board to work the plastic down.

over the panel. Running your hand back and forth rapidly over the panel, won't tell you a thing except that it isn't straight. Your hand will automatically tell your brain that it feels lumps and waves. Watch your hand as you move it slowly along the repair and concentrate on what is high and what is low. Let's say you're very close to having the panel perfect. It's a natural tendency to think that this is good enough, and when it is painted, it won't show. WRONG! Painting not only DOESN'T HIDE, IT HIGHLIGHTS DEFECTS.

This is where the amateur can often do a better job than a lot of body shops. Most body men work on a percentage of the total labor of every job; therefore, the quicker they finish one job, the quicker they can start another. If it is not perfect (just close), instead of "hitting it" one more time, they turn it over to the painter. Most body men know from experience how much they can get away with, and if the shop doesn't insist on perfect work, the customer gets a sloppy job. Since time should not be one of your motives, there is not excuse to anything but perfection.

Priming and Glazing

When you are sure the panel is straight, when it looks good and your hand tells you it is good, let's take one more step to insure it is not only good, but perfect Take a clean rag and wipe the panel clean. Now, shake the aerosol can or primer thoroughly as per the instructions on the label. Apply a medium coat of primer over the area you have just repaired. Be sure all the plastic is covered and just a few inches of the metal surround it. Don't go way out on the metal and onto the old finish edge, as you will just be wasting material. Let the primer dry; thirty minutes is usually sufficient.

When the primer is dry, take the small rubber squeegee and the tube of glazing putty and apply a thin covering of putty over the repaired area. Apply this material smoothly and quickly. You will notice that if you go back over an area that you had puttied just seconds before, it will tear the film of the first application. In other words, squeeze about a tablespoon of putty onto the edge of the squeegee and immediately, with one quick stroke, apply it the length of the repaired area. If there is still some putty on the squeegee after the first pass, drop down and wipe it on right below the first pass. When you have the area covered, leave it to dry for about an hour.

Clean the squeegee at once with lacquer thinner and a rag. If it takes longer than an hour for the putty to dry, you probably put it on too thickly. The purpose of glazing putty is to fill sandpaper scratches, small low spots in your work, and pin holes in the plastic.

When the putty is dry, take a paint paddle and cut it to nine inches with a wood saw or a hack saw. Now, take a piece of 3¾ in. x 9 in. (100-grit) sandpaper, and fold it over the shortened paint paddle lengthwise. Lay the covered paint paddle flat on the puttied area and sand it down until it is smooth. When you finish sanding, there shouldn't be very much putty left on the panel, as it was only applied to fill sandpaper marks, pin holes and very minute low spots. You should see most of the primer that you previously applied. I like to think of putty as nothing but thick primer. In the old days of body repair, scratches and voids were filled by priming heavily and sanding, sometimes as many as five or six times. With glazing putty, you do the same thing in one operation. When you have finished sanding the area with the paint paddle and the 100-grit paper, take another piece of 100-grit paper and fold it in thirds lengthwise. With the folded paper in your palm, very lightly go over your work with long smooth strokes.

Don't sand in any one spot but in long strokes the entire length of the repaired area. If you dwell on one spot, you will lose everything you have gained and finish with a wavy job. Take a clean rag and thoroughly wipe the area. Now, get down close to your work and carefully inspect it. Look for any imperfections or pin holes that may still remain. If you see any bad spots, get the putty and squeegee out and do these spots individually, with just enough material to do the job. In other words,

if you see a few pin holes, wipe the putty into the holes flush with the surface rather than put a big god on and have to go through the blocking procedure again. These areas should dry in just a few minutes. When dry, sand them smooth with 100-grit, being careful not to overdo it and damage the adjacent areas. Wipe the area down again and prime the entire area with a medium coat. When you apply the primer this time, prime over the old finished edge a couple of inches. This will prevent the metal from rusting until it can be painted.

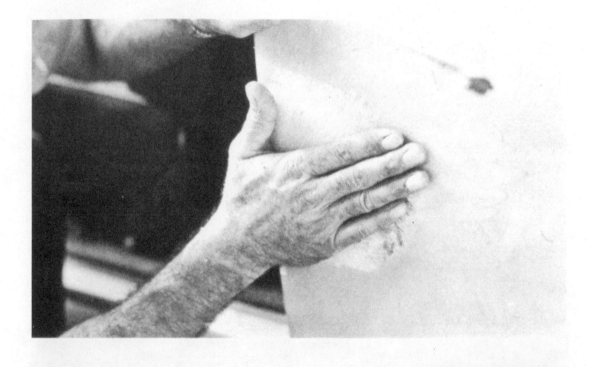

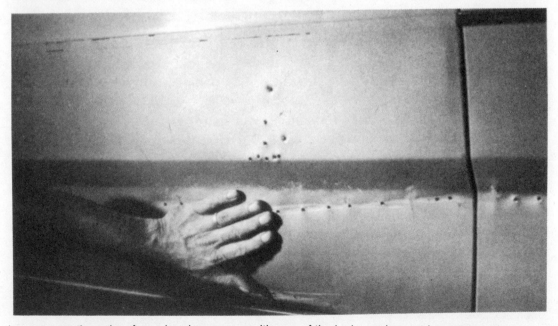

Learn to use the palm of your hand as a gauge. It's one of the body man's most important tools.

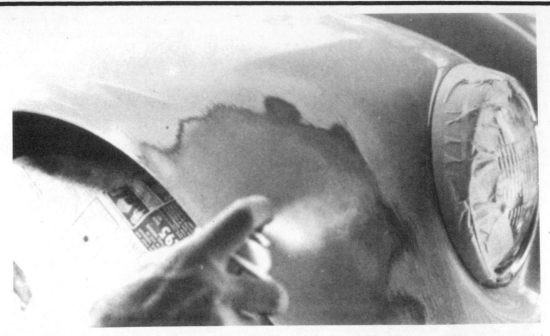

Allowing the first medium coat of primer to go way beyond the edge of the old finish just wastes material.

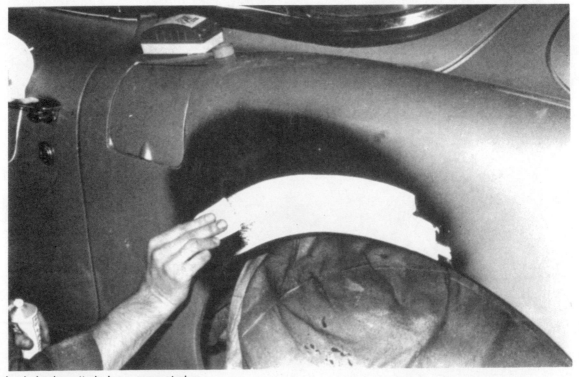

Apply body putty in long, even strokes.

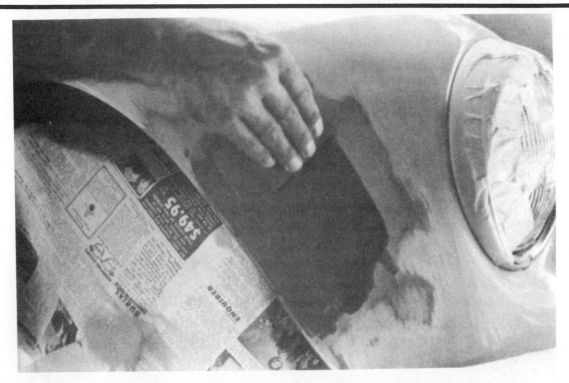

Apply glazing putty in one stroke applications. If you go over what you have already spread you will tear the previous application away from the surface.

Lacquer thinner is the best for cleaning putty from your squeegee. Be careful with this liquid, though, as it is more flammable than gasoline.

After the putty as dried, block sand with the shortened paint paddle and 100-grit paper. This removes scratches and small low spots.

Finish sanding with a piece of 100-grit paper folded in thirds. Use long even strokes. Sand very lightly.

KEY STEPS TO EASY BODY REPAIR

1. Study the damage before you start.
2. Try to imagine how the damage was done.
3. Work the panel back to shape slowly. Take your time.
4. When grinding back the old finish, go far enough so that no plastic will be on the old finish when you're through.
5. Learn to use the palm of your hand. A good body man can't work without it.
6. Don't depend on paint ot hide anything. If you can feel it, you will definitely see it when the job is done.
7. Glaze small imperfections in your plastic work-pin holes, scratches and very minor low spots with smooth quick strokes.
8. Block your glazing with the paint paddle and 100-grit sandpaper.
9. Prime lightly, covering all bare spots to prevent rust.

Folding 100-grit paper over shortened paint paddle for use in blocking glazing putty.

Repairing Minor Surface Scratches

REPAIR ONE

Just about every car or truck has minor scratches, superficial rust spots or other surface imperfections in the paint. These 2 rust spots on a Blazer fender were caused by spilled battery acid, and can be easily repaired in this stage without the use of body filler, before they rust through the sheetmetal.

REPAIR 1

Repairing Minor Surface Scratches

TIME REQUIRED: 30 minutes–1 hour

TOOLS

No hand tools required

MATERIALS

*Clean rag or tack cloth
*Solvent
*320 and 400 grit sandpaper
*Primer and paint
 Rubbing compound
 Masking tape and newspaper

*Starred items are packaged individually or in kit form by major manufacturers of auto body repair products and are available from auto supply and accessory stores.

Step 1. Minor scratches and surface rust such as these can usually be repaired without using body filler

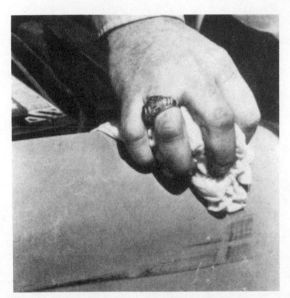

Step 2. Wash the area to remove all traces of dirt and road grime. Wash it with a Prep-Sol, Formula 409 or some other solvent to remove the coating of wax, so that the paint will stick

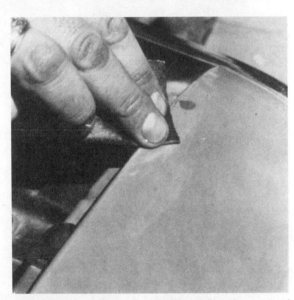

Step 3. Small rust spots and scratches like these require only light sanding. Start with 320 grit

Step 4. Finish the sanding with a piece of 400 grit wetted from a bucket of water. Wet sanding will feather the edges of the surrounding paint. For large areas you should use a sanding block, but it's not necessary for small jobs

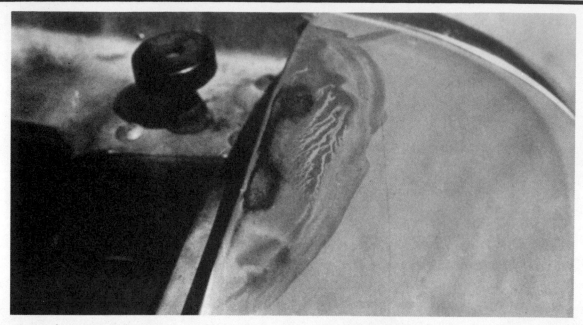

Step 5. It should look like this when you're finished wet sanding. Wipe off the water and run your hand over the area-you shouldn't feel any bumps or ridges. If you do, more wet sanding is needed to feather the edges

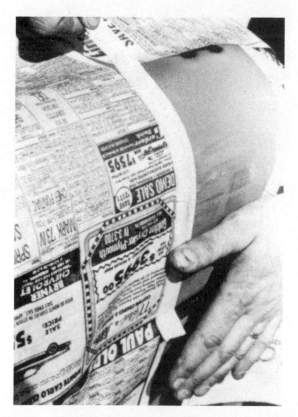

Step 6. Once you have the area sanded to your satisfaction, mask the surrounding area with masking tape and newspaper. Be sure to cover any chrome

Step 7. If you haven't painted before, practice on a piece of scrap metal. Keep the can moving to avoid runs or sags. The primered areas should look like this when you have finished. It's better to spray several light coats than one heavy coat. Let the primer dry for several minutes between coats. Make sure you've covered all the bare metal

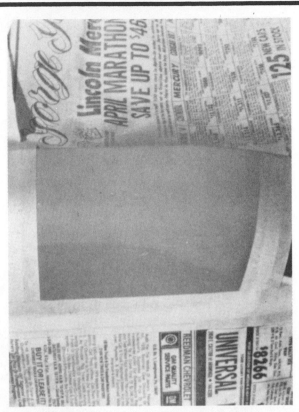

Step 8. After the primer has dried, sand the area lightly with wet 400 paper, wash it off and let it dry. Your final coat goes on next, so make sure the area is clean and dry

Step 9. Wipe the primered area dry with a clean rag and spray the finish coat of paint. Make the first coat a light coat (known as a fog coat). Keep the pain can moving smoothly 8-12 inches from the surface. Be sure to cover the area

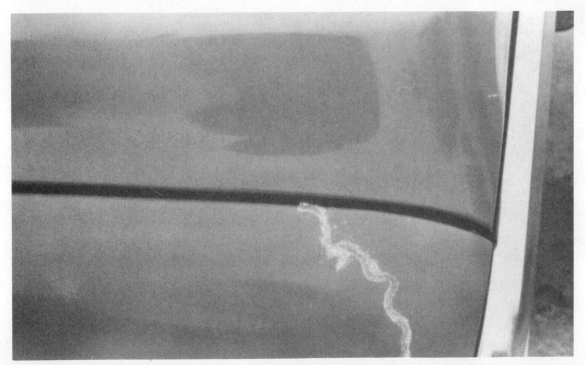

Step 10. Let the paint dry for 15 minutes before removing the masking tape. Let the paint dry for several days before rubbing it out with fine rubbing compound. This will blend the overspray into the existing paint to make the repair indistinguishable. Don't rub too hard or you'll cut through the paint

Deep Scratches and Minor Dents

REPAIR TWO

Almost every car falls prey to a deep scratch or minor dent at some time in its left. They can result from parking lot incidents, scraping the garage, vandalism or very minor accidents. These blemishes are almost always deep enough to require the use of body filler, but rarely are deep enough to pull the metal out with a puller or hammer it out from behind the panel.

This type of repair is easy to make and can save you anywhere from $50–75 at body shop prices.

REPAIR 2

Repairing Deep Scratches and Minor Dents

TIME REQUIRED: 1–1½ hours

TOOLS

Electric drill
Grinding attachment
Body file
Safety goggles

MATERIALS

*Body filler and hardener
*Sanding block
*Spreader
*80, 100, 200 and 320 sandpaper
*Primer
 Paint

*Starred items are packaged individually or in kit form by major manufacturers of auto body repair products and are available from auto supply and accessory stores.

Step 1. This dent (arrow) is typical of a deep scratch or minor dent. If deep enough, the dent or scratch can be pulled out or hammered out from behind. In this case no straightening was necessary

Step 2. Using an 80-grit disc on an electric drill grind the paint from the surrounding area down to bare metal. This will provide a rough surface for the body filler to grab

Step 3. The area should look like this when you're finished grinding

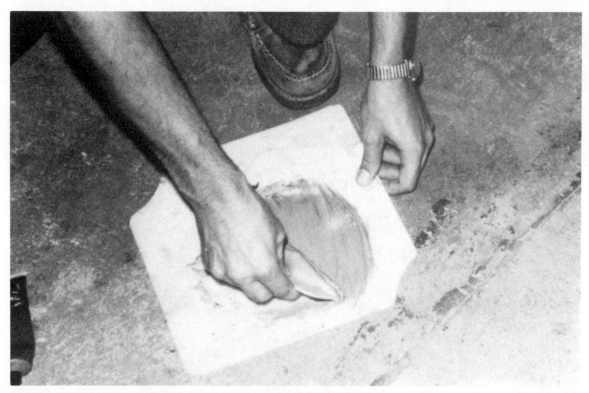

Step 4. Mix the body filler and dram hardener according to the directions

Step 5. Spread the body filler evenly over the entire area. Be sure to cover the area completely

Step 6. Let the body filler dry until the surface can just be scratched with your fingernail

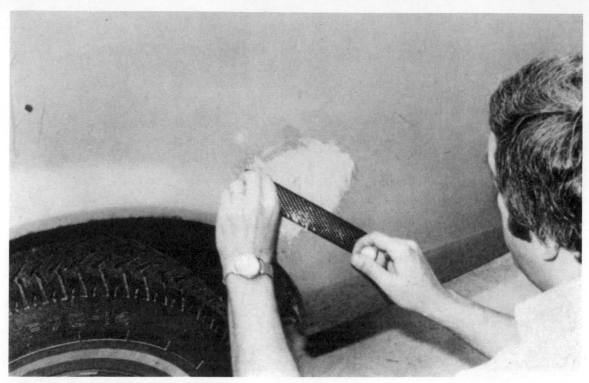

Step 7. Knock the high spots from the body filler with a body file

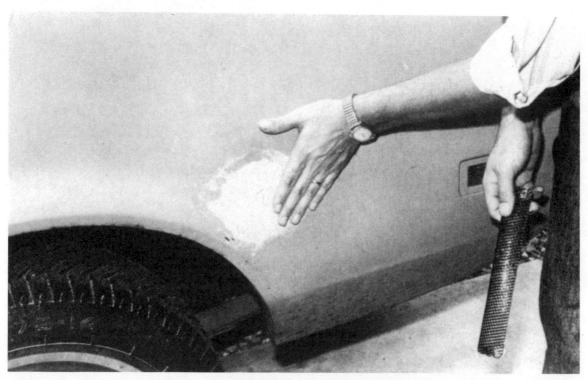

Step 8. Check frequently with the palm of your hand for high and low spots. If you wind up with low spots, you may have to apply another layer of filler

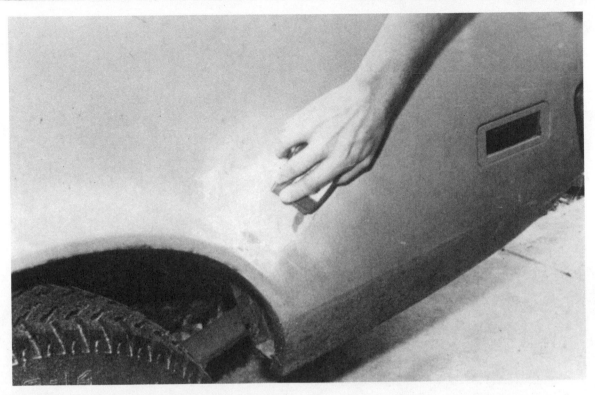

Step 9. Block sand the entire area with 320 grit paper

Step 10. When you're finished, the repair should look like this. Note the sand marks extending 2–3 in. out from the repaired area

Step 11. Prime the entire area with automotive primer

Step 12. The finished repair ready for the final paint coat. Note that the primer has covered the sanding marks (see Step 10). A repair of this size should be able to be spotpainted with good results. See the sections on "Prepping for Paint" and "Painting Techniques"

Small Fender Dent

REPAIR THREE

This creased Volkswagen fender, is a classic parking lot dent. Careless parkers will leave you little reminders like this of their thoughtlessness. Notice that the exposed, bare metal has already begun to rust. These dents are usually too deep to simply fill in. They should be pulled out with a dent puller.

REPAIR 3

Repairing Small Fender Dents

TIME REQUIRED: 1½–2½ hours

TOOLS

Electric drill
Grinding attachment
Body hammer
Body file
Safety goggles

MATERIALS

Paint paddle
*Body filler and hardener
Sanding block
*Spreader
*80, 100, 220 and 320 grit sandpaper
Squeegee
*Primer
Paint

*Starred items are packaged individually or in kit form by major manufacturers of auto body repair products and are available from auto supply and accessory stores.

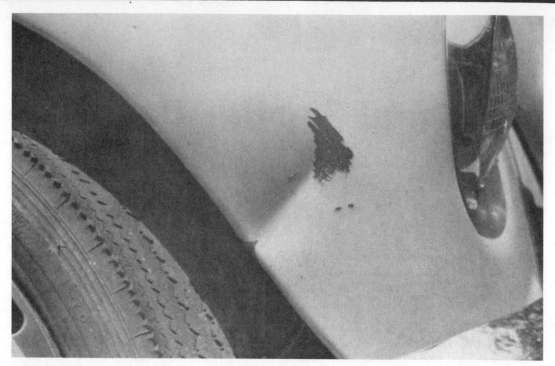

Step 1. Study the panel and read the stress lines. A little thinking here can often save a lot of work

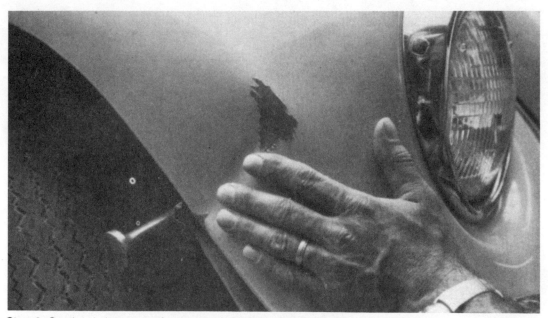

Step 2. Cautiously bump out the crease using the palm of your hand to feel you way

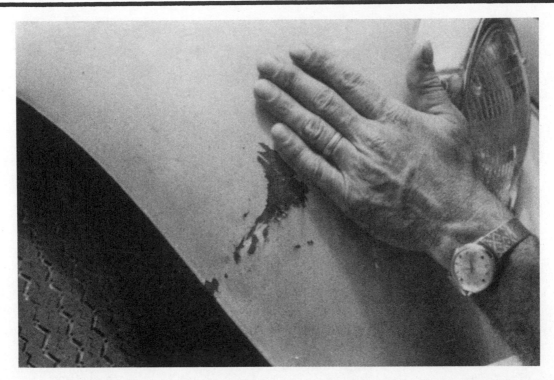

Step 3. Think straight! As you move your hand along the panel, read what your palm is telling you about the surface

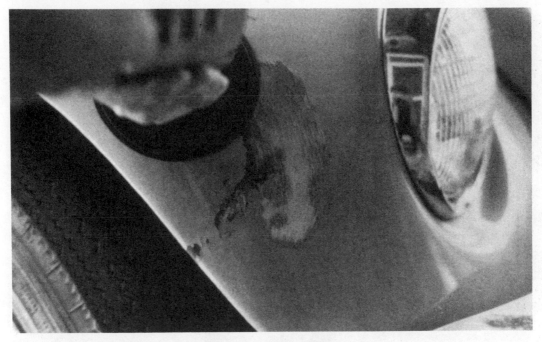

Step 4. Remove the old finish with a drill and grinding attachment

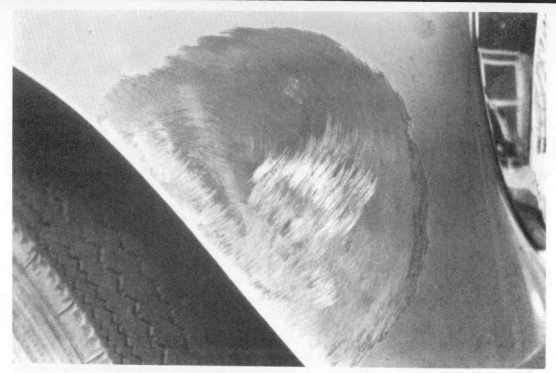

Step 5. The area should look like this when you are finished grinding

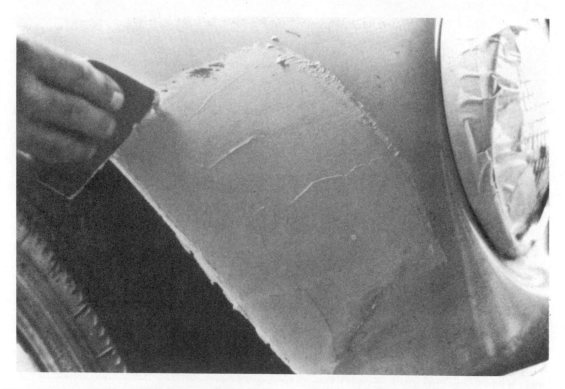

Step 6. When the panel is ground clean (above) mix the plastic (see Section 1) and apply plastic as quickly and as smoothly as possible (below). Mask off the chrome trim

Step 7. File the plastic before it gets too hard

Step 8. Using a sanding block for small jobs or a sanding board for larger ones, work the plastic down to about the desired height

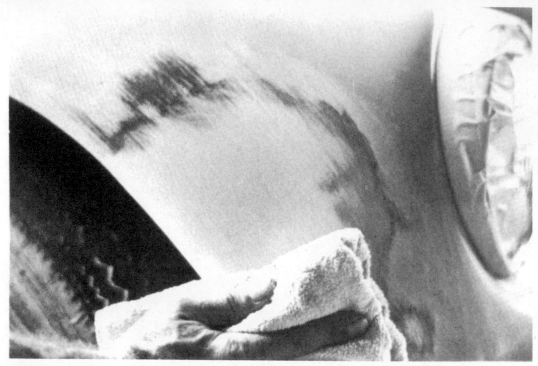

Step 9. Wipe the area with a clean rag or tack cloth

Step 10. Recoat the area with plastic body filler

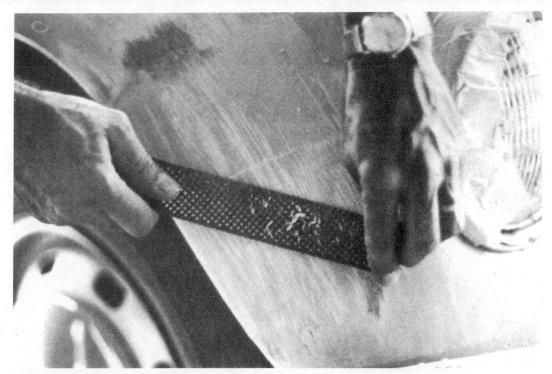

Step 11. Use your file as soon as the plastic becomes solid

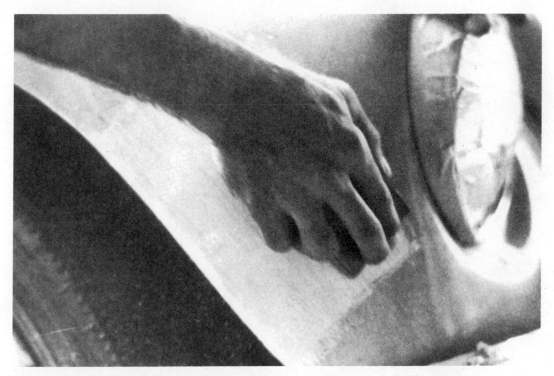

Step 12. Work the plastic down to within a hair of the desired height

Step 13. Finish sanding with a piece of 80-grit folded in thirds. Use long smooth strokes

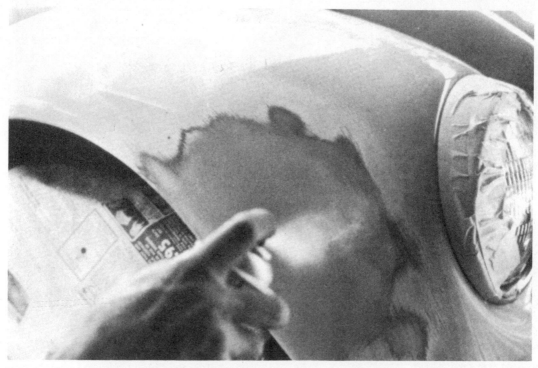

Step 14. Prime the repair area with a medium coat

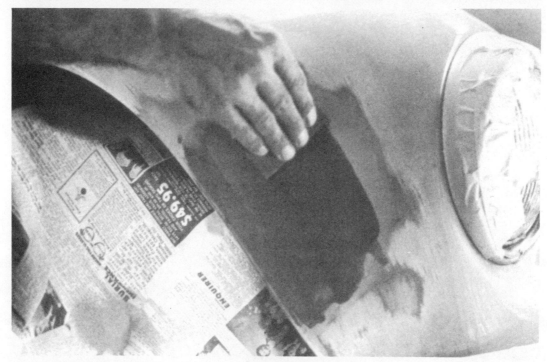

Step 15. Apply glazing putty with a squeegee

Step 16. After the glazing has dried, block sand with a paint paddle and 100-grit paper

Step 17. Finish sanding with a piece of 100-grit paper folded in thirds

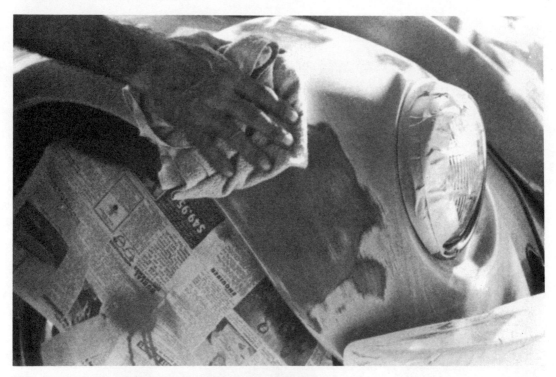

Step 18. Clean the entire area with a clean rag or tack cloth

Step 19. Re-prime the entire area

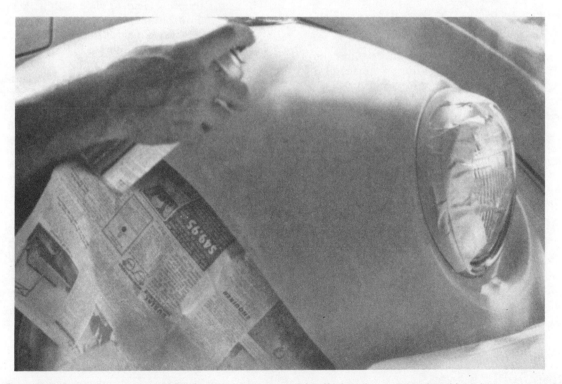

Step 20. Be sure to prime out over the old finish edge to prevent rusting if it is going to be painted later by someone else. If you are going to finish painting the panel yourself you are ready to finish sanding the primer. See the section on "Prepping for Paint" and "Painting Techniques"

Rust Problems

RUST PROBLEMS

In these days of soaring transportation costs, owners are hanging onto their cars as long as possible. Thousands of cars 10 years or older are still providing faithful service showing little or no evidence of body or structural deterioration. On the other hand, there are probably an equal number of cars and trucks taking up space in junkyards, victims of body or frame rust. Between the 2 extremes are hundreds of thousands of cars and trucks with varying degrees of rust, that not only makes the body unsightly (and possibly dangerous), but also reduces the car's value in the resale market.

CAUSES OF RUST

Rust is an electrochemical process. It works on ferrous metals (iron and steel) from the inside out due to exposure of unprotected surfaces to air and moisture. The possibility of rust exists practically nationwide-anywhere humidity, industrial pollution or chemical salts are present, rust can form. In coastal areas, the problem is high humidity and salt air; in snowy areas, the problem is chemical salt (de-icer) used to keep the roads clear, and in industrial area, sulphur dioxide is present in the air from industrial pollution and is changed to sulphuric acid when it rains. The rusting process is accelerated by high temperatures, especially in snowy areas, when vehicles are driven over slushy roads and then left overnight in a heated garage.

Automotive styling also can be a contributor to rust formation. Spot welding of panels creates small pockets that trap moisture and forms an environment for rust formation. Fortunately, auto manufacturers have been working hard to increase the corrosion protection of their products. Galvanized sheet metal enjoys much wider sue, along with the increased use od plastic and various rust retardant coatings. Manufacturers are also designing out areas in the body where rust-forming moisture can collect.

PREVENTING RUST

To prevent rust, you must stop it before it gets started. On new cars, there are 2 ways to accomplish this.

First, the car should be treated with a commercial rustproofing compound. There are many different brands of franchised rustproofers, but most processes involve spraying a waxy "self-healing" compound under the chassis, inside rocker panels, inside doors and fender lines and similar places where rust is likely to form. Prices for a quality rustproofing job range from $100–250, depending on the area, the brand name and the size of the vehicle.

Ideally, the vehicle should be rustproofed as soon as possible following the purchase. The surfaces of the car or truck have begun to oxidize and deteriorate during shipping. In addition, the car may have sat on a dealer's lot or on a lot at the factory, and once the rust has progressed past the stage of light, powdery surface oxidation rustproofing is not likely to be worthwhile. Professional rustproofers feel that once rust has formed, rustproofing operations offer a 3–5 year warranty against rust-through, but will not support that warranty if the rustproofing is not applied within 3 months of the date of manufacture.

Undercoating should not be mistaken for rustproofing. Undercoating is a black, tar-like substance that is applied to the underside of a vehicle. Its basic function is to deaden noises that are transmitted from under the car of the areas where rust is likely to form. It simply cannot get into the crevices and seams where moisture tends to collect. In fact, it may clog up drainage holes and ventilation passages. Some under coatings also tend to crack or peel with age and only create more moisture and corrosion attracting pockets.

The second thing you should do immediately after purchasing the car is apply a paint sealout. These are petroleum based products marketed under a wide variety of brand names. It has the same protective properties as a good wax, but cover the paint with a chemically inert layer that bonds to the paint, to seal it from the air. If air can't get at it, oxidation cannot start.

The paint sealant kit consists of a base coat and conditioning coat that should be applied every 6–8 months, depending on the manufacturer. The base coat must be applied before the car is waxed, or the wax must first be removed.

Third, keep a garden hose handy for your car in winter. Use it a few times on nice days during the winter for underneath areas, and it will pay bid dividends when spring arrives. Spraying under the fenders and other areas which even carwashes don't reach will help remove road salt, dirt and other build-ups which help breed rust. Adjust the nozzle to a high-force spray. An old brush will help break up residue, permitting it to be washed away more easily.

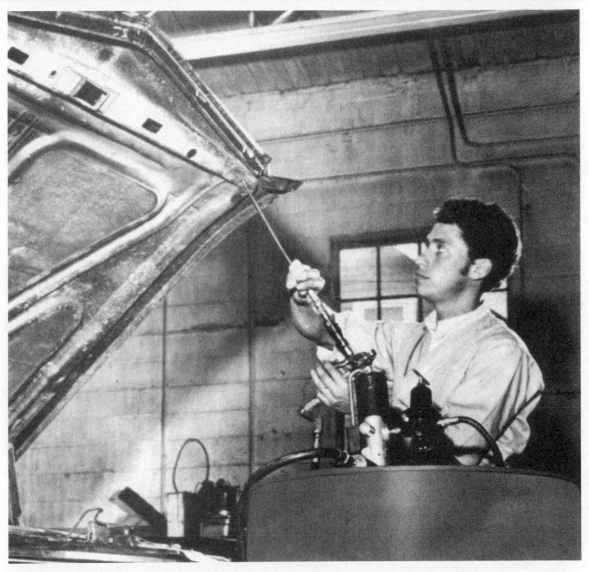

Professional rustproofing jobs are expensive, must be done within 3 months, but will protect hard to reach areas

It's a somewhat messy job, but it will be worth it in the long run because a car's rust often starts in those hidden areas.

At the same time, wash grime off the door sills, and, more importantly, the under portions of the doors, plus the tailgate if you have a station wagon or truck. Applying a coat of wax to those areas at least once before and once during winter will help fend off rust.

When applying the was to the under parts of the doors, you will note small drain holes. These holes often are plugged with undercoating or dirt. Make sure they are cleaned out to prevent water build-up inside the doors. A small punch or penknife will do the job.

Water from the high-pressure sprays in carwashes sometimes can get into the housings for parking and taillights, so take a close look, and if they contain water, merely loosen the retaining screws and the water should run out

Do-It-Yourself Rustproofing

Professional rustproofing jobs consist of drilling holes in exactly the right places through which the rustproofing is sprayed, by special equipment. Naturally, the location of the holes is different on each model, which requires precise specifications and the equipment is not expensive, which somewhat justifies the big price.

The alternative to a professional rustproofing job is a do-it-yourself kit, at a fraction on the cost of a professional aftermarket job. The kits consist of aerosol spray cans of rustproofing, plastic wands to reach inside panels, doors and fenders, and small rubber or plastic plugs to close the access holes that must be drilled.

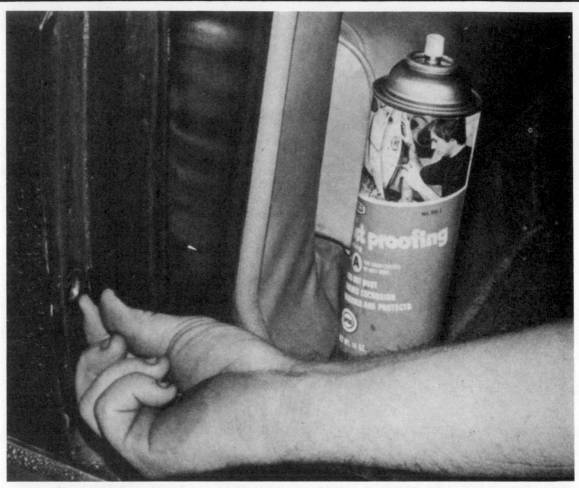

Do-it-yourself rustproofing kits contain aerosol cans of rustproofing compound, plastic wand to reach out-of-the-way areas and rubber plugs to seal access holes

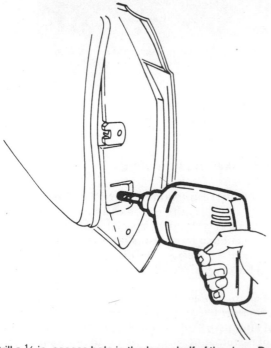

Drill a ½ in. access hole in the lower half of the door. Be sure there is nothing behind the door and the windows are rolled up

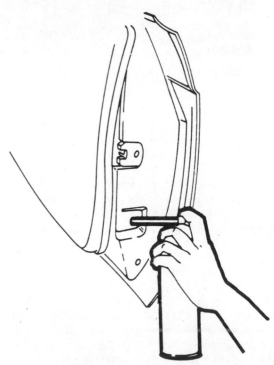

Attach a wand to the spray can and insert in the door as far as possible. Coat the entire inside metal door surface

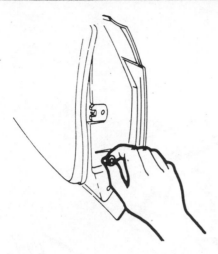

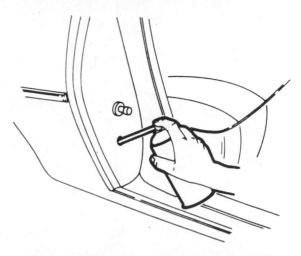

Plug the drilled hole with a ½ in. rubber or plastic plug. Repeat the operation for all doors and tailgates

The quarterpanel can normally be reached through the trunk or through an access hole drilled in the front part. Follow directions for the insides of doors

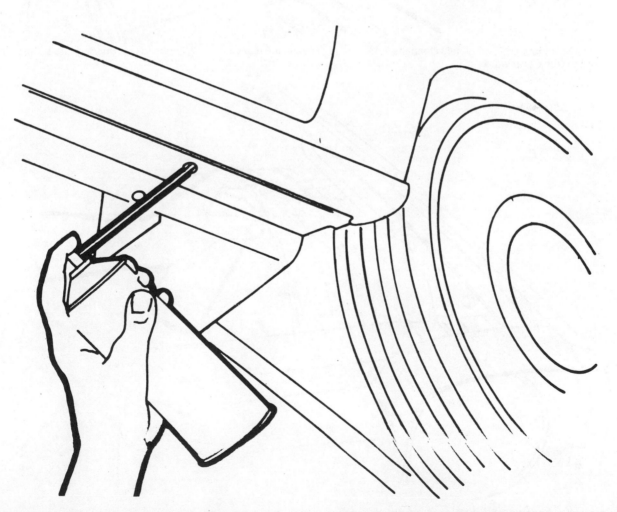

Rocker panels are one of the most rust-prone areas and access depends on the individual can. There may be drain or access holes; if not, you'll have to drill access holes

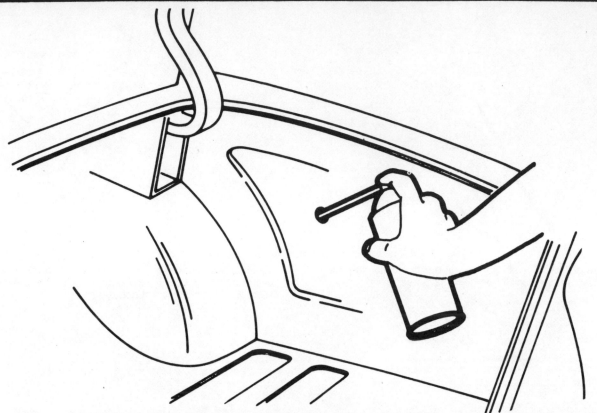

Remove the floor mats and completely clean the trunk. Spray between the rear wheelwell, floor and rear quarterpanels. Spray the bottom of the trunk and walls

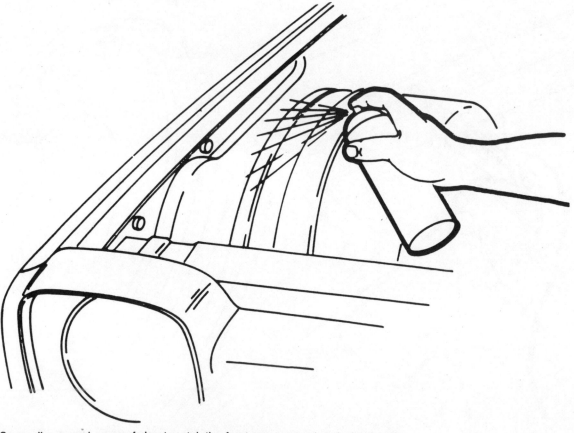

Spray all exposed areas of sheet metal, the front quarterpanel and wheel wells

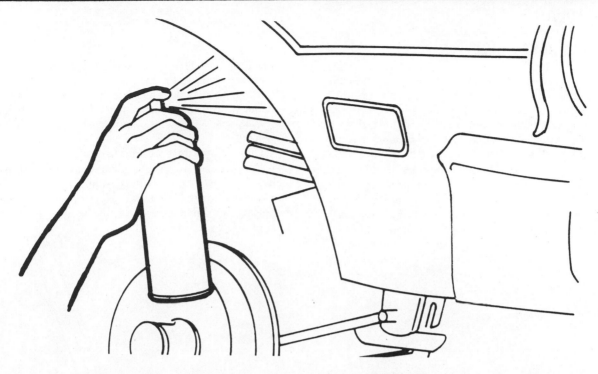

Remove the wheels and cover the brake drums or discs. Spray the entire inside of the fender liner after cleaning away all dirt

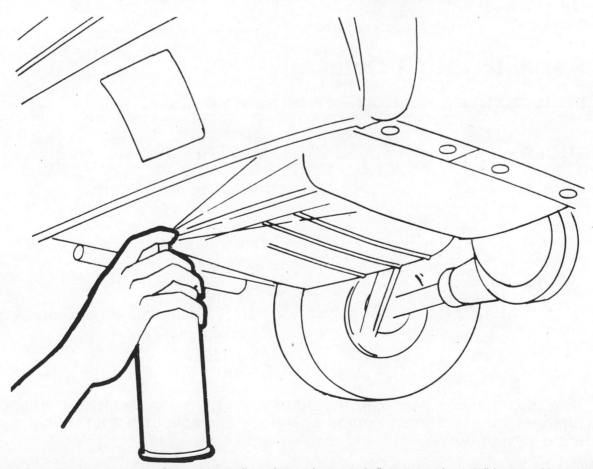

Block the wheels and support the car. Clean all loose dirt and spray the gas tank, floor pan and accessible parts of fender wells. Do not spray brake drums, drive shaft, exhaust system, shock absorbers or rubber parts

REPAIRING RUST HOLES

Rust if the number one enemy of your car. It is the hardest problem to stop from happening and the hardest to cure once it has happened.

One thing you have to remember about rust. Even if you grind away all the rusted metal in a panel, and repair the area with any of the kits available, EVENTUALLY the rust will return. There a 2 reasons for this. One, rust is a chemical reaction that causes pressure under the repair from the inside out. That's how the blisters form. Two, the back side of the panel (and the repair) is wide open to moisture, and unpainted body filler acts like a sponge. That's why the best solution to rust problems is to remove the rusted panel and install a new one or have the rusted area cut out and a new piece of sheet metal welded in it place. The trouble with welding is the expense; sometimes it will cost more than the car is worth.

One of the better solutions to do-it-yourself rust repair is the process using a fiberglass cloth repair kit (shown here). This will give a strong repair that resists cracking and moisture and is relatively easy to use. It can be used on large or small holes and can be applied even over contoured surfaces.

REPAIR 4

Repairing Rust-Outs

ESTIMATED TIME REQUIRED: 1½–2 hours depending on size

TOOLS

Electric drill
Sanding attachment
Scissors
Grease pencil or marker
*Mixing stick
*Mixing tray

MATERIALS

Grinding disc (35 grit)
*Repair jelly
*Cream hardener
*Fiberglass cloth
*Release film
*Sandpaper in 80, 100, 220 and 400 grits
*Glazing compound (topcoat)
*Spreaders
Primer
Spray paint

*Starred items are packaged individually or in kit form by major manufacturers of auto body repair products and are available from auto supply and accessory stores.

Step 1. Rust areas such as this are common and can be easily patched

Step 2. Grind away all traces of rust with a 24-grit grinding disc. Be sure to grind back 3–4 in. from the edge of the hole down to bare metal and be sure all traces of rust are removed

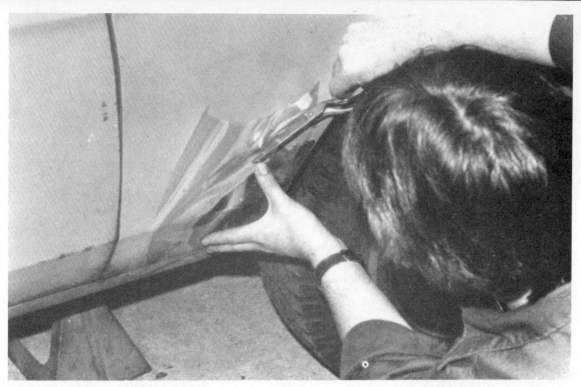

Step 3. If you are going to sue the release film, cut a piece about 2 in. larger than the area you have sanded. Place the film over the repair and mark the sanded area on the film. Avoid any unnecessary wrinkling of the film

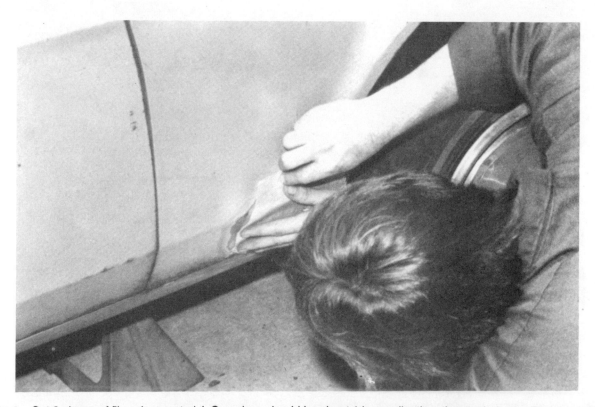

Step 4. Cut 2 pieces of fiberglass material. One piece should be about 1 in. smaller than the sanded area. The second piece should be 1 in. smaller than the first. Use sharp scissors to avoid loose ends

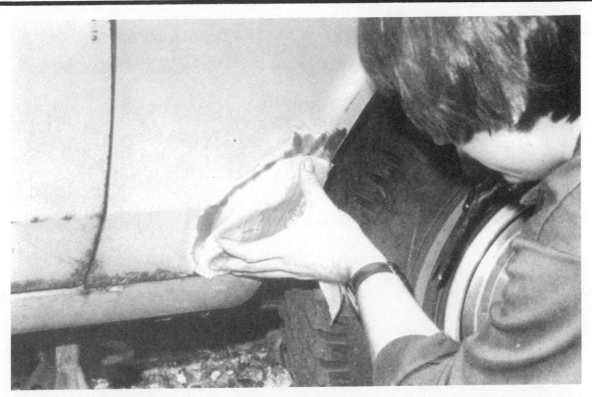

Step 5. Check the dimensions of the release film and fiberglass cloth by holding them up to the repair area

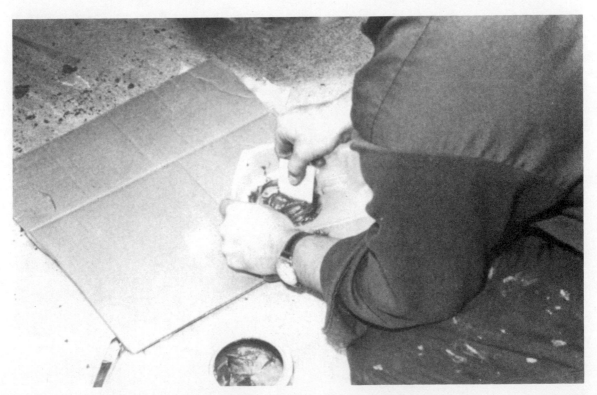

Step 6. Stir the repair jelly and place enough to saturate the fiberglass material or fill the repair area in the mixing tray. Add a 3 in. ribbon of cream hardener for each ounce of repair jelly and mix until the consistency is uniform

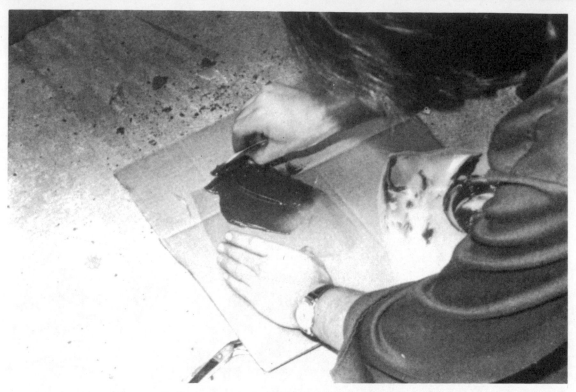

Step 7. Lay the release sheet on a flat surface and spread an even layer of filler, large enough to cover the repair

Step 8. Lay the smaller piece of fiberglass cloth in the center of the repair jelly. Spread another even coat of repair jelly larger over the fiberglass cloth and repeat the operation for the larger piece of cloth. If fiberglass material is not used, spread the repair jelly on the release film concentrated in the middle of the repair

Step 9. Place the repair material over the repair area, with the release film facing outward

Step 10. Use a spreader and work from the center outward smoothing the material, following the contours. Be sure to remove air bubbles

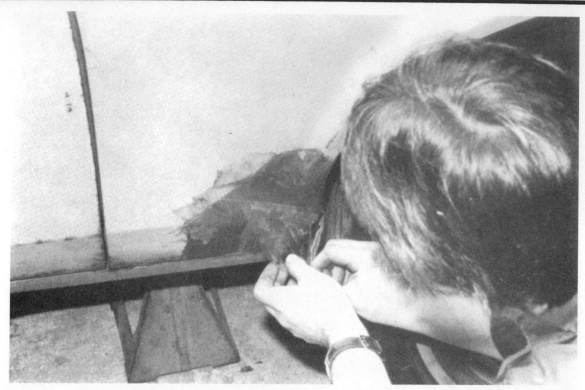

Step 11. Wait until the repair has dried tack-free and peel the release sheet off the repair. The ideal working temperature is 65–90°F. Cooler temperatures or high humidity may require additional curing time

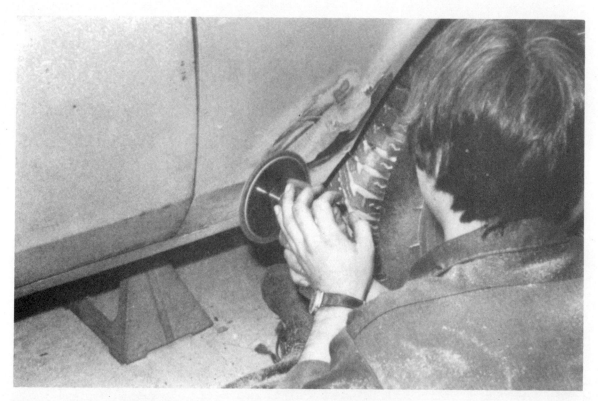

Step 12. Sand and feather-edge the entire area. The initial sanding can be done with a sanding disc

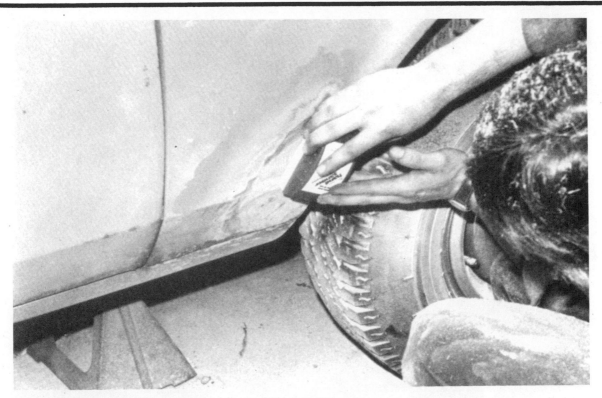

Step 13. Finish the sanding and feather-edging with a block sander

Step 14. For a smooth finish, and to prevent the glass matte from showing through, mix some topcoat with cream hardener and apply it directly with a spreader

Step 15. Sand the finish coat with finishing sandpaper

Step 16. When you're finished the repair area should look like this

Step 17. To finish this repair, grind out the surface rust along the top edge of the rocker panel

Step 18. Mix some repair jelly and cream hardener (see Step 6) and apply it directly over the surface. When it dries tack-free, block sand the surface smooth

Step 19. Sand the repair. When finished the whole repair should look like this. Note the taped door edge preparatory to painting

Step 20. Spray the entire area with a primer coat

Step 21. The repair is now ready to be painted with a finish coat. See the Chapters on "Prepping for Paint" and "Painting Techniques"

Creased Panel and Door Edge

REPAIR FIVE

This little crease in the Volkswagen's door is easily repaired using a dent puller. This 17 step procedure will restore the car's beauty and value at a fraction of the cost to have it repaired in a body shop.

REPAIR 5

Repairing a Creased Panel

TIME REQUIRED: 1–1½ hours

TOOLS

Electric drill
Grinding attachment
Drill bit (½ size of end of the dent
  puller)
Body file
Sanding block
Safety goggles

MATERIALS

*Plastic body filler and hardener
*Glazing putty
 Clean cloths or tack rag
 Paint paddle
*Sanding paper in 80, 100, 220 and
   320 grits depending on whether
   you're going to paint it yourself
*Primer
 Paint
 Squeegee
*Spreader

*Starred items are packaged individually or in kit form by major manufacturers of auto body repair products and are available from auto supply and accessory stores.

Step 1. Evaluate the damage. There is no way to tap this out from the inside, so it will have to be pulled out with a dent puller

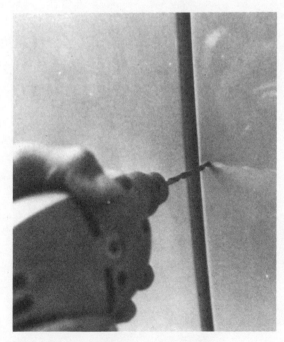

Step 2. Drill holes along the stress line

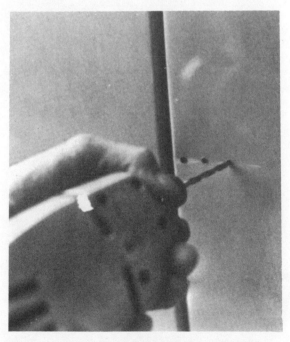

Step 3. Holes should be spaced one inch apart

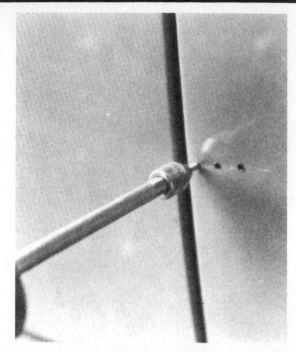

Step 4. Use the dent puller to bring the panel back to its original shape

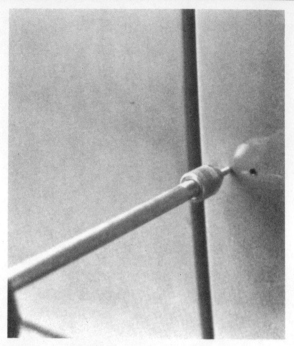

Step 5. Several light taps in each hole will keep the panel even. If it is still too low, repeat the step

Step 6. Mask the door edge and grind the old finish back

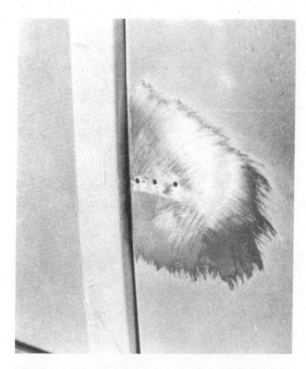

Step 7. After grinding the area should look like this

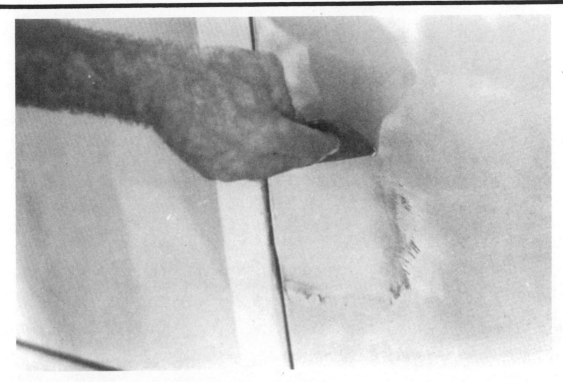

Step 8. Mix and apply the first coat of filler using a spreader

Step 9. File off any high spots as soon as the plastic becomes solid

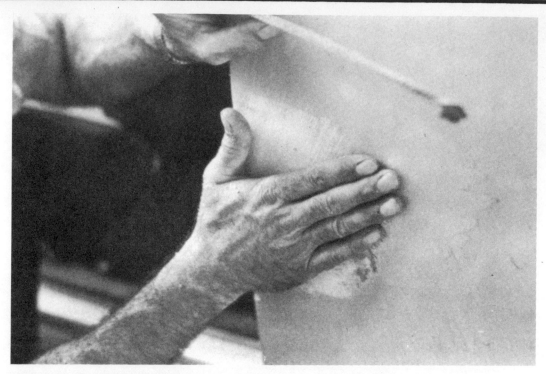

Step 10. Think straight. Find the highs and lows with your most valuable tool—the hand

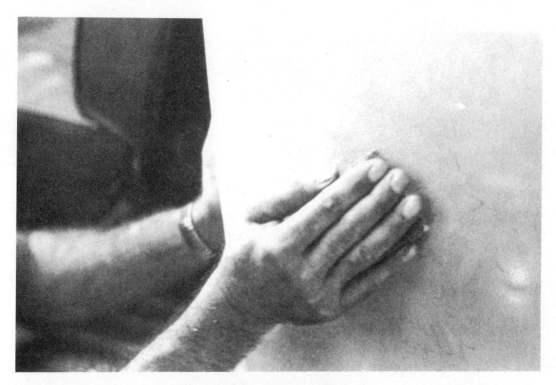

Step 11. Fell the high spots with your hand and the sandpaper

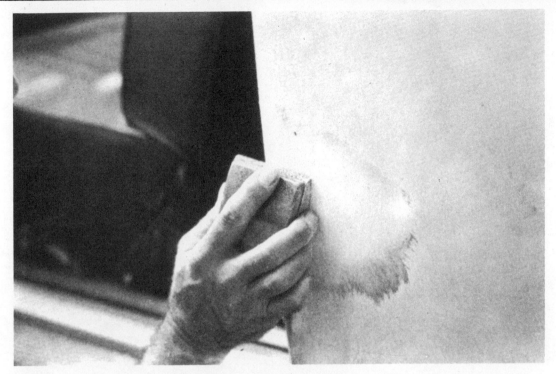

Step 12. Work the plastic down with the appropriate sanding tool

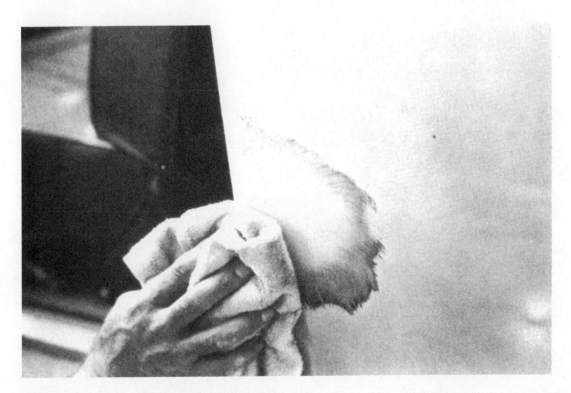

Step 13. Wipe the repair area clean with a rag

Step 14. Mask the area and prime it with a medium coat

Step 15. Apply the glazing putty with a squeegee

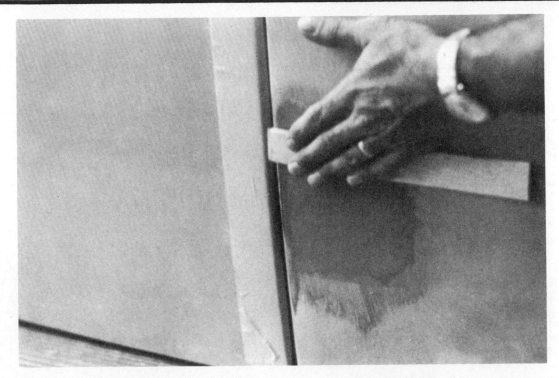

Step 16. Block sand the area with 100-grit paper wrapped around a paint paddle

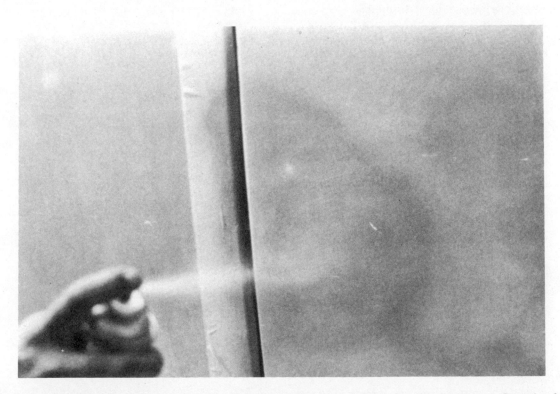

Step 17. Prime the entire area. You are now ready to finish sand and paint the area. See the sections on "Prepping for Paint" and "Painting Techniques"

Dented Trunk Lid or Hood

REPAIRS SIX AND SEVEN

The following two repairs differ only in that the panels are functional. The hook and the trunk lid, or deck lid as it is sometimes called, must open and close properly, so in addition to straightening the sheet metal, you have to align the panel so that it fits squarely in the opening it covers. This is not difficult, but will take some time and adjustment to get it right. As in the previous jobs, take your time and think the problem out.

Whenever you are working on a hood panel or deck lid, follow these basic steps.

1. Straighten the dent or damage that has been done to the panel by pulling or knocking it out as described in other repairs.
2. When the dent is roughed out and before you apply the plastic filler, align the panel so it fits the opening properly. There are several adjustments that can be made here. Though they seem impossible at first, take your time and follow the step-by-step photos.
3. When you have the dent roughed out and the panel aligned properly in the opening, apply your filler as you did before. The only other difference with these panels

(hoods and trunk lids) is that they are very visible to anyone looking at or driving the car. So do an extra special job so that your work is sure not to show. The best compliment any body man can be paid is for someone to say, "You can never notice his work."

One word of caution here for safety's sake. Upon repairing the hood panel, check the hood latch assembly. If there is any damage or if the latch doesn't seem to work well, go to the dealer and buy a new unit. Many a hood latch has been repaired enough to get by only to have the hood fly open at high speed, creating all kinds of havoc. Don't take the chance to save the low price of a new latch assembly.

The same problem exists with the trunk latch assembly. It is not likely to become a life and death situation, but if you try to repair a trunk latch that should really be replaced, you may find yourself unable to get into your trunk. This could be really frustrating after a thirty-mile drive to your favorite fishing spot when you find you can't get to your fishing gear on the inside. Replace latches that appear to be bad.

REPAIR 6 AND 7

Repairing a Dented Trunk or Hood

TIME REQUIRED: 2–3 hours each

TOOLS

Electric drill
Drill bit (½ size of end of dent puller)
Grinding attachment for electric drill
Dent puller
Open end adjustable wrench
Screwdriver
Socket wrench
Body file
Safety goggles

MATERIALS

*Plastic body filler and hardener
*Glazing putty
Clean cloths
Paint paddle
Sanding block
*Sanding paper in 28, 80, 100, 220 and 400 grits
Block of wood
*Primer and paint
*Spreader

*Starred items are packaged individually or in kit form by major manufacturers of auto body repair products and are available from auto supply and accessory stores.

REPAIRING A DENTED TRUNK LID

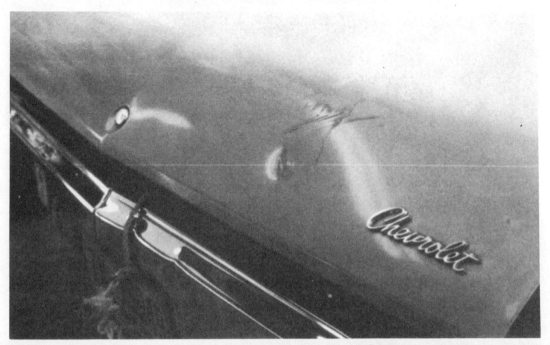

This trunk lid was hit just above the bumper. Follow the proper steps in repairing it. Pull out the dent, align the lid in the opening and metal finish the dent

Arrow shows how the impact knocked the lid out of alignment

The same deck lid at another angle. Note the trunk lid-body seam (arrows). The lid is pushed up at the upper arrow. When properly aligned, the gap in this seam will be even

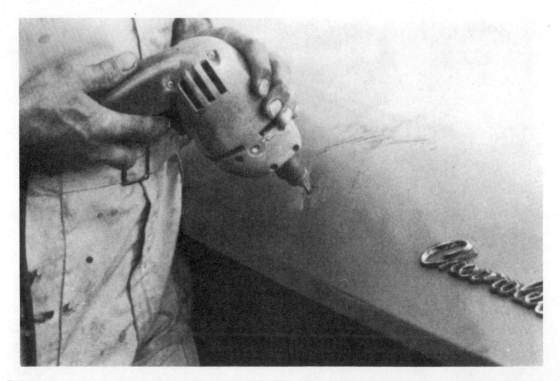

Step 1. Before attempting to align the lid, rough out the dent. This will remove any unseen stress in the lid. Make your holes for the puller with a drill. It may be possible to push the dent out from inside. See Crumpled Rear Quarterpanel

Step 2. Bring the lid panel back to its original position with the puller

Step 3. Grind back the old finish, using an electric drill and grinding attachment with 28 grade paper

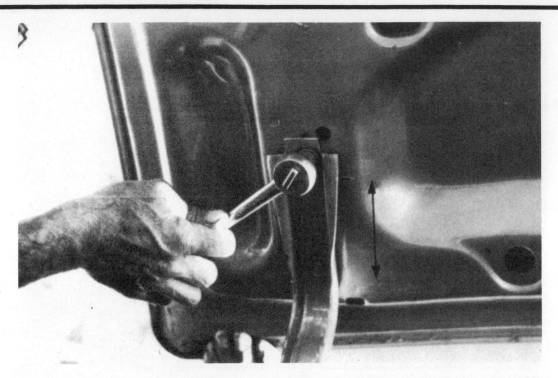

Step 4. Before applying plastic filler, align the lid in the opening. Arrows show the adjustment direction

Step 5. After the lid is properly aligned, the gap in the seams will be even. Continue making minor adjustments until the gap is even all the way around

Step 6. In cases where the leading edge of the lid is too high or too low, you will have to bend the hinges. To lower the leading edge (front of lid), simply open the trunk lid fully and then force it up

Step 7. To raise the leading edge of the trunk lid, use a wooden block as shown and force the lid down. Do one side at a time. The hinge will bend at the arrow

Step 8. To raise or lower the rear edge of the lid, simply adjust the latch mechanism. On this model, the latch assembly is in the lid and adjustes from side to side. The striker is on the rear body panel. The arrows show direction of adjustment

Step 9. On some cars, the adjustment locatins are reversed from those shown in Step 8

Step 10. Mix and apply the body filler. When it has dried sufficiently, cut it down with a body file (cheese grater)

Step 11. When the high spots have been removed with the body file, work it down with a block sander and 100 grit paper

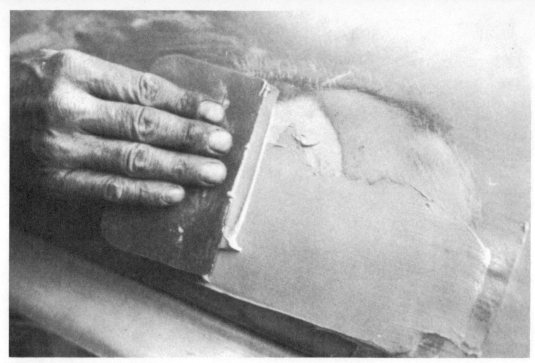

Step 12. Apply another coat

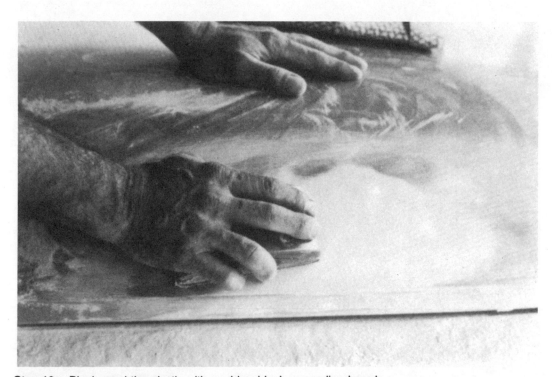

Step 13. Block sand the plastic with a rubber block or sanding board

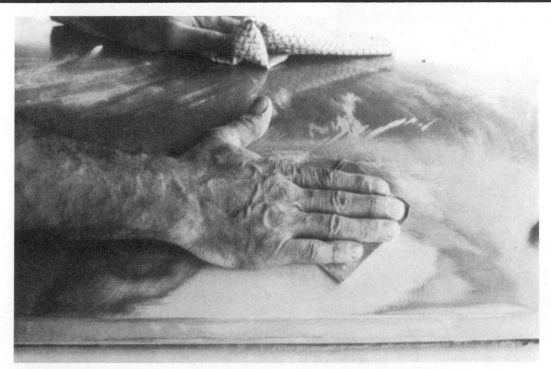

Step 14. Just before priming, sand the area smooth with a piece of 100-grit in the palm of the hand

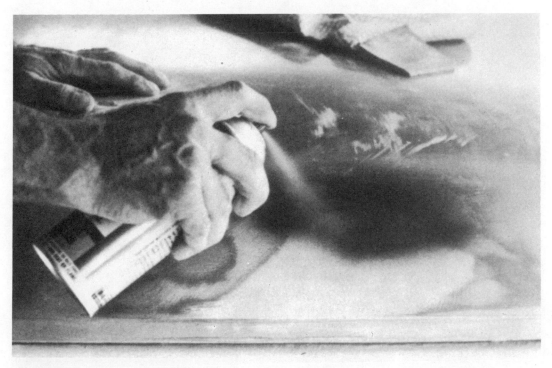

Step 15. Prime the area as in other repairs

Step 16. After the primer dries, coat the area with glazing putty

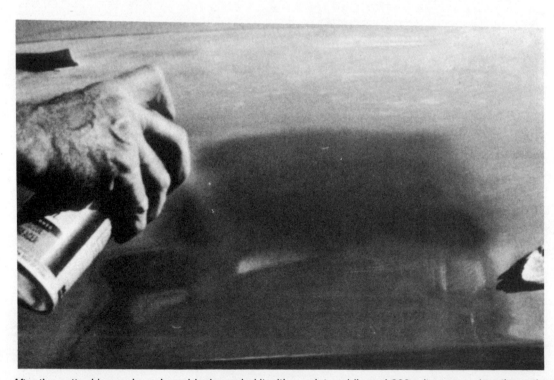

Step 17. After the putty dries and you have block sanded it with a paint paddle and 220-grit paper, prime the entire area and prepare it for painting

REPAIRING A DENTED HOOD PANEL

This repair involves the hood panel. This panel was hit in the right front knocking it out of alignment on the left side

The same basic procedures will be used to make this repair as were used to repair the dented trunk lid

Step 1. Drill holes for the dent puller at the stress line(s)

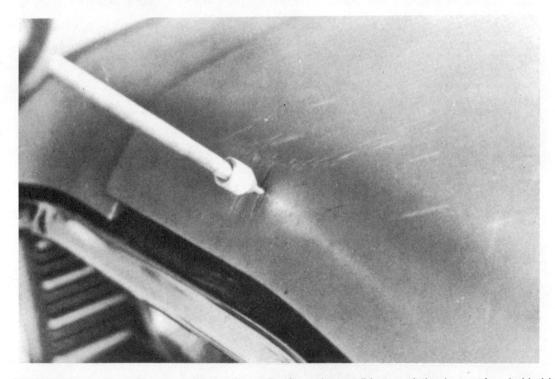

Step 2. Straighten the dent by pulling it out with the dent puller. It may be possible to push the dent out from behind (see Crumpled Rear Quarterpanel)

Step 3. Grind the old finish back

Step 4. Before you apply any plastic, align the hood in the opening. There are usually four bolts on each hinge. The two bolts holding the hood to the hinge adjust the hood forward and back. The two bolts that hold the hinge to the fender control the height of the rear edge of the hood. See the repair on aligning body panels for illustrations and more details

Step 5. Once the hood is properly aligned, the hood-fender seams should look like this. Note that the gaps are equal on both sides and are level with the fender panels

Step 6. Hood height is adjusted as shown. Turn the lock shaft clockwise to lower the front of the hood. Turn counterclockwise to raise the front of the hood

Step 7. Be sure the hood latch is operating properly. A bad hood latch is dangerous. When the hood is fitting and operating properly, you can metal finish the damaged area as in the previous repair ("Repairing a Dented Trunk Lid") and be ready to paint

Crumpled Rear Quarter Panel

REPAIR EIGHT

At first glance, this damaged Oldsmobile Toronado rear quarterpanel looks like a job that belongs in a body shop. However, you can repair this panel yourself with patience and careful attention to these instructions.

This job would cost several hundred dollars to have it repaired professionally. All it will cost you is these tools, materials and your time.

REPAIR 8

Repairing a Crumpled Rear Quarter Panel

TIME REQUIRED: 4–6 hours

TOOLS	MATERIALS
Hammer	*Plastic body filler and hardener
Body hammer	*Glazing putty
Block of wood	Rag or tack cloth
Yardstick	Paint paddle
Electric drill	*Spreader
Grinding attachment	Squeegee
Body file	*Sandpaper in 36, 80, 100, 220 and
Sanding board and block	320 grits depending on whether
Safety goggles	you're going to paint it yourself
	*Primer
	Paint

*Starred items are packaged individually or in kit form by major manufacturers of auto body repair products and are available from auto supply and accessory stores.

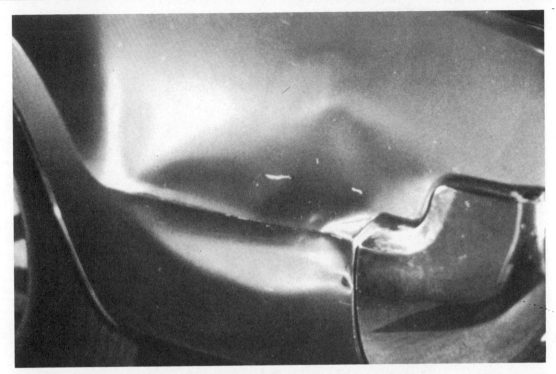

This job looks bad, but can be repaired if you think it out and proceed slowly

Step 1. Study the damage. Look at the other side of the car and study the lines of the undamaged panel

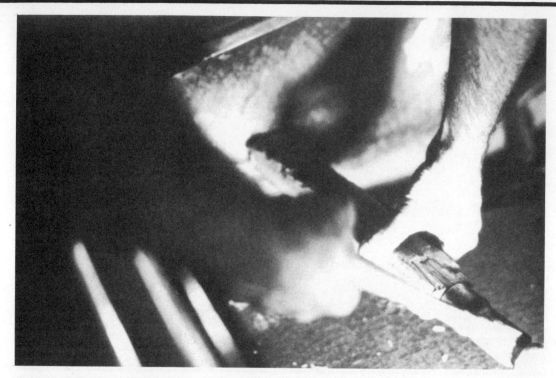

Step 2. Return the panel to its original position by tapping it out with a block of wood and a hammer

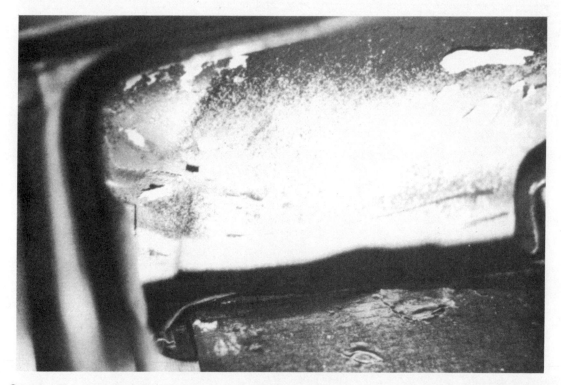

Step 3. This job was easier because access to the back side of the panel was possible through the trunk

Step 4. Shape the panel. When a panel is hit this hard, you have low areas (small dents) and high spots (arrows)

Step 5. Work the high spots down as you bring the panel back to its original shape

Step 6. On large areas like this, use a yardstick to locate highs and lows and check body lines

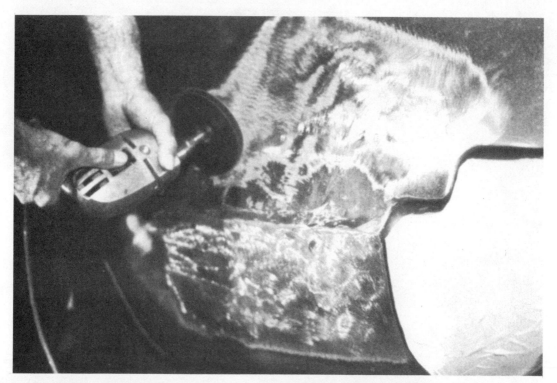

Step 7. Grind off the old finish. After grinding, you may find small areas that are still not right. Correct them now

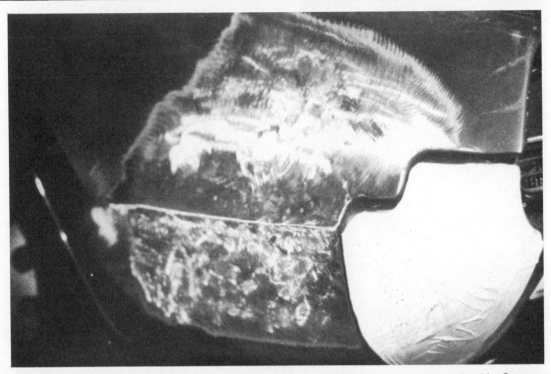

Step 8. Correct the high spots. When you are finished shaping and grinding the area should look like this. Compare the shape to the undamaged side

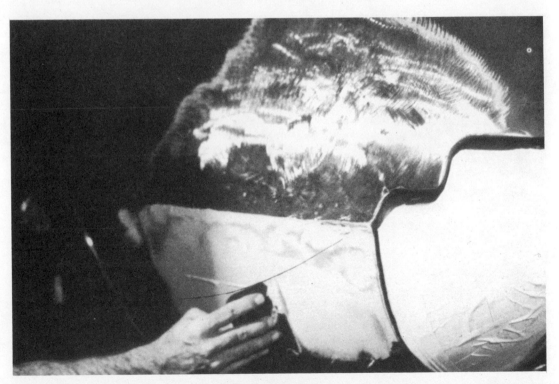

Step 9. With the finish ground back (above) tin the metal with small amounts of plastic on a spreader (below)

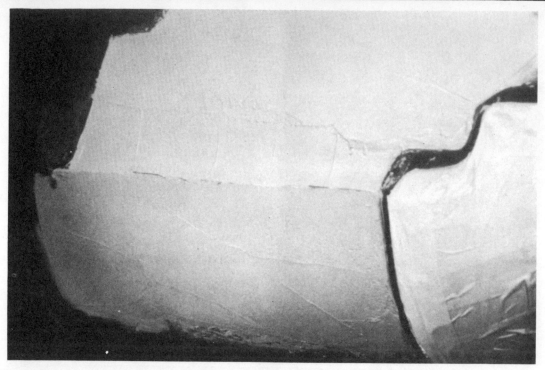

Step 10. Spread the plastic as smoothly as possible

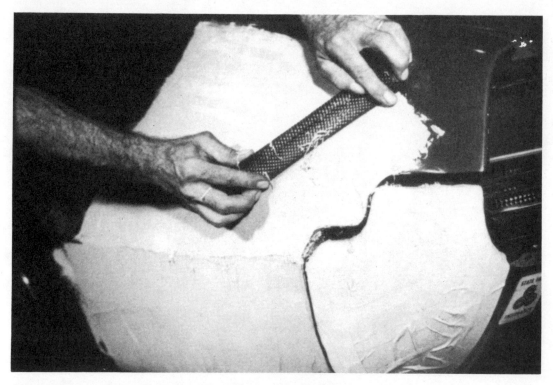

Step 11. Knock off the high spots with a file

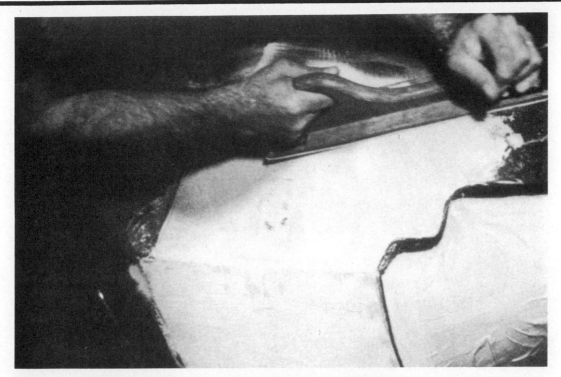

Step 12. Work the plastic down with a sanding board and rough paper

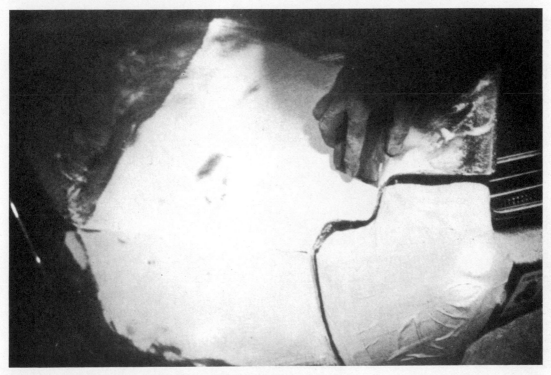

Step 13. Finish smaller areas with a sanding block

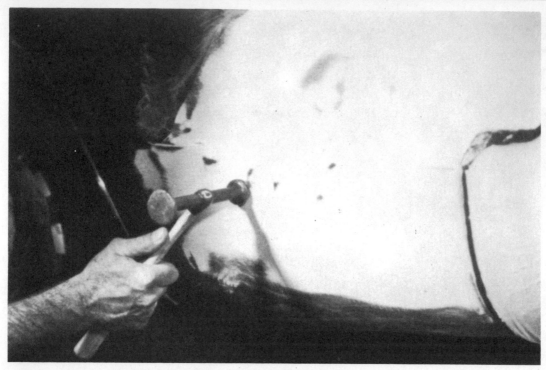

Step 14. High spots in the metal will become apparent as you sand. These can be tapped down with a body hammer before the next coat of filler is applied

Step 15. On a curve such as this body line, a piece of 17 in. x 2⅔ in. (36-grit) sandpaper rolled into a tube shape does a great job

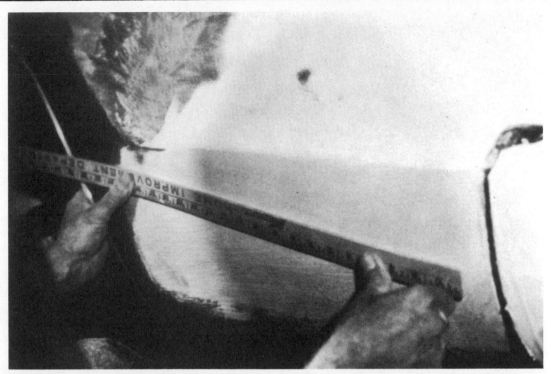

Step 16. Use the yardstick to be sure the lines are shaping up correctly and to show high and low spots. Run your hand over the rear to visualize the low and high spots

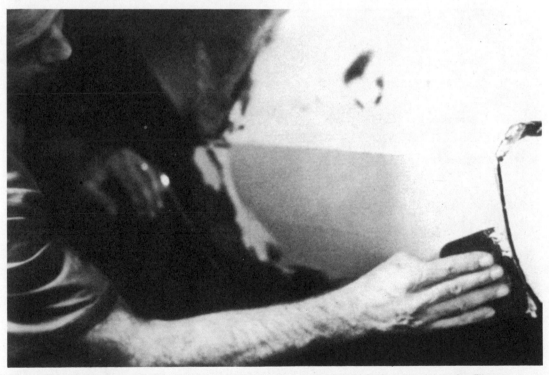

Step 17. Recoat the area with body filler. Keep the low areas in mind when applying the filler

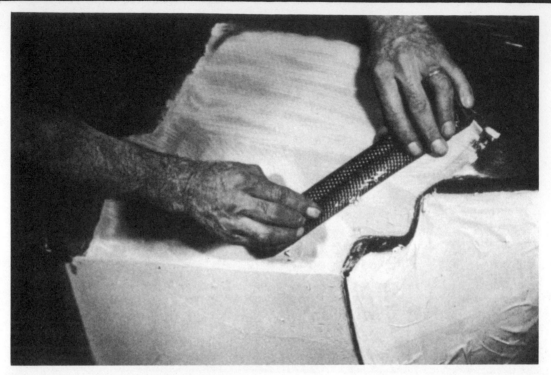

Step 18. Knock off any high spots with the file

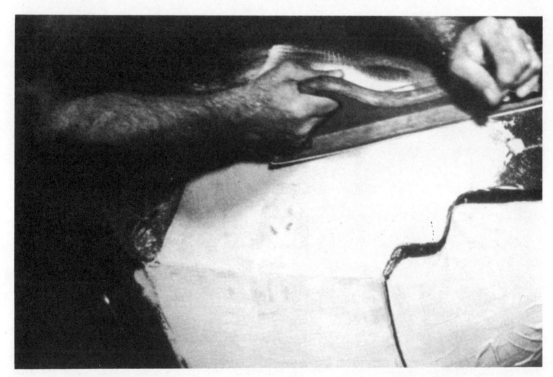

Step 19. Work the plastic down with sanding board and block. If a third and fourth application are needed, don't feel bad

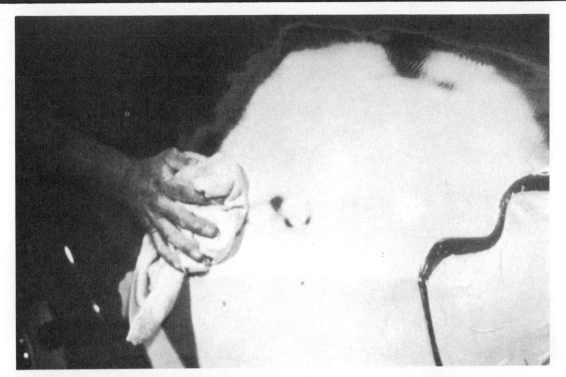

Step 20. When you have the desired surface wipe it clean with a rag or tack cloth

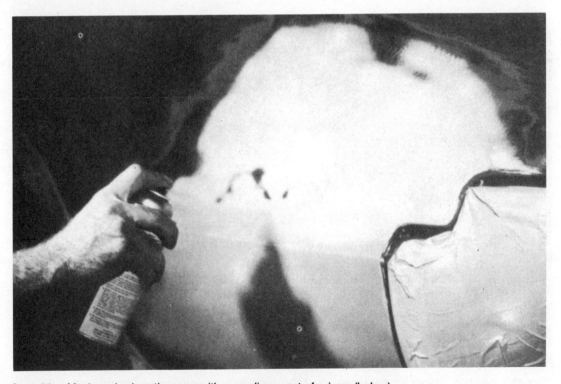

Step 21. Mask and prime the area with a medium coat of primer (below)

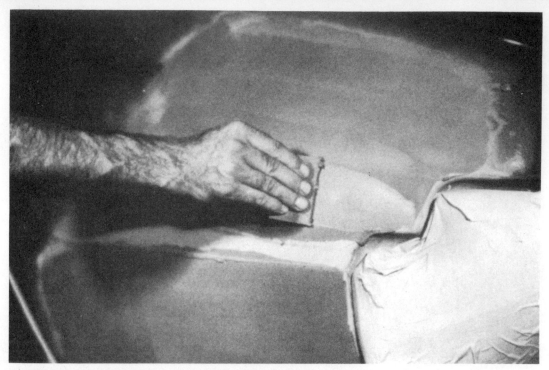

Step 22. Glaze the area in one-stroke applications

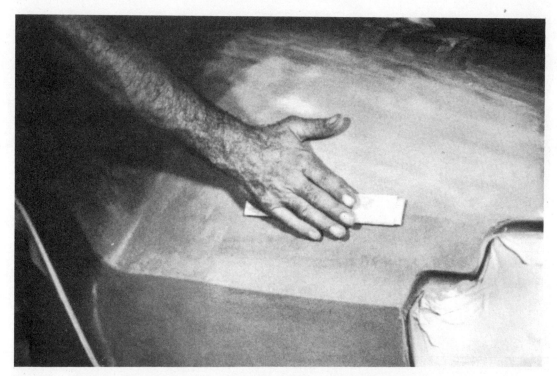

Step 23. When dry, block sand the area with 100-grit sand paper wrapped around a paint paddle

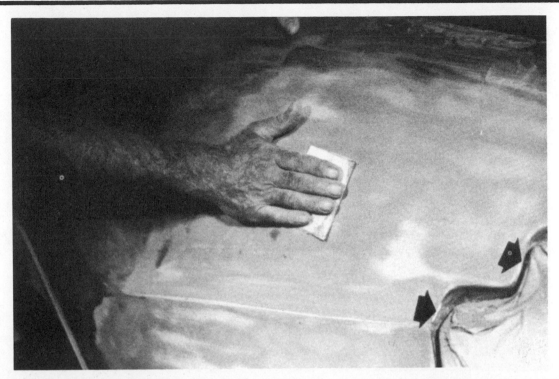

Step 24.   Finish sand with 100-grit folded in thirds. Use long, light, even strokes. Be sure edges are straight, and don't allow excess material to build up (arrows)

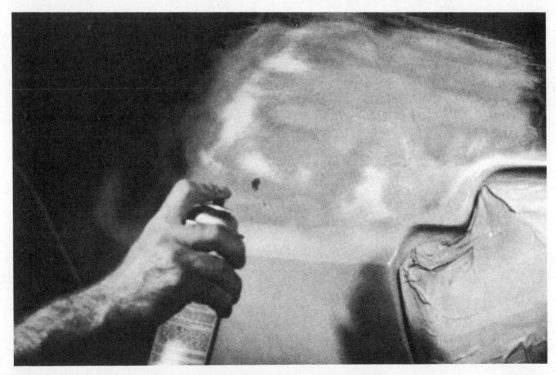

Step 25.   Prime the entire area, being sure that all bare metal is covered

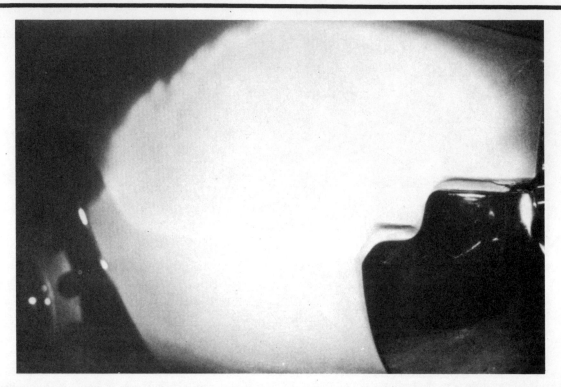

Step 26. The finished product ready for paint. See the sections on "Prepping for Paint" and "Painting Techniques"

Damaged Door and Front Quarter Panel

REPAIR NINE

This Dodge Dart was a victim of overnight street parking. This is a typical gouge or dent that must be repaired using a dent puller and body filler techniques. Most of the work involved with this repair is returning the panel to its original shape. Work slowly and use the other side as a guide.

REPAIR 9

Repairing a Damaged Door and Front Quarterpanel

TIME REQUIRED: 5–7 hours

TOOLS

Electric drill
Drill bit
Dent puller and body hook (if necessary)
Screwdriver
Grinding attachment for electric drill
Wire brush attachment for electric drill
Body file
Sanding block or board
Safety goggles

MATERIALS

Body molding adhesive
Clean clothes
*Sanding paper 28, 80, 100, 220, 320 and 400 grits
*Body putty and hardener
*Spreaders
*Glazing putty
*Primer
Paint

*Starred items are packaged individually or in kit form by major manufacturers of auto body repair products and are available from auto supply and accessory stores.

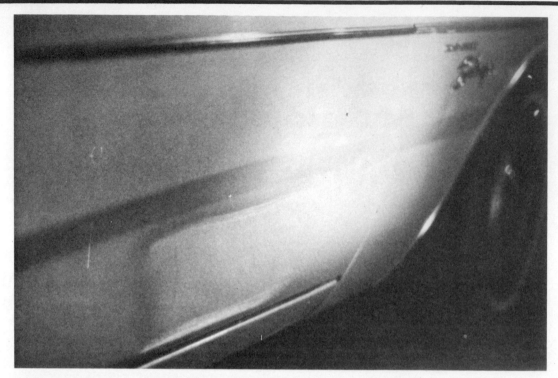

This is a typical gouge, but with a little patience you can easily do it at home

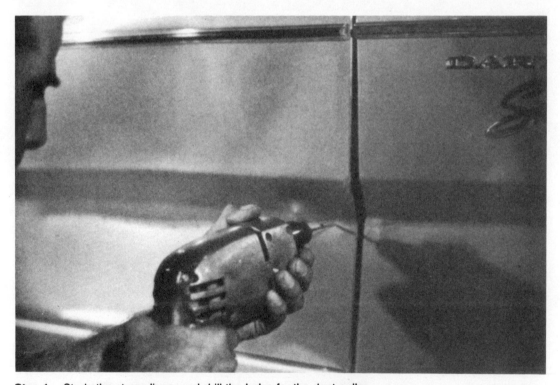

Step 1. Study the stress lines, and drill the holes for the dent puller

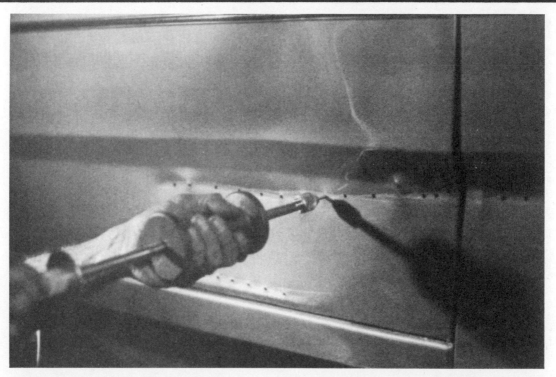

Step 2. Gradually work the panel back into position. As you are using the dent puller, watch what the rest of the panel is doing

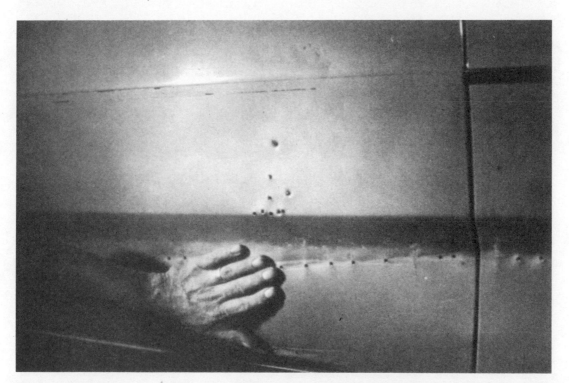

Step 3. Use the palm of your hand to find highs and lows. Work them out as smooth as possible as you go

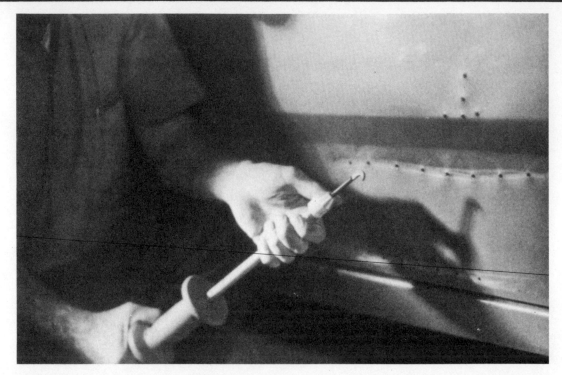

Step 4. This body hook tool is very handy and comes with some dent pullers. It is used when you can get behind the edge of the damaged panel

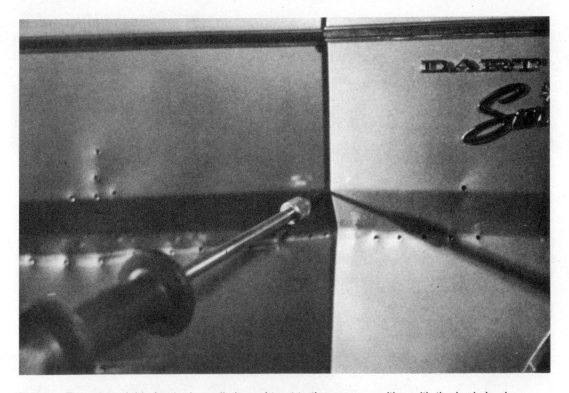

Step 5. The edge of this fender is easily brought out to the proper position with the body hook

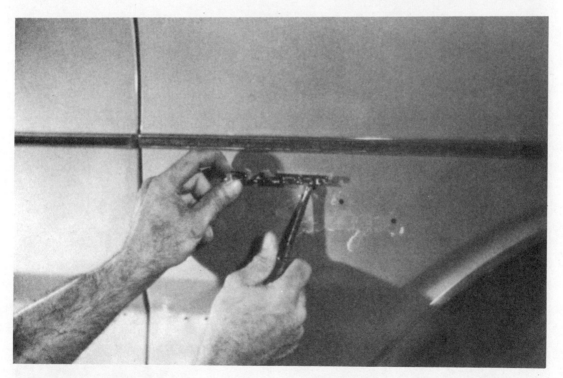

Step 6. Most emblems are fastened to the body by means of barrel type fasteners. They are easily removed with a small screwdriver, but be careful you don't break the emblem

Step 7. This is the latest type of side molding. It is easily replaced with a good trim adhesive

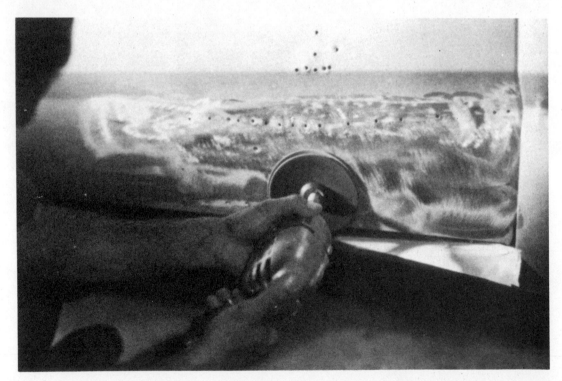

Step 8. Begin the grinding operation when you are sure the panel is as close to the original as you can bet it. use a 28 or 35 grit grinding disc

Step 9. Grind the old finish well back from the damage. Notice that one panel at a time is finished

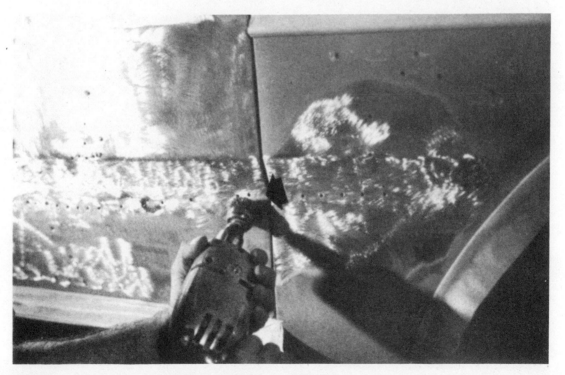

Step 10. Use a small wire brush for hard-to-get-at places

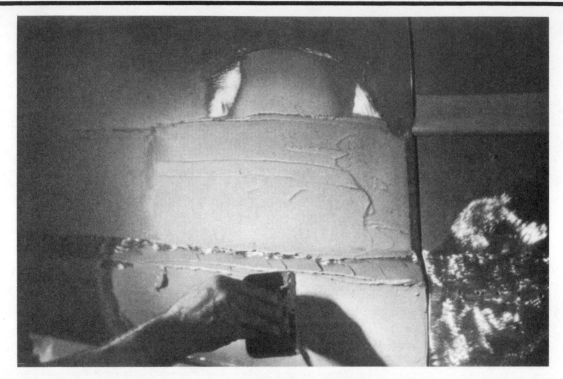

Step 11. Mix the plastic and spread it as smoothly and quickly as possible. On panels with sculptured lines such as this, concentrate on those lines first. Then do the low spots on the flat portions of the panel

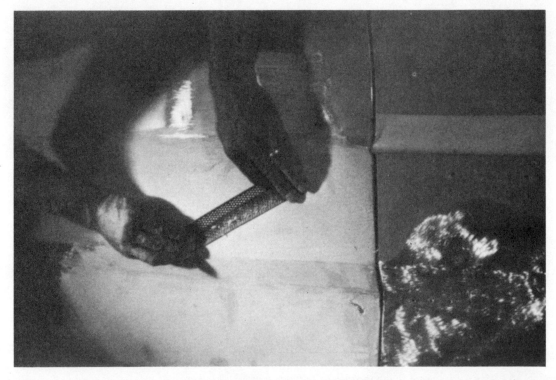

Step 12. Work the plastic down with a file as soon as it becomes solid. Notice that only one panel at a time is finished. This way the plastic doesn't get too hard on one panel while you are working on the other

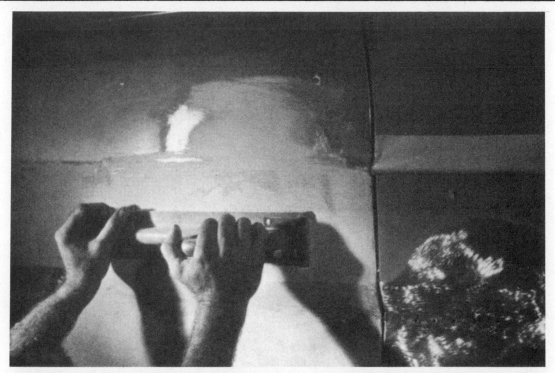

Step 13. Use a sanding board with 80 and 100 grit paper on large areas like this to obtain straight panels

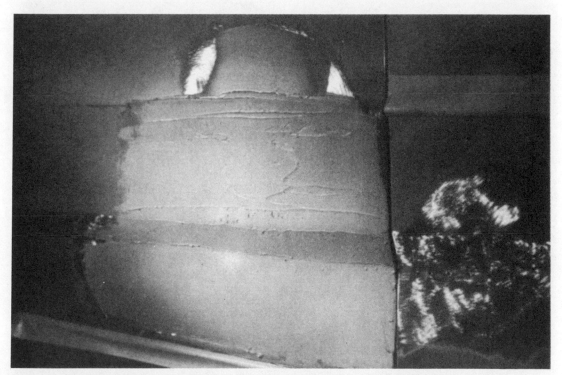

Step 14. Recoat the panel as many times as necessary to obtain smooth contours

Step 15. After the first panel is done, start on the second

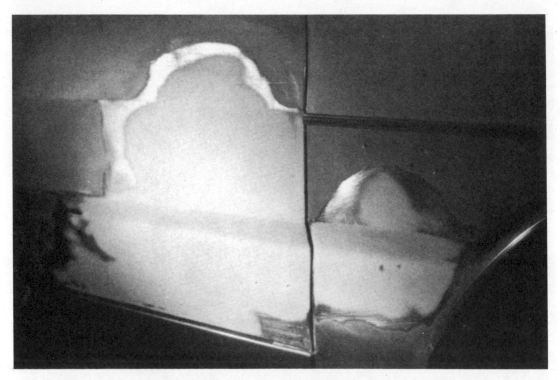

Step 16. After a few hours, your panels should look like this. Prime and glaze as in the previous repairs, and you're ready for paint. When a large surface is involved it's probably better to paint the entire panel and door rather than try to match the paint and blend it in

Repairing Fiberglass Panels

REPAIR TEN

Many panels on today's cars are made of fiberglass to reduce weight and resist the elements. The front nosepiece, the rear quarterpanel extensions spoiler and smaller panels are frequent places to encounter fiberglass. The crack in the fender of this early Corvette and the procedures used to make the repair are also typical of any fiberglass body panel.

NOTE: *Many people are allergic to the fiberglass dust produced by sanding. Be sure to work in a well-ventilated area, wear a protective dust mask and clothing that covers your arms and legs.*

REPAIR 10

Repairing Fiberglass Panels

TIME REQUIRED: 2–3 hours

TOOLS

Electric drill
Grinding attachment for electric drill
Body file
Protective dust mask
Safety goggles

MATERIALS

* Polyester resin
* Hardener
* Spreader
* Fiberglass mat (cloth)
  Sandpaper in 80, 100, 220 and 400 grit
  Grinding disc (35 grit)
* Plastic filler and hardener
* Body putty

*Starred items are packaged individually or in kit form by major manufacturers of auto body repair products and are available from auto supply and accessory stores.

Step 1. The crack in the fiberglass panel of this 1959 Corvette is typical of the repair to almost any fiberglass panel

Step 2. Use an 80 grit grinding disc on an electric drill and grind the paint down to bare fiberglass. Use the edge of the grinding disc to remove all loose material from the crack

Step 3. When you've finished, the area should look like this. Notice that the edges of the crack have been leveled inward to form a "V" for better adhesion

Step 4. Use scissors to cut a piece of fiberglass cloth to roughly the shape of the sanded area (no larger). For more strength, depending on the size of the crack, you can also cut a smaller piece of cloth to fill the crack

Step 5. Follow the directions and mix the resin and hardener

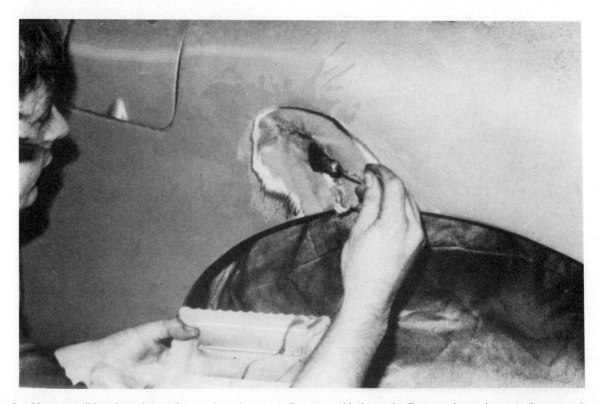

Step 6. Use a small brush and coat the crack and surrounding area with the resin. Be sure the resin coats the area where the patch will be applied

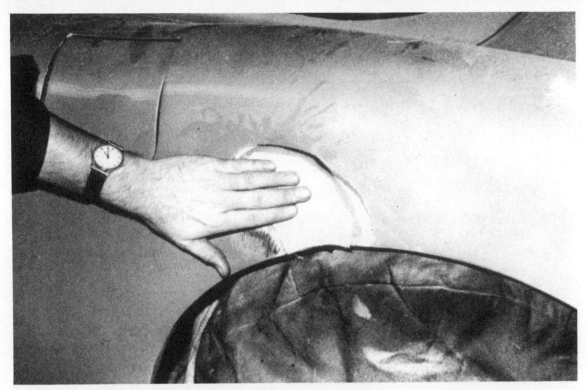

Step 7. Lay the piece(s) of fiberglass cloth in place over the crack

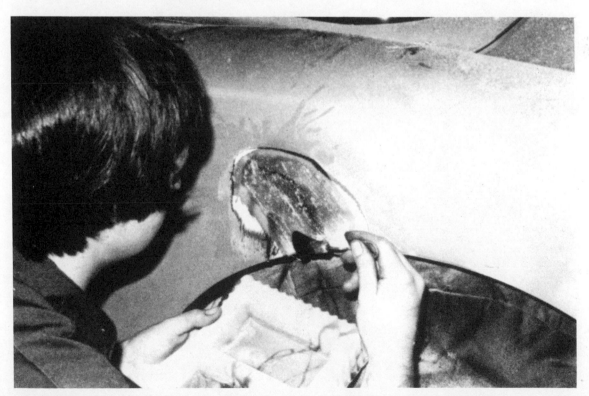

Step 8. Use a small brush and saturate the fiberglass cloth with the resin. Be sure to saturate it thoroughly and cover the edges of the fiberglass cloth

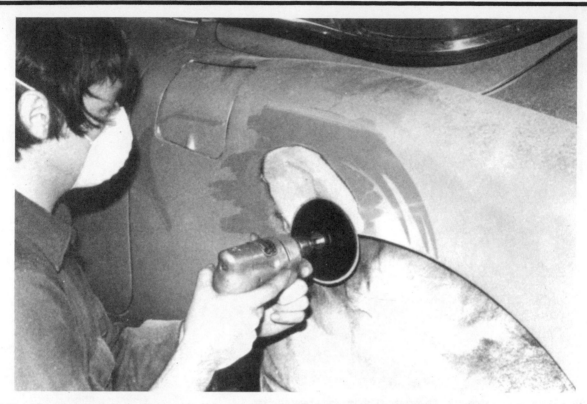

Step 9. Allow the repair to dry thoroughly. Using the electric drill and a medium grit sandpaper disc, sand the entire repair area

Step 10. When you're finished, the area should look like this. Check with your hand for high or low spots. Minor bubbles in the cloth can be sanded away and filled later

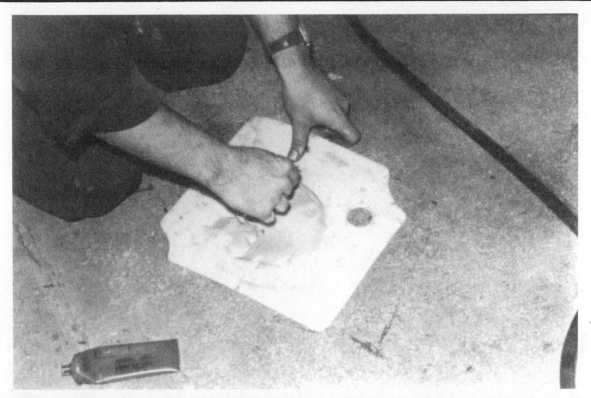

Step 11. Mix some plastic body filler, following the directions on the container

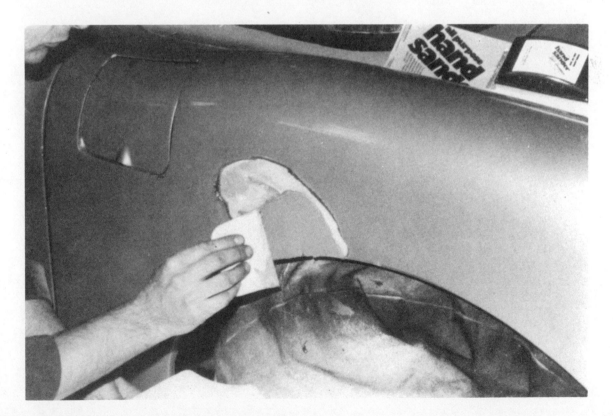

Step 12. Apply the body filler using a medium size spreader. Apply the filler in long, even strokes, making sure you cover the entire sanded area

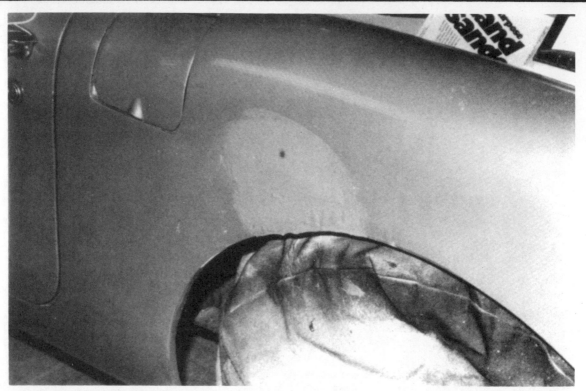

Step 13. Properly applied, the body filler should look like this when you've finished applying it. Allow the filler to dry until you can nick the surface with a fingernail

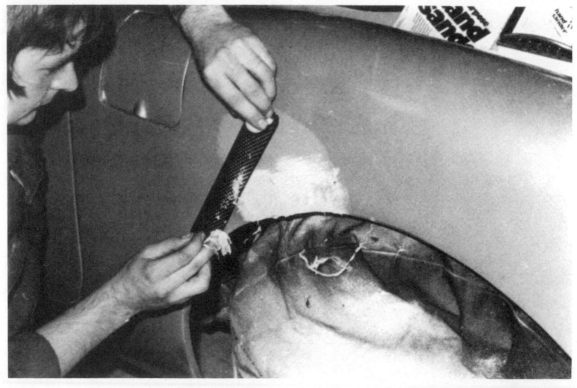

Step 14. Use a body file to knock the high spots, you may have to let the filler dry and apply another coat of filler, and cut it down with the file again

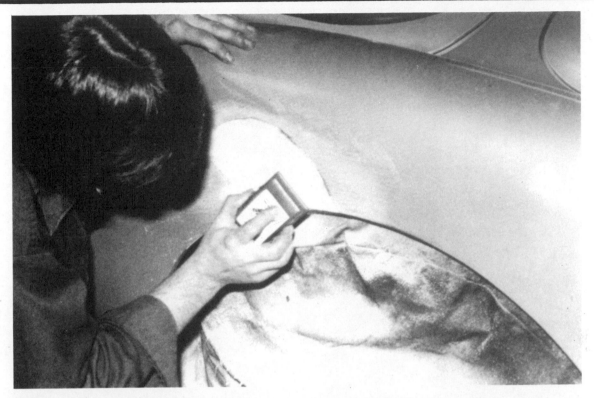

Step 15. Using a sanding block and medium grit paper, block sand the entire area smooth

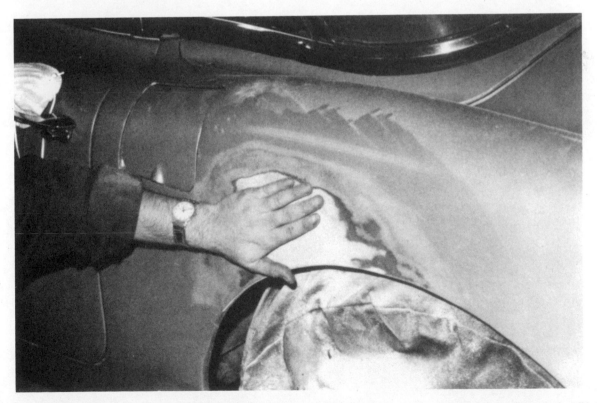

Step 16. Check with the palm of your hand to be sure the entire area is smooth. Note where the sand marks extend well beyond the repair area to be sure the edges are feather-edged

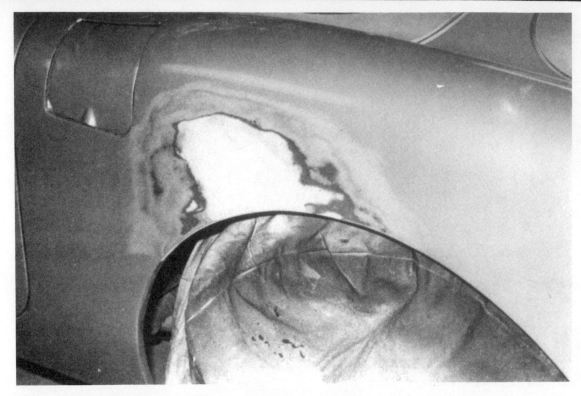

Step 17. When you're ready to primer, the entire area should look like this

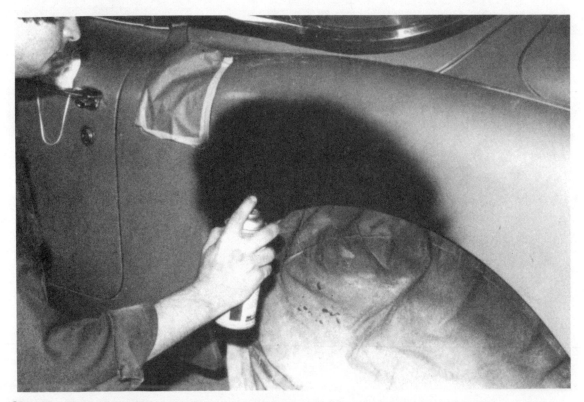

Step 18. Mask off any chrome or trim pieces adjacent to the repair and prime the entire area

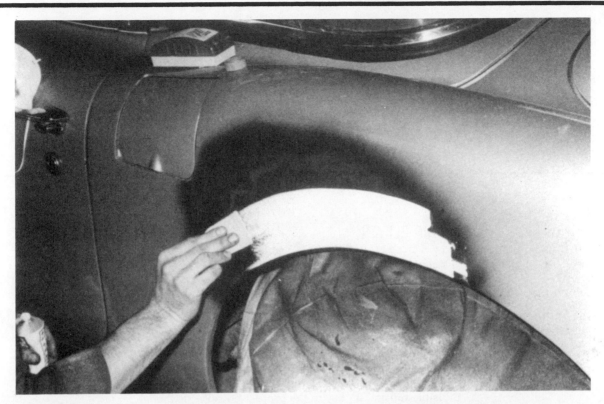

Step 19. When the primer is dry, apply glazing putty over the primed area. The glazing putty is applied direct from the container to fill in minor surface imperfections. It should be applied in long, even strokes, using just enough putty for a light coat. Try not to go over areas where you have already applied putty. When you've finished the area is ready for final sanding with 400 grit paper, in preparation for paint. This particular paint job was left to a body shop because (1) the car was silver, one of the most difficult colors to spray and match and (2) the entire panel was to be repainted for as close a match as possible

Vinyl Top Repairs

REPAIR ELEVEN

Your car's vinyl top is extremely decorative and vulnerable to damage. The vinyl fabric can be torn, cut or cracked either from abuse or neglect.

To have a new vinyl top put on your car is an expensive proposition, running well over $100.00. Fortunately, if the damage is small, it can be repaired using repair and restoration products especially for vinyl tops.

The procedure shown here is basically the one used by major car manufacturers, and can produce an almost invisible repair. The key to the process however, is the "Micro-Heat Beam curing tool", which although inexpensive (about $15) is currently available only from the manufacturer, Repair-It Industries, Inc. A household iron or other type of heating device will burn or overheat the surrounding area, resulting in an unsatisfactory repair. The other repair materials can be purchased separately.

REPAIR 11

Repairing a Vinyl Top

TIME REQUIRED: ½–1 hour depending on size of repair

TOOLS

Razor blade
Thin bladed spatula
*Heat curing tool (see above)

MATERIALS

*Backing fabric
*Graining paper
*Vinyl repair compound
Vinyl Top dressing

*Starred items are available in kit form directly from the manufacturer. All items except the heating tool are also available locally.

Step 1. Assess the damage. This small tear is typical of minor vinyl top damage

Step 2. Clean the damaged area and remove any loose threads with a razor blade or razor knife. Trim the damage neatly using the same razor blade or knife. Cut a piece of the backing fabric approximately $\frac{1}{4}$ in. larger than the damage. Using a small spatula, push the backing fabric under the damaged area. For damaged areas smaller than $\frac{1}{2}$ in., backing is not necessary

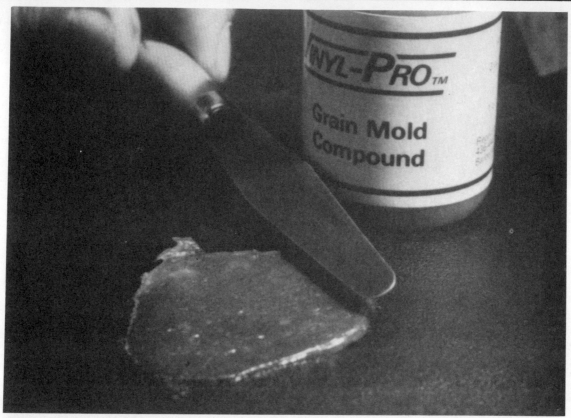

Step 3. Mix and match the color of your vinyl repair compound to the color of the vinyl being repaired

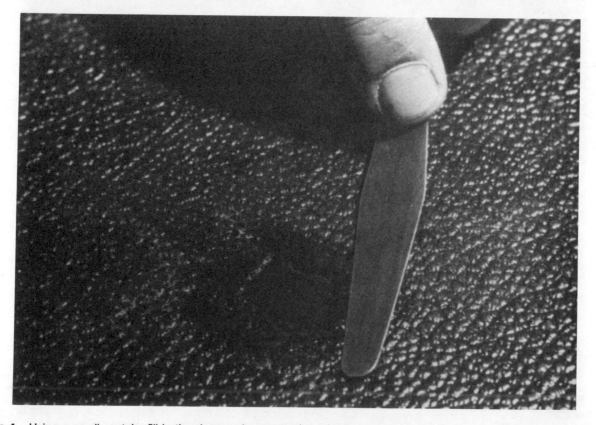

Step 4. Using a small spatula, fill in the damaged area evenly and remove any excess compound from the area. On deep grained vinyl tops, the center of the damaged area should be filled slightly higher than the edges. This will create a slight mound in the center of the repair, to allow it to accept the deep grain necessary

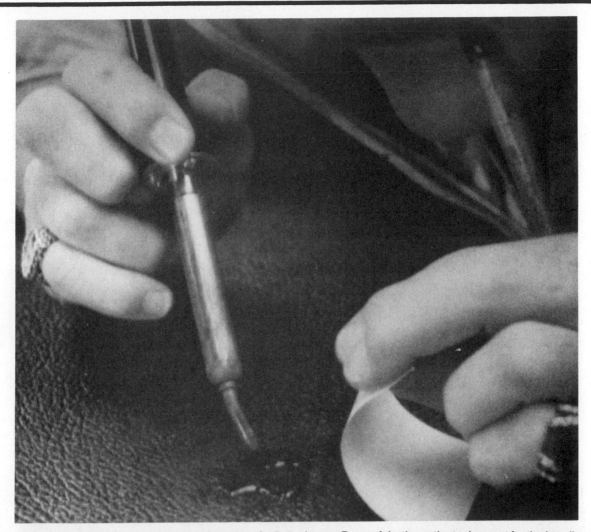

Step 5. Plug in the heat curing tool and allow it to warm for 3–5 minutes. Be careful — the entire tool except for the handle will get very hot. Hold the tool about $\frac{1}{8}$ in. away from the repair compound and insert the plastic hose tip in your mouth. Select a piece of grain paper that matches the grain of your vinyl fabric and hold it with your other hand next to the area being repaired

Step 6. Blow into the plastic tube and move the heat curing tool in a circular motion over the vinyl repair compound. The repair compound will get very hot and will probably smoke slightly. If the repair compound does not get hot enough (smoke slightly), it probably will not accept the grain from the grain paper. Instantly press the grain paper down on the hot repair compound and leave it there for a full minute. After it is cool, remove the grain paper and examine the repair. Any underfilled areas or small defects can be corrected by filling in the repair and repeating Step 5. Refill and regrain as often as necessary

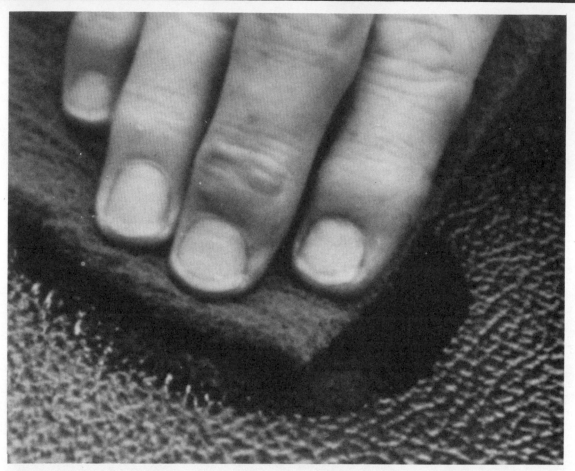

Step 7. Use a conventional vinyl top dressing to restore the shin over the repaired area

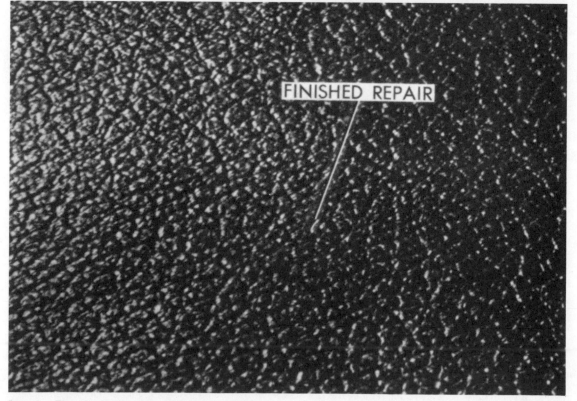

FINISHED REPAIR

Step 8. The repaired area is practically invisible

Aligning Body Panels

REPAIR TWELVE

Depending on the type of body repairs that are made and the location of the damage, it may be necessary to make some minor adjustments on doors, trunk lids or tailgates. The adjustments shown are typical examples of most cars.

DOORS AND HINGES

Doors

If a door must be removed and reinstalled, or simply adjusted you should matchmark the position of the hinges on the door pillars. The holes of the hinges and/or the hinge attaching points are usually oversize to permit alignment of doors. The striker plate is also moveable, through oversize holes, permitting up-and-down, in -and-out and fore-and-aft movement. Fore-and-aft movement is made by adding or subtracting shims from behind the striker and pillar post. The striker should be adjusted so that the door closes fully and remains closed, yet enters the lock freely.

Door Hinges

Don't try to cover up poor door adjustment with a striker plate adjustment. The gap on each side of the door should be equal and uniform and there should be no metal-to-metal contact as the door is opened or closed.

1. Determine which hinge bolts must be loosened to move the door in the desired direction.
2. Loosen the hinge bolt(s) just enough to allow the door to be moved with a padded pry bar.
3. Move the door a small amount and check the fit, after tightening the bolts. Be sure that there is no bind or interference with adjacent panels.
4. Repeat this until the door is properly positioned, and tighten all the bolts securely.

HOOD, TRUNK OR TAILGATE

As with the doors, the outline of hinges should be scribed before removal or adjustment. The hood and

trunk can be aligned by loosening the hinge bolts in their slotted mounting holes and moving the hood or trunk lid as necessary. The hood and trunk have adjustable catch locations to regulate lock engagemnt bumpers at the front and/or rear of the hood to provide a vertical adjustment and the hood lockpin can be adjusted for proper engagement.

The tailgate on the station wagon can be adjusted by loosening the hinge bolts in their slotted mounting holes and moving the tailgate on its hinges. The latchplate and latch striker at the bottom of the tailgate opening can be adjusted to stop rattle. An adjustable bumper is located on each side.

The door hinge holes, either where they bolt to the body or the door, are enlarged to permit adjustment horizontally and vertically

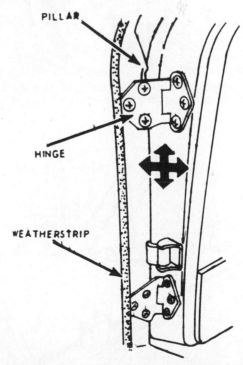

The door hinge holes, either where they bolt to the body or the door, are enlarged to permit adjustment horizontally and vertically

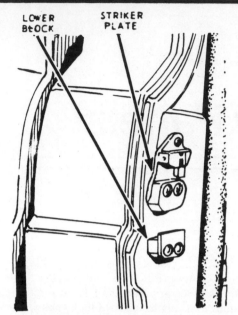

The door striker (attached to the body pillars) can be adjusted for proper lock engagement

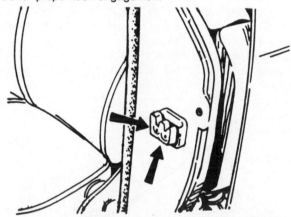

The striker plate and lower block are attached to the door and can also be adjusted for positive lock engagement

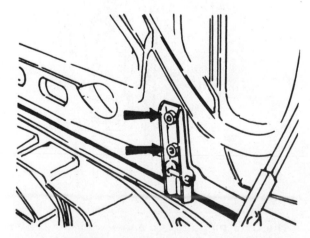

The hood or trunk hinge bolts (arrows) can be loosened to permit fore-and-aft adjustment

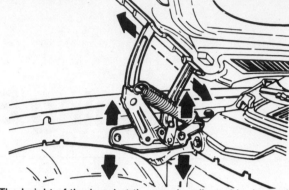

The height of the hood at the rear is adjusted by loosening the bolts that attach the hinge to the body and moving the hood up or down

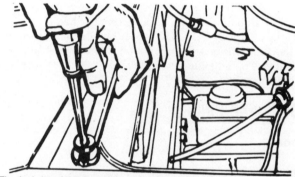

The height of the hood can also be adjusted with stop screws at the front and/or rear of the hood

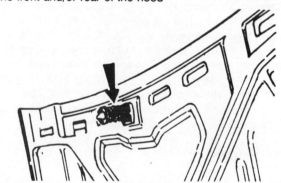

The end of the hood pin (arrow) is slotted and locked in place by a nut at the base of the pin. The pin can be turned in or out for proper lock engagement, after loosening the locknut

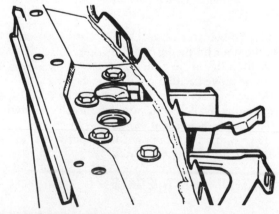

The base of the hood lock can also be repositioned slightly to give more positive lock engagement

Removing Headlights, Tail Lights and Lenses

REPAIR THIRTEEN

In the course of making body repairs, it is often necessary to remove exterior lights and lenses in order to effect repairs or paint a panel.

There are many different exterior lighting arrangements, but basically only 2 ways to gain access to the lights.

Headlights are usually held in place by a retaining ring which may or may not be covered by part of the grille or nosepiece. The screws are almost always accessible from outside the car.

Turn signals, tail lights and parking lights are covered by a plastic lens. The lens retaining screws may be accessible from outside or they may have to be reached from behind the panel or through the trunk. In some cases, the entire housing may have to be removed from inside the trunk before the lens can be removed.

The following photos are typical examples of removal techniques.

SINGLE HEADLIGHT

This single headlight on a Mustang II is typical of those held in place by a retaining ring covered by a trim piece.

Step 1. Remove the trim ring retaining screws. Don't disturb the headlight aiming screws located behind cut-outs in the trim ring (arrow). Remove the trim ring

Step 2. Remove the screws holding the retaining ring in place. Again, don't disturb the plastic headed headlight aiming screws

Step 3. Some retaining rings have one or two small rings that must be removed with pliers

Step 4. Remove the retaining ring

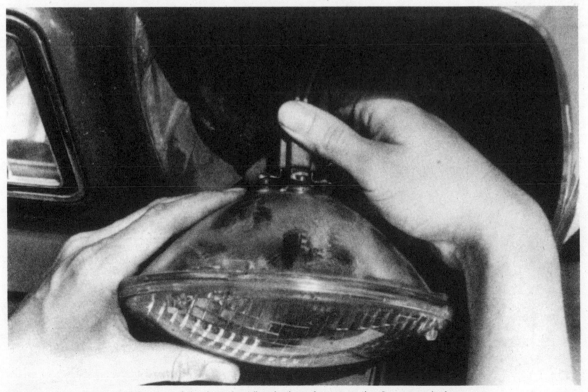

Step 5. Slide the headlight out of the housing (bucket) and remove the 3-pronged plug

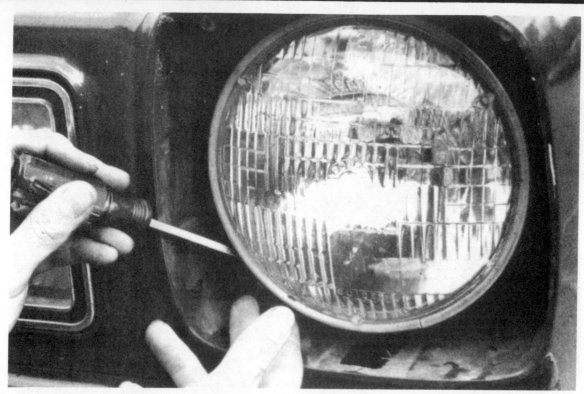

Step 6. The headlight can be installed in the same manner as it was removed. A screwdriver can be used to hook the springs in position

DUAL HEADLIGHTS

The dual headlights on this Chevrolet are typical of those that are accessible after removing a portion of the grille.

Step 1. The trim piece on this Chevrolet is part of the grille and must be removed for access to the headlight retaining ring. Don't disturb the headlight adjusting screws (arrows)

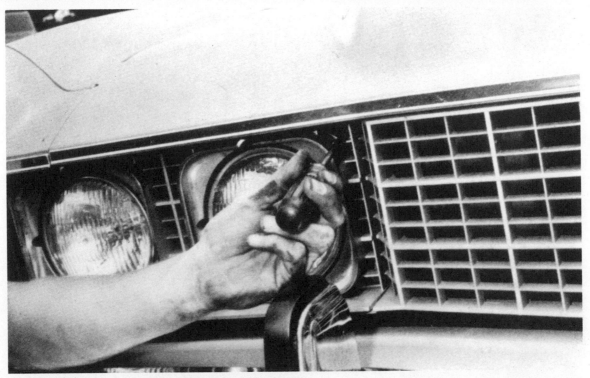

Step 2. Remove the screws holding the trim piece in place

Step 3. Remove the trim piece to expose the headlight retaining ring(s)

Step 4. Remove the 3 screws securing the headlight retaining ring. Don't disturb the plastic-headed headlight aiming screws (arrows)

Step 5. Remove the headlight retaining ring and pull the headlight out of the bucket

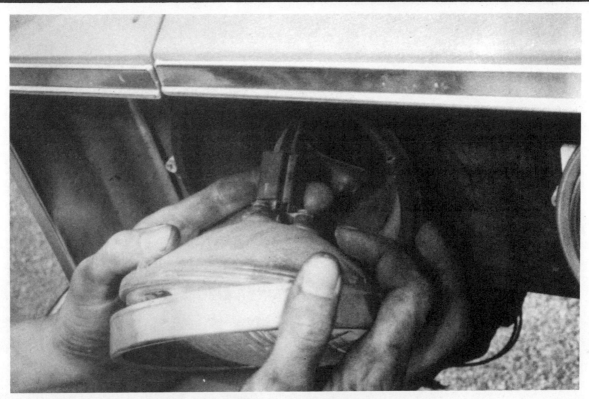

Step 6. Remove the 3-bladed plug from the back of the headlight

SIDE MARKERS AND PARKING LIGHTS

Most parking lamp and side marker lenses can be removed from outside the car. In some cases, the retaining nuts are located behind the fender panel. These 2 examples are typical of common types.

The rear side marker lens on this Vega also serves as the bulb housing. Remove the 2 screws holding the lens/housing to the fender and unsnap the bulb socket from the lens

The front side marker lens on this Datsun was removed after removing 2 screws. If it is necessary to remove the lamp housing, it is held to the fender with sheet metal screws. Be sure you don't damage the gasket when removing the lens

TAIL LIGHTS AND TURN SIGNAL LENSES

In most cases, the lens is removed from outside the car and the housing itself is removed from inside the trunk. In some cases, the entire housing can be removed from outside the car.

The entire rear taillight housing can be removed from this Plymouth Volare after removing 4 screws. Pull the lens and housing from the fender and unsnap the bulb holder from the housing

To remove the rear taillight lens from this Vega, remove 4 screws holding the chrome ring and the lens in place. The housing is removed from inside the car

Installing
Body Side Molding

REPAIRS FOURTEEN AND FIFTEEN

Next to rust and collision, crowded parking lots are your car's worst enemies. The dents and dings from careless shoppers opening their doors against your doors and fenders can be just as expensive as a minor accident. Body side moldings serve the dual purposes of dressing up the appearance of your car and protecting it from the hazards of parking lots.

Body side molding kits are available in almost any well stocked parts store from a variety of manufacturers.

There are two basic types—self-adhering or rivet-on—available in 3 widths and in more than 30 colors to match almost any OEM color. Self-adhesive types typically come in rolls of narrow (approximately ½ in. wide), medium (¾–1 in.) and wide (1¼–1¾ in.) widths, while rivet-on styles are normally available in 6 ft. lengths of wide and narrow widths only.

Enough to do an average size car will cost from $10–15 and can be installed by anyone in about an hour, using commonly available hand tools. The only tool you might not have in your collection is a rivet gun (for rivet-on types) that can be rented or purchased inexpensively.

The last step is to carefully remove the masking tape, leaving you with a professional installation that will protect your car from parking lot dings and dents.

There are a few precautions that should be followed when performing any adhesive molding installation.

1. Let new paint age for at least 1 week before installing any adhesive molding.

2. Don't wash the car for at least 48 hours following the installation. This will allow the adhesive backing to "set" for a permanent job.

If, for any reason, you should want to remove the molding, use a bug and tar remover to soften the adhesive and remove the molding. Any adhesive that remains can be removed with Formula 409, Prep-Sol or rubbing alcohol.

REPAIRS 14 AND 15

Installing Body Side Moulding

TIME REQUIRED: ½–1½ hours

TOOLS

Grease pencil (china marker)
Tape measure or yardstick
Single edged razor blade
Electric drill ⎫
Rubber mallet ⎬ Rivet-on
Shears ⎬ type only
Rivet-gun ⎪
Screwdriver ⎭

MATERIALS

Clean rag
Solvent (wax remover)
Masking tape
Rivets (rivet-on type only)
Body side molding kit

INSTALLING ADHESIVE BODY SIDE MOLDING

Step 1. The car should be on a reasonably level surface and parked in the shade. Direct sunlight will make the adhesive backing too sticky and difficult to reposition. Use a steel tape and china marker to mark the position of the molding. It will generally be placed along the widest part of the car

Step 2. Lay a strip of masking tape along the entire length of the car using the marks you've just made as a guide. Sight down the length of the tape to be sure it is straight. The top of the tape will act as a guide for the molding

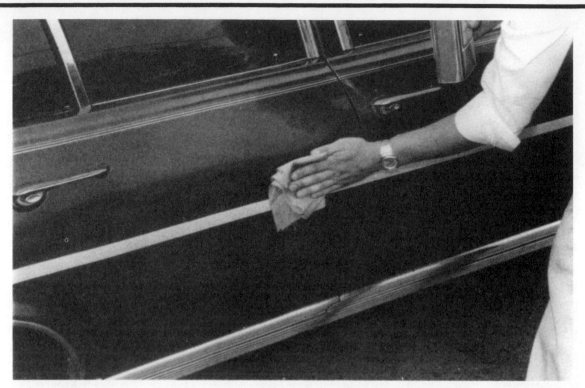

Step 3. Use a clean rag and a solvent to strip the wax from car where the molding will be applied. This is the most important step-you must get all the wax off. Prep-Sol or household Formula 409 are good solvents, although rubbing alcohol will work with more rubbing effort

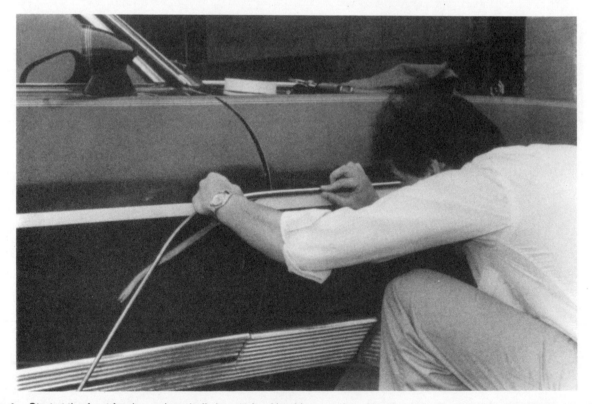

Step 4. Start at the front fender and peel off about 1 ft. of backing at a time. Use the tape as a guide for the molding, and don't press too hard, so the molding can be repositioned if necessary

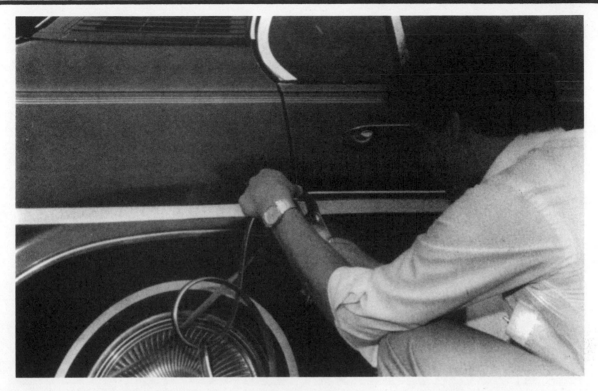

Step 5. When you get to the rear quarter panel, cut the molding in the center of the gap between the door and quarter panel. You can cut the molding with garden shears or a single edged razor blade

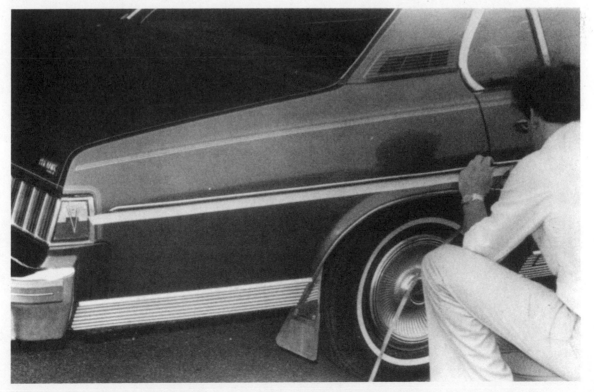

Step 6. Start the other spear end at the rear of the car and work towards the front, as you did in Step 4

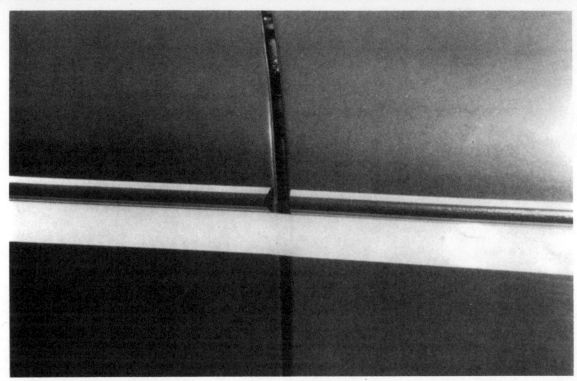

Step 7. Finish the installation by checking your work and trimming the molding ends. Use a razor blade to trim the molding at the trailing edge of the door square. The end of the molding on the leading edge of the door (arrow) should be trimmed at a 45 degree angle, so the molding will not "catch" when the door is opened. Go along the entire length of molding and bear down hard with the heel of your hand

INSTALLING RIVET-ON BODY SIDE MOLDING

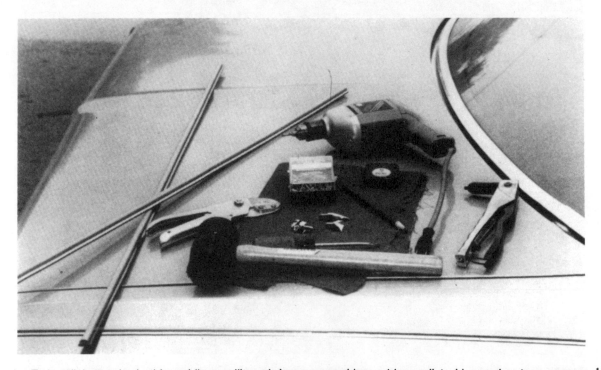

Step 1. To install rivet-on body side molding you'll need shears, screwdriver, rubber mallet, china marker, tape measure, $\frac{1}{8}x\frac{1}{4}$ in. grip rivets and an electric and an electric drill with a $\frac{9}{64}$ in. bit. It's easiest to use a drill bit $\frac{1}{64}$ in. larger than the rivet shank

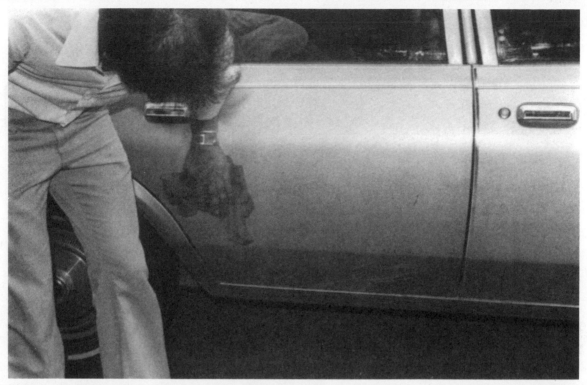

Step 2. Rivet-on molding can be installed on any temperature surface, but some molding manufacturers use a small adhesive strip to make installation easier. In these cases, it is advisable to wipe the car clean with a rag to allow the temporary adhesive to hold

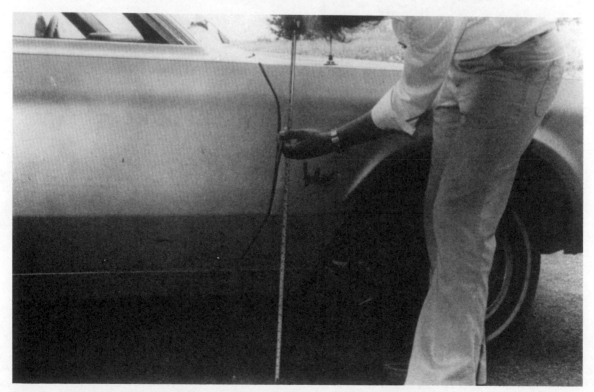

Step 3. Mark the fenders and doors at the widest part of the car with a china marker

Step 4. Assemble a piece of molding and track, and mark the length required. Be sure to leave enough on each end (usually about ½ in.) for the caps and spears. Cut the molding to the size required. After cutting and measuring the first side, you can use these to make duplicate pieces for the other side

Step 5. Remove the molding from the track. If the track has an adhesive strip, peel off the backing and position the track according to the marks you made in Step 3. If there is no adhesive strip, someone will have to hold the track in position. Be sure it is where you want it before drilling holes

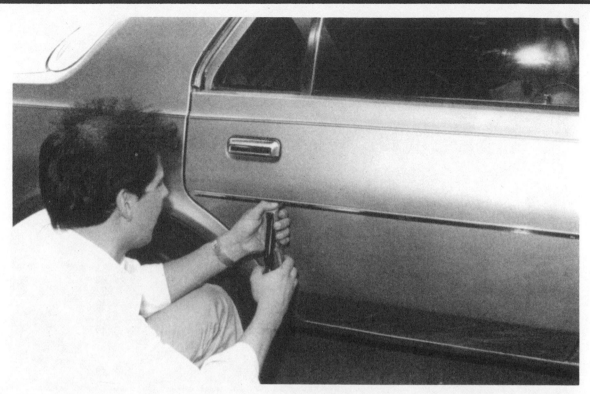

Step 6. Using the holes in the track as a guide, drill each hole and an additional hole ¾ in. from each end. Using a rivet gun, install the rivets. Be sure to squeeze the rivet tightly

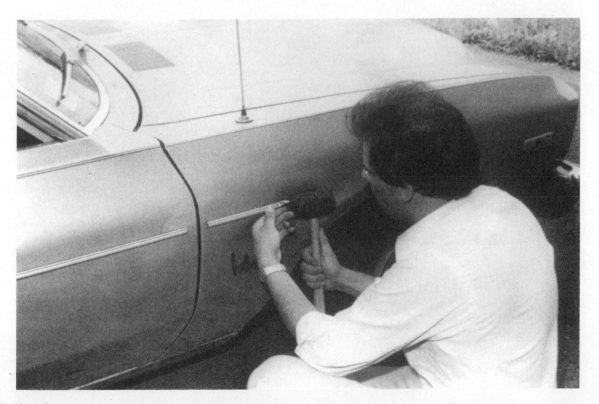

Step 7. Install the plastic molding in the track and finish the job by installing the end caps and spears. It may be necessary to tap the caps and spears into the track with a mallet

Step 8. The finished job gives a neat, original equipment look that will last the life of the car

Preparing Your Car for a New Paint Job

PREPARING YOUR CAR FOR A NEW PAINT JOB

Unless you have, or have access to, the necessary equipment, you would be wise to leave painting an entire car to profesionals. You'll get a far better job, and it won't cost much more than it would for you to rent or buy the equipment and purchase the materials. Your largest saving will result from preparing the car for painting. If you get the car ready to paint at home, you can (1) get a perfect job because you can take all the time you need to get it right, and (2) save yourself about two-thirds of the cost of a new paint job. What most people don't know is that most of the high cost of completely refinishing an automobile is the labor of preparing it for spraying. The actual time it takes to spray a car is only about one-half hour. So . . . if your car is destined for a bright, new, shinh finish, roll up your sleeves and let's get started. If you follow the simple procedures and take your time to do it right, you can stand back and look at a beautiful finished product. If you really want to paint the car yourself, see the Chapte ron Painting Techniques.

There are four basic steps to follow when completely refinishing an auto.

1. Pre-clean the complete body from bumper to bumper with a good pre-cleaning solvent.

2. Feather-edge all nicks, scratches and slight imperfections in the old finish. If you have done any body work using this book as a guide, then all of the old finish edges that were ground back must be feather-edged at this time. Spot prime all these areas and block sand them with a paint paddle and 220-grit open face sandpaper.

3. Sand the complete car with 320-grit open face sandpaper.

4. Using masking tape and newspaper, tape off all areas that are not to be painted such as bumpers, moldings, glass etc.

The following instructions for preparing your car for refinishing include many professional techniques so that the finished product will be nothing short of perfect. There is only way to do a iob, and that way is, of course, the right way. Otherwise, the material you purchase and the time and energy you spend will be wasted.

LIST OF MATERIALS

This list of supplies includes everything you will need to prepare your car for refinishing. They can be purchased at any auto supply or auto paint supply store, and most large discount stores. When you buy these supplies, do not purchase the paint. The paint is supplied by the shop that is going to apply the finish. The reason for this is that different painters use different brands. They are used to their favorite brand and do their best work with it, so let them buy the paint. You will need:

One gallon of pre-cleaning solvent.
Two or three wooden paint paddles.
Three rolls of $\frac{3}{4}$ in. masking tape.
Twelve sheets of 220-grit open face sandpaper.
Twelve sheets of 320-grit open face sandpaper.
One or two spray cans of lacquer base primer.

Don't over-buy on these items, as you can always go back for more if you run out.

STEP 1—PRE-CLEANING THE BODY

The very first step in preparing the car for refinishing is to remove all foreign substances from the old finish, including wax, road tars, tree sap, etc. They must be completely removed to insure that the new paint film will completely adhere to the old finish.

For this job you need a good pre-cleaning solvent. Before you use the solvent, read the label and do exactly as it says with no short cuts. This is a very important step if you expect your new finish to last. Do one panel at a time, such as a complete fender, so as not to miss a spot accidentally that could give trouble later.

Most pre-cleaner labels will tell you to wipe an area with solvent on a clean rag and, while the surface is still wet, wipe it dry with a clean rag. The rag dampened with the solvent loosens the foreign substance and the clean dry rag wipes it form the old finish. This leaves it clean and ready for the following operations. Change rags often. When you are certain you have done this first step completely, move on to Step 2.

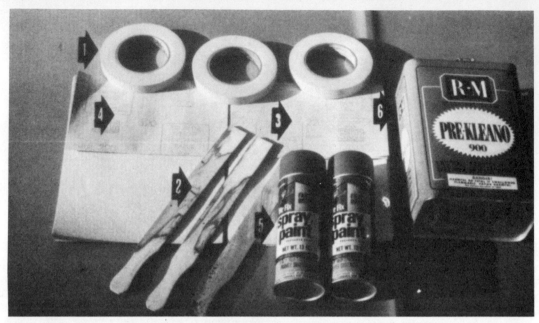

Materials needed to prepare your car for a new paint job

This high contrast photo shows the wet area when using the precleaner. Do about 12 square inches at a time. Apply the cleaner, and while the area is still wet, wipe dry

STEP 2—FEATHER-EDGING, SPOT PRIMING AND BLOCK SANDING

The second step is feather-edging the old finish wherever it is broken or interrupted; for example, a stone bruise or a nick where someone has opened a car door into the side of your car, etc. You must also feather-edge any areas where you have done body work and have ground the old finish back to make room for your metal finishing. The reason for this is very obvious if you think about it for a moment. First of all, think of the old finish as having some degree of thickness. A coat of paint is only a film covering the metal, but it does, in fact, have thickness. Any interruptions, such as scratches or chips, will cause a hole in the film. If you were to cover this hole in the old finish with a coat of bright shiny paint, it would be highlighted.

What you have to do is build the hole or low area back up to the level of the old finish with primer. Sand the area of the hole to taper the abrupt edge of the hole gradually out to the level of the old finish. When this is done, simply spot prime a couple of times and, when dry, block sand with 220-grit sandpaper and a paint paddle. Feel the area with the flat of your hand. If it is perfectly smooth, go on to the next area. If you still feel a slight low spot, prime it again and block it down when dry.

The illustrations show such nicks and scratches and just how they are treated.

A. Feather-edge the hole or scratch in the old finish with 220-grit paper and paddle so that it gradually tapers out to the level of the old finish.

B. Spot spray with lacquer-type primer, two or three coats, allowing each coat to dry before applying the next one.

C. Block sand with the 220-grit paper and paddle when the primer is dry.

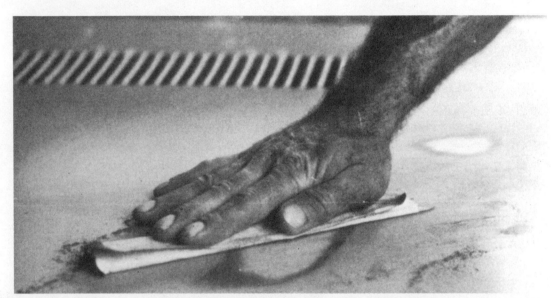

Feather-edging a typical nick or hole in the old finish with 220-grit and paint paddle

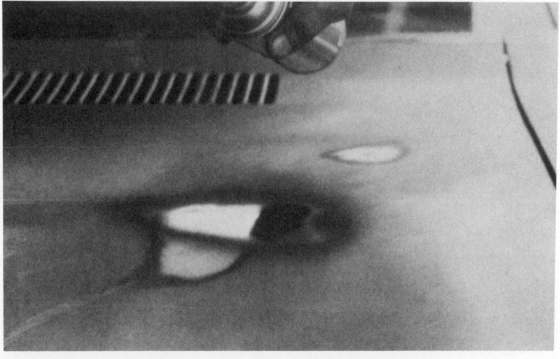

Priming the area just feather-edged to bring the void up to the level of the old finish

I've talked about doing a job and doing it well, without taking any shortcuts. Well, here is a short cut to certain failure, one I have seen many times, both in profesional shops and on do-it-yourself jobs. Instead of going through the sand and prime operation step-by-step, glazing putty is wiped into these small imperfections and when dry, leveled off with the old finish. This sounds easy, but that glob of filler that is wiped into the hole in the old finish is destined to become a pop-out. It will do just that, pop-out and take the paint that is covering it along.

The reason this method doesn't work is very simple. When you feather-edge the damage in the old finish, tapering the abrupt edge gradually out to the level of the

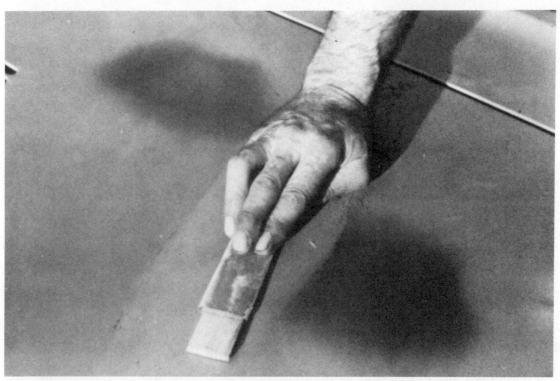

Block sanding with the same 220-grit paper and paddle. If the void can still be felt, repeat the operation

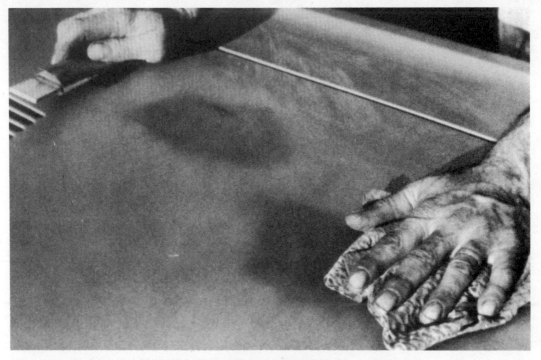

When properly done, the finish should be smooth and look like this

old finish, and apply primer, it becomes a part of the film covering the metal. When one stuffs a gob of putty in the hole, it is not part of the film, as it has definite edges. It becomes only a sort of plug or insert in the old finish. When the new paint is applied, with all its "chemical hotness", the putty or filler becomes soft and sooner or later is dislodged. This, of course, leaves you with the same hole.

A similar process is used for a large area such as one

that you have repaired. The edge of the old finish has to be gradually feather-edged and the metal finished area has to be built up with primer and then the entire area block sanded with a paint paddle and 220-grit sandpaper. Once these damaged areas in the old finish are taken care of, you are ready to go on to Step 3. Be certain to do a good job on Step 2. This is where most do-it-yourselfers fail.

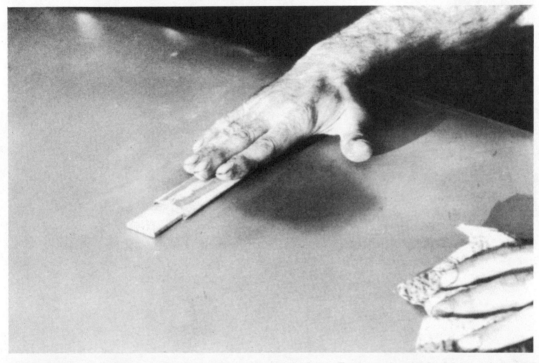

The same treatment is given to all holes, nicks and scratches in the old finish. Feather-edge the bad spot, prime, and block sand to make the area level with the old finish

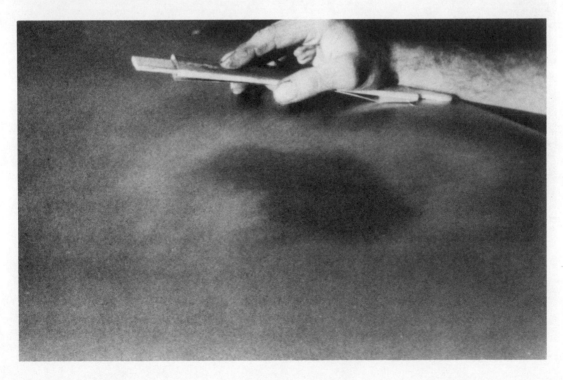

A good example of scratches in the old finish

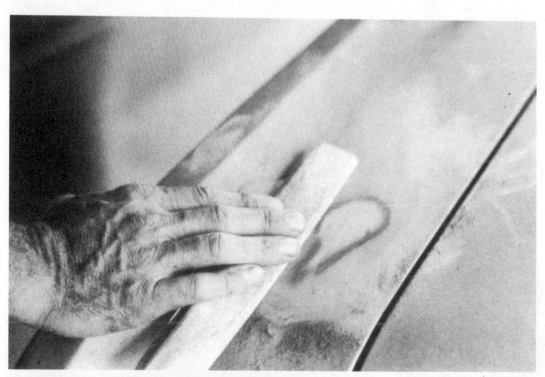

Feather-edge the scratches with 220-grit and paddle

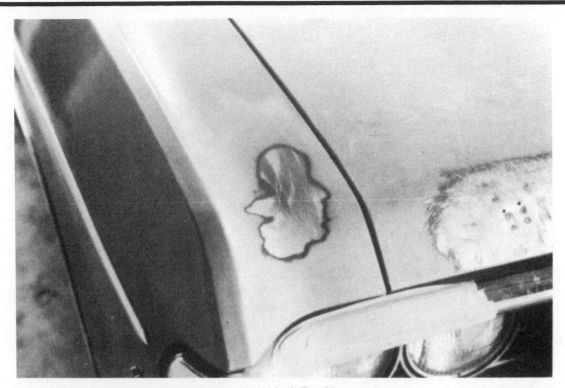

Properly feather-edged, the scratches area should look like this

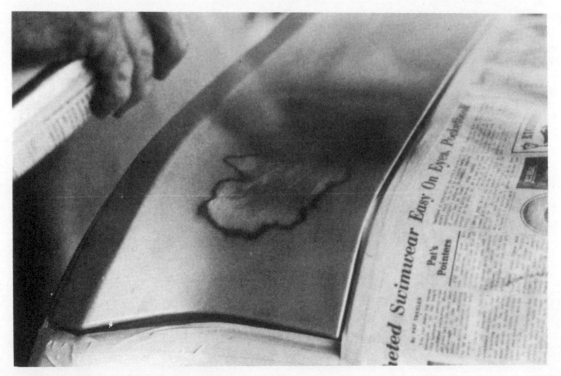

Temporarily mask off the area and prime it

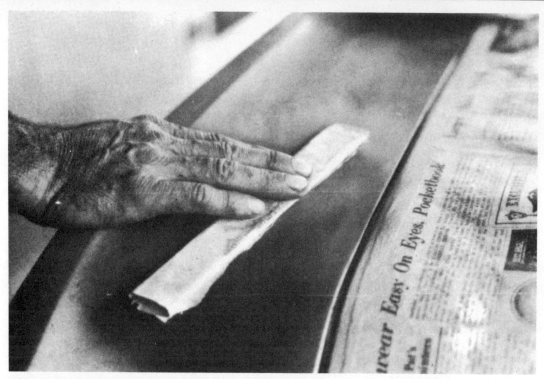

After primer is dry, block sand the are. If you can still feel the void, repeat the operation

If you've made any body repairs, these must also be feather-edged

Repaired area should look like this before priming

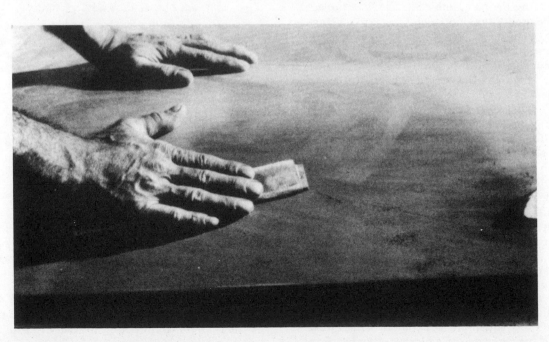

Prime all metal finished areas after feather-edging. When primer has dried, block sand with 220-grit and paddle. If the area is still not smooth, reprime and block sand again. Keep repeating this operation until the area is smooth and you can feel no imperfections with the palm of your hand

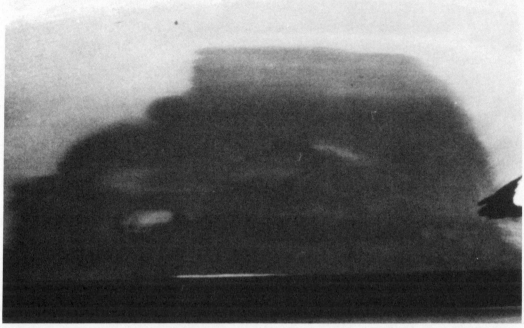

The area is primed again, since portions of metal and filler show through. It will be sanded again when you sand the complete car

STEP 3 — SANDING THE COMPLETE CAR

Step 3, sanding the complete car, is another project that should be done panel-by-panel. Do one panel completely before going on to the next. This step is the next-to-most-tedious part of preparing to refinish, but it is, in fact, just about the most important. The better you do this step, the better the finish you're going to end up with, and most important, the longer it will hold up. Take a sheet of 320-grit open face sandpaper and fold it in half from the top to the bottom. Crease it, and tear the paper in half. Take one of the halves and fold it in thirds. This gives you a good sized piece for palming. Start sanding on any panel, snading in straight lines back and forth. As the paper tends to build up with sanding dust, knock it against your free hand to reduce clogging. Sand an area about twelve inches square until the old finish is completely dull and you feel no imperfections as you run your hand over your work. The reason for sanding until the old finish is completely dull is to insure complete bonding of the new finish. Of course, you are feeling with your free hand to detect any small nicks or foreign matter that might be in the old finish.

Continue until the entire car is sanded. Care must be taken to sand every square inch of your car's sheet metal, right up to the very edge of moldings, door handles, hood emblems, etc. If you are having trouble sanding close to the edge of these items without scratching them,

tape them over temporarily to protect them. If rust appears to be creeping out from under any of these trim pieces, it may be best to remove them. When you have them off, you can sand the finish down to bare metal and prime as in the fether-edging process. Otherwise, do not remove these items and disturb their factory installation. Getting in close to items like windshield wiper shafts where they go through the cowl, door handles, door locks, etc. is very time consuming, but very necessary to prevent your new paint job from peeling in just a few months, so do it. Sand the entire surface no matter how hard it is to get at, if you want a top-flight professional job. On the feather-edged areas and the areas that you repaired, continue to sand just as you are sanding the rest of the car. Look closely at these areas for grinder marks and coarse sandpaper scratches.

If you sand through to bare metal, reprime that area and work around that spot until it dries. Then go back and sand it again. Usually, you won't be able to feel these marks in the primer. You have to look closely for them, and they must be sanded out. If they are not taken care of they will show in the finished product.

When you have sanded the whole car, just to be sure of your work, go back and check the areas that were feather-edged and primed and any areas that were repaired. These are trouble sport that can ruin an otherwise good job. When you have doublechecked your work and are satisfied with it, you have completed Step 3.

You're now read to sand the complete car with 320-grit paper and lots of patience

Tear the sandpaper in half, and then fold each half in thirds

Sand in straight lines back and forth in an area about twelve inches square. Sand until the old finish is completely smooth and full. Sand over all the areas that were primed as well. Be sure all the scratches and imperfections are sanded out on these areas

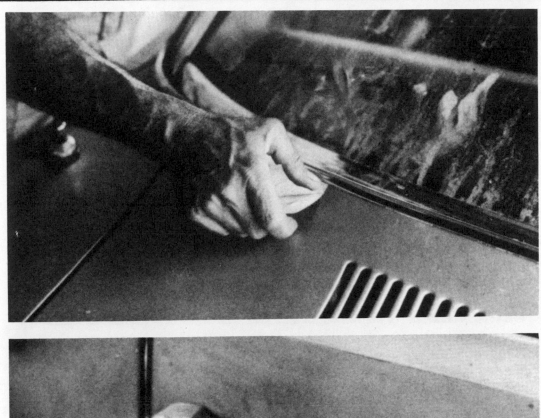

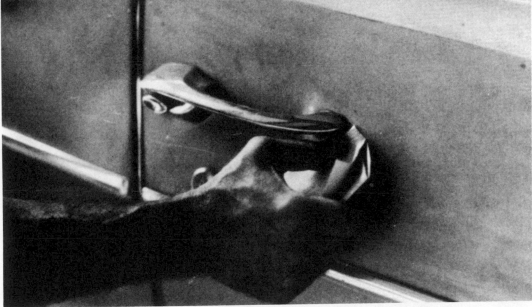

When sanding the complete car, be careful to sand right up to the very edge of moldings and door handles. If you don't, the paint will soon peel from these areas

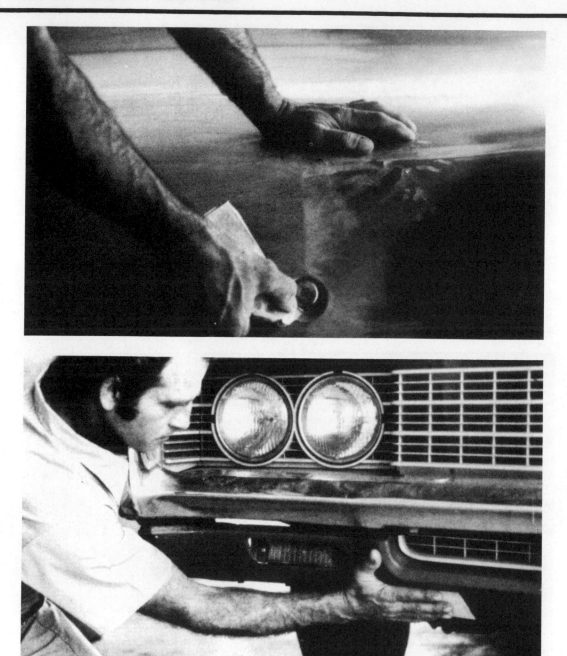

Here are two areas that are hard to get at, but they must be sanded if you want a good paint job

STEP 4—MASKING THE CAR

This is a fairly simple operation but is probably the most tedious. If it is done quickly, items like chrome moldings, emblens, window glass will get paint on them and look thoroughly shabby when the job is finished. A poorly masked car is the result of amateur work. There is no set rule for masking, as we all do it differently. The end result is the important factor.

1. All items that are not to receive paint must be completely masked with tape and/or paper. This includes windows, bumpers, and vinyl tops. Be as neat as possible. Avoid pockets in the paper where dust can gather and cause a dirty finished product.

2. For safetty's sake, no windows or lights of any kind should be masked until the car is driven to the shop that will do the painting. If the car is to be driven some distance to the shop, don't paper the grille or the car may overheat. Don't expect the painter to do it though or the price will go up! Do it yourself when you have the car at the shop.

3. Do not mask until a day or two before taking the car to the shop. The longer masking tape stays on the car the harder it will be to get off. Don't let the car get wet once you start masking. Water can get trapped and then blown out on the finish as the painter is applying the paint.

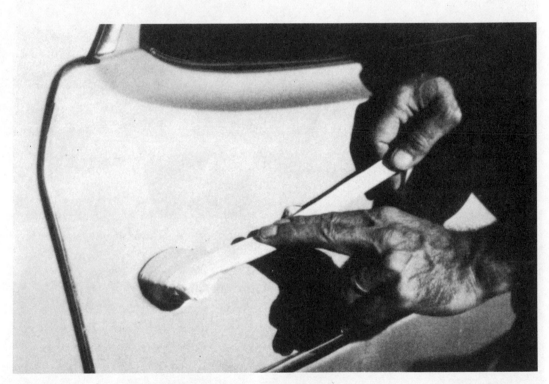

Taping a door handle. It is better to leave a small part of the handle exposed than to get too close to the body and possibly pull the fresh paint off when you untape the car

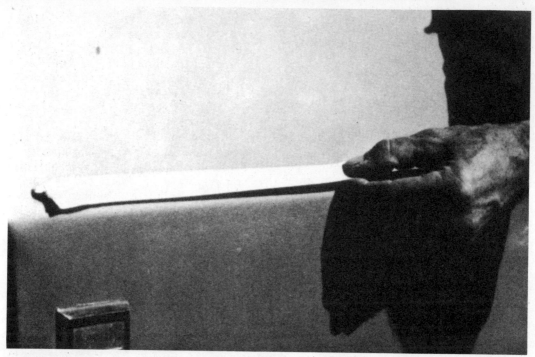

Tape moldings in the same manner as door handles. Be sure that the tape doesn't touch the body

A typical masked section. Notice that all taping is neatly done

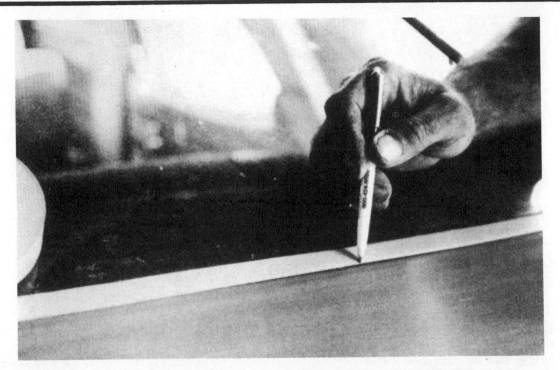

The pen reminds you not to get any tape on any part of the sheet metal to be painted. Naturally, when you untape the car that portion under the tape wouldn't have any paint on it

Taping is a time-consuming job, but it must be done. Some emblems can be removed and some can't. Take your time and do it right

When taping an antenna, don't spiral the tape, instead, tape the length of the unit. It will be much esier to remove the tap.

When taping the windows, be very neat and avoid pockets and folds in the paper that can trap dirt and cause a dirty final product.
CAUTION: Do not tape windows or lights until the car is at the paint shop

STEP 5—GETTING THE CAR PAINTED

By now you should be just about ready for paint. If you are going to pain the car yourself, see the chapter on Painting Techniques. If you are going to have someone else paint the car, and haven't already lined up someone to do the job, call around to do your pricing rather than taking the car to different shops. Like everything else, price is not the only consideration. After all the work you've put in, quality is equally important. Your best bet is to look in the Yellow Pages of your phone book and jot down two or three addresses of independent body shops. Don't bother going to any of the new car dealers, as they are always loaded with work, and probably wouldn't do your job.

Talk to your friends or people at a local body shop. Frequently there is someone locally who works as a painter in a shop and "moonlights" out of his own garage at nights. Don't forget to contact the local franchised paint shops, as most do quality work at reasonable prices. Frequently you'll find that many body shops send their work to these painters, rather than paint an entire car themselves.

When you talk to the man at the shop, say, "I have prepared my car for painting and would like to know how much you charge for applying a sealer coat and spraying the paint".

Be sure they are planning to seal your old finish before they paint, as sealing is important for good adhesion, good gloss, and good coverage of any minor imperfections you may have missed.

One thing to remember when you ask about getting your paint work done: The people you are dealing with are professionals. They are always busy and are trying to make money. Use the humble approach, and don't try to make them think you are an old hand at their game. They'll find you out before you have said ten words. Simply tell them you have prepped your car and you would like them to refinish it. If they brush you off, thank them for their time and go to another shop. It will mean they have more work than they can handle. When you find a shop that will look at your car or panel, they will see you have done a good job and will give you a price.

CARE AND MAINTENANCE OF A NEW FINISH

After your car is repainted, put back any items you removed prior to painting such as moldings or emblems. For the next thirty days be very careful of the new finish, as it will be soft and quite vulnerable to nicks and scratches. Keep the car out of the hot sun as much as possible, and keep the finish free of dirt. To wash the car for the first two weeks, just rinse it off with clear water from a garden hose and wipe it dry with a clean, soft cloth. After two weeks you may wash the car with clean, soft rags and a mild soap solution. Be sure the soap is mild! Do not use harsh detergents!

Do not wax the car for at least thirty days, as the new finish has to breathe in order to dry peoperly. Before you wax the car, see the chapter on body care.

Painting Techniques

PAINTING TECHNIQUES

Painting an automobile or an entire panel is a skill gained from years of experience. There is far more to painting than simply squeezing the trigger on the pain gun and hoping for the best.

Once you have completed the body repairs and primed the repair area you're ready to think about the finish coat of paint, and whether you are going to "shoot" the paint yourself or have it done professionally. There are several factors to consider:

There are basically 3 kinds of repair where paint is concerned-spot finishing, panel finishing and complete repaint jobs. The vast majority of minor auto body work falls into the spot refinishing category, which is easily handles by an aerosol spray can. These are inexpensive, easy to use and will produce quality finishes.

Repainting an entire panel is usually necessary after fairly extensive body work or in cases where a spot repair will be difficult to match the exact color. This is frequently the case with silver cars or those with metallic paint finishes. An entire panel is usually painted with a commercial spray gun and compressor, which can be rented, borrowed, or is available to purchase in do-it-yourself models from manufacturers of power equipment.

Repainting an entire car should be done with a spray gun and compressor.

EQUIPMENT

Of primary importance is a clean, dry place to work. Dirt and dust have an affinity for wet paint and nothing will give your fresh paint job a worse looking surface than dirt and dust that settle in the paint.

For larger repairs, a compressor and spray gun can be purchased, rented or borrowed. The most common types of spray equipment are the syphon cup spray gun, in which trigger action controls both air and paint flow and the electric compressor with a storage tank reservoir. This equipment is frequently designed for automotive use and will produce excellent results when used properly.

REFINISHING SYSTEMS

The refinishing system is basically the type of paint being used. The choice will be made from one of the 4 basic systems below.

Acrylic Lacquer

Acrylic lacquer is relatively easy to apply and dried quickly. It provides excellent color and gloss, but does require more application time, as it must be applied in several color coats. Its cost is also slightly more and it must be buffed and compounded to bring up the high gloss.

Synthetic Enamel

Synthetic enamels require fewer top coats, do not need compounding or buffing and cost less than other enamels. They dry to a high gloss, but require more drying time.

Acrylic Enamel

Acrylic enamels combine the best features of the Synthetic enamels and acrylic lacquer. They are easy to apply, dry quickly and no compounding or buffing is necessary. Acrylic enamel dries to a hard, durable finish but should be recoated with sealer after about 6 hours. Coat is between acrylic lacquer and synthetic enamel.

Urethane Enamel

Urethane enamel is one of the newest, most sophisticated automotive finishes. It is expensive, but gives all the advantages of acrylic enamel, but is highly resistant to chemicals, nicks and scratches.

BEFORE YOU BEGIN TO PAINT

There are several important preparatory steps you must take prior to actually painting that will go a long way toward assuring a satisfactory job.

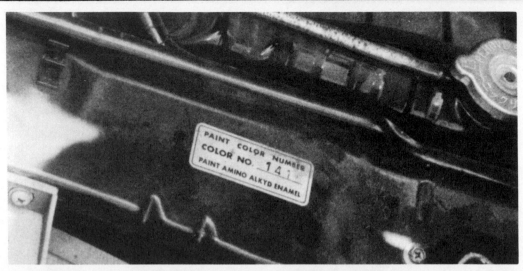

The paint code is usually located on a metal tag affixed to the radiator support, door pillar or similar place. Check the paint code to be sure of the exact color

Check the Paint Type & Color

The paint code is usually listed on a special tag affixed to the car either under the hood or on the door post. This code is the exact color for the original equipment paint on the vehicle. The code should be used when purchasing paint unless you plan to change the color. The reason for this is that some types of paint are incompatible without the use of special sealers.

Acrylic lacquer, for instance, can be used over old lacquer and acrylic lacquer with little surface preparation, assuming that the old finish is not rusted, severely checked, or otherwise deficient. Acrylic lacquer can also be used over enamel, but first it is generally recom-

mended that the enamel be sanded thoroughly and sprayed with a sealer to assure good adhesion and minimize sand scratches marring the finish.

If you aren't sure which type of old painted surface you are working with, moisten a cloth with lacquer thinner and rub the finish. If it dissolves easily with little or no rubbing, it is lacquer; if it dissolves easily with considerable rubbing, it is acrylic lacquer; if it doesn't budge even with brisk rubbing, it is enamel.

Armed with the paint code and type of paint, you can purchase aerosol spray cans from a rack or you can purchase paint in bulk from your automotive paint supplier.

Check the application book from the paint supplier for the exact color and code that you need

Do-it-yourself paints for small repairs are sold in spray cans or small bottles for touch-up work

SURFACE PREPARATION

Aerosol Spray Can (Small Areas)

Once the repair is made and the area primed you are ready to paint. Just be sure the surrounding paint is clean and dry, and all wax is removed.

Spray Gun (Larger Areas)

1. Remove the old finish—Several methods can be used. Among them are power sanding, hand sanding or specially formulated liquid paint removers. On fiberglass surfaces, it is safer to sand the paint, rather than use paint remover.

2. Metal preparation—This is the most important step for good paint adhesion. Remove all traces of corrosion from the surface, by sanding. Wash the surface with a wax or grease remover and follow this with a metal conditioner and rust inhibitor to remove invisible rust.

Wipe the entire panel with a tack rag to remove dust and dirt. Coat the bar metal with primer or primer surfaces.

3. Fiberglass preparation—Fiberglass should be treated the same as metal, except that it is not corrosive and does not require treatment for rust. Thoroughly clean the surface with wax and grease remover.

Sand exposed fiberglass with 220 grit paper by hand and wipe the surface dry with clean rags. Wipe the entire surface with a tack rag, and prime the exposed surfaces.

4. Preparation of old paint—Wash the entire surface with wax and grease remover. Sand out any defect in the old finish and feather-edge all edges. Reclean the surface and treat the metal areas as above. Prime or seal the old paint as follows:

If the old surface is enamel use an all-purpose primer-surface followed by acrylic enamel or acrylic lacquer.

If the old finish is lacquer, prime the surface with all-purpose primer-surfacer followed by enamel or lacquer.

If the old finish is acrylic, prime the surface with all purpose primer-surfacer followed by acrylic lacquer or acrylic enamel.

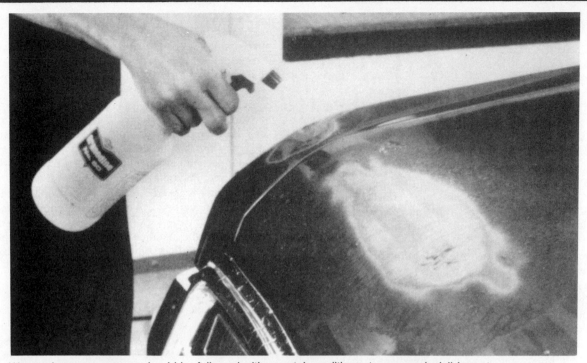

Wax and grease remover should be followed with a metal conditioner to remove invisible rust

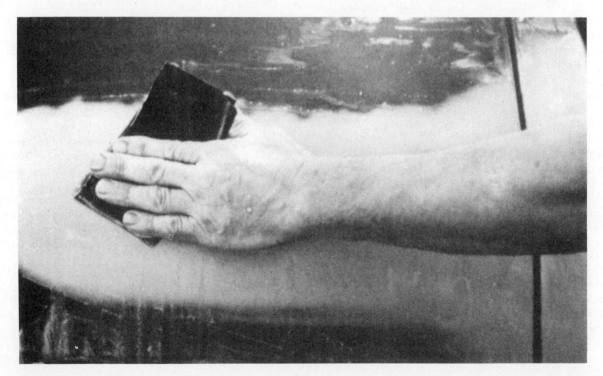

A primer-surfacer should be sued to prime and seal the old paint. Finish the primer-surfacer by wet sanding with 400 paper

2 MINOR BODY REPAIR

PAINTING TECHNIQUES

There are several important things to remember for a good paint job regardless of whether you are spraying from a can or spray gun.

Spraying Viscosity (Spray Gun Only)

The material should be thinned to spraying viscosity according to the directions on the can. Use the recommended thinner or reducer.

Measurement of the thinner is the only way to do the job adequately. Because appearance is affected by the temperature, the way the paints runs off the stirring paddle is not a reliable method of determining viscosity.

The amount of reduction should be the same regardless of temperature. At higher temperatures the viscosity of the reduced material will be lower but this is offset by a faster evaporation rate of the thinner as it travels between the gun and the surface. The result is that the paint reaches the surface at the correct viscosity.

The reverse is true in a cold shop. Reduced paint is a little thicker, but evaporation in the air is less so that the paint reaches the surface at the proper viscosity.

Temperature

The temperature at which paint is sprayed and dries has great influence on the overall quality. This involves not only the surrounding air temperatures but the temperature of the surface as well. The surface should be approximately the same temperature as the surrounding air temperature. Spraying warm paint on a cold surface or spraying cool paint on a hot surface will completely upset the paint characteristics. The rate of evaporation on a hot summer day is approximately 50% faster that it is on an average day with an air temperature of 72°F. Appropriate thinners or reducers should be used for warm and cold weather applications, as recommended by the manufacturers.

Film Thickness

In general, the thicker the film applied, the longer the drying time.

The difference in film thickness will show up plainly in enamel colors. A lacquer that can be sanded in 30 minutes will take over an hour if sprayed twice as thick.

The reason is that the thicker the film the greater the depth of paint from which the thinner or reducer must work its way out, and, in enamels, the greater the distance the oxygen from the air must penetrate.

You should develop a technique so that the paint will remain wet long enough for proper flow-out, and no longer. Heavier coats are not necessary, and they may produce sags, curtains or wrinkles.

The amount of material sprayed on a surface with one stroke of the gun will depend on width of fan, distance from gun, air pressure at the gun, reduction, speed of stroke, and selection of thinner or reducer.

Distance

Spray guns are designed to give the best performance at a distance of 8–12 in. from the surface. If the spraying is done from a shorter distance, the high velocity of the spraying air tends to ripple the wet film. If the distance is increased beyond that there will be a greater percent of thinner evaporated, resulting in orange peel of dry film and, adversely affect color where matching is required. A slower evaporating thinner will permit more variation in the distance of the spray gun from the job, it will produce runs, if the gun gets too close. Excessive spraying distance also causes a loss in materials due to overspray.

Strokes and Overlapping

If the gun is tilted toward the surface so that the fan pattern is not uniform, or if the gun is swung in an arc, varying the distance from the nozzle to the work, the paint will go on wetter where the nozzle is closer to the surface and drier where it is farther away. The gun should be at right angles to the job at all times. Do not fan the gun and do not use wrist motions if you want a uniform film. The only time it is permissible to fan the gun is on a small spot spray where the paint film at the edges of the spot should be thinner than the center portion. Work to a wet edge by using a fifty percent overlap and direct the center of the spray fan at the lower or nearest edge of the previous stroke.

PAINTING WITH AEROSOL SPRAY CANS

1. Before painting, shake the can for almost 1 minute to thoroughly mix the paint. The paint is mixed when you can no longer hear the agitator ball inside the can.

2. Hold the can 8–12 in. from the work.

3. Spray with smooth strokes, keeping the can the same direction from the work and perpendicular to it.

4. Apply several thin coats, about 30 seconds apart. The final coat should appear glossy.

5. Let the paint dry thoroughly and inspect the surface. Runs or an orange peel surface can be sanded out, reprimed and repainted. If the surface is uniformly glossy and to your satisfaction, no further painting is necessary.

6. Allow the final coat to dry thoroughly. Don't be in too big a hurry to remove the masking tape, as this only produces paint ridges and lines.

7. You are now ready to blend the new paint job with the surrounding area.

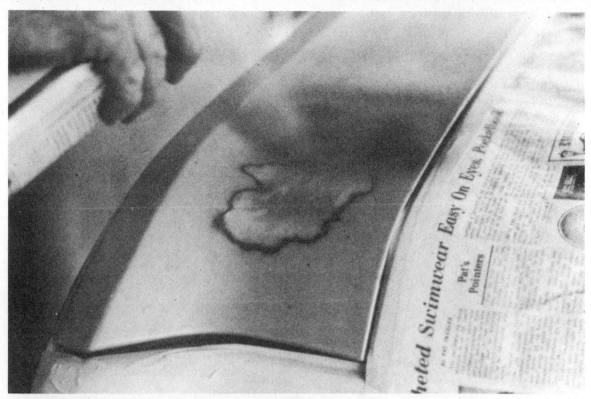

Aerosol spray cans should be held 8–12 in. from the work

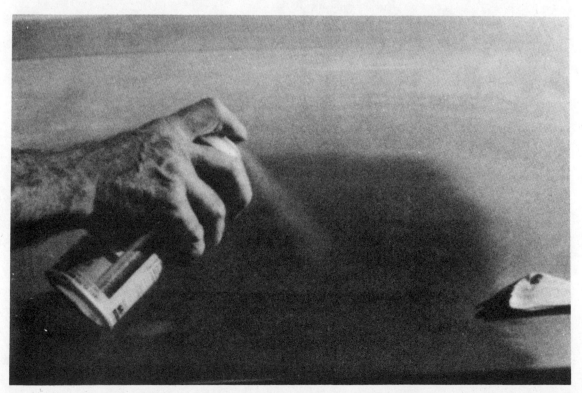

Keep the can perpendicular to the work and spray with long even strokes. Apply several thin coats about 30 seconds apart

PAINTING WITH A SPRAY GUN

1. Mix the paint and thinner accurately. Eyeballing these measurements is not good enough.

2. Use the recommended thinner and equipment as specified by the manufacturer of the paint.

3. Air pressure is very important to a good paint job. Be sure you are using the proper recommended pressure at the gun by consulting the chart.

4. Experiment on an old piece of sheet metal to find the right combination of air pressure, distance and film thickness before you begin to paint.

5. Spray a light (fog) coat, followed by heavier, color coats.

6. Overlap the paint coats by 50% for best coverage.

7. Keep the gun moving at an even speed, perpendicular to the surface.

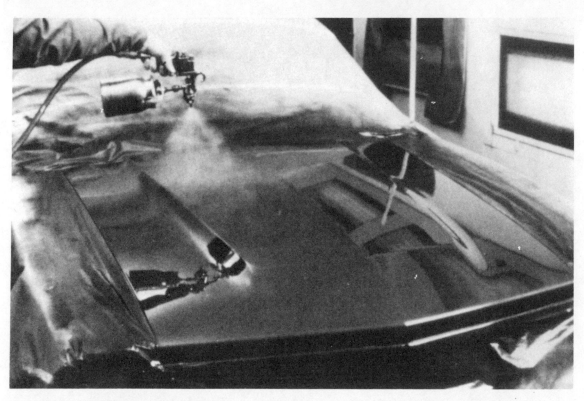

Keep the gun perpendicular to the surface

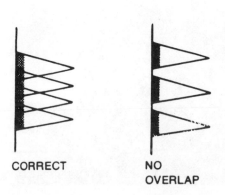

CORRECT   NO
               OVERLAP

For good coverage, coats should be overlapped

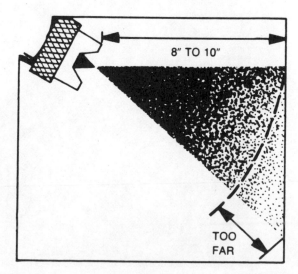

8" TO 10"

TOO FAR

If the gun is not kept perpendicular to the surface, paint coverage will be spotty and thin in places

ESTIMATED AIR PRESSURES AT THE GUN

Air pressure instructions are based on at-the-gun pressures. While the dial at the regulator indicates air pressure, there is a drop in air pressure at the gun, the amount of which is affected by the size and length of hose, snap hose connectors and hose conditions. For a close estimated at-the-gun pressure, this table may be used.

Pressure Reading (Lbs.) At Gage		Pressure At-The-Gun For Various Hose Lengths					
		5 ft	10 ft	15 ft	20 ft	25 ft	50 ft
¹⁄₄ Inch Hose	30	26	24	23	22	21	9
	40	34	32	31	29	27	16
	50	43	40	38	36	34	22
	60	51	48	46	43	41	29
	70	59	56	53	51	48	36
	80	68	64	61	58	55	43
	90	76	71	68	65	61	51
⁵⁄₁₆ Inch Hose	30	29	28½	28	27½	27	23
	40	38	37	37	37	36	32
	50	48	47	46	46	45	40
	60	57	56	55	55	54	49
	70	66	65	64	63	63	57
	80	75	74	73	72	71	66
	90	84	83	82	81	80	74

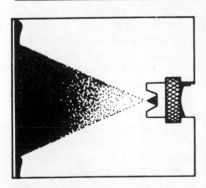

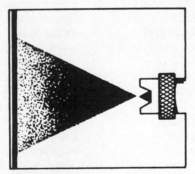

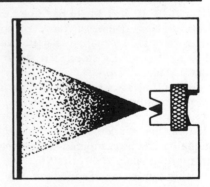

WRONG
Thin coat, rough, dry, no lustre.

REASONS
Gun too far away
Paint too thin
Too much air
Stroke too fast
Not enough overlap

CORRECT
Medium coat, good flow-out with hardly any orange peel and no sags.

REASONS
Gun clean and properly adjusted
Gun distance proper
Stroke okay
Overlap 50%

WRONG
Heavy coat with sags, ripples or orange peel.

REASONS
Dirty air nozzle
Gun too close
Paint too thin or too thick
Low air pressure
Stroke too slow
Too much overlap

Experiment on an old piece of sheet metal to get the right combination and "touch"

BLENDING THE NEW PAINT

For a practically invisible repair, it will be necessary to blend the new paint into the old using very fine rubbing compound.

The final paint coat should be allowed to dry for at least 48 hours (lacquer and acrylic) or 30 days (non-synthetic enamel) before using rubbing compound.

Wet the entire painted area thoroughly with water. Fold a clean cloth into a pad and work a little fine rubbing compound into the pad, which should be very wet. Don't use too much compound.

Lightly rub the entire panel, old and new finish, with horizontal strokes. Never use a circular motion. Start at the top of the panel and work to the bottom using lots of water. The panel will be left with a residue of compound which can be wiped off with a dry cloth, wiping in the same direction that you rubbed. Then wet a cloth and wipe the panel until all compound is gone.

Compare the smoothness of the surrounding paint and the new paint. It should be about even. If not, wet sand the new paint lightly with #600 paper, and compound again. Clean the area and buff it with a clean cloth until the entire panel has a uniform sheen.

Wash the panel clean and polish; unless you have used enamel paint, which should not be waxed for at least 6 months.

SPECIAL PROBLEMS

Clear Coat Paint

In recent years, many car makers have been using a clear coat finish on many of their car lines. The end result is an eye catching depth to paint jobs, particularly to many of the metallic or irridescent glamor colors. But these clear coats are proving to be traps for the unwary repairing auto body damages. Here's why:

Many owners fail to realize that the vehicle had a clear coat on top of it's color. This type of finish is known as 2-stage, or 2-phase.

2-phase painting is not new. At the turn of the century painters were applying this system on cars, trucks, and carriages. Color was applied by brush. When it was fully dried, it was then sanded with pumice stone. Pumice cutting quality can be compared with a very fine sandpaper of approximately 1000 grit. When the painted surface was fully sanded and cleaned the paint would look extremely dull. Clear varnish was then brushed on. Instantly it brought out the color in full deep gloss. This system was, and still is, superior to the normal gloss that remains on just a color application. Wax and similar polishes applied on color can highlight the gloss, but they are not as lasting, or as glossy, as a clear finish can be.

Today, the 2-phase system is basically the same. Apply color, make sure its surface is free from all imperfections, and then apply a clear coat to magnify the color.

Clear varnish is no longer used for automotive applications. Today's clear is a see-through paint. There are various types of clears. There's a clear coat that is used as a protective coating on interior nonferrous metals like aluminum, a clear that covers and highlights a color, and a clear that can be used for blend coating.

Many cars arrive with OE (original equipment) clear coat finishes over the color coat. Just about the only way to know if a car you are working on has clear coat or not is to check in trunk and engine compartment areas for evidence of clear coat termination. You may be able to lift a small chip of clear off with a finger nail.

Look carefully for evidence of peeling at the edges of the original clear coat application on the car body. If a chip of clear coat can be pried away from the underlying color coat you've got a clear-coat-finished car on your hands.

For the inexperienced, it's possible to check if a car has a clear coat on it through the paint code, which will be found on the body number plate. Don't assume all late model cars-even metallic finishes-are clear coated. Check with the local car dealer of the brand in question or ask the body shop, if they have one, or the parts department, if the subject vehicle has OE clear coat on it.

This is a good example of a job that is not for the do-it-yourselfer. Application of clear coat paint and repainting of panels that are clear coated should be left to professionals.

Stone Resistant Coatings

In recent model years cars have been arriving on the street with a new customer convenience option. It's a stone-chip resistant coating which preserves the cosmetic appearance of the lower body panels and protects them against stone damage- which can lead to rust damage. This new coating is virtually undetectable, and must be taken into account when making lower body damage repairs to a late-model car with this feature.

Some two years ago, car makers began applying a special coating between the metal and top coat. This abrasion-resistant coating may be called "stone-guard" or "gravel protector" finished by some car makers. Whatever the name, the material used is usually a clear vinyl coating that is similar to smooth undercoating. The color coat is applied on top of the coating and thus becomes cushioned from stone pecking. IF the paint does chip, the stone guard finish does not. Its basic purpose is to prevent rust from setting in.

This body repair person must be aware of this type of coating, because it is virtually impossible to featheredge the lower areas. The sandpaper becomes quickly clogged, and blending just won't take. As with any other type of body and paint work, a lack of knowledge about any job can ensure its becoming a disaster. One method of testing is to press the surface with a pin. Remember the resistant coating is some 15–20 mils thick. It should have a cushiony feel.

Remove color and coating with a heat gun. Use a scraping tool to get the coating off once it is softened from the heat. Be extremely careful that heat application does not cause metal warpage.

After the bulk of the finish has been removed, clean the area with either a grinder or power sander.

This is an example of another paint job that should be left to a professional who has the skill and the experience to do a quality job.

Body Care

BODY CARE

Now that you've restored your car's body and paint to something resembling its original finish, you should give some thought to keeping it that way.

There are hundreds—maybe thousands—of products on the market, all designed to protect or aid your car's finish in some manner. There are as many different products as there are ways to use them, but they all have one thing in common-the surface must be clean.

WASHING

The primary ingredient for washing your car is water, preferably "soft" water. In many areas of the country, the local water supply is "hard" containing many minerals. The little rings or film that is left on your car's surface after it has dried is the result of "hard" water.

Since you usually can't change the local water supply, the next best thing is to dry the surface before it has a chance to dry itself.

Into the water you usually add soap. Don't use detergents or common, coarse soaps. Your car's paint never truly dried out, but is always evaporating residual oils into the air. Harsh detergents will remove these oils, causing the paint to dry faster than normal. Instead use warm water and a non-detergent soap made especially for waxed surfaces or a liquid soap made for washing dishes by hand. Other products that can be used on painted surfaces include baking soda or plain soda water for stubborn dirt.

Wash the car completely, starting at the top, and rinse it completely clean. Abrasive grit should be loaded off under water pressure; scrubbing them off will scratch the finish. The best washing tools are sponges, cleaning mitts or soft towels. whatever you choose, replace it often as they tend to absorb grease and dirt.

Other ways to get a better wash include:

• Don't wash your car in the sun or when the finish is hot.

• Use water pressure to remove caked-on dirt.

• Remove tree-sap and bird effluence immediately. Such substances will eat through wax, polish and paint.

One of the best implements to dry your car is a turkish towel or an old, soft bath towel. Anything with a deep nap will hold any dirt in suspension and not grind it in to the paint.

Harder cloths will only grind the grit into the paint making more scratches. Always start drying at the top, followed by the hood and trunk and sides. You'll find there's always more dirt near the rocker panels and wheelwells which will wind up on the rest of the car if you dry these areas first.

CLEANERS, WAXES AND POLISHES

Before going any farther you need to know the function of various products.

• Cleaners—remove the top layer of dead pigment or paint.

• Compounds—rubbing compounds are used to remove stubborn dirt, get rid of minor scratches, smooth away imperfections and partially restore badly weathered paint.

• Polishes—polishes contain no abrasives or waxes; they shine the paint by adding oils to the paint.

• Waxes—is a protective coating for the polish.

Cleaners

Before you apply any wax, you'll have to remove oxidation, road film and other types of pollutants that simply washing will not remove.

The paint on your car never dried completely. There are always residual oils evaporating from the paint into the air. When enough oils are present in the paint, it has a healthy shine (gloss). When too many oils evaporate the paint takes on a whitish cast known as oxidation. The idea of polishing and waxing is to keep enough oil present in the painted surface to prevent oxidation, but when it occurs; the only recourse is to remove the top layer of "dead" paint, exposing the healthy paint underneath.

Products to remove oxidation and road film are sold under a variety of generic names-polishes, cleaner, rubbing compound, cleaner/polish, polish/cleaner, self-polishing wax, pre-wax cleaner, finish restorer and many more. Regardless of name there are two types of cleaners-abrasive cleaners (sometimes called polishing or rubbing compounds) that remove oxidation by grinding away the top layer of "dead" paint, or chemical cleaners that dissolve the "dead" pigment, allowing it to be wiped away.

Abrasive cleaners, by their nature, leave thousands of minute scratches in the finish, which must be polished out later. These should only be used in extreme cases, but are usually the only thing to use on badly oxidized paint finishes. Chemical cleaners are much milder but are not strong enough for severe cases of oxidation or weathered paint.

The most popular cleaners are liquid or paste abrasive polishing and rubbing compounds. Polishing compounds have a finer abrasive grit for medium duty work. Rubbing compounds are a coarser abrasive and for heavy duty work. Unless you are familiar with how to use compounds, be very careful. Excessive rubbing with any type of compound or cleaner can grind right through the paint to primer or bare metal. Follow the directions on the container-depending on type, the cleaner may or may not be OK for your paint. For example, some cleaners are not formulated for acrylic lacquer finishes.

When a small area needs compounding or heavy polishing, it's best to do the job by hand. Some people prefer a powered buffer for large areas. Avoid cutting through the paint along styling edges on the body. Small, hand operations where the compound is applied and rubbed using cloth folded into a thick ball, allow you to work in straight lines along such edges.

To avoid cutting through on the edges when using a power buffer, try masking tape. Just cover the edge with tape while using power. Then finish the job by hand with the tape removed. Even then work carefully. The paint tends to be a lot thinner along the sharp ridges stamped into the panels.

Compounding by machine or by hand, only work on a small area and apply the compound sparingly. If the materials are spread too thin, or allowed to sit too long, they dry out. Once dry, they lose the ability to deliver a smooth, clean finish. Also, dried out polish tends to cause the buffer to stick on one spot. This in turn can burn or cut through the finish.

When rubbing out blemishes or just polishing paint, work in straight lines-there's less risk of rubbing through the paint

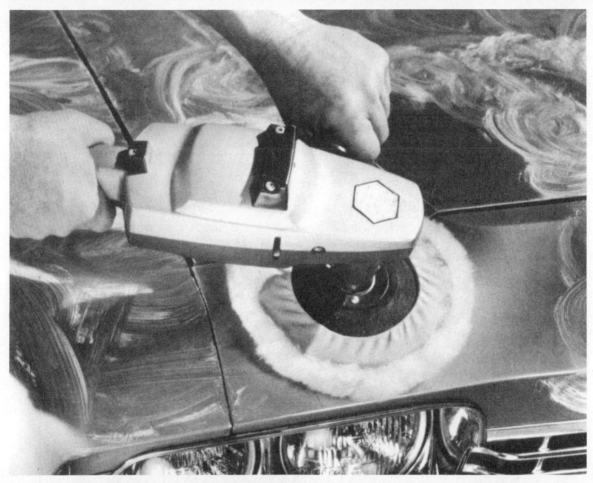

Use a polish or wax sparingly when power buffing. Liquid or paste should be spread evenly, because the pad must operated on wax or polish, not bare paint. If not, the pad could burn the paint

BEFORE YOU BEGIN TO BUFF

See also the buffing potion of the "Detailing" section. Brighter shines and longer buffing bonnet life are well worth the extra effort it takes to keep the pads in good condition. Bonnets are usually either wool pile or lamb's wool. The pile bonnet will last longer than the lamb's wool, especially under constant use on a buffing machine. But the lamb's wool is softer and gives a glossier shin than pile. So lamb's wool is normally saved for the final finish of a wax job.

Poor care of a buffing bonnet not only shortens the life of the pad, but results in a poor polish job. Proper care, though, can nearly double the useful life of a bonnet.

Brand new bonnets especially those with finer texture, tend to lint. Before using one on a car, attach the bonnet to the machine and hold it against the edge of a work bench. Run the machine at about 500 rpm for a minute to remove most of the surface lint.

After buffing about four times remove the pad and clean it thoroughly. Use lukewarm water and a mild detergent. Never use hot water. It makes even pre-shrunk wool shrink more, and curls the edge as well.

A word of caution about synthetic buffing bonnets: they are not intended for direct use on a car's finish.

They are quite abrasive and can cut away the topmost layer of paint.

Waxes and Polishes

Your car's finish can be protected in a number of ways. A cleaner/wax or polish/cleaner followed by wax or variations of each all provide good results. The 2-step approach (polish followed by wax) is probably slightly better but consumes more time and effort. Properly fed with oils, your paint should never need cleaning, but despite the best polishing job, it won't last unless it's protected with wax. Without wax, polish must be renewed at least once a month to prevent oxidation. years ago (some still swear by it today), the best wax was made from the Brazilian palm, the Carnauba, favored for its vegetable base and high melting point. However, modern synthetic waxes are harder, which means they protect against moisture better, and chemically inert silicone is used for a long lasting protection. The only problem with silicone wax is that it penetrates all layers of paint. To repaint or touch up a panel or car protected by silicone wax, you have to completely strip the finish to avoid "fisheyes".

Under normal conditions, silicone waxes will last 4–6 months, but you have to be careful of wax build-up from too much waxing. Too thick a coat of wax is just as bad as no wax at all; it stops the paint from breathing.

Combination cleaners/waxes have become popular lately because they remove the old layer of wax plus light oxidation, while putting on a fresh coat of wax at the same time. Some cleaners/waxes contain abrasive cleaners which require caution, although many cleaner/waxes use a chemical cleaner.

WAX, WHAT IT IS

Hydrocarbon is found in a lot of places but the most interesting variety for people trying to preserve paint is a Brazilian palm called the Carnauba. The vegetable wax extracted from this plant has an unusually high melting point, 185°F.

The thing that makes wax so good for protecting surfaces is its hydrophobic character—it rejects water. And the things which cause paint to deteriorate include water, light and air.

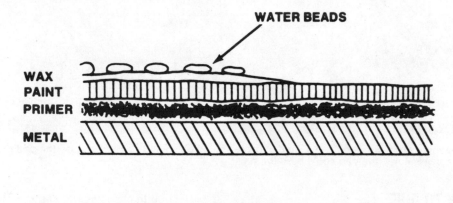

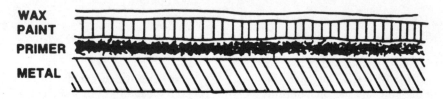

The film of wax applied to a surface will not exclude these completely, but it does slow the attack. Detergents tend to remove wax in spite of the fact that it will not readily dissolve in water. To help it get through several washings, a chemical called aminofunctional-silicones is added to the blend of waxes. The wax is blended to get toughness in an extremely thin film.

The layer of wax is perhaps only one molecule thick at some points. While this is difficult to measure, it isn't hard to detect. And the method used even by experts is the water beading test. If water "beads" on the surface, the wax layer is present. If it doesn't bead, it's time to clean and wax again.

Applying a Wax or Polish

You may view polishing and waxing your car as a pleasant way to spend an afternoon, or as a boring chore, but it has to be done to keep the paint on your car. Caring for the paint doesn't require special tools, but you should follow a few rules.

1. Use a good quality wax.
2. Before applying any wax or polish, be sure the surface is completely clean. Just because the car looks clean, doesn't mean it's ready for polish or wax.
3. If the finish on your car is weathered, dull, or oxidized, it will probably have to be compounded to remove the old or oxidized paint. If the paint is simply dulled from lack or care, one of the non-abrasive cleaners known as polishing compounds will do the trick. If the paint is severely scratched or really dull, you'll probably have to use a rubbing compound to prepare the finish for waxing. If you're not sure which one to use, use the polishing compound, since you can easily ruin the finish by using too strong a compound.
4. Don't apply wax, polish compound in direct sunlight, even if the directions on the can say you can. Most waxes will not cure properly in bright sunlight and you'll probably end up with a blotchy looking finish.
5. Don't rub the wax off too soon. The result will be a wet, dull looking finish. Let the wax dry thoroughly before buffing it off.
6. A constant debate among car enthusiasts, is how wax should be applied. Some maintain pastes should be applied in a circular motion, but body shop experts have long thought that this approach results in barely detectable circular abrasions, especially on cars that are waxed frequently. They advise rubbing in straight lines, especially if any kind of cleaner is involved.
7. If an applicator is not supplied with the wax, use a piece of soft cheesecloth or very soft lint-free material. The same applies to buffing the surface.

Special Surfaces

One-step combination cleaner and wax formulas shouldn't be used on many of the special surfaces which abound on cars. The one-step materials contain abrasives to achieve a clean surface under the wax top coat. The abrasives are so mild that you could clean a car every week for a couple of years without fear of rubbing through the paint. But this same level of abrasiveness might, through repeated use, damage decals used for special trim effects. This includes wide striped, wood-grain trim and other appliques.

Painted plastics must be cleaned with care. If a cleaner is too aggressive it will cut through the paint and expose the primer. If bright trim such as polish aluminum or chrome is painted, cleaning must be performed with even greater care. If rubbing compound is being used, it will cut faster than polish. Thus the possibility of getting into trouble is increased.

If you attempt to protect these more-porous-than-usual surfaces, don't turn to low-luster furniture waxes.

They aren't formulated for automotive finishes. They may even cause damage.

Just the opposite gloss problem is found with acrylic finished. They have their highest gloss as sprayed. Abrasive cleaners will dull the finish. The best way to clean these newer finishes is with a non-abrasive liquid polish. Only dirt and oxidation, not paint, will be removed.

Taking a few minutes to read the instructions on the can of polish or wax will help prevent making serious mistakes. The information on the label is there because it is important. Not all preparations will work on all surfaces. And some are intended for power application while others will only work when applied by hand.

Don't get the idea that just pouring on some polish and then hitting it with a buffer will suffice. Power equipment speeds the operation. But it also adds a measure of risk. It's very easy to damage the finish if you use the wrong methods or materials.

Caring for Chrome

The same advice applied to normal cleaning of chrome as well as paint, but there are special products for chrome if you live in areas where rust forms easily (shore, heavy rain or snow areas).

Read the label on the container. Many products are formulated specifically for chrome, but others contain abrasives that will scratch the chrome finish. If it isn't recommended for chrome, don't use it.

Never use steel wool or kitchen soap pads to clean chrome. Be careful not to get chrome cleaner on paint or interior vinyl surfaces. If you do, get it off immediately.

INTERIOR CARE

One way to preserve the new car feeling is to keep the interior clean and protected. You have to use some common sense and not let the dirt accumulates. The more dirt that gets ground into carpeting and seats, the faster they will wear out. Keep the seats wiped down and the rugs vacuumed.

Cleaning Fabric and Vinyl

There are a number of products on the market that will clean vinyl or fabric interiors, but mild soap and water is still one of the best (and cheapest) cleaners and should be used at least 3–4 times a year. Household cleaners like 409, Fantastik and multi-purpose cleaners such as Armor All will also clean vinyl well. As with any cleaner, test it in an out-of-the-way place, before using it.

A whisk broom or vacuum cleaner will keep the rugs clean and free of loose dirt build-up. To clean the carpet, rug shampoo can be used as well as the foamy types in an aerosol can, but the foam types are more of a spot cleaner than an overall cleaner. When working with chemicals and spot removers, be sure that you follow directions on the product and work in a well ventilated area.

HOW TO REMOVE STAINS FROM FABRIC INTERIOR

Please refer to the "Stain Removal" portion of the "Detailing" section.

Type of Stain	How to Remove It
Surface spots	Brush the spots out with a small hand brush or use a commercial preparation such as K2R to lift the stain.
Mildew	Clean around the mildew with warm suds. Rinse in cold water and soak the mildew area in a solution of 1 part table salt and 2 parts water. Wash with upholstery cleaner.
Water stains	Water stains in fabric materials can be removed with a solution made from 1 cup of table salt dissolved in 1 quart of water. Vigorously scrub the solution into the stain and rinse with clear water. Water stains in nylon or other synthetic fabrics should be removed with a commercial type spot remover.
Chewing gum, tar, crayons, shoe polish (greasy stains)	Do not use a cleaner that will soften gum or tar. Harden the deposit with an ice cube and scrape away as much as possible with a dull knife. Moisten the remainder with cleaning fluid and scrub clean.
Ice cream, candy	Most candy has a sugar base and can be removed with a cloth wrung out in warm water. Oily candy, after cleaning with warm water, should be cleaned with upholstery cleaner. Rinse with warm water and clean the remainder with cleaning fluid.
Wine, alcohol, egg, milk, soft drink (non-greasy stains)	Do not use soap. Scrub the stain with a cloth wrung out in warm water. Remove the remainder with cleaning fluid.
Grease, oil, lipstick, butter and related stains	Use a spot remover to avoid leaving a ring. Work from the outside of the stain to the center and dry with a clean cloth when the spot is gone.
Headliners (cloth)	Mix a solution of warm water and foam upholstery cleaner to give thick suds. Use only foam—liquid may streak or spot. Clean the entire headliner in one operation using a circular motion with a natural sponge.

Type of Stain	How to Remove It
Headliner (vinyl)	Use a vinyl cleaner with a sponge and wipe clean with a dry cloth.
Seats and door panels	Mix 1 pint upholstery cleaner in 1 gallon of water. Do not soak the fabric around the buttons.
Leather or vinyl fabric	Use a multi-purpose cleaner full strength and a stiff brush. Let stand 2 minutes and scrub thoroughly. Wipe with a clean, soft rag.
Nylon or synthetic fabrics	For normal stains, use the same procedures you would for washing cloth upholstery. If the fabric is extremely dirty, use a multi-purpose cleaner full strength with a stiff scrub brush. Scrub thoroughly in all directions and wipe with a cotton towel or soft rag.

Repairing Seats and Dash

Vinyl seats and dash are subject to cracking and tearing with hard use. Wear and tear in those areas is very noticeable but not too difficult to repair. Cloth covered seats are harder to repair, unless you're handy with a tailor's needle and thread. If you're not and the seams are coming apart, invest in a set of seat covers in lieu of a trip to the upholstery shop.

Any retail auto store sells pre-fitted seat covers at a fraction of the cost of new upholstery. Seat covers are sold as "fits-all" (universal application) or more expensively by make and model of car. Be sure to check if the covers fit bench or bucket seats, or split back seats. The covers are tied or wired under the seats.

Burn marks in vinyl seats, arm-rests and dashboards can be repaired with the help of a good vinyl repair kit. Rips in the vinyl and seams that have come apart are slightly more difficult but are well worth the time and effort in the end.

About the best way to repair a rip is to heat both sides of the tear with a hair drier. Lift up the material and place a 2 in. wide strip of fabric tape under one side of the vinyl.

Stretch the other side over the tape and line it up carefully. When you have if lined up, press down. Hold it in place while someone applies the vinyl repair liquid over the are to be repaired. Let it dry completely before using it. The repair should look like new and last quite a while.

Other methods of repairing vinyl involve vinyl repair compounds that require heat. The kits contain a repair compound, applicator and several different graining papers. If the hole is deep, it will have to be filled with foam or anything to provide a backing.

Rug Care

Before doing anything about cleaning carpets, thoroughly vacuum everything to remove all loose dirt. The foaming type of rug shampoo (aerosol cans) are good for spot cleaning.

Overall cleaning can be done with 1 pint of upholstery cleaner in 1 gallon of water. If the carpet is faded, spotted, or discolored, add an upholstery tint to the solution. To get the right color shade add tint in small quantities and test the solution by dipping a white cloth in and wringing it out. The color will usually dry a shade or 2 darker.

Apply the solution with a stiff brush and scrub the carpet vigorously, in one direction. When it dried, fluff the carpet with a dry brush.

Salt stains (from winter weather) can be removed by soaking the stained area in a heavy solution of table salt and water. Soak the stained area to loosen embedded salt with a stiff brush, if necessary, and wash the entire carpet. You may have to repeat this several times.

Glass

Interior glass should be cleaned at least once a week to remove deposits from smoke and other films.

Water alone will seldom cut through the haze from cigarette smoke and usually only succeeds in rearranging the film.

Household, blue-liquid cleaners for glass work best. In the absence of these, or for stubborn dirt, use about 4 tablespoons of ammonia in 1 quart of water.

Clean the excess dirt and grime with a paper towel. Apply the cleaner and use a paper towel to clean the dust and dirt from the glass and another to polish the glass.

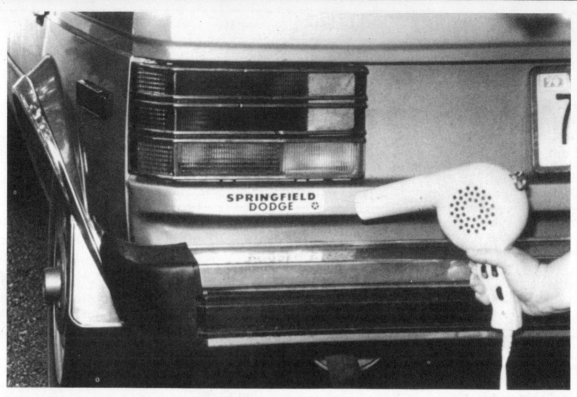

A hair drier will often soften the adhesive used to apply stickers

To remove overspray and masking tape residue from glass; use a strong professional type glass cleaner.

Exterior glass surfaces are best cleaned with commercial window cleaning solutions. Smears, bugs and road tar can be removed with a rubber or plastic scraper and window cleaner. Don't use razor blades (except as below), putty knives or steel wool.

To remove stubborn stickers, scotch tape or masking tape, wet a paper towel or cloth with cigarette lighter fluid and moisten the residue.

Let it soak in and very carefully scrape it away with a single edge razor blade. Stubborn stickers can also be removed by heating them with a hair dried to soften the adhesive.

Clear Plastic

If you have any clear plastic, use a plastic cleaner that has no harsh abrasives. Inexpensive plastic polishes are available that will remove minor scratches and restore the finish.

Keeping the Interior Clean

Once you've gone to the trouble of cleaning up the interior, it'll be worth your while to keep it clean. It makes it much easier to clean up the next time around.

Common sense plus these tips will help keep the interior clean.

• Vacuum the carpets regularly. The hardest thing to get out of carpets is ground in dirt.

• If you don't have floor mats, invest in a set. They are a lot cheaper to replace than carpets and take a lot of wear the carpets normally get.

• Don't be too heavy handed with waxes, polishes and dressings. Too much buildup of wax and polish only traps more dirt.

• Don't use dressings or wax on dirty vinyl. Spend a little time to clean it properly before applying a vinyl dressing.

• A combination cleaner/protectant or saddle soap used on vinyl will keep it soft and pliable, but will also makes the seats slippery. A good buffing with a soft cloth will reduce the slipper feeling.

• If your fabric upholstery is fairly new, and absolutely clean, Scotchguarding will keep stains from setting in the fabric and make them easier to clean. But, if the fabric is already dirty or old, you're only wasting your time.

• If possible, park your car in the shade. If you can't park in the shade, at least cover the seat back and dash if they will be in the sun's rays.

• Clean spots and stains as quickly as possible before they have a chance to set in the material. You stand a better chance of completely removing the stain if you remove it while it's wet.

Auto Body Refinishing Terms

Abrasive – A hard grit used for sanding or grinding.

Adhesion – The ability of the paint or primer to stick to the surface to which it is applied

Air-dry – Allowing paint to dry at ambient (surrounding) temperatures, without the aid of an external heat source

Aluminum oxide – A metallic abrasive used to manufacture sandpaper and sanding discs

Atomize – The extent to which a spray gun breaks up paint into a fine mist, fog or spray

Binder – The ingredient in a paint that holds the pigment particles together

Bleeding – A lower (older) color coming through a fresh coat of paint

Blistering – The formation of bubbles on the paint surface

Blushing – The formation of a whitish or misty appearance on the finish color

Chalking – The appearance of a white powder of a paint surface as it weathers and ages

Checking – Short, very fine crack lines that appear in the paint film

Compound – An abrasive paste or liquide that smooths and polishes the painted surface

Crazing – Many fine cracks in the paint surface, resembling crow's feet

Cross-hatch coat – Checkerboard application of paint to be sure of a continuous paint film. One medium coat is usually followed by a second medium coat in a perpendicular direction

Curing – The final drying stage where the paint reaches maximum strength

De-grease – Wiping with a clean cloth saturated in a solvent. This is essential to good paint adhesion

Die-back – In a lacquer finish, the loss of gloss after compounding, caused by continued evaporation of thinner

Dry-spray – Atomized paint that does not dissolve into the material being sprayed. It is caused by holding the gun too far from the work, too much air pressure or a solvent that evaporates too fast

Evaporation – Solvents in the paint escaping to the air

Feather-edge – The tapered edge of the paint where it meets the metal. The edges should be tapered or slanted so that no edge will be felt when a finger is passed over it

Ferrous metals – Metals made from iron (steel). Nonferrous metals are aluminum alloys, brass, copper or magnesium

Finish coat – The final color coat

Fish eyes – Small pits that form in the finish coat, usually due to insufficient or improper cleaning of the old coat

Flash – The fits stage of the drying process where most of the solvent evaporates

Flash time – The time required for a coat of paint to lose most of its solvent through evaporation

Fog coat – A fully reduced (thinned) paint that is sprayed at higher than normal air pressure or with the gun held at a greater distance than normal from the work. The object is to obtain a fast flash-off (evaporation) of thinner with minimum penetration of thinner into the old paint

Glazing – Use of special putty to fill minor imperfections

Gloss – The ability of a paint to reflect images when polished

Hardener – Chemical added to plastic filler to induce hardening

Hiding – The ability of a paint to obscure the surface to which it is applied

Metallic paint – Finish paint colors that contain metallic flakes in addition to pigment

Mist coat – Usually the final color coat, produced by over-reducing with a slow evaporating thinner. It is generally used to blend in the final overlap areas

OEM—Original Equipment Manufacturer

Orange peel—A rough paint surface, resembling the skin of an orange caused by the paint spray failing to flow together

Original finish—The paint applied to vehicle when it is built by the manufacturer

Overlap—The part of the spray band that covers the previous application of paint. A 50% overlap on each stroke is generally recommended

Overspray—The fine mist of paint on areas where it is not wanted (glass, moldings, other painted surfaces, etc). The tell-tale mark of a car that has been painted or had body work done

Oxidation—One of the processes by which enamel paint cures, by combining oxygen in the air with the paint film. This process dried and continues to harden enamel for several weeks. Oxidation also results in chalking in older paint

Paint film—The actual thickness of the paint on a surface

Pigment—Finely ground powders in the paint that give it its color

Prime coat—Primer or surfacer applied to the old paint or bare metal before the finish coat is applied

Primer—The surfacer that acts as a bond between the metal surface or old paint and the color coat

Reducer—The solvent that is used to thin enamel

Sanding block—A block of rubber or plastic to which the sandpaper is fastened, offering the operator a good grip. The block should be used for most sanding jobs because it distributes the pressure evenly and gives a more uniform surface

Sand scratches—The marks left in metal or in the old finish by abrasives. They may also show in the finish coat due to lack of filling or sealing

Sand scratch swelling—Solvents present in surface scratches that cause the old finish to swell

Sealer—An intercoat between the top coat and the primer or old finish, giving better adhesion

Settling—Pigment in the paint collecting at the bottom of the spray gun container

Shrinkage—The shrinking of automotive paint as it dries. All automotive paints shrink, and if scratches or surface imperfections have not been properly filled, they will show up as the paint shrinks into them

Single coat—A coat of paint, with each stroke overlapping the previous stroke by 50%

Solids—the ingredients (pigments and binders) of the paint that remain on the surface after the solvents evaporate

Solvents—A fluid that dilutes, liquefies or dilutes another liquid or solid. Solvents include thinners, reducers and cleaners

Spot glazing—Filling minor imperfections (sand scratches)

Substrate—The surface that is to be finished (painted). It can be anything from an old finish or primer to an unpainted surface

Surface dry—A condition in which the outer layer (surface) of the finish dries while the underneath remain soft and not thoroughly dried

Stress lines—Low areas in a damaged panel, usually starting at the point of impart and travelling outward

Tack coat—The first coat of enamel that is allowed to dry until "tacky" usually about 10–30 minutes, depending on the amount of thinner used. The surface is "tacky" when it will not stick to the finger when light pressure is applied

Tack rag—A cloth impregnated with a non-drying varnish that is used to pick up dust and dirt particles

Thinner—The solvent used to thin lacquers and enamels to the proper consistency for application

Undercoats—All of the products used to prepare the surface to receive color coats (primers, surfacers, putties, sealers, etc.)

Water-spotting—Drops of water that mar the finish before it is thoroughly cured

Weathering—The change in appearance of paint caused by exposure to the elements

Automobile Sheet Metal: Steel and Aluminum

This chapter will provide information about the material used in making automobile body sheet metal parts. Prior to the world-wide shortage of oil, which arose in the early 1970s, mild steel was the only material used. Legal restrictions and economic pressures resulting from the shortage have forced automobile manufactuers to develop more fuel-efficient automobiles. The manufacturers took the two obvious approaches to the problem: one, to develop more fule-efficient engines; two, to develop lighter automobiles that would require less fuel consumption from any engine. The drive to reduce weight affected all components of the automobile, but was most effective with the parts made of stamped sheet metal, because it outweighs all other materials. Mild steel parts have been reduced in weight and size as much as possible, aluminum has been substituted for steel where practical, and thinner but much harder steels are being substituted for many body structural parts. For the first time since the beginning of the mass production of automobiles, the repairman is forced to widen his skills so that he can work new metals.

It is impossible to predict the ultimate design of the automobile of the distant future, but it is reasonable to assume that the present trends will continue for some time into the immediate future. Mild steel probably will continue to be the basic material for most automobiles for long years to come. The use of aluminum and lighter, harder steels will surely increase, and the time could come when some automobiles are built with one or the other as the primary material. If so, the transition will be gradual rather than abrupt. Revolutionary changes must come slowly in any large industrial operation.

Any discussion of automobile body construction must consider the use of plastics and plastic-reinforced materials. Use of these materials started long before the oil shortage developed and has accelerated rapidly since. The materials manufacturers and the automobile companies have many experimental and development programs working to produce lightweight substitutes for steel. The possibility of a non-metallic automobile body structure cannot be ruled out, but it is still in the future. If and when it comes, it will not cause an overnight change in the entire automobile industry. Plastics and other non-metallic materials, however, are outside the scope of this text and will not be discussed further.

In the following non-technical discussions of steel and aluminum, the intention is to interpret the technical language of the metallurgist and engineer into plain language for the repairman, to provide basic information about the material with which he will work. Sections on the general subject of steel include a discussion of the nature of steel, with emphasis on the properties that determine whether it is *hard* or *soft*, an explanation of grain structure, an explanation of plasticity as it applies to steel, an explanation of the tendency of steel to harden further as it goes through plastic deformation, and an explanation of the plastic limits of various grades of steel.

Sections on the general subject of aluminum follow the pattern used for steel, because it has some degree of the same properties. Pure aluminum is basically a soft metal. Other elements are combined with aluminum to produce an alloy with sufficient rigidity to permit its use in automobile body or chassis parts.

On the specific subject of *sheet metal*, which encompasses both steel and aluminum, included are the essential properties of either metal that make it suitable for automotive use, a brief explanation of the process by which any metal can be made into sheets, and a brief explanation of the stamping process by which metal sheets are made into body panels and parts.

STEEL

An exact definition of steel is difficult, because it is made in many grades for use in almost countless products. The fact that it can be produced with special properties to meet almost any need has made it the world's most important industrial alloy. The different grades of steel are produced by varying the combination of basic materials, or *elements*, used in its manufacture. Some of these elements are common to all grades of steel; others are used only to impart special properties to a particular grade or type of steel.

A broad definition of steel often is used in which it is described as a commerical form of iron containing carbon as an essential alloying element. The amount of carbon in steel is very small in comparison to the amount of iron; it is rarely ever more than 1.7 percent, and most often it is much less. It is the amount of carbon that determines the hardness and strength of a particular grade. Mild or soft steel has the least carbon, less than 0.23 percent; this type is also called low carbon steel. Medium steel has from 0.25 to 0.60 percent carbon. High carbon steel has over 0.80 percent carbon.

Other elements also common to all grades of steel, though found in only very small amounts, are manganese, silicon, phosphorus, and sulfur. Still others are added to produce special properties such as toughness, corrosion resistance, high strength, wear resistance, and so on.

The original steel available to the automobile industry when it entered the mass production era was relatively hard. It was adequate to the needs of the times, but the demands of styling led the automobile manufacturers to demand better materials to make more complicated shapes and make them faster. Essentially, this meant softer but tougher steels made available by lowering the carbon content, use of special alloys, and improving manufacturing methods. Use of softer steels does not imply that the strength of the automobile structure was made weaker, because, as explained more fully in later sections, the metal is stiffened by the stamping process in forming the panels. Further strength can be provided where needed by using welded-on reinforcements or heavier metal.

The state of the art of sheet metal forming limits the use of the thin, hard steels to relatively simple shapes such as frame members, reinforcements, and inner body parts. This is not a static situation, however; historically, progress of the automobile industry has been as much a matter of improving manufacturing methods as of improving the product. There is good reason to believe that improved methods of sheet metal forming will extend the use of hard steels far beyond today's limits.

GRANULAR STRUCTURE OF STEEL

The properties of any piece of steel—hardness, weldability, strength, and so on—are the result of the particular combination of elements that make it up. These elements are not combined in a smooth, uniform mixture such as found in glass, however. Steel is made up of tiny grains.

The individual grains of steel are large enough to be seen with the aid of a microscope, if the sample has been prepared properly. In preparation, the surface is polished and etched with acid to bring out the shape of the individual grains. The grains will form a pattern called the grain structure. A photograph of a steel sample prepared in this manner and magnified 150 times is shown in Figure 1-1.

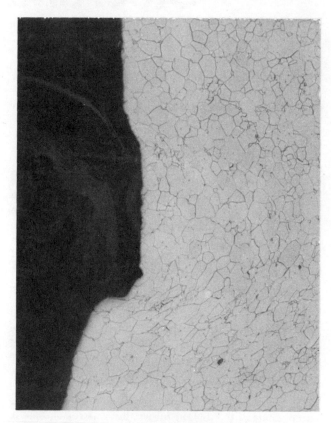

1-1 Grain structure of steel, magnified 150 times after polishing and etching with acid.

The grain structure of a particular grade of steel will vary according to the way it has been heat treated and worked. The changes follow a definite pattern, however, so that a microscopic test of grain structure can be used to determine important information for the metallurgist and engineer. The condition of the grain structure of any piece of steel determines the extent to which it can be bent or formed. To change the shape of the piece, it is necessary to change the shape and position of every grain in the affected area. In mild steel, which bends easily, the individual grains can withstand a considerable amount of deformation and movement. In harder steels and many other common metals, this amount is much less. In all steels, there is a definite limit of such action, and when it is reached the piece breaks.

A simple demonstration of the action of the grains in a piece of sheet metal can be made by bending it back and forth several times rapidly. There will be noticeable increase in temperature because of internal friction among the grains.

1-2 Typical stretcher strain pattern.

SHEET STEEL

The properties of sheet steel that make it suitable for use in body panels are due to the combination of elements in its composition and the way it was processed in the steel mill. It is essential that sheet steel for a particular part be soft, or pliable enough to withstand the necessary deformation required to make it by existing manufacturing methods. Complicated shapes require very soft, low carbon steel. Less complicated shapes can be made of harder, higher-carbon-content steel. In years past spot heating has sometimes been used to soften panel areas, because the design required deformation beyond the limit of the then available low carbon steel. This was usually an interim step between successive stamping operations on the same panel. The purpose was to relieve the grain structure; the heated piece was partly cooled before going to the next stamping operation.

There is often a very definite surface difference in the metal used for inner and outer panels. Many of the inner panels show patterns of wavy lines on the surface, called *stretcher strains* (Figure 1-2). These patterns are duplicated exactly on both sides of the metal. They are the result of yielding under tension when the panel is stamped. These lines may have almost any pattern; some may look like fern or grass leaves, others like the branches of a tree. Sometimes they have the appearance of worms pressed into the surface. Successive parts coming from the same stamping press will have different patterns; some may have no marks at all.

Metal used for outside panels is processed in the steel mill prior to stamping so that it will not form stretcher strains; otherwise, excessive labor would be necessary to file or power-sand the panel smooth. Inner panels that cannot be seen are not harmed by the presence of these marks, so the metal used to make them need not be processed. There is no difference in strength or in the way such metal can be worked when it is being straightened, so stretcher strains are not a problem to the repairman.

WORKING PROPERTIES OF SHEET STEEL

Certain properties or characteristics of sheet steel which vary for different grades of steel, determine and limit the manner in which it may be worked. Automotive sheet metal requires primary properties that will permit it to be formed into the shape of the various panels and be fabricated by welding. It also must have a surface with which paint can form a lasting bond. Strength and surface texture are related to the primary properties discussed in the following paragraphs.

The desired properties of sheet steel are determined by manufacturing requirements. These same properties, however, permit and limit the work that may be done by the repairman, and for that reason they should be studied so hat they become ingrained in his thinking on the job. Those that directly affect his work are (1) plasticity, (2) work hardening, and (3) elasticity.

Although each of these properties will be dealt with separately in the following pages, it must be remembered that they are all closely related in that they are different aspects of the effect of force applied to sheet steel. The key point in this relationship is the *yield point*, which may be defined in terms of the amount of force that any piece of metal can resist without bending or otherwise deforming. The yield point has been reached when enough force has been applied to cause deformation.

Plasticity

Plasticity is the property of any metal or other material that permits it to change shape when sufficient force is applied to it. Plasticity permits the flat sheet to be reshaped into any of the body or other stamped parts with one stroke of the press. Since in this process the sheet metal is subjected to tremendous forces, without sufficient plasticity it would break or split. A high degree of plasticity is required to make some of the complicated shapes found on the surfaces of present-day automobiles.

Changing the shape of a sheet of metal may be called *plastic deformation*. The amount of plastic deformation that a piece of sheet metal can undergo without breaking is related to its hardness. Harder grades of steel cannot withstand as much plastic deformation as can the softer grades. Although closely related, however, softness and plasticity are not necessarily the same. It would be possible to have two pieces of steel of equal softness, but one could have a greater degree of plasticity than the other.

The opposite of plasticity is rigidity. The best example of metal with no plasticity is cast iron, which is used for engine blocks because it will not bend or deform in any way. A cast-iron part designed to withstand the forces that will be applied to it will maintain its shape permanently. Instead of bending, it will break under a severe overload.

Plastic deformation takes place under both tensive and compressive forces. The property that permits deformation under tension is *ductility*. The property that permits deformation under compression is *malleability* (not to be confused with malleable iron, which is cast iron heat-treated to give it some degree of the malleability of steel). The result of deformation under tension is *stretching*. The result of deformation under compression, or pressure, is *upsetting*.

Plasticity is important to the repairman because both stretching and upsetting take place in various areas of most of the damaged panels with which he works. This is explained in much more detail in the section dealing with the effects of force on sheet metal.

Work Hardening

The common term used to describe the plastic deformation of steel without the use of heat is *cold working*, or sometimes the more simple term *working*. These terms are used in all discussions that follow. Any area of *any metal* that has been bent, upset, stretched, or changed in shape in any way below a temperature of approximately 500°F. (260°C.) has been cold worked; above that heat level, the effect gradually lessens until it is lost at red temperature.

The amount of cold working possible for a certain piece of steel has a limit; when worked past this limit, it breaks. As cold working approaches this limit, the metal becomes progressively harder. This causes a corresponding increase in stiffness and strength. This increased hardness is called *work hardening*.

A very simple experiment can be performed to demonstrate the effect of work hardening. A 1¾ in. piece of soft utility wire may be used. It has essentially the same properties as automotive sheet steel and is small enough so that it can be stretched by hand. To perform this experiment, tie one end of the wire to a rigid support and the other end to something that will serve as a handle. Best results will be obtained if the wire used is several feet in length, because the increase in length will be more apparent. Measure the overall length, then

stretch the wire until it breaks. The total increase in length should be close to 25 percent.

A noticeable increase in stiffness can be felt by bending a section of the stretched wire between the fingers and comparing it to the stiffness of another section of the same wire that has not been stretched. This increase in stiffness is due to the strain on the individual grains. For the wire to grow thinner and longer, it is necessary for the individual grains to grow longer and smaller in diameter. It is this distortion of the shape and position of the individual grain that causes the metal to work harden. When comparing the stiffness of the stretched wire to that of the unstretched wire, the full increase is not apparent because stretching reduces the diameter of that piece. If an unstretched wire of the smaller diameter were available for comparison, the difference would be more evident.

This experiment can be carried out under more scientific conditions by supporting the wire overhead and attaching weight, in increasing amounts, to the lower end. If this is done, it will be found that when enough weight is added to reach the yield point, the wire will stretch a short distance and stop. It will then be necessary to add still more weight to cause further stretching. This can be repeated several times, each time with additional weight, until the limit is reached and the wire breaks. The need for additional weight is proof of additional strength resulting from the stretching. Each time the wire is stretched, the yield point is raised slightly.

This experiment can be carried further by using a strip of automotive sheet metal and the proper equipment. A hydraulic body jack and sheet metal clamps, such as those shown in use in the repair section of this book, are satisfactory for the purpose. If the proper gauges are available to record the force used, it will be found that a strip of mild steel will more than double in strength if it is stretched to the breaking point. This is illustrated in Figures 1-3 to 1-7.

Figure 1-3 shows a strip of metal 1 inch (25.4 mm) wide and 0.037 inch (0.93 mm) thick set up in clamps. A length of salvage steel tape has been clamped to it at one end, and crayon marks, 8 inches (203.20 mm) apart, have been aligned with the 1- and 9-inch marks of the tape. Note that the gauge hand is slightly below the 0 mark of the gauge.

In Figure 1-4, the jack has been extended enough to stretch the strip ⅛ inch (3.17 mm), as indicated by the crayon mark of the right side which is one eighth past the 9-inch mark. Note that the gauge hand now reads slightly over 1,000 pounds.

In Figure 1-5, the jack has been extended enough to stretch the strip inches (44.45 mm), as indicated by the crayon mark now at the 10¾ inch mark. Note that the gauge pressure has built up to about 2,100 pounds, approximately double the force needed to stretch the strip the first eighth. It was expected that the strip would break soon after this picture was taken, but after the jack had been extended another ¾ inch (19.05 mm), the picture in Figure 1-6 was taken. This shows a reading of approximately 2,500 pounds on the gauge, which was the maximum.

1-3 *(Top)* Tensile test of body sheet metal strip. The gauge hand registers 0. Arrows indicate crayon marks on the strip, 8 inches (approx. 200 mm) apart and aligned with numerals 1 and 9 on the tape.

1-4 *(Bottom)* Strip stretched ⅛ inch (approx. 3 mm). The gauge registers slightly over 1,000 pounds on the jack.

1-5 *(Top)* Strip stretched 1¾ inches (approx. 45 mm). The gauge registers 2,100 pounds—more than twice the original yield point.

1-6 *(Bottom)* Strip stretched 2½ inches (approx. 63 mm). The gauge registers 2,500 pounds, the maximum pressure reached.

Figure 1-7 shows the strip stretched another ⅜ inch (9.52 mm), and the gauge reading has dropped back to 2,000 pounds. Note that the strip has begun to fail by narrowing sharply close to the clamp on the left end. The actual breaking point is not shown, but only a little more stretching was needed; the gauge pressure dropped rapidly as the piece was stretched from the point shown in Figure 1-7.

Both the amount of stretching and the increase in yield strength obtained with the strip in these illustrations are more than can be expected normally. Failure at twice the first yield point, in this case about 2,000 pounds, would be more probable. In fact, another strip cut from the same piece of sheet stock did yield at the lower figure. The significance of this test is that unworked sheet steel elongated more than 25 percent and, in doing so, increased in strength more than 100 percent. (Actual figures for the strip shown are 34 percent increase in length and 150 percent increase in strength; however, they are probably higher than can be expected with most available sheet steel.)

The harder, thinner sheet steel coming into use for some body parts can be expected to stretch less and to

build up resistance to further stretching more rapidly than milder steel. Its use is a radical departure from previous design practices of the automobile industry, caused by the need to reduce weight. It is reasonable to assume that the weight reduction efforts will continue; it seems equally reasonable to assume that various grades of harder steel will come into use as the industry gains experience with it.

Another example of work hardening is shown in Figure 1-8. This strip of mild steel was bent double by pressing on the ends and then straightened by resting the bent area against a solid surface and pushing the ends apart. When bent double, this piece was in the shape of the piece shown in the left in Figure 1-9. The work hardening caused by the first stiffened the metal in the bent area. The additional stiffness resisted the straightening action, causing two new bends to form on each side of the first one.

The importance of understanding how metal stiffens, making it stronger, in areas that are bent or otherwise worked, cannot be over-emphasized in the study of sheet metal repair. It is the basis of practically all damage. Some work hardness will be found in any undam-

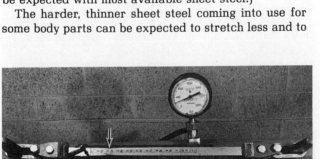

1-7 Strip beginning to break at arrow.

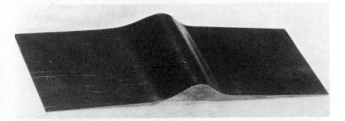

1-8 Typical buckle formed by bending and straightening a piece of sheet metal.

aged automobile body panel; it is the result of the cold working done in the die that originally formed the panel. The bending caused by a collision adds still more work hardening in the areas affected. More, sometimes much more, will be added by the cold working used as the metal worker straightens the damaged area. Excessive work hardening caused by working the metal improperly will make the job more difficult.

Elasticity

Automotive sheet metal has a limited amount of *elasticity*, which may be defined as the ability of an object to regain its original shape after a deflecting force has been removed. Reducing this to a simpler statement as it applies to automotive sheet metal, elasticity may be considered as the tendency of the metal to spring back after a force has been applied to it and released.

Elasticity is not the exact opposite of plasticity, but the two properties are closely related. Very soft steel has very little elasticity but a high degree of plasticity; the opposite is also true to a large extent. However, it would be possible for steel having low elasticity to have varying degrees of plasticity. In the example of stretching shown in Figures 1-3 to 1-7, the shown strip has stretched more than another cut from the same stock, showing differences in plasticity in the same material.

Any metal has an *elastic limit*. Going back to the simple definition of elasticity above, the eleastic limit is the point at which enough force has been applied to overcome some of the tendency to spring back. This is the yield point. However, even though yielding relieves some of the elastic strain, there is always enough of it left to cause a partial spring-back. This may be proved by bending any piece of metal as the piece shown in Figure 1-8 was bent. There will be partial spring-back when it is released.

This partial spring-back tendency makes it highly desirable for the metal worker to learn to recognize the elastic strains in the damaged panels on which he works. The work should be planned to take advantage of any spring-back tendency that is present. Spring-back will be found in almost any area that is still relatively smooth but has been carried out of position by buckles formed in adjoining areas. Some areas will spring back to shape if released by relieving the distortions in the buckled areas that hold them out of place.

ALUMINUM

The use of aluminum in automobile body construction seems to many experienced repairmen to present new and difficult metal repair problems, to the point that some consider aluminum panels not repairable. This reaction is not surprising, because it is human nature to distrust and avoid new routines. But there is no reason for the student to share this distrust as he begins his training, because he has not yet developed routines to cling to. He will find that working aluminum and working steel are in many ways quite similar, but each has its own combination of properties that govern repair procedures. If these properties are understood, skill in working aluminum should develop as fast as it does for steel. The fact that aluminum requires a "finer touch" may make the student more sensitive to the problems of working steel and make him a better performer on both metals.

The adoption of aluminum as one of the automobile body construction materials should be regarded as permanent—at least, until some as yet undiscovered element or process comes along. Ignoring world politics, the world's supply of petroleum is finite. The development of substitutes for petroleum motor fuels is based on an economy that is governed by relatively high-cost petroleum. Whether the world's supply of petroleum runs out in the twentieth century or lasts for centuries to come, the return of relatively low-cost petroleum-based motor fuel seems remote, if not impossible. Use of aluminum provides one of several ways to build lighter automobiles that require fewer quantities of relatively expensive fuel. The student entering the automobile collision field should be aware that his services may not always be limited to working on steel. Both steel and aluminum may eventually be replaced by other substitutes; but, for the foreseeable future, at least some skill should be acquired on aluminum as well as steel.

THE GRADES OF ALUMINUM

The term aluminum, as it is used normally, refers to some alloy of aluminum and several other metals. Pure aluminum is too soft for most industrial uses. But, just as iron can be combined with other elements to produce various grades of steel, aluminum can be combined with many of the same elements—silicon, copper, manganese, magnesium, zinc, chromium, titanium, and even iron—to produce alloys having special properties for special purposes. The aluminum industry produces well more than a hundred different alloys, referred to here as grades. Of these, only a few are suitable for use in automobile body panels. It is reasonable to assume that, as experience is gained with aluminum use on mass production, more suitable grades will be developed.

Sheet aluminum suitable for body panel use must have sufficient strength or rigidity for the specific panel. In addition, it must have properties that permit it to be stamped into shape by mass production methods, withstand 180-degree bends in making hem-flanges, and have a smooth surface to which paint can adhere as well as it does to steel. Some of the weight advantage of pure aluminum, as compared to steel, must be sacrificed to produce an alloy that meets these requirements. Pure aluminum weighs approximately one third as much as steel, but the addition of other elements to produce a metal suitable for body use increases the weight, because most of those added are considerably heavier. Allowing for the extra weight and probable design differences required for aluminum, it is possible to make body panels that weigh approximately one half of what they would if made of steel. This is a distinct advantage, which the body designer will use, when necessary, to meet the demand for reduced weight. The limits of possiblity are established by safety and manufacturing problems.

Safety for the body structure is, primarily, a matter of protection for the passengers if and when the automobile suffers physical damage due to collision, upset, or other causes. Safety requirements are established by law and approved by the automobile industry. No automobile manufacturer would knowingly design an unsafe automobile because the repercussions from both legal sources and the general public would be financially devastating. The first use of aluminum in the current weight-reduction program has been in hood panels and deck lids, areas where the passengers are least exposed in an accident. Aluminum could be used in door assemblies if sufficient reinforcement was provided to meet safety requirements.

Aluminum cannot be joined directly to steel, particularly by welding, because corrosion will develop. This eliminates the use of steel for reinforcing parts, and thus eliminates the use of aluminum for the large area panels. Aluminum could be joined to steel by using mechanical fasteners and providing insulation between the contact surfaces, but that would eliminate the advantage of welding, and the cost would be prohibitive. For these reasons, the current use of aluminum is limited to separate assemblies that attach to the main structure by bolts or other mechanical fasteners. If aluminum is ever adopted for the main body structure, it will probably be an all-welded aluminum structure. The possibility of this should not be ruled out, particularly in the luxury automobile field, because there is little evidence that the demand for such automobiles will diminish in the future. As the aluminum industry and automobile engineers find ways to retain the weight-saving features of aluminum and improve its strength, its competitive position as a substitute for steel will improve proportionally.

WORKING PROPERITES OF SHEET ALUMINUM

For aluminum to be an economically feasible substitute for steel in automobile body manufacture, grades must be available that either can be worked by existing methods for steel or require the minimum development of new methods. Aluminum grades must perform in much the same manner as steel when it is pressed into shape, welded, assembled, and painted. Ideally, the grade selected would have properties identical to those of steel. In practical use, the alloys available have varying degrees of those properties, sometimes more and sometimes less. For that reason, the properties of aluminum are discussed by comparing them to the properties of steel.

Elasticity

Pure aluminum, being quite soft, has much less elasticity than steel. When it is mixed with other elements to produce an alloy that can be used as a substitute for steel, the hardness and corresponding elasticity are increased, but neither reaches a degree equal to that of steel, when compared on the basis of volume. It would be possible to use extra-thick aluminum to acquire equivalent strength, in terms of rigidity, but to do so would defeat the purpose of the substitution. All grades of aluminum suitable for body use have less elasticity and hardness than steel.

Plasticity

Aluminum has more plasticity than steel. It will stretch, upset, bend, and tear more easiy than steel. To the repairman, this means it will suffer more damage in collision and react differently to the force he applies when repairing collision damage. Also, it means that he must use more care in applying force to aluminum than to steel to avoid adding to the existing damage.

Work Hardening

Aluminum tends to work harden differently from the sheet steel used in body construction. Although softer, aluminum of the grades suitable for automobile body panels can withstand less deformation without breaking than the steel it replaces. But this is more a problem for the body engineer than for the repairman. The engineer must select a grade of aluminum that can be pressed into shape without breaking in the draw die. The work hardening that occurs in the stamping operation as the panel is formed affects the entire panel area. Even though some areas are affected more than others, none are worked to the total limit of the aluminum, or the panels would break and become scrap.

The work hardening caused by a damaging impact can be quite severe, but in most cases it is limited to small areas where the metal has not been severely worked in the manufacturing operation. Examination of a typically damaged panel—if there is such a thing— would reveal that most of the severe buckles are in the relatively flat sections that have had very little working when stamped. The most severe cold working of the aluminum in the stamping operation is in the sharp bends, particularly the 180-degree bends in hem-flanges, and the few high crown areas. When these areas are affected by a severe impact, more breakage can be expected than for similar damage to a steel panel.

EFFECT OF HEAT ON SHEET METAL

Heat, from one source or another, is involved in many of the repair operations performed on the sheet metal panels of an automobile. The most common source of heat is the oxyacetylene welding torch. Another source is friction, resulting from power-driven abrasives such as the disc-sander. Because of the different characteristics of the two metals, the effects of heat on aluminum and steel are discussed separately.

EFFECT OF HEAT ON SHEET STEEL

The repairman should understand the effect of heat on steel over the full temperature range from normal ambient temperature to the melting point, which is over 2,600°F. (1,427°C.); but most of his concern is in the temperature range from 400°to 1,600°F. (204°to 871°C.). Heat above this temperature range is not, or at least it should not be, used, except for welding. Except for the effect of welding temperatures on grain structure, the temperature above 1,600°F. (871°C.) will not be considered.

Three separate effects of heat are to be considered: (1) scaling, (2) changes in grain struture, and (3) expansion and contraction. These effects occur at the same time, but for study purposes it is easier to consider them separately.

Scale and Heat Colors

A light film of scale, which is iron oxide, will begin to form on steel when it is heated to 430°F. (221°C.). If the surface is clean and bright, it will be visible as a pale, yellow coloring. As increased further, the color deepens progressively through straw, brown, purple, light blue, and dark blue, which is reached at approximately 600°F. (315°C.).

Further heating will cause the dark blue to fade into a gray or greenish shade until the first reddish glow appears at approximately 900°F. (482°C.). Above this temperature the colors usually are described as blood red, dark cherry, medium cherry, or full red, which is reached at approximately 1,550°F. (825°C.). Above this, the red color increases in brightness through salmon, orange, lemon, light yellow, and white, which is reached at approximately 2,000°F. (1,093°C.). At approximately 2,600°F. (1,427°C.), steel melts.

The colors below the red heat range will not be affected by the light in which they are viewed, because they are simply a film that coats the surface. They can be used as an indication of the approximate temperature of the surface, essential in many of the straightening and shrinking operations the repairman uses.

However, the way we see the colors in the red range is affected to some extent by light conditions, because those colors are a form of light. Metal that appears to be at bright red heat in dim light will not appear to be so bright in sunlight. This can be confusing, because shop lighting conditions can vary widely at different hours of the day. This is not a critical problem, but it is well to learn to make allowance for light conditions when doing work where temperature is important, particularly in shrinking operations.

Metal heated to the higher temperature range will accumulate a heavy scale on the red-hot area unless it is protected from the air. When the metal is heated with the oxyacetylene torch flame, the scale will be much heavier on the underside than on the side to which the flame was applied, because the gases burned in the flame exclude air and prevent oxidation. The scale on the protected side does not begin to form until the flame has been removed, but the underside is subjected to the attack of oxygen in the air as soon as the proper temperature is reached.

Although the formation of scale is an acutal burning of the metal, it is impractical to attempt to prevent its formation in the normal use of heat on sheet steel. Most spots are heated only once, so the effect is not of great importance. Nevertheless, it is desirable to avoid heating the same area of metal to high temperature repeatedly. Each reheating will cause some loss of metal by oxidation, so that after enough reheatings, the piece is weakened because part of it has been burned away. Such reheating and consequent metal loss rarely occurs in normal repair operations, however.

EFFECT OF HEAT ON GRAIN STRUCTURE

A progressive change in grain structure takes place when steel is heated from room temperature up to the melting point. The structures that result have a direct effect on hardness. Hardness and strength are so closely related that they are almost the same thing; therefore, the structure also affects strength.

The effect of heat on mild steel, such as automotive sheet, is more limited than it is on higher carbon steels. The carbon content of mild steel is too low for the metal to harden to any appreciable extent by heat treating; the effect of heat on it is almost completely limited to softening or *annealing*. Higher carbon steels may be annealed or hardened by following the proper procedure.

Work hardening of automotive sheet steel as a result of cold working was explained earlier. It can be completely relieved by heating to slightly above the bright red heat range. When the metal is turning to a salmon color, it has reached 1,600°F. (871°C.). Metallurgists call this point the *critical temperature*, because the grain structure undergoes a complete rearrangement. The new grains have none of the effects of working that hardened the old grain structure, because they have been entirely reformed. Cooling from this temperature to normal by exposure to air will leave automotive sheet steel in a very soft or annealed condition.

The effect of annealing is illustrated in Figure 1-9. These two pieces of metal were cut from the same sheet and were bent in the same manner, by pressing on the ends. The only difference is that the piece on the right had a band of metal annealed across the width before it was bent. This was done by passing the flame of a welding torch across it just fast enough to bring the metal to a salmon red heat, just slightly above bright red, and allowing it to cool to normal temperature before bend-

1-9 Effect of heat on bending. The piece on the right was heated to bright salmon red; the piece on the left was not heated. Both were bent by pushing the ends together.

ing. Note that all of the bending has taken place within the area affected by the heat, and that it has bent in a much shorter radius than the unheated piece on the left. The shorter radius bend is due to the loss of strength caused by the annealing.

The pieces of steel shown in Figure 1-9 were cut side by side from flat stock that had not been worked in any way other than the cold rolling they were given in the steel mill. The same metal would show an even greater effect if it first had been through a stamping operation that would have cold worked it further. Similar pieces cut from a salvage panel would show greater resistance to bending than the unheated one. The heated piece would bend the same whether it had been further worked or not, because the work hardening would be lost.

Figure 1-10 shows the same piece of metal after it had been straightened and further cold worked by hammer-on-dolly blows over the annealed area. The entire area was covered with closely spaced, hard hammer blows to ensure uniform and severe cold working. Bending was done by pressing on the ends, just as the previous ones, shown in Figure 1-9 were bent. Note that the previously soft area has become so stiff that it has bent less than the unheated piece in Figure 1-9. It is now the stiffest area in the strip.

Part of this work hardening was the result of the bending and straightening; the rest of it was the result of the hammer-on-dolly work. More work on this area with the hammer-on-dolly would make it even harder. However, there is a limit to the hardening that can be obtained by cold working mild steel; further working past that point would cause the metal to break when bent.

The discussion so far has been limited to the effect on the metal of heating up to the critical temperature fol-

lowed by slow cooling. Fast cooling, by immersing the heated metal in water, will tend to harden any steel. The hardening effect on automotive sheet steel is very slight, however, too little to have any practical significance. On higher-carbon steels, such as would be used in a punch or chisel, the hardening effect is of great importance; such tools would be useless unless they were properly hardened by heating and quenching.

A simple experiment performed with a strip of mild steel will show another effect of cold working. Bend it back and forth rapidly, and it will get quite hot, due to internal friction. Also, a slight increase in stiffness will be felt at first, but this will drop off and the strip will break if bending continues long enough.

The hardening effect gained by *quenching*—immersing hot steel in water or oil—results because the rapid loss of heat traps the metal in its finest, hardest grain structure. The hardness that can be obtained is directly related to the amount of carbon in the steel; however, the increase in hardness tends to level off when the carbon content exceeds 0.6 percent. Most ordinary hand tools are made of steel having less carbon than this.

Another characteristic of higher-carbon steel is that it reaches the critical point at lower temperatures than mild steel. Steel used in a chisel will reach the critical point at about 1,450°F. (788°C.), when it will be between cherry and bright red when viewed in bright light. Steel of the quality used in chisels will be too hard and brittle when quenched from bright red to normal temperatures. This is corrected by reheating to a much lower temperature and requenching, in an operation called *drawing* or tempering. The reheating would be up into the color range, usually light or dark blue. The old-time blacksmith's method of tempering tools such as chisels was to heat an inch or more of the end up to bright red; he then quenched part of the red-hot metal by dipping the end into water, keeping the tool moving

1-10 Effect of cold working. This is the same piece shown on the right in Fig. 1-9 after straightening, working the annealed area with hammer-on-dolly, and rebending.

up and down to avoid a sharp break-line between the hot and cold metal. When the end cooled enough to stop boiling off water, he scratched the scale off quickly, so he could see the color change as heat flowed back into the end, and when the shade he wanted reached the tip, he plunged the complete tool into the water. This same procedure can be used in the repair shop to reclaim many dull or soft tools. Heat from the welding torch and either a pail of water or a quantity of oil are all that is needed. To be safe, quench the tool in oil first. If that does not make it hard enough, redo it using the water. If the tool is made too hard, it will break in use and be ruined.

The effect of heating above the critical point, into the orange or white range, is to set up a coarse and weak grain structure. Such a structure always is formed in the metal next to a weld. Most so-called weld failures occur in this area, rather than in the weld proper. Unless this condition is removed by reheating or cold working, the area becomes the weakest in the welded panel. More detailed information on the proper treatment of this area is found in Chapter 5 on Welding.

A very common mistake is to overheat a section of metal that is to be straightened. Many sharp kinks are found that will straighten best if heat is applied, but best results will be obtained if heating stops at or below the critical point. Where overheating has occurred, it can be relieved by allowing the area to cool and then reheating to the critical temperature.

Free Expansion and Contraction

Expansion is the increase in size that occurs in nearly everything when its temperature is raised. Contraction is the decrease in size that occurs when the temperature drops. Some materials expand and contract more than others. Automotive sheet steel expands and contracts more than many other materials, particularly non-metallic substances.

The amount of expansion and contraction of anything is expressed in *linear* measurement; length, width, and thickness are the linear measurements used to measure size or volume. As expansion occurs, each of these dimensions increases at the same rate. The rate at which 1 inch of linear dimension increases when the temperature is increased or decreased 1°F. is called the coefficient of expansion. In the metric system, the coefficient of expansion is expressed in terms of the change of 1 centimeter caused by a change of 1°C. in temperature.

The coefficient of expansion of automotive sheet steel in the temperature range from normal to 1,500°F (816°C.) is approximately six millionths of an inch per degree. Above that range it is less, decreasing to practically nothing at the melting point. This may seem to be an amount so small that it has no significance. However, it is a matter of simple mathematics to determine that 1 inch of steel heated to 1,500°F. (816°C.) will expand 0.009 inch (0.23 mm); 10 inches (254 mm) heated 150°F. (65.5°C.) will expand the same. This becomes a matter

of great importance, particularly when something acts to restrict the movement caused by expansion.

It should be kept in mind that the expansion takes place in all directions. Reference was made to 1 inch of steel. This inch could be measured in length, width, or thickness. Expansion would be equal in all three if the application of heat were uniform. Although 1-inch thickness is never found in sheet metal construction, the expansion in thickness would be proportional for the fractional part of an inch that it measures.

RESTRICTED EXPANSION

When sheet metal expands, it pushes outward in all directions. When a condition exists that tends to restrict this outward push, tremendous forces can be generated. The exact amount of such force will be governed by the amount of restriction offered, the amount of heat, and the strength of the metal expanding. If sufficient heat is applied to a small area, the result will be serious heat distortion, as shown in Figure 1-11.

In the case of a spot heat application to sheet metal—which includes nearly every repair operation in which heat is used—the restriction to expansion is offered by the surrounding metal that is either unheated or at a much lower temperature. The restriction is only to the expansion of surface area. No similar restriction is offered to the expansion of thickness.

The limit of outward push is established by the force required to cause the particular area to bend or buckle. Once buckling has started, further expansion will not increase the outward push, because it will be taken up in the buckle. This condition is further complicated by the fact that as the temperature rises, the resistance to buckling is lowered proportionately; thus, as the metal expands, it begins to push up into a higher and higher bulge.

The same piece of metal shown in Figures 1-11 and 1-12 was scribed with parallel lines before heat was applied, so the heat distortion could be seen better. Note

1-11 *(Top)* Heat distortion due to spot heat application.

1-12 *(Bottom)* The same piece of metal as shown in Fig. 1-11 after cooling.

that, in Figure 1-11, the buckle is lightly higher than in Figure 1-12, which shows the piece of metal after cooling. This buckle remains because the expansion of the heated area has caused a bend strong enough to resist the tension set up by cooling. The tension tends to pull the buckle out, but it is never as effective as the pressure of expansion. This is because of the time lag between the development of highest pressure and tension. Rapid cooling in this very short time restores the strength in the distorted area so that much greater resistance is offered when tension develops.

The heat experiment shown here was performed on a piece of unworked metal. A similar experiment on a flat body panel would create a similar but probably smaller condition, because the outer edges would not be free to flex with the expansion of the hot spot. After cooling, such a spot on a body panel may cause hollow buckles to form on opposite sides of the heated area. If such buckles do form, they will be in the direction of the greatest curvature of the panel.

A distortion much different in appearance would be caused by heating an area of metal reinforced by its shape in such a way that it tends to resist swelling—for example, a section of a panel with a bead pressed into it. The bead is too stiff to swell; instead, most of its expansion would be taken up as an upset into the heated spot. When such an area cools, it will draw sharp buckles into the adjoining metal. The upset in the stiffer area will serve as a drawstring on the adjoining metal surface.

An explanation frequently offered for heat distortion is that it is the result of relieving existing strains in the metal. An experiment similar to the one shown in Figures 1-11 and 1-12 has proved this to be untrue. The experiment involved several pieces of metal of the same size, three of which were annealed by heating and long cooling in a heat treat furnace. An experiment similar to the one shown in Figures 1-11 and 1-12 was then performed. No appreciable difference could be seen in the amount of heat distortion on the annealed pieces and the unannealed pieces. As the result of this experiment, it appears that the primary cause of heat distortion is the restriction offered by the adjoining, cooler metal.

The three photographs in Figure 1-13 indicate the importance of very slight changes in the length of flat, or very nearly flat, panel surfaces. In the upper photograph, a flat strip of sheet metal is shown lying on a flat surface and fitting exactly between square blocks on each end. In the center picture, the strip has been lifted out, a 0.005-inch (0.127 mm) feeler gauge placed against the edge of one block, and the strip fitted back into place. Note that the thickness of the feeler gauge added to the length of the strip has caused it to bulge upward nearly ¼ inch (6.35 mm).

In the lower picture, the strip has been fitted back into place without the feeler gauge, but it has been expanded by passing a torch flame along its length. Note that it has bulged upward about twice as high as it did when the feeler gauge was in place. This amount of bulging has been obtained without heating the strip enough to cause it to discolor.

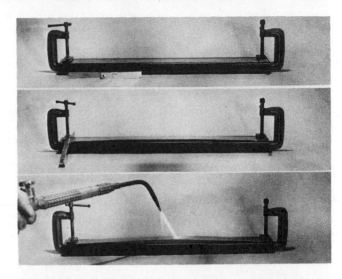

1-13 *(Top)* Demonstration of the effect of a slight increase of length of a section of flat metal. *(Center)* A 0.005-inch (0.127 mm) feeler gauge has been added to the length of the flat strip. *(Bottom)* The strip has been heated but kept below red heat.

The significance of these three photographs is in what they reveal concerning the need for precise length restoration if flat metal is to remain flat after it has been heated. The feeler gauge in the center photograph shows that only a few thousandths of an inch will create a bad wave. The torch application in the lower photograph shows that only slight heating will cause much more difference in length.

The same amount of expansion would be obtained by heating a much smaller area to a much higher temperature. This was done in heating the metal sheet shown in Figures 1-11 and 1-12. Of course, the effect would not be the same on a narrow strip as on a wide piece of metal because the strip, being free to move, does not offer the restriction to expansion that the larger piece does. Thus, the strip would not tend to distort nearly as much when heated as the surface of a panel would under the same conditions.

The repairman must understand the effect of heat distortion. Heat concentrated on a small spot causes the metal to push outward against the adjoining, cooler metal. This resistance will cause the heated spot to bulge and shorten, because it is under a compressive strain. Then, when the surface cools, the heated spot remains shorter, tending to have a gathering effect on the adjoining metal surface. In relatively flat panels, this effect may be enough to cause buckles to extend on each side of the heated spot for several inches.

A very common mistake is to think of metal affected in the manner just described as being stretched. Stretching is dealt with in greater detail in later sections, but we can quickly demonstrate a condition similar to stretching by folding a pleat in the edge of a piece of paper. The shortening effect of the pleat will cause the adjoining paper to bulge. The fact that only a few thousandths of an inch of upset will cause an appreciable bulge in a flat surface indicates how important it is to be able to differentiate between heat distortion and stretching.

EFFECT OF HEAT ON ALUMINUM

The following discussion of the effects of heat on aluminum is separated into these closely related topics: (1) melting points of different alloys, (2) heat conduction, (3) scaling, and (4) expansion and contraction.

Melting Point

The exact melting point of aluminum varies with the composition of the alloy involved, but all alloys melt in the temperature range in which steel is just beginning to show red heat in bright light. The lowest temperature at which any aluminum alloy melts is approximately 1,150°F. (621°C.), and the highest is over 1,200°F. (649°C.). All grades of aluminum retain the distinctive aluminum color when heated from normal temperature almost to the melting point. Unlike steel, which goes through a wide range of colors before melting at white heat, aluminum indicates melting only by the appearance of tiny bubbles and a slight greying, sometimes called an ashen appearance. The molten aluminum retains its distinctive aluminum color unless heated far beyond any practical heat range.

Scaling

Aluminum differs from steel in that it does not form a scale that varies in color and thickness as it is heated from approximately 430°F. (221°C.) to red hot. Instead, a thin scale, aluminum oxide, forms on aluminum; it has properties much different from those of scale on steel.

An important characteristic of aluminum oxide is that it forms a protective layer over the surface of the metal. If it did not, oxygen in the air would continue acting on the metal until it was all consumed, leaving nothing but aluminum oxide. The formation of aluminum oxide can be seen on pure aluminum by watching closely as the surface is scraped with a knife blade. The scraping action breaks the existing surface film, revealing a much lighter-colored metal. The lighter color darkens almost instantly as oxygen attacks it and replaces the scraped-off film. This same action takes place on the various aluminum alloys, but is easier to see on the pure metal.

The film of aluminum oxide, or scale, complicates welding and brazing procedures, because it remains in place at the temperature at which such work is done. Flux is required to break down the oxide before aluminum can be either welded or brazed.

Expansion and Contraction

In comparing the expansion and contraction of aluminum to steel, consideration must be given to three basic differences in the properties of the two metals: (1) aluminum conducts heat approximately twice as fast as steel, (2) aluminum expands approximately twice as far as steel; the contraction by volume will be equal to the expansion, but the linear contraction may be different, and (3) aluminum yields at lower temperature than steel.

The rapid conduction of heat in aluminum, as compared to steel, presents repair problems, because most of the heat applications involved are to a relatively small area; in most cases heat will be applied with welding equipment, although occasionally overheating may occur if a power-driven abrasive tool is held too long in one spot. A much larger area expands more rapidly than would be expected by a person whose experience was limited to steel.

Restricted Expansion is involved in any spot heat application. Experiments such as the ones shown in Figures 1-11, 1-12, and 1-13 would not produce quite the same results if performed on aluminum. The metal surface would rise higher, even though heated to a lower temperature, in Figures 1-11 and 1-13, but the remaining bulged area would be less than shown in Figure 1-12.

Linear expansion and contraction may not always be the same because, as the metal expands, upsets occur at relatively low temperatures. Once an upset has formed, it will not be released by cooling. The overall expansion and contraction will be equal, but the shape and dimensions of area will change.

Heat conduction in aluminum is approximately four times as fast as it is in steel. The effect of this is that heat spreads over a much larger area when it is caused either by welding operations or by friction when power-driven abrasives are used on it. The repairman should consider this as heat absorption. Any spot heat application below the melting point will require more heat, or take longer, to reach a given temperature than a similar application to a similar piece of steel.

The rapid conduction of heat by aluminum is an advantage in some instances and a disadvantage in many others. At least to some degree, it is a limiting factor in using heat to shrink stretched areas, and compared to the same operations performed on steel, it produces different heat distortion, or warpage, patterns caused by welding operations. These differences are partly offset, or minimized, by the fact that all operations involving heat are performed on aluminum at lower temperature levels than similar operations on steel.

Heat conduction should not be considered a major problem or difficulty, but techniques suitable for steel must be refined to be suitable for use on aluminum. A part of the refinement is to recognize that the nature of aluminum places some limits on what can be done with heat, as compared to steel.

Weldability

In the discussion of steel and its properties, weldability was taken for granted and not discussed as a separate topic. Welding of both metals is discussed in detail in Chapter 5, but brief mention of some of the differences in their welding problems is made here.

The primary difference is in the melting point temperatures. The exact melting temperatures of both vary according to their composition, but aluminum melts at or above 1,150°F. (621°C.), which is approximately one half the melting temperature of steel. At this relatively low temperature there is very little color change to indicate that it is close to melting. The surface becomes ashen in appearance and tiny bubbles appear on the surface just before it melts; there is no emission of light. At the higher melting temperature of steel, it glows white hot, giving off considerable light. The welder can judge the melting point of steel much more easily than that of aluminum.

A second difference is in the need for flux. Aluminum is always covered by a thin layer of scale that melts at a higher temperature than the metal does. The flux breaks this scale down by chemical action to bare the metal so that filler metal can be added. Steel does not require flux for fusion welding.

Finally, particles of molten steel seem to have an attraction for each other, which aluminum lacks or has to a much smaller degree. The combined differences make aluminum more difficult to weld than steel, but aluminum welding techniques can be developed by any person who has learned to weld steel.

MAKING SHEET METAL PANELS

The sheet metal panels of the automobile are made by dies that form and trim the metal to shape. The dies are mounted in huge presses that are the operating or power unit. We may consider the methods used for pressing steel and aluminum to be the same. Any real differences are manufacturing problems that do not concern the finished product.

Different types of dies are required to perform all the operations involved in making any of the larger panels of the automobile. The panel has to be formed, or *drawn*, into shape; this is done in the *draw die*, Figure 1-14. After being drawn, it has to be trimmed, flanged, and pierced. These operations may be performed by separate dies, or they may be combined; the complexity of each individual panel is the determining factor.

Knowledge of the action of the draw die is helpful in understanding the effect that force can have on automobile sheet metal, whether steel or aluminum. The plastic properties that permit either metal to be permanently deformed in the draw die also permit them to be permanently deformed by the force of a collision and also by the forces the repairman uses in correcting the collision damage.

Operation of the draw die includes two separate actions: clamping the sheet metal blank around the outer edges, and pushing the male die against the center area of the sheet metal blank to form it. These actions are illustrated in Figures 1-15 and 1-16, which

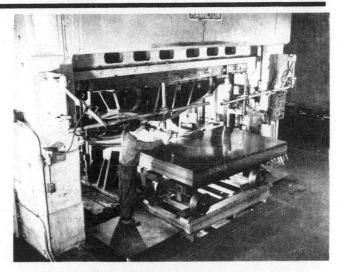

1-14 Typical draw die mounted in a draw press.

represent a cross-sectional view of a die stamping circular metal pan. The basic principle of stamping such a pan or a hood or roof panel is essentially the same.

Figure 1-15 represents the die in the open position, with a sheet metal blank in place ready to be pressed. The press that operates this type of die has two separate actions: the first raises and lowers the movable clamp ring; the second raises and lowers the male die. These actions are timed so that the clamp ring pressure is maintained throughout the entire downward stroke of the male die. Thus, the male die draws the edge of the blank inward through the clamp ring as it shapes the panel.

The pressure on the clamp ring must be adjusted properly. If it is too tight, the metal will break instead of drawing inward around the die; if it is too loose, the metal will wrinkle as it is drawn inward. However, when this pressure is correct, sufficient metal will be drawn through the clamp ring to permit a smooth, unbroken panel to be formed. It is here that manufacturing techniques are varied to suit the different operating problems of aluminum and steel.

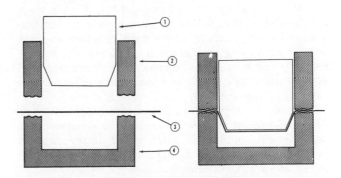

1-15 *(Left)* Cross-sectional sketch of a simple draw die in operation: 1, male die; 2, movable clamp ring; 3, sheet metal blank; 4, stationary clamp ring.

1-16 *(Right)* Cross-sectional sketch of male die at the bottom of a stroke.

3 SHEET METAL REPAIR

In stamping a part with a complicated shape, the draw die exerts a tremendous tension of the sheet metal even though some of it is relieved by the movement through the clamp ring. This tension is enough to cause a slight spring-back after the die pressure is released.

The press action is completed when the clamp ring and male die return to the positions shown in Figure 1-15. The drawn panel is then removed, a new blank put in place, and the operation repeated.

The action of the draw die produces a piece of sheet metal that has the overall dimensions and shape of the finished part, but instead of being properly trimmed and flanged, it is surrounded by the excess metal that has been held between the clamp rings. To remove this excess, the piece then is put into a trim die, which is simply a shear built to the proper shape for the particular part. The excess metal trimmed off in the trim die is useless for other purposes because of the beads pressed into it and the working it has undergone in being pulled through the beaded surfaces of the clamp rings. In any large pressroom operation, this scrap is baled and shipped back to the steel mill.

Up to the point of trimming, the operations in making the round pan and a body panel are approximately the same. The differences lie in the shape of the dies and the fact that the die with the more complicated shape would have more complicated operating problems. For example, the clamp rings for a hood panel would follow its outer edge, and the male die would have the exact shape of the inside of the hood. In some cases, trimming the edge of the automobile panel is all that is needed; in others it is necessary to form special flanges.

The action of a flanging die is to fold the edges of the panel to shape. The widely varied types and shapes of flanges used on the different panels of the automobile make it necessary that such dies be designed to perform a specific operation. These dies are never interchangeable from one operation to another; some are very simple, others quite complicated. Detailed information on this type of die is beyond the scope of this book, however, and will not be considered further.

The important fact to gain from the preceding discussion of die operation is that any die-stamped panel is left in a state of *tension*. As pointed out, there is some spring-back as the die pressure is released, but the tendency to spring back is not relieved completely by this action. Remaining in the panel are locked-up forces, properly called *residual stresses*, that continue to pull against the shape. Being less than the strength of the metal in which they are found, these stresses have no effect unless the panel is weakened in a spot or area. The presence of such stresses may be demonstrated easily by cutting through a flat section of any stamped panel. The edges of the metal adjoining the cut will pull out of shape. A straightedge laid across the cut will show that the edges have dropped below the original contour.

The amount of residual stresses remaining in the panel is governed by the amount of stretching required in drawing it. Panels that have been subjected to minor forces may be expected to have fewer stresses than those subjected to much greater forces. Also, the condition will not be uniform over the entire surface of any particular panel.

Since the natural condition of the residual stresses in a panel is a slight state of tension, it should be remembered that when a damaged panel is repaired properly, it is restored to a state of tension. This matter will be considered in much greater detail in later sections on metal finishing and shrinking with heat.

BASIC SHAPES

The effect of a damaging force on a panel is governed by the shape, size, and reinforcements of that panel. Many different areas on the surface of an automobile have the same or similar shapes, and even though such panels vary in both size and the kind of reinforcements that support their outer edges, they may be expected to form the same damage patterns when subjected to similar damaging forces.

The similarity of shapes is more readily understood when the various areas of the panel are considered separately. The overall shape of the panel is a combination of the various areas representative of the basic shapes. The shape of a particular part, such as a door or hood panel, may vary for different year models of the same automobile, but it still is a combination of the basic shapes.

By classifying panels according to basic shapes, it is possible to establish basic damage patterns and related repair procedures. These can be applied to any sheet metal panel, whether it is on past, current, or future models.

Another factor that makes it desirable to classify panels according to shape is that it is rare for the damage to extend to the entire area of a panel. The repair problem will be confined to a portion of the larger panels, and the repairman need only concern himself with the portion that is damaged. There is always a direct relationship between the basic shape involved and the damage pattern that results.

There are different damage patterns for a basic shape, because damaging forces may be applied in many different ways. However, two different panels of the same basic shape will be damaged in a similar pattern if the damaging forces are the same. Damage patterns are discussed in the following chapter.

An easy way to describe shape is to consider the curvature of the length and width of an area separately. The shape of any particular area may be described accurately by placing two curved lines, at right angles to each other, over the area. In establishing these lines, length would lie along the front-to-rear length of the automobile. Width would be taken either vertically, as on the side of the automobile, or crosswise, as on the top or bottom. Front- and rear-end panels having their length in the crosswise direction to the automobile would be considered whichever way their overall shape would suggest.

The combined effect of the shape of length and width

1-17 Example of high crown panels. Most of the surface is high crown except the flat cowl side and reverse crown at headlight.

will be considered as the *crown* of the area of the panel being discussed. Four basic classifications are used to describe the crown of any panel: (1) low crown, (2) high crown, (3) combined high and low crown, and (4) reverse crown. Examples are shown in Figures 1-17 and 1-18.

High Crown

Surfaces in the high crown classification have enough curvature to give the impression of rounding shape in both directions. The curvature in both directions may not be the same, but in both cases it is enough to be obvious.

True high crowns were very common in the automobiles built in the early years of the automobile industry, but became less common immediately following the end of World War II. The weight reduction program caused by the world oil shortage of the early 1970s started a trend toward plainer, boxier shapes having even fewer high crowns than before. Those that are found are relatively small and usually in such locations as roof panel corners, rear end of quarter panels, and sometimes on the front end of hood panels.

As with the low crown, it is difficult to define exactly the amount of curvature necessary for a surface to be classified as high crown. Defined in terms of stiffness, it cannot be flexed out of shape by hand pressure; when enough force is applied to a high crown to push it out of shape, it will not spring back when the pressure is released. Examples of high crown are shown in Figure 1-17.

Metal in high crown areas has been worked by the draw die more severely than low crown metal, and for that reason it is slightly stronger due to additional work hardening.

Low Crown

Panels in the low crown classification have very little curvature; many of them can be found that are straight in the lengthwise direction. The impression gained from a glance at a small area is that it is a flat surface. For all practical purposes, the repairman must treat such panels as though they were flat. Figure 1-18 shows the shape of typical low-crowned panels.

The best examples of low-crowned panels are door lower panels, quarter lower panels, fender skirts, hood tops, and the center area of roof panels. Of this list, the roof panel has the least appearance of being flat because if has more curvature both lengthwise and crosswise than most other low crown panels. However, it is also the largest panel on the automobile, which causes it to react to a force, either damaging or repairing, as if it were flat. This is because the load-bearing strength of such long, slight curves is very low.

It is difficult to define exactly the amount of curvature that a panel can have and still be considered low-crowned. It is easier to define in terms of springiness or elasticity. The surface of an undamaged low-crowned panel will spring or flex out of shape when hand pressure is applied to it and snap back when the pressure is released.

In some cases, the entire area of a panel will be in the low crown classification; in others, only a portion will be low-crowned; the rest of the area may blend into any combination of the other basic crowns.

Combined High and Low Crown

The rounding edges of many low crown areas are actually low-crowned in one direction and high-crowned in another. Many such panels, like doors and front fenders, are very nearly flat lengthwise but curve away very sharply in the crosswise or width direction

1-18 Examples of low crown panels. The door and quarter panel are relatively flat but blend into sharp reverse crowns at the upper and lower edges.

along the edges. Many such surfaces can be compared to a portion of the outside of a cylinder.

Combined low and high crown surfaces have the strength characteristic of the high crown rather than the low crown surface. Although relatively flat in one direction, the relatively short radius of the curvature in the other provides strong bracing to resist force.

Reverse Crowns

In contrast to the other crowns, one curve of the reverse crown is hollow when viewed from the outside. This may be considered an inside curve, because the center point of the curve is on the side from which it is viewed. Usually, the inside curve has a relatively short radius as compared to the radius of the outside curve. It is quite common to find considerable variation in the radius of the inside curve of a reverse crown that runs the length of a panel. The outside curve will usually have a relatively long radius. Variations of either of these conditions will be found.

The reverse crown presents a particular repair problem because of its strength. A simple bend is not possible, because the two curves are braced against each other. A collapse of the metal surface is necessary for a bend to occur. As a result, damage in a reverse crown is usually severe as compared to damage in either a low or high crown. However, when damage does occur, often it is localized in one or more small areas. Because the reverse crown is stiffer, damage tends to spread less than it will in the other crowns.

Examples of reverse crowns can be seen in Figures 1-17 and 1-18.

REINFORCING METHODS

The strength of crowned panel surfaces on an automobile body is not enough to provide the rigidity necessary to hold alignment of parts and resist the strains of normal operation. The desirability of keeping weight down to the minimum rules out the use of heavy reinforcing members; this has always been important to good body design, but its importance has increased tremendously with the demand for more fuel-efficient automobiles. This demand has placed even greater emphasis on the development of lightweight reinforcements using minimum amounts of material.

Reinforcements are of three basic types: (1) those formed in the surface of an inner or outer panel, (2) those welded to the panel, and (3) those made by bonding inner and outer panels together with thermosetting or catalyst-activated adhesives; this is relatively new, as compared to the first two, and is discussed in more detail later in this section.

The reinforcements formed in a panel are the flanges, beads, and offsets used primarily for stiffness. Examples are such sections as the flange on the lower edge of a fender skirt and the ribs or beads on door inner panels and floor pans; reinforcements of this type

are essentially stiffeners intended to prevent vibration or flexing. Welded-on reinforcements are usually channel or box section pieces that serve as structural members. Examples include roof rails, windshield headers, and the crossbars used under the floor pan, among many others.

Body engineers design light structural members of thin sheet metal by taking advantage of the stiffening effect of an àngular bend. A strip of sheet metal has relatively little strength to resist bending when force is applied to it at right angles to the surface. The same strip can support far greater loads when it is turned so that the load is applied to the edge instead of to the flat surface. A flange turned on the edge of flat sheet is, in effect, an attached strip. The far greater resistance to bending of the edgewise strip is added to the relatively low strength of the flat sheet.

The reinforcing effect is greatest when the flange is turned away from the load and least when turned toward it. These two conditions are illustrated in Figures 1-19 and 1-20. In Figure 1-19 the outer edge of the flange is under tension and cannot yield except by breaking or stretching. The inner edge of this flange is under a compressive force that would tend to buckle it if it were free; attachment to the flat sheet prevents buckling. In Figure 1-20, the opposite is true. The attached edge of the flange is under tension, and the outer edge is under compression; unsupported, the outer edge is free to buckle as the flat sheet bends. A second flange has been added in Figure 1-21, making a channel.

Maximum strength can be obtained by adding the fourth side to the three-sided channel, making what is

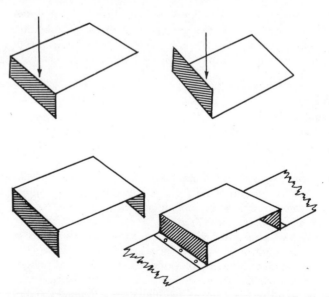

1-19 *(Top, left)* Flange turned away from the load, indicated by the arrow

1-20 *(Top, right)* Flange turned toward the load, indicated by the arrow.

1-21 *(Bottom, left)* Channel formed by adding a second flange.

1-22 *(Bottom, right)* Box construction.

1-23 Cutaway section of roof and box construction roof rail. Roof rail construction varies widely.

1-24 Cutaway section of typical rocker panel; showing box construction.

commonly termed a box construction. Figure 1-22 is representative of a very commonly used form of box construction. It is essentially a channel with narrow flanges turned on the outer edges of the wide flanges. These narrow flanges serve as a means of welding to the broad section of sheet metal. The crossbars on the underside of floor pans are excellent examples of this type of box construction.

Box construction is not limited to the square shape shown in Figure 1-22. The possible variations of the shape of such parts, usually called members, are almost limitless. Regardless of shape, however, box construction offers more strength than can be obtained by any other method used to provide reinforcement in automobile bodies.

An actual cutaway section of a typical roof and roof rail is shown in Figure 1-23. This is true box construction, as is the cutaway rocker panel shown in Figure 1-24.

Adhesive bonding of inner to outer panels started in the years following World War II as a means of prevent-

ing flutter in large, nearly flat areas of sheet metal. It has been used primarily on hoods and deck lids, but one manufacturer has used it on roof panels. Wherever it is used, an inner panel is required to serve as the support for the outer; the inner panel may have pressed-in reinforcements and cut-out sections, but will be designed so that the bonding points will be close to the outer.

The adhesive is a viscous material that forms artificial rubber when subjected to heat or when a catalyst is added to it. In factory assembly, blobs of the material are put on one panel, in a predetermined pattern, and the other panel is put in place. The panel will later go through a heated paint drying oven, which will provide the heat required to cure the adhesive. When a catalyst is used, the material cures immediately.

Adhesive material used to install windshield glasses, either the caulking or the tape type, can be used to reattach a broken bond whenever necessary.

Collision Damage

When a collision occurs and damage results, it is because the sheet metal was subjected to more force than it could resist. The study of collision damage is complicated by the fact that it is the result of an impact instead of normal wear. Each case of damage is an individual problem to be solved by the repairman. This is in sharp contrast to the repair of the operating units of the automobile, because similar units develop similar problems, so that exact procedures can be prepared and published in a shop manual or service bulletin for the mechanic to follow. In solving his problems, the repairman must be guided by what he knows about the effect of impact force on the particular metal involved and the repair methods that may be used to restore it to original shape.

This chapter explains the basic damage conditions that result when impact force is applied to the basic shapes. By understanding these basic conditions, it is possible to reduce a highly variable situation to a combination of basic patterns. Training and experience allow us to see the damage on any panel as a combination of these conditions instead of as just a tangled mess of sheet metal.

To grasp these basic factors, it is necessary to understand the relationship of shape to the effect of force on it. This relationship is a variable factor, because it involves different speeds, impact angles, size and rigidity of the impact object, and the construction of the area affected. The use of different metals, mild steel, hard steel, and aluminum, may seem to complicate the prob-

lem. This should not be a matter of great concern; the repairman's problems are with panels that are repairable. Panels of different metals may suffer more or less damage under the same conditions, but shape and force will react in much the same manner regardless of the type of sheet metal involved.

This chapter has been arranged so that the relationship of shape to the effect of force on it is discussed first. This is followed by a list of the basic conditions and a discussion of the physical effects of each. The chapter concludes with an explanation of the variable factors of speed, angle, rigidity, and so on, and how they are related to the severity of the damage conditions.

EFFECT OF FORCE ON SHAPE

The term *impact*, as used here, means the force involved when an automobile strikes, or is struck by, another object. The other object may be another automobile, but could be anything. To cause damage, the *impact object* must strike the *impact area* hard enough to overcome its elasticity, meaning that it will not spring back. The deeper the impact area is driven in, the wider its effect spreads. As it spreads, force from the impact either pushes or pulls on the adjoining surface, depending on the shape of the areas affected. This spreading action is referred to in later sections as the *flow of force*.

Figure 2-1 shows the outward flow of force from a direct impact on a combination high and low crown. The solid lines AA and BB represent vertical and lengthwise cross sections of a typical panel. The arrow C represents a direct impact on the intersection of the cross section lines. The dotted lines show the effect of the impact on the original shape, and the arrows indicate the flow of force. Note that the arrows under the high crown point outward, indicating that the force following this path has pushed outward against the adjoining metal; the arrows under the low crown point inward, indicating an exactly opposite effect.

An impact on a high crown always can be expected to push outward against the adjoining metal; the same impact on a low crown always can be expected to pull inward on the adjoining metal. When these crowns are combined, as they are on most body panels, the effect of pushing and pulling will act along lines as shown. The panel's material will not change the flow of force; steel, aluminum, or a non-metallic substitute will react in the same manner. The strength of the material involved, however, will determine the extent of damage; softer material will be driven in farther and damaged more than a hard material.

The reaction of any sheet metal when subjected to a force that pulls will be different from that to a force that pushes on it. Pressure on the opposite edges of a sheet toward the center will cause it to crumple because of its low resistance to bending. An outward pull on the same edges will draw it tight, and no further effect will occur unless enough force is applied to exceed the metal's yield strength. For this reason, the damage conditions found in a high crown area will be different from those found in the adjoining low crown area, even though both are the result of the same impact.

THE BASIC DAMAGE CONDITIONS

Force spreading from the impact point into other areas of the panel or into other panels causes damage by changing the shape of the areas affected. The nature of such damage varies too widely to attempt to establish what could be called a typical condition. However, when a detailed examination is made of the damage area, it will be found to be a combination of the following basic damage conditions: (1) displaced areas, (2) simple bends, (3) rolled buckles, (4) upsets, and (5) stretches. The combination is called the *fold pattern* in this book.

Displaced Areas

In almost every case, examination of a damaged panel will reveal that parts of the area are not affected by bending or other distortion. Such areas are part of the overall damage only because they have been pushed out of position. Quite often they are under an elastic strain that, when relieved, will allow the area to snap

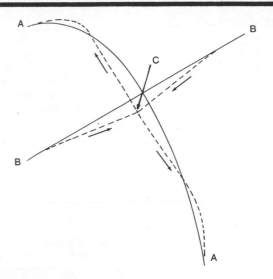

2-1 Showing the flow of force from a direct impact on a combination high and low crown surface.

back into shape. Such areas may be considered displaced. Much of the center area of the door panel shown in Figure 2-2 is displaced. Such an area is sometimes called *elastic metal*, because it will tend to snap back to place if the buckles holding it are relieved properly. The word "elastic" in this sense is technically wrong, because all metal is elastic. The area should be considered under an elastic strain, or springy.

It is important to recognize all displaced areas and plan the repair procedure so that the buckles holding them out of place will be relieved properly. Large displaced areas often can be released so that there is little or no repair work except on the buckled areas that hold them.

One measure of the severity of any damage is in the amount of displaced metal that makes up the damaged area. It is obvious that an area that can be made to snap back into shape will not require as much straightening work as a similar-sized area that is badly bent and distorted.

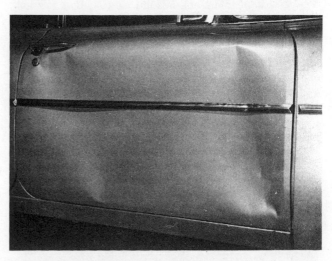

2-2 Displaced metal. Much of the center area will snap back into shape when the sharp buckles are relieved.

3 SHEET METAL REPAIR

Simple Bends

As the surface of a panel collapses under impact, it folds. Some of the folding is the result of simple bends, particularly in relatively flat areas. A simple bend is essentially a long, usually narrow, area of metal that has served as a pivot for the movement of the adjoining metal and in doing so has changed shape.

The deformation in a simple bend is due to the opposing action of tension and pressure forces. As force, which tends to cause bending, is applied to a piece of sheet metal, it causes tension on the outer surface and pressure on the inner. Bending occurs when the force is enough to overcome the metal's resistance to this tension and pressure. Under normal conditions, the outer surface of the bend is *stretched* and the inner is *upset*. Upset means shortened, and stretched, obviously, means lengthened. The bending action is illustrated in Figure 2-3.

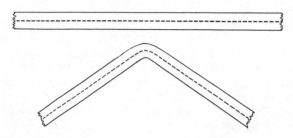

2-3 Enlarged cross section of a piece of sheet metal before and after bending. The outer surface is stretched, and the inner surface is compressed. The center line remains unchanged.

If stretching occurs on the outer surface and upsetting occurs on the inner, it is quite apparent that somewhere in between the metal would not be affected by either. The dotted center line in Figure 2-3 represents this unaffected part, which is actually a plane, located approximately in the center of the thickness. The metal on each side of this plane is solid, so that both tension and pressure are resisted equally at the start of the bending. When breaking occurs in a sharp bend, however, it appears on the outside, because the action tends to pull it apart. The inner surface will be at the breaking point but will not separate until the bend is straightened.

In studying the effect of bending, it is essential to direct attention to the very small unit of metal instead of being concerned with the entire panel. Figure 2-4 represents an enlargement of a piece of sheet metal slightly less than ½ inch (13 mm) long and ⅓ inch (18 mm) wide. The lines on its surface are spaced apart the thickness of the metal. Thus, if flat, each square formed by these lines represents one face of a cube joined on four sides to similar cubes.

In Figure 2-5, A and B represent a much greater enlargement of one of these cubes before and after bending. In A, the upper and lower halves are exactly the same size and shape; in B, bending has distorted the

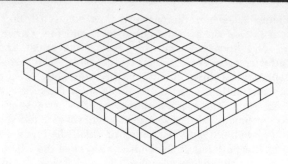

2-4 Enlarged piece of metal with lines scribed on the surface, representing interconnected cubes.

square into the shape of a wedge. The upper and lower halves are still the same in bulk, because nothing has been taken away or added, but they are different in shape, the upper being stretched and thinned and the lower being pressed together and thickened.

The total amount of metal involved in a simple bend is determined by its length and how sharply it is formed. Quite often an area several inches long and a fraction of an inch wide, made up of many sections of metal the size of the cube illustrated, is affected. The effect of bending on various sections throughout such an area would vary considerably. It follows logically that to straighten such an area, force must be applied so that these effects are relieved, regardless of the extent of individual section distortion.

Hinge Buckles

A hinge buckle is one form of a simpe bend. There is no major difference, but the term hinge suggests a straight, simple bend that has served as a pivot point for one section of a panel to swing around another. Many simple bends are curved, particularly when they have been formed into a curve by pressure flowing out from an impact area.

Rolled Buckles

The rolled buckle is so named because of the rolling action that occurs in much of the area of a panel as it collapses under an impact. This action is similar to the pivot action of a hinge buckle, except that the pivot

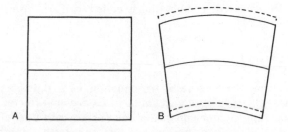

2-5 The shape of a single cubical section (A) before and (B) after bending.

point travels across an area instead of remaining in one place. An example of a severe rolled buckle is indicated by arrow 1 in Figure 2-6. Less severe rolled buckles are indicated by the arrows 2 and 3. The sharp dent between 1 and 3 is a direct impact area from which spread the force causing the rolling. This example is from an older car, because rolled buckles as severe as this one are becoming quite rare, due to the design trend to squarer bodies. They still occur, however, and represent one of the repairman's major problems in straightening panels.

The distinctive feature of a rolled buckle is two ridges running together at an angle. These ridges are generally sharply formed at the meeting point, which is usually in the area where a low crown blends into a combination low and high crown. On each side of the meeting point, the sharpness of these ridges will be reduced gradually, until in many instances they will blend into the shape of the adjoining surfaces. This is not true of the rolled buckle shown here, however, because the ridges are in an area of metal that is quite high crowned in both directions, and the dent is quite deep.

As the buckle rolls into the high crown area, flattening of the crown forces the meeting point of the two ridges above the proper level of the panel. Referring to Figure 2-1, this is the raised effect shown by the dotted line AA. The rolling action always causes a valley section to form between the two ridges; this valley forms a stiff prop under the raised area.

The damage caused by a rolled buckle can vary from a condition no more severe than a simple bend to one of the worst conditions with which the repairman will work. The severity of the distortion of the individual rolled buckle is governed by the amount of force that caused it. The rolling action starts as a curved ridge around the impact point and moves, or rolls, outward. The shape of this ridge is relatively smooth until it reaches the point where the low crown blends into a combination crown. At this point, the inner surface of the ridge collapses, forming the valley buckle. If the roll-

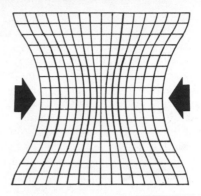

2-7 Enlarged drawing showing the effect of force pushing from opposite directions on a section of metal approximately ½ inch (13 mm) square.

ing action stops here, the damage is not much more severe than a simple bend. If there is sufficient force to drive this rolling action farther into the higher crown, the damage will be severe. This is the case with the buckle indicated by arrow 1 in Figure 2-6. Note that a path of flaked-off paint has been left by the rolling action. This path is referred to as the break-over path because of the breaking or collapsing action that occurs as it forms.

The metal in the break-over path will be upset. The next section deals with the exact nature of upsetting, whether caused by a rolled buckle or otherwise.

Upsets

An upset occurs when opposing forces push against an area of metal and cause it to yield; in yielding, the surface area will be reduced and the thickness increased proportionally. Forces that cause an upset may act only from two opposite directions, as indicated in Figure 2-7, or they may act against a central point from several directions. To identify an upset, remember that one or both of the surface dimensions of the affected area will be reduced.

The effect and importance of an upset will be better understood if one remembers that it usually is restricted to a relatively small area. Figure 2-7 can be considered as representing the same section of metal surface represented by Figure 2-4. Reducing this enlarged drawing to the dimensions of most sheet metal found in the automobile body would indicate a piece about ½ inch (13 mm) square and about 0.037 inch (9 mm) thick. Larger areas of metal can be upset, but the tendency to buckle and relieve the pressure limits the upsetting effect to areas not too much larger than this. The break-over of a severe rolled buckle may be much longer but usually not much wider.

Many drawings of various shapes could be used to illustrate the effect of upsetting. However, each would be similar to the three in Figure 2-8. A represents a small cubical section of sheet metal before the upsetting force application. B represents the same section after

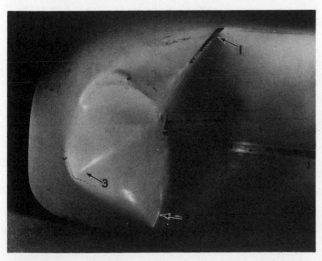

2-6 A typical example of rolled buckles. Arrow 1 points to the break-over path of the most severe buckle. Arrows 2 and 3 indicate less severe buckles.

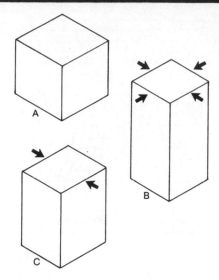

2-8 Effect on a small, cubical section within the upset area. In A, the cube is shown before force has been applied. In B, pressure has been applied from four sides. In C, pressure has been applied from two sides.

force application from all four sides. Note that the top surface is shown much smaller, and the height, which would be the thickness, is much greater. C represents the same section after force application from two sides only. Note that only two sides of the top surface are shown smaller, and the height, or thickness, is less than in B.

Upsetting a single section no larger in area than its thickness would not have a significant effect on the shape of a panel. When this effect is spread over an area ½ inch (13 mm) wide and much longer, it is an important factor. The series of photographs in Figure 1-13, showed that as little as 0.005 inch (0.127 mm) would cause an unacceptable bulge in a flat strip. The drawing in Figure 2-7 does not represent any specific upset, but the amount of upset shown would not be uncommon. Considering that this drawing represents an area of metal approximately ½ inch (13 mm) square, the upset shown would be many times more. Such a spot anywhere on the surface of a low crown panel would draw wrinkled-type buckles on each side of it.

Figure 2-9 represents the upsetting effect of most rolled buckles. The offset in the lower section of these parallel lines represents the point reached by the break-over path. The resistance of the adjoining metal tends to force the metal together; lines scribed on the panel before the buckle was formed would have this shape after the break-over action passed between them.

Upsetting is not limited to the effect of the damaging force. The piece of metal shown in Figure 2-10 has had a ridge formed in it by bending and straightening; this is a typical buckle left after any piece of metal has been bent double and then opened up again without work being done directly on the ridge which forms. The section in the center was flattened by hammering it down as it lay on a flat surface. Note that this section has been lowered until it is about level with the metal on

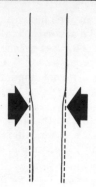

2-9 Upset effect in the break-over path of a severe rolled buckle. The break-over action would reach the point where the solid and dotted lines converge.

either side. Flattening this section caused far greater upsetting than would be found in almost any rolled buckle. The repairman who does not know that he should avoid hammering sharp ridges will make upsets of this type and add damage to damage.

The metal referred to in this discussion of upsetting is mild steel. Aluminum, being a softer metal, will upset more than steel under the same circumstances. Harder steel would upset less.

Stretches

Stretch, the exact opposite of upset, occurs when an area of metal is subjected to force in tension greater than its yield strength. The result is an increase in surface area. Sheet metal is considered stretched whether the increase of area is caused by an increase of either length or width, or both.

Stretching also can be the result of the improper use of tools, particularly the hammer and dolly block. (These are the repairman's most important tools *if* he will learn to use them properly.)

Stretching occurs under conditions and usually in areas different from those of upsetting because it is the

2-10 An upset section of a crease-type buckle, made by hammering the buckle as the piece lay on a flat surface. No heat was used.

result of tension instead of pressure. The most common type of stretching is a gouge. Small, point-type gouges may be seen in the impact area of the dented deck lid in Figure 2-6. A much more severe crease-type gouge is shown in Figure 2-11.

When the exact difference between stretched and upset metal is recognized, the problems of stretched metal become relatively simple. Stretched areas of metal rarely rise above the surface level to cause unacceptable bulges. When they do, they are usually caused by something within the automobile being thrown against the underside of the panel during the collision. The repairman who has learned the proper technique of shrinking metal finds these areas relatively easy to repair. Gouged areas are frequently filled, because the fill can be blended into the surface area easily in most cases. However, the decision as to whether a particular gouge should be filled or straightened by shrinking should not be made without considering the conditions. In some cases, filling is all that is required; in others filling can be a mistake.

False Stretch

The term false stretch refers to a condition often mistakenly considered as stretched metal. It occurs when a severe rolled buckle is straightened without relieving the upset condition in the break-over path. As shown in Figures 2-8 and 2-9, the metal in the break-over path may be squeezed enough to cause upsetting. The incorrect use of a hammer on a sharp ridge can add to the upset. Driving a severe rolled buckle out by hammering on the underside will have a drawstring effect on the undamaged metal adjoining it, similar to that shown in Figure 2-10. We can illustrate this condition by folding a small pleat in the edge of a sheet of paper and mashing it flat. The surface of the paper adjoining the pleat will bulge upward because of the drawstring effect of the pleat. Release the pleat, and the surface will flatten. An upset in the break-over path of a severe rolled buckle, if not relieved in straightening, will similarly affect the adjoining panel surface.

The technique of avoiding false stretch, or at least minimizing it, is explained in Chapter 3 and emphasized

2-11 A crease-type gouge, the result of a high-speed impact by a small, rigid impact object.

in the discussions of straightening procedure in other chapters. The procedure for shrinking unavoidable false stretches is discusses in Chapter 4, along with other shrinking procedures.

VARIABLE FACTORS IN COLLISION

Even though all collision damage is made up of the same basic conditions, few damaged areas are exactly alike. Because the damage from any collision is unique, the repairman is forced to determine his own procedure. He can do this best if he has been trained, or has trained himself, to determine the fold pattern and apply opposite force to reverse the damage. An important part of this training is to learn what to look for when inspecting the damage. The trained eye will see a pattern in what seems a mess to the untrained eye.

Analyzing the job consists of determining (1) the area that received the impact, (2) an approximation of the total force of the impact, and (3) a check on the paths the force might follow to cause related damage at points distant from the impact area. In the analysis he should look for (1) the angle of the impact, (2) the relative speed of the impact object, (3) the size, rigidity, and approximate weight of the impact object, and (4) the construction of the area receiving the impact.

These will be referred to in later discussions as the *variable factors*. They determine the nature of the damage resulting from any collision. It is easy to determine the extent to which each factor has contributed to the total. From this is a simple step to visualize the actual movement of the metal as it folded. The key to good repair procedure is a matter of reversing this movement.

IMPACT ANGLE

The impact angle means the angle at which the impact object collided with the automobile; or, put another way, the angle at which the automobile collided with the impact object. Often, both are moving. Whether or not the impact object is another automobile is of no consequence, except that it determines the nature of the surface which caused the damage. The reason the impact angle should be considered is that it determines the direction of the flow of force from the impact area into the structure, where it may cause related damage.

With everything else equal, a direct impact will cause more damage than a glancing one, because the full force will be absorbed. It was shown in Figure 2-1 that the force that flows outward from a direct impact will be in tension on a low-crowned surface and in pressure on a high-crowned surface. A much more variable situation results when the angle of impact becomes much more oblique, as shown in A, Figure 2-12. The colliding object may either dig into the surface or glance off. If it digs in instead of slipping, it tends to push, or crumple, the surface ahead of it and to pull on the sur-

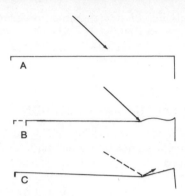

2-12 Showing the effect of an impact from a sharp angle. Figure A indicates the angle of approach. B shows the effect when the impact object digs into the surface, pushing metal ahead of it and drawing metal behind it. C shows the effect when the impact object glances instead of digging in; this is essentially the same as a direct impact.

face behind it, often carrying it along as shown in B. A severe damage of this type can be difficult to straighten. However, when the impact glances off, as shown in C, the damage is usually minor.

Another typical damage result from a glancing impact occurs when the object slips instead of holding, leaving a path of dented, sometimes deeply gouged metal as shown in Figure 2-11. It was pointed out in the section on stretched metal that gouges of this type are stretched, often very severely, because tremendous force has been concentrated on a very small area.

A quite different damage condition occurs when a panel having a combination crown, such as a quarter panel, door, or fender, is subjected to a direct impact on

2-13 Buckle formed by the collapse of a section of metal under pressure.

2-14 A .22-caliber rifle bullet hole in a piece of sheet metal.

one end. In this case most of the entire panel is subjected to pressure that will tend to collapse it. Typically, the smooth areas simply fold out of shape, but sharply crowned areas will crumple, or collapse, accordion fashion, if the pressure is great enough. An example is shown in Figure 2-13.

RELATIVE SPEED OF THE IMPACT OBJECT

The speed of impact should be considered as relative because essentially identical damage results whether the damaged automobile moves against a standing object or is struck by a moving object. When both are moving toward each other, as in a head-on collision, the relative speed equals the combined speed of both.

The speed of impact is important because of inertia. Stated briefly, inertia is the tendency of any stationary object to resist being put in motion, or of a moving object to continue moving. An excellent example of the effect of inertia is shown in Figure 2-14. The hole in this piece of metal was made by a .22-caliber rifle bullet. A hole can be shot in a body panel because of the speed at which the bullet travels. A much heavier object could exert the same amount of force at a much lower speed, but instead of piercing the panel, it would crush the surface. The difference is a matter of time; under the impact of the heavier but more slowly moving impact object, the panel has more time to move inward and spread the effect over a larger area.

A general idea of the speed of the impact is important in analyzing damage, because it indicates the extent to which force has penetrated into the structure to cause related damage. A high-speed impact on the front end of a fender may cause severe damage at the point of impact but not affect the alignment of the fender to the hood and door. Impact by a heavier object traveling a lower speed may cause less damage at the impact area, but may break the fender loose from the cowl, causing the fender to move back against the door. The trained repairman would know, by the appearance of the damage, that he also should check the alignment of the cowl hinge pillar; it may have shifted enough to prevent proper door alignment.

SIZE, RIGIDITY, AND WEIGHT

In addition to the impact angle and speed, the size, rigidity, and weight of the impact object have a great bearing on the type of damage. Again, as in the analysis of impact angle and speed, the repairman need not concern himself with the *exact* size, degree of rigidity, or weight. He is interested only in whether the impact object was large or small, rigid or yielding, or extremely heavy or very light.

The preceding example of the bullet serves as an illustration of the small, relatively rigid, but lightweight impact object. As a contrasting example, consider the effect of a roll-over accident in which the automobile lands on one side in soft earth. It is possible for the automobile to bounce as it continues to roll without causing severe visible damage. However, bends or misalignment may be found in the reinforced parts supporting the panels that received the impact, because the soft earth spreads the impact force over enough panel surface area to avoid severe overloading of any one point. Some of the impact force will be absorbed in displacing soft earth, but much of it will be transferred through the adjoining metal into the reinforcements.

An entirely different type of damage would result if the automobile were to roll into something hard and unyielding, such as a tree stump or rock. The effect would be much more severe, because there would be no cushioning effect. Severe distortion in the impact area would absorb some of the force, reducing misalignment in adjoining sections; force expended at one point cannot travel on and cause additional damage elsewhere.

CONSTRUCTION

The rigidity of the area receiving the impact determines to a large degree the nature of the damage and the extent to which it spreads. For example, a direct impact on the center of a door panel would spread over the entire area, but the same impact on the reinforced pillar section of the same door would probably cover much less area. The reduction in area concentrates the force of the blow. There is no easy way in which the severity of damage in one area can be compared with the other, but it is obvious that greater misalignment would occur from the impact on the pillar section. Similar examples could be pointed out over the entire surface of the body.

In analyzing any damage, it is essential to consider whether the impact has struck an area that is quite rigid or one that will yield readily. The effect on the rigid area will tend to cause severe distortion that spreads over a relatively small area; the opposite will be true of a similar impact on an area that will yield easily. To the untrained observer, however, the larger damage may appear to be more severe because of its size. The trained repairman should never make the easy mistake of judging the severity of damage on the basis of size alone.

Tools and Basic Operations

A knowledge of the proper use of the tools of the trade is necessary to understand the procedure of repairing even the simplest dent. Tools of some kind are required for every operation in straightening and preparing a damaged panel for repainting. Some of these operations require tools that normally are classified as shop equipment because of size and cost; others require only such items as may be classified as the repairman's hand tools. Both types of tools require the development of skill in their use. However, skill in the use of shop equipment is primarily in knowing where to use it. For example, comparatively little manual skill is required to set up a body jack, but it must be set up so that it will push against the right spot, or it may do more damage than good. On the other hand, skill in the use of hand tools requires both knowledge and manual dexterity.

This chapter deals with the repairman's hand tools and the basic operations performed with them. The tools are discussed first, then the basic operations in which they are used. This has been done to explain the purpose of the individual tool and what may be expected of it before giving instruction for its use on an actual repair job.

Hand tools may be classified according to basic use, either straightening or metal-finishing. Of course, some tools may be used in both basic operations, but the primary use will be in one or the other. This chapter has been organized with this in mind. The first section deals with the metal-straightening tools and the basic straightening operations, the second with the basic

metal-finishing tools and the basic metal-finishing procedures.

METAL-STRAIGHTENING TOOLS

To straighten damaged sheet metal, force is applied to restore it to original shape. This becomes a matter of straightening bends and relieving distortions. Tools used for this purpose are the means of applying the necessary force.

Metal-straightening hand tools apply force by one or more of three ways: (1) striking a direct blow on the metal surface, (2) resistance to a direct blow struck on the opposite side of the metal, and (3) as a lever used to pry against the surface, usually on the inside.

It would be impractical to list every tool available for use in straightening sheet metal, but considered basic may be (1) bumping hammers, (2) dolly blocks, (3) bumping spoons, (4) body spoons, (5) pry or pick tools, (6) caulking tools, and (7) screw-equipped slide hammers.

Development of manual skill in the use of these tools is essential for the student who wishes to become a good repairman. This requires an understanding of the purpose of the tools and practicing to become proficient in their use.

BUMPING HAMMERS

Bumping hammers are made in a wide range of

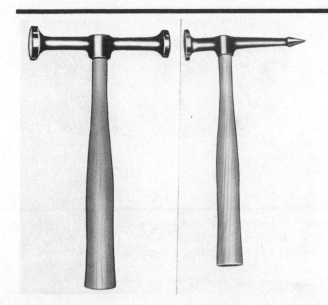

3-1 General-purpose hammer, sometimes called a dinging hammer.

3-2 Combination bumping and picking hammer.

styles, sizes, and combinations by the various manufacturers of body tools. Two very common styles are shown in Figures 3-1 and 3-2.

The distinguishing feature of all bumping hammers is the one head which is quite wide and nearly flat on the working face. The width of this head may vary on different types of hammers, but most of the popular ones will be approximately 1½ inches (38.1 mm). The most common shape for this head is round, but some are made square. Having an exact size and shape of the hammer, however, is not as important as having a hammer that is satisfactory to the person using it.

The large, nearly flat face serves to spread the force of a hammer blow over a fairly large area of the metal surface. This is essential in working with soft sheet metal. A smaller face or one having a high crown would tend to mark the metal when striking a hard blow on a spot backed up by the dolly block. The large, nearly flat face has the additional advantage of taking care of slight errors in aiming the hammer blow. This is particularly important in working on low crown panels.

The shape of the slight crown on the large face is important. The ideal surface is almost dead flat in the center, blending into a crown around the outer edges. This flat center spot may be from ¾ to 1 inch (19 to 25 mm) in diameter. The outer edges should be rounded off enough to prevent making a sharp edge mark when a blow is struck with the hammer turned slightly from the proper angle.

In selecting a bumping hammer, it may be difficult to obtain one that fits this description exactly; if so, it is better to accept one that is nearly flat over the entire area, because it is much easier to round off the edges than to flatten the center. The edges may be honed down with a piece of fine, water-resistant sandpaper wrapped around a stick of wood or a steel strap. Start with 220 or 260 grit and finish with 400 grit paper. A

mirror finish can be put on the hammer face in this manner with very little effort. The same procedure can be used to maintain the hammer face when it becomes marked by rough use.

The opposite end of the bumping hammer is almost always different from the large head. The combination hammer (Figure 3-2) is the type most widely used, and is as much a metal-finishing hammer as a bumping hammer. However, the hammer having the smaller round head (Figure 3-1) is an essential tool in straightening panels if its use is properly understood.

The small head is usually not used with the dolly block. It should have a much higher crown than the large head. It is used primarily to work out high spots and ridges in low-crowned panels. Light blows with this head, placed uniformly over the surface of a springy ridge, will straighten it easily. If the face of the hammer is properly polished, it is possible to work out many such areas so that they will require very little extra work to metal-finish.

The same blow struck with the large head will not straighten springy areas nearly so well, because the large head spreads its force over too large an area. Instead of making a very slight bend at the point of contact, the force of the blow is wasted in flexing the surrounding metal. The smaller, higher-crowned head reduces the area of contact enough to do more straightening and less flexing. It is simply a matter of straightening a large area a little at a time.

Much more detail in the use of the bumping hammer will be found in later chapters.

DOLLY BLOCKS

Dolly blocks vary so widely in size and shape that no general description can be applied to all of them. The purpose of all dolly blocks, however, is the same. They are used either as a striking tool or as a back-up tool for the bumping hammer. In both cases, the dolly normally is used on the underside, or inside, of the panel.

Four of the most common types of dolly blocks are shown in Figures 3-3–3-6. Of these, the most frequently

3-3 *(Left)* General-purpose dolly block.

3-4 *(Right)* Low crown general-purpose dolly.

used will be the general-purpose dolly shown in Figure 3-3. This dolly has a variety of curves over its surface, but its primary working face is the broad, smoothly curved upper section. The smaller, rounded lower section has some use as a working face but serves mostly as a hand hold.

The low-crowned, general-purpose dolly shown in Figure 3-4 is similar to the one in Figure 3-3, but its use is more limited. A dolly of this shape is very valuable when repairing low-crowned panels, but the working face will not fit into the shape of higher crowns.

The heel dolly (Figure 3-5) and the toe dolly (Figure 3-6) are both special-purpose tools. Being thinner, both of these may be used in narrow quarters where the larger general-purpose dolly cannot enter. They also provide a smooth, flat surface with sharp, right-angle edges for working flanges and sharp bends. Both of these are convenient tools to have; for various jobs, one will be better suited than the other.

Many other dolly blocks that are not discussed here are available, and many are as well suited to the job of metal-straightening as the ones shown. Preference of a skilled repairman for a particular dolly block is a personal matter. It is much more important that the dolly block be satisfactory to the user than it is for him to use a particular one.

Used as a striking tool, the dolly is essentially a hand-held, handleless hammer. It is good practice to use a dolly in this manner to drive out simple dents. As the metal is brought out, the hammer is then brought into use as needed.

3-5 Heel dolly block.

3-6 Toe dolly block.

Used with the bumping hammer, the dolly is actually much more than just a back-up tool. Its primary purpose is to provide a reaction to the force of a hammer blow. When used properly, the dolly tends to raise the spot of metal that is in contact with its working face. This is true, regardless of whether it is directly under the spot struck by the hammer or a short distance away. These operations are explained in detail in later sections of this chapter.

A very common misunderstanding of the use of a dolly block can be described as the anvil theory. Followers of this theory consider the dolly as a broad, smooth, anvil-like tool to be held on the underside of a buckle so that the metal can be driven down against it. The idea is very similar to the operation of straightening a bent nail by laying it on a flat surface and driving the bend down.

The rather widespread acceptance of the anvil theory accounts for the large number of dolly blocks available that have only one curve to the working face. In the cross direction, the working face will be flat. It is true that some metal-straightening may be done in this manner, but it is not as effective as a properly shaped dolly

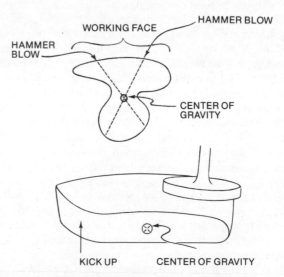

3-7 *(Top)* Balance characteristics of a general-purpose dolly block. A hammer blow on almost any part of the working face will be directed toward the center of gravity.

3-8 *(Bottom)* Balance characteristics of the toe dolly block. A hammer blow on either end will tend to cause the other to kick up, because the center of gravity acts as a pivot.

used correctly. A dolly with the right crown on the working face will result in both faster and better work.

Two factors that must be considered in selecting a dolly block are weight and balance. For normal operation, the weight of the dolly block should be at least three times that of the hammer. This difference in weight is needed because the dolly is at rest when the hammer blow strikes. The weight provides the inertia to resist the force of the hammer blow.

Balance is simply a matter of the distribution of weight. This is illustrated in Figures 3-7 and 3-8. Note that the general-purpose dolly (Figure 3-7) is shaped so that it is in balance regardless of where on the working face a hammer blow is struck. The toe dolly (Figure 3-8) is in balance only when a blow is struck on its center area. A blow on either end will tend to cause it to roll, or kick, so that much of the effect of its weight is lost.

This is not to say that an unbalanced dolly is no good. Such dollies are special-purpose tools to be used where the better-balanced tools cannot enter. In the places where they are needed, they are the best tools available.

SPOONS

The term spoon is applied to so many body tools that it is difficult to define. However, a spoon is usually a bar of steel that has been forged flatter and thinner on one end, sometimes on both ends. It may be bent into a variety of shapes, depending on its intended use. The forged end, or ends, serve as a working face to use against the metal; the rest of the bar serves as a handle.

Spoons serve three basic purposes:

1. To spread the force of a hammer blow over a large area. Such spoons are commonly called dinging or bumping spoons.
2. As a dolly block in areas in which the inner construction limits access to the inner side. These are commonly called body spoons.
3. As a prying or driving tool. Heavy-duty body spoons are usually more satisfactory for this purpose than the lighter dinging spoon.

The use of body spoons has declined as the automobile body has grown more complex in construction and shape. Use of spoons, particularly those classed as body spoons, requires a considerable degree of skill. This has caused many repairmen to rely on filling and panel replacement instead of straightening and metal-finishing panels that would require use of spoons. The acceptance by the industry of methods of working metal from the outside and the almost total use of plastic filler instead of body solder filling has caused many repairmen to adopt the mistaken attitude that spoons are obsolete tools.

The discussion of spoons is limited, because they have become relatively little-used tools. However, it is emphasized that the person who will make the effort to obtain a set of body spoons and learn to use them will be repaid many times in increased skill and productivity.

3-9 Low crown bumping spoon.

His problem may be to find them; he may have to make his own.

The low-crowned bumping spoon in Figure 3-9 is a very valuable tool for smoothing out soft ridges. Its use is shown in Figure 3-36, but it should not be used on sharp ridges of the type shown in Figure 3-37. Ridges such as this should be straightened by other means and the bumping spoon used only in the final smoothing operations.

The primary use of the bumping spoon is on low ridges in fairly stiff combination crown areas. Its purpose is to spread the force of a hammer blow over a larger area than the face of a bumping hammer will cover. It is not particularly well suited to use on nearly flat areas, such as door panels, because it will tend to flex the surrounding metal instead of straightening the ridge. In general, the face of the bumping hammer is a better tool on low crowns than the spoon.

The body spoons shown in Figures 3-11–3-15 are general-purpose tools that deserve more use than they often get. Used properly, they will reduce the number of holes punched for the dent puller screw and often produce a better-quality job with less labor. Although the use of such tools has declined, the reader is urged to investigate and experiment with them as part of his skill development.

Two suggested uses of body spoons are shown in Figure 3-10. The long, thin spoon in A can be used where inner construction prevents the use of a dolly block, as shown here, but it is equally useful as a pry tool. On many jobs the inner construction that makes the long, thin tool necessary also provides a base to rest the tool against for both uses. B shows another spoon of different shape used for the same purpose. Where construction permits, this spoon serves better as a substitute dolly block than the one in A, because its shape provides a better back-up, but there are many uses for both.

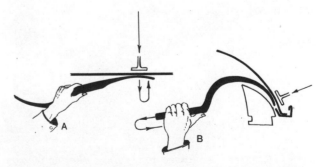

3-10 Balance characteristics of body spoons. A: This spoon has no balance, because the weight does not support the working face. B: This spoon has good balance.

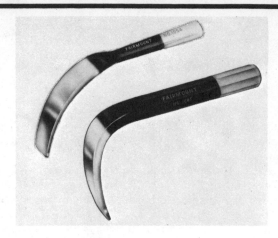

3-11 *(Top)* Pry spoon.

3-12 *(Bottom)* General-purpose body spoon, originally called a turret top spoon.

The spoon in Figure 3-11 is primarily a pry tool, but it can be used as a bumping spoon in reverse crowns.

The spoon in Figure 3-12 is for general-purpose body work. It serves as a pry tool, substitute dolly block, and an offset driving tool (Figure 3-13). It has many uses of this type in various parts of the body and fenders.

The spoons in Figures 3-14 and 3-15 are quite large and heavy. They are excellent tools for both prying and as substitutes for a dolly block in any area where there is room to get them into place behind the inner construction.

The spoon in Figure 3-16 is intended for rough service. It works particularly well as an offset caulking tool.

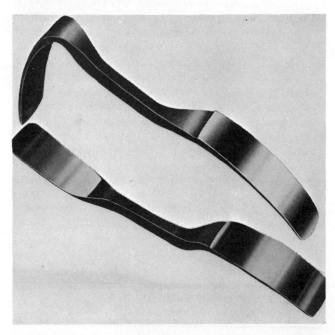

3-13 *(Top)* General-purpose body spoon. Working face on both ends and an extra length make this spoon particularly useful on door and deck lid panels.

3-14 *(Bottom)* Large offset spoon.

3-15 Rough service spoon.

CAULKING, DRIVING, AND BENDING TOOLS

So many special-purpose tools are used for straightening sheet metal that it would be impossible to list them all. The three tools shown in Figures 3-17–3-19 are typical. Many others are used for the same or similar purposes.

The tool shown in Figure 3-17 is for caulking. It resembles a blunt, wide-bladed chisel, but it is used for reshaping short-radius bends or narrow, flat surfaces. A wide variety of caulking tools is needed to do the various caulking jobs normally found when repairing severely damaged panels. These tools may be of different lengths, and the shape of the working ends may vary from almost sharp to wide and flat.

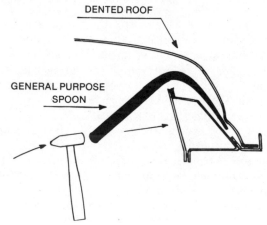

3-16 A general-purpose spoon being used as a driving tool.

The tool shown in Figure 3-18 is a special-purpose caulking tool for straightening flanges. It is particularly suited to straightening the bead section of fenders, but it may be used on any flange that is turned away from the operator's side. In use, one end is hooked into the flange to be straightened, and the other end is held by the operator as he strikes hammer blows on the bar, close to the panel.

3-17 Caulking iron.

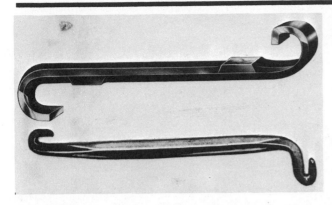

3-18 *(Top)* Special flange straightening and offset caulking tool.

3-19 *(Bottom)* Flange bender, rarely available but easy to make up.

The tool shown in Figure 3-19 is intended for working flanges. This particular tool would not be readily available, but it and the one shown in Figure 3-18 are examples of tools that the repairman can make for personal use, using salvage steel shafts from the scrap pile.

A complete set of pry tools is shown in Figure 3-20. A pry rod in use is shown in Figure 3-21. In this operation, the rod is inserted through an enlarged drain hole, but many panel areas can be reached through open inner construction, particularly the wheelhousing area of quarter panels or doors after disassembling the trim panel. In general, use of pry tools is preferable to the use of the dent puller, described in the following section, on any spot within practical reach and with a suitable fulcrum available to pry against.

SLIDE HAMMERS

Specially equipped slide hammers have several uses in metal work, the most common as a dent puller in panel areas where inner construction blocks access to the under side. These pullers are equipped with a metal screw held firmly in place by a retainer. To use, a hole is

3-21 Use of pry rod through an enlarged drain hole in the lower edge of a quarter panel.

either punched or drilled in the dent, the screw is driven into the hole, and the sliding weight is snapped back against the stop to lift the area. A typical dent puller is shown in Figure 3-22.

It is recommended here that the hole be pierced in the panel with a sharp-pointed scratch awl, instead of drilled. As illustrated in Figure 3-23, the awl makes a depression in the surface, which stiffens the surrounding area. This stiffened area will lift a much larger spot and has less tendency to rise above the correct level (B). A drilled hole does not have anything to stiffen the surrounding metal, so the edge is lifted higher than it should be. The common practice is to grind the paint off of the area after the dent puller has been used. These high edges will be ground off, thinning the metal and enlarging the hole.

Hooks of various types are available or can be made up by the repairman to extend the usefulness of most slide hammers. To use, the screw retainer is removed and the hook threaded to the end of the hammer shaft. One special use is shown with the weld-on pull tabs, shown in Figure 3-24. These tabs are attached to the panel with an electric resistance spot welder and are recommended, instead of the metal screw. The first-time user is cautioned to use care when removing them; they break off easily if twisted as though they were

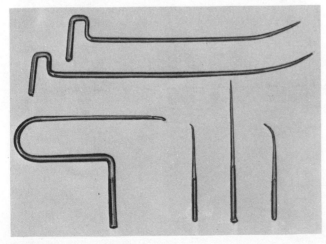

3-20 Set of pry tools.

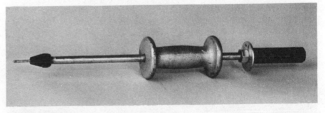

3-22 Screw-equipped slide hammer, commonly called a dent puller.

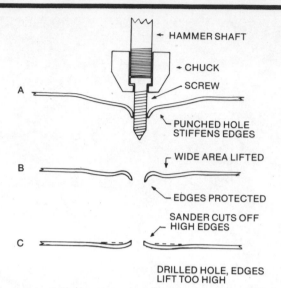

- HAMMER SHAFT
- CHUCK
- SCREW

A

- PUNCHED HOLE
  STIFFENS EDGES

- WIDE AREA LIFTED

B

- EDGES PROTECTED

- SANDER CUTS OFF
  HIGH EDGES

C

DRILLED HOLE, EDGES
LIFT TOO HIGH

3-23 Advantage of piercing instead of drilling holes for dent puller. A, punched hole is stiffened and provides extra screw contact. B, punched hole lifts wide area and edges are protected from sander. C, edges of drilled hole are lifted too high and will be ground off, enlarging hole and thinning metal.

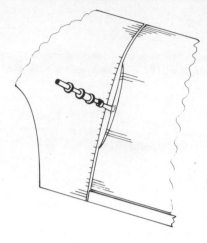

3-25 Slide hammer with wide hook used to straighten forward edge of front door.

screwed on, but will break a hole in the panel if simply bent back and forth. The procedure for welding these tabs on is explained in more detail in the resistance spot welding section of Chapter 5.

A slide hammer equipped with a wide, relatively thin hook used to straighten the forward edge of a front door is shown in Figure 3-25. These edges can be driven out with a hammer and some type of driving tool by working from the inside, but the repairman cannot see the result. With the slide hammer on the outside, it is easy to align the door edge with the fender.

SPOT WELD CUTTERS

A spot weld cutter kit is shown in Figure 3-26, and Figure 3-27 shows a cutter in use. The various-sized cutters thread onto the end of the mandrel. The sharp-pointed retractable pin extends through the center of

the cutter and acts as a guide. A center-punch mark in the center of the weld should be made to keep the point in place.

In use, the cutter is chucked in an electric drill and pressed against the weld, cutting a circular hole through the upper of the two pieces welded together. The depth of cut can be adjusted by a stop screw in the mandrel, which requires adjustment only when changing from one thickness of metal to another.

The cutter leaves the cut-out piece of the weld still attached to the underpanel. This may be ground off, using a disc sander, or, if the parts are to be rejoined, the slot can be brazed.

WELD-ON PULL TABS

The weld-on pull tabs in Figure 3-24 are a specialty item used only with an electric resistance spot welder and are discussed more in that section of the welding chapter. They are preferable to a metal screw-type panel puller, because it is not necessary to pierce the panel.

3-24 Slide hammer with hook used with weld-on pull tab.

3-26 Spot weld cutter kit.

3-27 Spot weld cutter in use.

They provide a means of straightening many damaged areas enough so that the metal can be finished satisfactorily with plastic filler without removing trim or piercing inner construction to make access to the inner surface.

These tabs can be broken off the surface and re-used, but may require repointing after two or three uses, because the point gets wider with each use. Removal procedure is explained in Chapter 5 on welding.

BASIC STRAIGHTENING OPERATIONS

This section explains and describes the uses of the straightening tools just discussed. The operations are referred to as basic, because they are essentially the same, regardless of the job. For example, the motions of using a hammer and dolly block are very much the same on any panel; the difference in procedure for panels having different damages is in the knowledge and judgment exercised in deciding where and how much to apply the basic operation.

It is suggested that the study of this section extend beyond reading it over once. It is easy for the beginner to fall into the trap of thinking that all he needs to develop manual dexterity is practice. Manual dexterity with his tools is an absolute must, but it is only a part of skill. The other, more critical, part is the knowledge and understanding with which he guides his hands.

Any discussion of the use of the hammer and dolly block should start by pointing out that they should not be abused. The working faces, particularly the hammer, should never strike *anything but sheet metal*. The hammer's working faces should be kept clean and polished with fine sandpaper so that it can be used on a painted surface without leaving marks to mar the reflective surface. Striking a punch or chisel with the hammer will damage it so that it will chop up the paint surface enough to make visual inspection almost impossible. Use another hammer for rough work.

A chopped-up working face on a dolly block may not be quite as bad as the same condition on the hammer, but it is definitely not desirable. Any marks on its surface will be imprinted on the underside of the metal when it is struck a hard on-dolly hammer blow. Many beginning students form a bad habit of tapping their hammer against the dolly block while studying the job. This is an unconscious action, but it should be watched for and avoided because of the damage it can do to both the hammer and the dolly block.

USE OF THE HAMMER AND DOLLY BLOCK

The bumping hammer and dolly block are discussed first, because they are the most important and versatile of the repairman's tools for straightening metal. They are also the easiest to misuse, because the difference between proper and improper use is often very slight. Misuse will cause additional damage. Also, many times it is possible to restore the surface appearance by either picking and filing or building a new surface with filler, even though the proper use of the hammer and dolly would do the same job better in less time. The fact that such work can be done "somehow" often leads the beginner to continue with less than the best methods. It is quite possible for the repairman to have good hammers and dolly blocks in his possession for many years without discovering their full usefulness.

The dolly block is used both with and without the hammer. Alone, it is an excellent tool for striking the inner surface to rough out simple dents or to complete the roughing out of areas being jacked into place. With the hammer, the combination becomes a highly efficient means of smoothing the roughed-out surface.

The dolly, when used with hammer, may be held directly under the spot struck by the hammer face, or it may be held to one side. These procedures are referred to as *hammer-on-dolly* and *hammer-off-dolly*. The dolly position should change as needed between hammer blows.

HAMMER-ON-DOLLY

The first step in learning to use the hammer-on-dolly is to develop the skill necessary to place the dolly under the metal and strike a hammer blow directly on it. This often seems to be an impossible task to the beginner but is actually an easy one to master, if practiced. It is easier for some persons than for others because it is essentially a matter of coordination between the hand and the eye. Even though the hand holding the dolly is out of sight under the panel, the student soon learns to bring any spot on the working face of the dolly into contact with the spot he intends to strike with the hammer. It becomes a reflex action to shift the dolly to the spot on which the eye is focused. Striking the same spot with the hammer should be simple, but the hammer must be held and swung properly.

The proper hammer grip is shown in Figure 3-28. The handle should be held lightly and the grip slackened as the blow descends on the metal. This is easy to do by forming the habit of gripping the handle with only the third and fourth fingers. The thumb aids in starting the blow, and the first two fingers are used to snap the handle back after the blow is finished. The blow starts with a snap action of the wrist rather than a full arm movement. The snap action will be easier if the handle is held at a slight angle to the forearm.

The hammer blow should strike the metal in the center of the broad face, and the contact should be exactly on the spot where the eye was focused in placing the dolly. If the hammer head is allowed to tip in any direction even slightly, the contact will be at the rim of the face rather than the center. Tipping the hammer will cause the blow to miss the intended contact spot by as much as half the width of the hammer face. The result is additional damage, because the edge of the hammer face makes a *chop mark* that must be repaired. An example of both proper and improper hammer-on-dolly

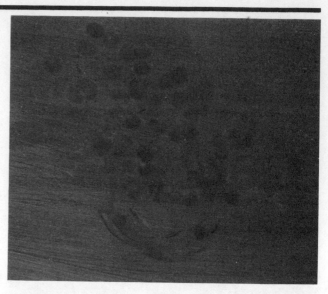

3-29 Proper hammer contact, rounded, smooth spots. Improper, half-moon shaped chop marks at lower edge.

work is shown in Figure 3-29. The surface of the paint was sanded lightly before this work was done so that the hammer contact spots would show clearly. It should be obvious that the round or oblong spots were made by a hammer striking the surface properly and the "half moon" chop marks were made by the edge of the hammer face. The first skill to develop is to place the dolly and aim the hammer so that a smooth contact is made with every blow.

The second skill required is to learn to gauge the force of the hammer blow and the pressure applied to the dolly so that they have the effect needed on that *particular* spot. It may be only a slight smoothing of a small rough spot, using very light hammer blows, or it may be actual stretching and raising, as illustrated in Figure 3-30. Stretching, as the term is used by repairmen, means hitting the dolly hard enough to thin it. Several spots scattered over an area will cause it to rise in a crown because its area has been increased. True stretching would be done by pulling lengthwise, but the effect is similar, so metal is called stretched when it has been crowned by hammering on-dolly.

3-28 Proper grip on hammer and dolly block.

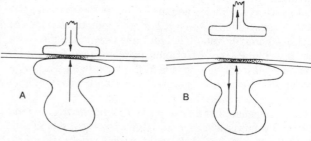

3-30 Action of a hammer-on-dolly blow. A represents the instant of impact. B represents a fraction of a second later when the hammer is moving away and the dolly has rebounded, lifting and stretching the metal.

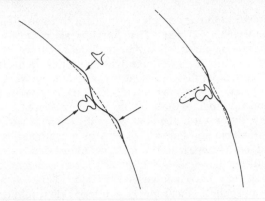

3-31 *(Left)* Using the hammer-off-dolly. The dolly should be held firmly against the low spot before the hammer blow falls.

3-32 *(Right)* The dolly rebounds after the hammer blow, increasing the lifting effect according to the hand pressure applied.

The force of a hammer blow on-dolly can be varied from less than enough to exceed the yield point of the metal to more, sometimes much more, than the yield point. Skill is required to sense just what each blow does to the particular spot struck. For example, a hammer-on-dolly blow on a small rough area, as illustrated in Figure 3-29, should be just short of the yield point if the intention is only to bring the low spot up and the high spot down without stretching. Hammer blows hard enough to cause actual stretching would be used to bring a larger but only slightly low spot up to the level of the adjoining metal. The procedure would be to cover the area with hammer-on-dolly blows in a regular pattern, striking hardest in the deepest area and reducing the force where the low spot blended into the adjoining surface. The harder the blow, the greater the hand pressure that should be applied to the dolly; the extra hand pressure would increase the secondary, lifting effect, as shown in Figure 3-30.

Any repairman skilled in use of the hammer and dolly block will develop the ability to gauge his hammer blows, sometimes without being conscious of it. The beginner who is aware that he should develop the ability and makes the required effort will develop it much more rapidly than if he just waits for it to come. It is partly a matter of feel, transmitted through the hammer handle, and partly sound. If the force does not exceed the yield point of the metal, the hammer blow is deflected almost instantly, with a sharp clear sound. However, any force that exceeds the yield point, causing the metal to stretch, is absorbed in the metal; the deflection of the hammer will be slightly delayed and deadened to some degree. At the same time, the sound will be slightly dulled. These differences would be unnoticeable to an uninformed bystander but very real to the repairman who has trained himself to detect them.

Skill in sensing the effect of the hammer blow and hand pressure on the dolly is important in any straightening operation, but it is critically important in working soft metal, such as aluminum, or mild steel that has been temporarily softened by heating so that it can be shrunk or otherwise worked. This is not as major a problem as it may seem, however, because it is much easier to feel the yield of the softer metal. The thinner but harder steels should present no more problem to the skilled worker than mild steel, because the greater hardness also raises the yield point so they will withstand more abuse.

HAMMER-OFF-DOLLY

Use of a hammer-off-dolly is to lower a high spot and raise a low spot with the force of a single hammer blow. It works because the elasticity of the metal permits an area of metal surrounding a hammer blow to flex inward. The dolly block resists this flexing action if it is in contact with any low spot within the affected area and, when manipulated correctly, returns considerable force to drive the low spot upward. The force returned is provided by reflex muscular action of the hand pressing the dolly against the metal. In effect, the hammer blow triggers a reflex blow by the dolly. These actions are illustrated in Figures 3-31 and 3-32. Note that the hammer is not shown in Figure 3-32 because it would have bounced away by the time the dolly could rebound.

Beginners often think learning to use the hammer-off-dolly is a difficult task because of the need to find and focus attention on two separate spots at one time, but it is really a rather simple problem that can be solved by practice. A person learning to drive an automobile often has a similar problem. At first there is doubt about how far to turn the steering wheel, but the problem disappears with practice.

It is important for the beginner to learn to sense the movement of the metal caused by the force of the hammer blow and rebound of the dolly. The metal moves more freely than when working on-dolly, because it does not have solid support, and the sound is duller. The movement is easier to feel through the hammer because of the greater travel.

The pressure exerted on the dolly is more important than it is when working on-dolly. Not being directly under the hammer, the dolly receives less impulse from the hammer blow. The beginner should learn to relax his hand pressure slightly at the instant of hammer contact, to permit slight travel of the dolly, then snap it back with added force. In this way the hammer will trigger a much stronger reflex action than it would otherwise.

The distance between the spots worked by the hammer and dolly affects the result. If the dolly is too far from the hammer, it does not receive enough impulse to trigger the reflex action needed to make it effective. No positive rule can be given on the maximum effective distance, because it will vary with different metals or even the same metal in different shapes. However, the most effective work will be done when the hammer and dolly are not more than 1 inch (25.4 mm) apart, and better results will be obtained when they are closer. When using a wide-faced hammer, this would bring the dolly

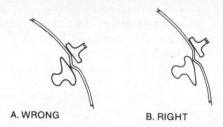

A. WRONG   **B. RIGHT**

3-33 Wrong and right dolly placement for close-in hammer-off-dolly blow. A is wrong, because dolly will interfere with hammer. B is right, because metal can flex around high crown of dolly.

contact under the outer rim of the hammer face. Whether or not they actually meet in on-dolly contact depends on the force of the hammer blow and the crown of the dolly in contact with the metal. The hammer blow can be gauged so that either it does not have enough force to make actual contact with the dolly, or if it does, it does not strike hard enough to exceed the yield point.

The two illustrations in Figure 3-33 show the incorrect and correct placement of the dolly crown for a close-in hammer-on-dolly blow. The position at A is definitely wrong because the dolly contact is shown in the center area of the working face. The crown is low at this point, and the lip of the dolly is in position to interfere with the hammer. B is correct. The crown of most general-purpose dollies is higher at this point—or at least it should be—and the dolly has been reversed so that there will be minimum interference with the hammer travel. These figures do not show the cross crown of the working face, but any good general-purpose dolly should have enough cross crown to limit the contact to a very small area. It was pointed out in the section on dolly blocks earlier in this chapter that a dolly having only one curve on the working face has limited use; it would be useless here.

A small dent in a combination high and low crown area is shown in Figure 3-34 and, after straightening by the hammer-off-dolly, in Figure 3-35. The only force

applied to the underside of this dent to raise it back to the proper level was a firm hand pressure on the dolly and the rebound action that resulted.

The procedure for straightening this dent is explained in detail, because it is the key to understanding the proper use of the hammer-off-dolly. It is particularly important to note that no hammer blows were struck on the right or left of the dent; all of the hammer work was done above and below it. As it was a combination high and low crown, metal was raised above and below the dent, but the sides were drawn down. Hammer blows would only drive it down further. Instead of accomplishing a repair, hammer blows on either side would tend to add damage to that already existing. A fraction of a second after the hammer blow, reflex action caused the dolly to rebound and strike the underside with considerable force, lifting it toward the proper level.

When this hammer-off-dolly procedure is understood properly, there should be no misunderstanding of the following rule: When using a hammer-off-dolly, a *hammer blow should never be struck except on metal that has been raised above the proper level.* This rule applies in every case. It is even more important to remember in straightening a severe rolled buckle than on this simple dent.

Following this same reasoning, the importance of this second rule should be understood: *The first hammer blows should fall on the high metal farthest from the dent, and following blows should work inward progressively.* On the minor dent shown in Figure 3-34, this is simply a matter of closing in from the raised crown areas above and below. When this procedure is used on a long rolled buckle, there will usually be some high metal to be worked in the low crown section, because the overall distortion is much greater.

BUMPING SPOONS

The skill required to use a bumping spoon with a hammer is relatively easy to acquire, compared to that

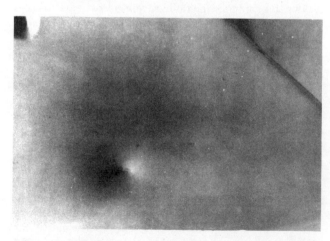

3-34 A small dent in a combination high and low crown section of a fender.

3-35 The dent in Fig. 3-33 after straightening by hammer-off-dolly blows.

needed to use the hammer and dolly block. The primary difference is that the spoon works as a part of the hammer blow instead of providing a secondary reaction to it, as the dolly block does.

The purpose of the bumping spoon is to spread the force of the hammer blow over a much larger area than the bumping hammer face can cover. It is best suited to straightening long, relatively smooth buckles, in which the distortion is comparatively light but is spread over a large area. Straightening could be done by using the hammer alone, but many light blows would have to be spread over the area, and it would be difficult to avoid making damaging hammer marks. The larger contact area of the working face of the spoon is much easier to control, so that such damage is kept to the minimum or avoided entirely. Also, this method is faster on jobs to which it is suited.

The shape, or crown, of the working face of the bumping spoon determines the exact use to which it is best adapted. A flat or nearly flat face is best for high-crowned or combination high- and low-crowned areas. Such areas are quite stiff and require considerable force to relieve the distortion that causes the buckle.

A spoon with a higher-crowned working face is best suited to buckles in low-crowned panels. The metal on each side of such a buckle will be springy instead of stiff, as on the high-crowned panel. The springiness reduces the support that the area provides for the buckle. The high-crowned spoon contacts only a small area, concentrating the force of the hammer blow on it; thus, it actually will straighten such an area better than a flat-faced spoon. The larger contact area of the flat spoon will tend only to spring the entire buckle.

The procedure for using either spoon is essentially the same. Figure 3-36 shows a bumping spoon in position. Note that the center area of the working face is in contact with the metal surface and that the hammer is directly over this spot. Note also that a ball-peen hammer is used instead of the bumping hammer; a good

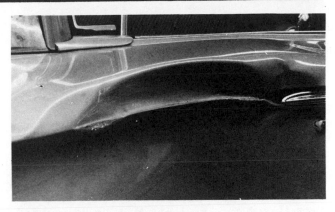

3-37 Ridge which is too sharp for use of the bumping spoon.

bumping hammer never should be used for such a purpose.

The handle of the spoon should be gripped lightly so that the hand does not tend to resist movement. Even though the spoon is being used on metal that is quite stiff, there will be some tendency for the entire area to flex with the hammer blow. The spoon must be free for this movement. If the hand resists downward movement of the handle (Figure 3-36), there will be a tendency to drive the opposite end of the working face down too far. This may cause damaging marks, particularly when using a spoon that has a flat working face.

Most of the damaged areas where a bumping spoon is the proper tool to use are too wide to be corrected with a single hammer blow. It will be necessary to strike a series of hammer blows as the spoon is moved back and forth across the buckle. On long buckles, work progressively down the length in a somewhat zigzag pattern.

In using a spoon on any buckle, start at the point of least distortion. On most buckles that remain after a rolled buckle has been worked out, this point would be as far from the break-over path as distortion could be detected.

The bumping spoon is most effective when used on a buckle under a strain that tends to straighten it. Such conditions will be found occasionally in minor damage on relatively flat panels. The experienced repairman learns to recognize the damaged panel that will snap back to shape after a buckle has been spooned down, leaving only minor damage actually to work out. However, such conditions are the exception rather than the rule. In most cases, the spoon should not be used until most of the unfolding has been completed by other means. Spooning out remaining buckles is very often the final straightening operation.

A very common mistake of the beginner is to use a bumping spoon on a buckle that is too sharp. Metal that has been folded over so that the buckle forms a sharp ridge, as in Figure 3-37, should not be spooned down, because it is too rigid. Striking the top of such a ridge may cause upsetting. After such a ridge has been partly straightened by the proper methods, described in later sections, the spoon would be a very logical means of finishing the straightening operation.

3-36 Bumping spoon in position for the hammer blow.

BODY SPOONS

Skill in the use of body spoons is entirely different from the skill required to use a bumping spoon and in most cases is more complicated. This is because the body spoon is used on the underside of the panel as either a substitute for the dolly block or as a pry tool.

The body spoon is never used for repairing any panel in which a dolly block has free access to the inner surface. Such a panel can be straightened better and faster with the dolly block. The use of the body spoon is made necessary by the inner construction found on many panels, which limits access so that only a relatively long, thin tool may be used. Without such a tool, the repairman would be forced either to cut out the inner construction or to depend entirely on filling to repair damage on such panels. With a good set of body spoons, he can repair many panels faster and with a minimum amount of filling or mutilation caused by cutting out and welding back inner construction.

Exact instructions for the use of the body spoons cannot be given, because the spoons are available in many shapes for use in many different areas and damage conditions. The discussion of procedure must be limited to general suggestions. This is less a handicap than it may seem, however, for the suggestions offered are simply variations of the basic procedure for using the dolly block. It is recommended that the beginner delay his practice with body spoons until he has had enough practice with the dolly block to develop some degree of skill. This should include some actual repair work on simple damage. At that time, the beginner's use of the body spoon will present far fewer problems than if he tries to use it before he develops the basic skill.

The body spoon may be used alone to pry out low metal or with the hammer. Used alone, it serves exactly the same purpose as the dolly block when the latter is used as a striking tool. Usually the main problems are to find a suitable fulcrum to pry against and to avoid making pry marks in the surface.

Used with the bumping hammer, the body spoon serves the same purpose as the dolly block. The difference is that the body spoon is more difficult to use and is less effective. This is because the working face of the spoon extends several inches from the hand; the sense of feel, which helps in locating the dolly block, is almost totally absent. The result is a tendency of the body spoon to wander after each hammer blow against it. This effect is greater from a hard hammer blow than from a light one. Thus an effective limit is placed on the force of the hammer blow, which in turn places a similar limit on the force of the rebound action of the spoon.

A second factor affecting the effectiveness of the spoon as a substitute for a dolly block is balance. This varies with the shape of the spoon, as was shown in Figure 3-10. A spoon having the working face at or close to a right angle to the handle may be in almost perfect balance, so that the only problem is the sense of feel. But a spoon having the working face parallel with the handle will have practically no balance at all. The rebound action obtainable with such a spoon is limited

for two reasons: (1), the operator's grip is at a mechanical disadvantage; and (2), very little of the weight of the spoon is under the working face to provide resistance to the hammer blow.

As with the dolly block, the choice of a body spoon is governed by the conditions of the panel to be repaired. Only to a limited extent can it be determined by personal preference. In many areas of the body, a well-balanced spoon would be useless, because its shape would prevent it from fitting into place. If work is to be done in such places, tools to do the job are needed. If it happens that a well-balanced tool can be used, fine; if it happens that an unbalanced spoon is all that can be used, it will be the best tool for the job.

BASIC REPAIR METHODS

It was pointed out previously that the repairman must examine the job to determine his procedure. In Chapters 7 and 8, which deal with much greater damage, this examination had been done by separate discussions on the inspection of the damage and planning the repair procedure. Coverage of this damage is not carried to that length, because it was selected to fit a predetermined procedure.

Careful attention should be given to the details of this damage, as it is essential for the student to learn to examine every one closely. Slight variations from one damage to another may make considerable differences in the procedure to be followed. The ability to recognize such differences and to know how they govern repair procedure may be regarded as an inspection and analysis that enable the repairman to read procedure for doing the job. The beginner may require considerable study to recognize simple features about a job that later will be recognized at a glance.

Whether the inspection of the job is done by a beginner or an experienced worker, it is a matter of looking for the fold lines, displaced sections, and distortions caused by the impact and determining the order in which they occurred. From this information and the knowledge of what may be accomplished with the basic

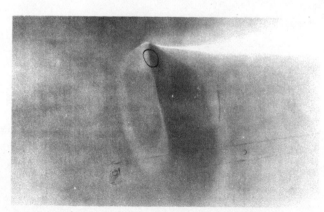

3-38 Rolled buckle dent in the side of a fender.

repair operations, it is a simple procedure to apply force to the damage so that these conditions are relieved.

A quick examination of the dent in Figure 3-38 reveals the following conditions:

1. It has been caused by a relatively light force.

2. It probably has been caused by a direct impact, but it could have been the result of force traveling through the length of the panel from a direct impact on the one end.

3. It is a minor but true example of a rolled buckle. A sharp ridge has formed, pushing a high spot into the high crown of it, but it has not rolled far enough to cause a break-over path of severely upset metal.

4. There has been little or no tension lengthwise of the panel.

This straightening operation is fairly simple—but it falls into two basic steps (called *phases* here and in the text following), just as all other straightening operations do. They are: (1) roughing out, or roughing, and (2) bumping.

The *roughing phase*, in this case accomplished by a few blows of the dolly block, takes very little time, but it is the most critical of the entire operation. When it is done properly, it will be a simple matter to get the high spot at the break-over point down to level. When done improperly, this high spot can be very difficult to remove, even though considerable extra effort is made in the bumping and metal-finishing operations, and it is quite probable that a high spot will show in the finished job.

The starting point of the roughing operation is marked by the black circle just below the break-over point (Figure 3-38). The first blow will be struck on the underside of the circled area; the following blows will be progressively lower.

This procedure is shown in much greater detail in Figure 3-39 in successive stages: (A) before starting, (B) after the first operation with the dolly, (C) almost roughed out, and (D) the completed job. The dotted line represents the original, and the solid line represents the damaged contour.

In A the dolly block, labeled 1, is shown in position to strike the first rough-out blow. Note that it is turned so

that the highest-crowned area of the working face will come into contact with the metal. This is necessary at this point because the blow will strike on the inside of the high-crowned surface. Three or four light blows were struck with the dolly before the action shown in B was started.

B shows the hammer, labeled 2, being used on the high break-over point. Use of the hammer is a follow-up operation. Driving the low metal out with the dolly block has pulled some of the high metal down. It also has left the area under a state of tension. The high spot will drop under the hammer blows until the tension is relieved. It is then time to drive out the surface more, as indicated by the dolly block, labeled 3, in B.

This action should be repeated several times to bring it to the condition shown in C. Each time the dolly is used on the underside, it tends to pull the high spot down. The hammer being used on the outside works with this tendency by driving the high spot down farther and preventing too much tension from building up in the area. If too much tension is built up, it will stretch the metal between the high point and the spot where the dolly block strikes. If this occurs, it will be very difficult to drive the high spot down to the contour shown in D.

Note that in both Figure 3-38 and A in Figure 3-39, the metal in the bottom of the deepest part of the dent is serving as a very rigid brace, or prop, under the highest point. This bracing effect always will be found in any rolled buckle. Instead of unrolling the buckle, hammer blows on the high spot would have caused severe upsetting similar to exaggerated example shown in Figure 2-7. The result would have been a surface very difficult to reshape properly.

It should be recognized that this work was started close to the farthest point that the rolled buckle reached in the high crown and moved progressively into the lower crown area. The result of this first series of steps is shown in Figure 3-40, a close-up view of the area circled in Figure 3-38 and a portion of the sharply buckled area below it; a crayon line has been drawn around the

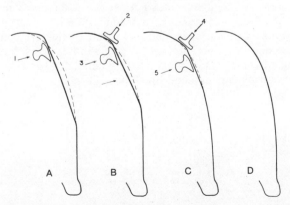

3-39 Four cross-sectional illustrations show the progressive steps in roughing out a simple dent.

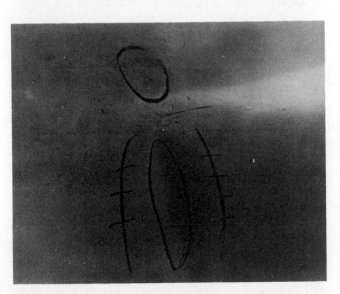

3-40 Close-up view of partly roughed-out surface.

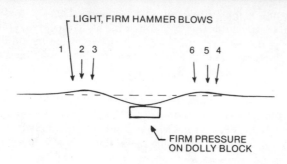

3-41 Cross section showing the pattern of off-dolly hammer blows used to straighten the remaining buckle in Fig. 3-40.

remaining sharp buckle in the center and two lines with cross marks drawn on the high ridge on each side. Note that the area within the original circle is quite smooth and unmarred, and the crayon line is still clear. This is the result of spending a few seconds polishing the bumping hammer with fine sandpaper.

It should be noted that the lower part of the valley tapers off into a displaced section. If a buckle had formed there, it would have been dealt with in the same manner before proceeding farther. The dashed line indicating original contour is shown higher on B than on A because the few dolly blows have relieved some of the displacement.

The continued action is shown in C. At this point the metal surface is in the condition shown in Figure 3-41. As much as possible of the displaced metal has been released; the remaining area must be worked out with the hammer and dolly block.

The marks on the panel in Figure 3-40, indicating areas of opposed strains, were put on before the photograph was taken. The long curved lines on each side are on surfaces that would spring back down if they were free. The sides of the surface within the long loop would close up and become slightly deeper if it was free for movement. These strains should be relieved by hammer-off-dolly work before driving the valley up farther.

The hammer-off-dolly operation is illustrated in Figure 3-41. Starting at the upper end, the dolly was held firmly against the valley while the hammer was used on each side, as indicated by the arrows. Note that the arrows are at slightly different angles so that the hammer face can follow the slight curvature of the surface. The hammer blows should be light but firm, meaning that the grip on the handle should not be released until the hammer contacts the surface.

The marked area was worked progressively from the upper to the lower end, keeping the hammer and dolly in the same relative positions. The valley was then driven up again, using the dolly as shown in Figure 3-39, and the off-dolly operation repeated.

These operations left the surface reasonable smooth, but some traces of the original ridge remained with low metal immediately below. The hammer and dolly were used spearately to drive the low surface up and the high surface down to restore the final overall contour. Some of the buckled area was worked with on-dolly hammer

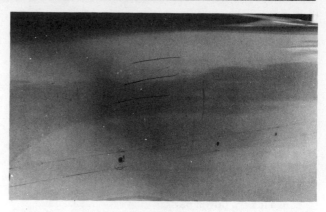

3-42 The straightened buckle, ready for metal finishing.

blows, using the flattest part of the working face of the dolly. The straightened surface, ready for metal finishing, is shown in Figure 3-42. The crayon marks were made before the photograph was taken to indicate the smoothness of the area. Similar marks on a rough area would appear wavy in a photograph.

METAL-FINISHING

Metal-finishing, as the term is used in automobile sheet metal repair, should not be confused with painting. Instead, it is the work of restoring final surface smoothness to damaged panels after straightening has been carried as far as practical. The primary need for metal-finishing is based on the fact that perfect straightening would require more time and a higher degree of skill than the value of most panels would justify.

The widespread use of plastic filler has led many persons in the body repair field to question the need for a beginner to learn metal-finishing. It is true that there are many workers in the field who have never tried to learn, but that does not prove them to be better mechanics for the lack; it does prove, however, that they are unable to complete even the most simple job without filler.

It is recommended that any beginner learn to finish metal, even though he may not use the skill extensively. Without it, he is starting his trade with a handicap.

Subjects discussed in the rest of this section are body files and their use, the disc sander, sanding discs, feeling for rough or low spots with the hand, and the beginner's problems in metal-finishing.

3-43 A 14-inch (approx. 35 cm) body file mounted on a wooden holder.

THE BODY FILE

A typical body file mounted on a wooden holder is shown in Figure 3-43. Practically all files of this type are 14 inches (35 cm) long, have teeth on both sides, and have holes in each end so that they may be bolted to some kind of holder. Both wood and steel holders may be used; it is a matter of which the user prefers. Wood has the advantage of causing less dulling of the teeth on the unused side, which is held in contact with the holder. Some kind of padding material to serve the same purpose is desirable with a steel holder.

Body files, for use on soft metals only, were intended originally for use on mily body sheet metal, aluminum, and body solder when it was in prevalent use. They can be used on most body fillers, but they dull rapidly when so used, because of the abrasive nature of the material.

Special-purpose body files are used, also. The most common of these is the half round (frequently called a shell file), which is used in reverse crowns. Specially bent files and shorter ones have been available, but are rarely seen since the use of body fillers has become widespread. None of the special files present any special problems in learning to use them.

Using the Body File

The beginner is cautioned that his body file should be used for *proof filing* as much as or more than for actual metal removal. An example of proof filing is shown in Figure 3-44, in which all of the lighter areas crisscrossed by file marks are at the proper level. The dark areas between the two large light areas are below proper level so that the file teeth bridged across them. Very slight raising of the low spots and refiling should restore the surface; proof filing has made a very accurate layout of the further straightening to be done.

The key in proper proof filing is in learning to stroke the file properly. If the file had been passed across the surface wood plane fashion, each stroke would have cut a single narrow line. As it is here, every low spot has been outlined clearly with a few file strokes, and very little metal has been cut away.

The technique in proper proof filing is easy to learn, and the beginner should not be permitted, or permit

himself, to file in any other manner. The proper file stroke is determined partly by direction on the panel and partly by the shifts made during the stroke.

The direction of the stroke is important because of the differences in lengthwise and crosswise crowns found in almost all panels. The file should lie on the panel so that it has the maximum bridging effect over low spots. If there is any difference in crown, it is obvious that the one nearest to flat will hold the teeth out of the low spots better than the higher one will. This is the reason for the following rule: *The file should be stroked in the general direction of the flattest crown of the panel.*

Cutting a wide area with a single stroke requires two simultaneous shifts of the file. As it moves forward, it should shift either right or left to widen the cut. At the same time, the cutting action should shift from the front end of the file to the rear. These two shifts are illustrated in Figure 3-45, A showing a shift to the left, and B showing a shift to the right to obtain a criss-cross effect. It is not necesary to criss-cross each stroke. In general, an area should be filed one way and then a few strokes made to check surface level.

Note that in both sets the cutting area is outlined at the front of the file at the start of the stroke, and an arrow within the outline points toward the rear. This outline is shown as having moved to the rear at the end of the stroke. Making this shift requires a slight crown in the panel or in the file. Filing in one direction, a combination crown that is dead flat requires a slightly crowned file if the work is to progress rapidly; the crown will permit the blade to rock slightly during the stroke to make the shift.

The beginner may find making the two shifts difficult at the beginning, but it becomes easy with practice. Once the skill is acquired, he will find it *easier* to metal-finish many small jobs than to take time to fill and finish them with plastic.

Any discussion of metal-finishing should include the

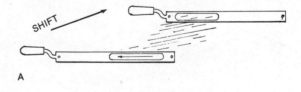

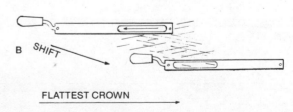

FLATTEST CROWN

3-45 Left shift of body file at A and right shift at B. Cutting area, outlined on file, should shift from front to rear on each stroke.

3-44 An example of proof filing to show up low spots.

problems with aluminum and thinner, but harder steels. Both present problems different from those of mild steel, which has always been the standard material of automobile bodies. Aluminum can be metal-finished with no difficulty other than extra care because of its softness. It is not practical to attempt to finish steel that is above a certain hardness, because the file and disc sander will not bite into it enough to make the effort worthwhile. Although metal that hard is not in use on any current body panels, it is reasonable to assume that it will come into use as the pressure for more fuel-efficient automobiles increases. Metal-finishing on such panels will, by necessity, be limited to covering the rough areas with filler.

Picking

Lifting the low spots shown up by filing is commonly called *picking*. It can be done with any blunt-ended tool, such as a pick hammer, the end of the body file, or any type of pry tool in areas where the underside of the panel cannot be reached otherwise. The effect of picking is shown in exaggerated detail in Figure 3-46. A shows a wavy surface before filing. B shows the effect of passing a file across the surface, just cutting the tops of the high spots. In C, the point of a pick hammer is in position to drive the low spots up to proper level to be filed off. Note that these spots are shown slightly above the level of the adjoining filed surfaces; otherwise, the file could not cut them. D shows the surface after the filing has been completed.

Picking, whether done with a pick hammer, pry rod, or other tool, is a precision straightening operation of spots that have been located accurately by filing. The beginner must develop the skill necessary to find the underside of the spot he is looking at and pick it just enough that it will be smooth when filed off. Obviously, picking too much or too hard will cause serious damage when the surface is filed or cut with the disc sander.

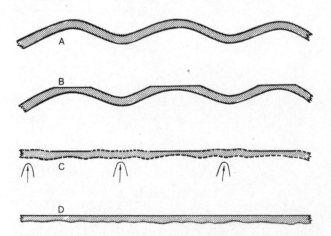

3-46 Cross section showing in exaggerated detail how filing and picking may be combined to produce a finished surface.

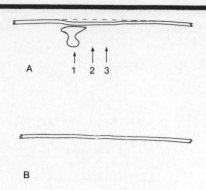

3-47 Dolly block used to raise large low areas instead of pick hammer.

These skills should be practiced on scrap panels before actual repairs are attempted.

The beginner has two problems in locating the underside of a low spot with the pick hammer, or other tool. One is that he is working "blind"; the other is that most people find it awkward to strike a hammer blow toward one's self. Neither problem is serious, but practice is required.

The first step is to position the eye so that light is reflected off the area to be picked; if necessary, rearrange the light. Next, bring the point of the tool (pick hammer or other) out into view and follow it with the eye as it is moved into position under the panel. When the desired spot is reached, or thought to be reached, touch the tool to the underside and hold the position momentarily before striking a light upward blow, and *hold the position*. If the light and eye position is right, the eye should catch the slight upward rise in the surface. The beginner may have to repeat this a few times to find where he *has hit*, but when he finds it, it is simple to move from there to the place he wants to hit. He must hold the position every time he hits, however; if the tool wanders away, it will be necessary to repeat the entire operation. It soon becomes as easy to hit the underside of a spot as it is to hit the side in plain view. The awkwardness of hitting toward one's self is soon forgotten.

The beginner should never work with a sharp-pointed pick hammer; the intention is to raise an area, but not to pierce the surface.

Lifting With the Dolly

A fairly large low area can be lifted with the dolly better than with the pick hammer, as shown in Figure 3-47. This is not practical on small low spots, but larger ones that can be reached with the dolly can be lifted faster and more smoothly than with the pick hammer or any other tool having a smaller contact surface.

The larger surface of the dolly crown raises a much larger area of metal without making a sharp pick mark. The surface can be filed more easily and faster with less mutilation. Note that Figure 3-47 shows the first blow being struck on the deepest point. The following blows should be placed over the area as needed.

THE BEGINNER'S PROBLEMS IN METAL-FINISHING

Almost all beginners at metal-finishing have the same problems, which must be solved before they can expect to make worthwhile progress. In every case the problems are caused by errors in procedure that are to be expected because of the lack of experience. To develop skill, the individual must be aware of the nature of these problems and be willing to be self-critical of his procedure to recognize and correct most of his errors; he cannot expect to correct them all, but he must correct the most glaring ones. Even the most skilled people are not error free. The most common errors made by the beginner metal-finisher are discussed separately in the following paragraphs.

Cutting too soon

The cutting operations, disc sanding and filing, must not be started until the surface has been made smooth enough that it will not be damaged. Either tool will remove very little metal when used on a relatively smooth surface, but will bite deeply into sharp ridges or high points that extend to any height above the surrounding surface. The sander is particularly bad in this respect, because of the speed of cutting. There is no way to set an exact standard of surface smoothness required before the cutting operations are started other than to advise the use of *common sense*. An uninformed casual observer should recognize when a panel surface is too rough to be ground or filed, and it is not unreasonable to expect the beginner to do as well.

Although an exact rule is not possible, a good practical rule is that the first cutting operation should contact at least one half of the total surface area being worked. But, this is a result; the surface must be judged before this operation is performed and the result anticipated before starting.

Picking too hard

After the low spots have been located, it is necessary to pick to raise them. They should be raised just enough to be smoothed off with the minimum cutting with either file or the sander. If the spot is larger than can be lifted with one pick mark, it should be picked several times over the area rather than given one or two harder pick blows. Cutting off excessively high pick marks will cause serious damage; the beginner often makes a good start and then ruins his surface by picking too hard.

Picking too much

Picking too much is, in most instances, the result of not having developed enough accuracy in picking to hit the intended spot quickly. It is important to do the least possible amount of fumbling around in finding the target area or spot. The first pick marks, made to find the target, should be very light so that they will not cause damage if they are off target. Furthermore, each pick mark stretches the surface slightly. Too many pick marks will cause a bulge above the proper surface level.

Filing too much

Each file stroke should increase the finished surface area slightly. When further file strokes do not reduce the unfinished area, it is time to stop filing and raise low spots.

Not following a pattern

When the area to be filed is larger than can be covered with normal file strokes, it is usually better first to proof file the entire area lightly, to detect major low areas, then concentrate the finishing effort on an area that can be covered with one file stroke. In general, this area should be on the highest crown, and the work should move progressively from high to low crown as the individual areas are completed. When working a large area of uniform low-crowned surface, it is desirable to work progressively around the edges so that the final finishing is done in the center area.

Not filing enough

When a low spot has been picked, all of the pick marks should be removed by filing before further picking is done. The beginner who finds the surface growing rougher rather than smoother can be sure that he is either not filing enough or picking too much, or both.

Not correcting bad picking

Any pick mark in an already finished area should be straightened, or put back down, before any filing or disc sanding is done. In high crown areas this can often be done with the small end of a combination hammer; in low crown areas it sometimes helps to make a *very light* on-dolly hammer blow against a flat dolly block surface. Simply cutting the high spot down causes unnecessary and often serious mutilation of the metal.

Locating High and Low Spots

The experienced repairman constantly checks the surface he is working on for high and low spots. The beginner who wants to become experienced should make every effort to develop this ability as quickly as possible. High skill is not involved; it is necessary only to learn two tricks: one is to know how to look at the reflections off of the panel surface, and the other is to learn how to feel high and low spots.

Reflections

Judging the surface by reflection works best when the paint is glossy, but the paint can be quite badly scratched or marred before it becomes unusable. The trick is to position the eye so that light from a spot source—window, ceiling light, or a portable lamp—is reflected from the area in question. By moving the eye back and forth, the spot of reflected light will move along the surface. If the surface is smooth, the movement of the reflection will be equally smooth; if the surface is rough, the reflection will dance around or break up. Even the slightest imperfection can be seen easily by anyone in this manner.

The surface condition can be judged by reflection in the metal-finishing operation even though the paint has been entirely removed. This is discussed in more detail in the section on metal-finishing.

Feel

Fine surface irregularities cannot be determined as accurately by feel as they can be reflection, but such determination is an important skill that the beginner should develop. The hand should be laid flat on the panel so that it contacts the surface lightly from the heel of the palm to the fingertips, and the fingers should be spread slightly. Feeling is done by drawing the hand backwards so that the fingertips trail. The trailing fingertips will feel the rise and fall as they pass over the various high and low spots. The same irregularities can be felt on the forward stroke, but most persons find the sensation is sharper on the back stroke.

There should be little difference in the ability to feel with either hand, but most right-handed persons sue their left hand more than their right for this purpose. It is a matter of personal preference.

Straightedge

The beginner is advised to use a straightedge at the start, but should not become dependent on it. As he learns to look at and feel the surface, he will find that its use will be a waste of time.

METAL-FINISHING ALUMINUM

Aluminum can be metal-finished in the same manner as steel, but much more care is required. As aluminum is softer, small high spots will be cut off by either the file or disc sander. Obviously, the surface must be made quite smooth before any cutting operation is started. A coarse-grit sanding disc used over a rough area to remove paint, as it would be on steel, could leave a similar area of aluminum with multiple perforations. If used at all, the grit should not be allowed to penetrate to the metal. On lacquer-painted panels, lacquer-removing solvent is much safer than sanding, but is hardly practical when large areas of paint must be removed.

Discs coarser then 80 grit should not be used on aluminum. Heavy-duty sanders, if used, must be operated very carefully to avoid grinding through or overheating. A high-speed polisher is preferable to a light-duty sander, because it runs at lower speed. With any sander or polisher, the surface should be watched carefully and quenched at the first sign of overheating; on flat surfaces it may be necessary to quench between passes.

The body file will load up quickly with aluminum, making it necessary to clean the teeth every few strokes. Filing should be done in exactly the same manner as on steel, but less pressure can be applied, because the surface will flex under the file more than will steel. Fortunately, a file too dull to cut steel easily will work well on aluminum.

The finished surface can be hand sanded or buffed; a rotary type, air-powered sander should be used, with reduced pressure to slow it down.

Plastic body filler can be used on aluminum in the same manner that it is used on steel, but more care is required in cleaning the paint off rough surfaces, and "cheese grater" planes should not be allowed to contact the metal surface. These planes will not scratch steel, but they will gouge aluminum. Other than these precautions, the procedure for finishing plastic filler on aluminum is exactly the same as on steel.

Obviously, the beginner should develop some skill on steel before attempting to finish an aluminum panel.

THE DISC SANDER

The portable disc sander commonly used in sheet metal repair is shown in Figure 3-48. It operates on the 110-volt, 30-ampere power used for lighting and other power tools. Sanders are available that operate on the higher-voltage power lines, but their use is restricted mostly to industrial operations larger than the average body shop. Air-powered sanders are used by some shops, particularly large ones. They are powerful and lighter in weight for the same capacity, as compared to the electric machine.

Care of the Disc Sander

Proper care is an important factor in the life of any disc sander. Rough handling must be avoided; do not drop the machine or pick an electric one up by the cord. When not in use, the machine should be laid down or hung up so that it does not rest on the edge of the pad, causing it to warp and vibrate in operation.

Overheating is probably the most common cause of

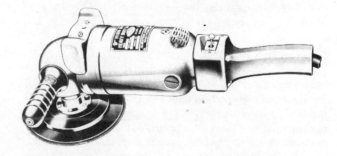

3-48 A 9-inch (approx. 23 cm) heavy-duty disc sander.

serious damage to an electric sander. Although it may be the result of too heavy use of a light-duty machine, it is most commonly the result of clogging the motor ventilating system. All portable electric power tools circulate air through the motor by means of a fan. The air passages in a sander tend to clog more than most electric tools because disc sanding is a dusty operation. Any electric sander should be cleaned periodically.

A sander should never be laid down while the pad is still turning. Serious injury can be caused if any part of the body comes into contact with the still turning pad. Furthermore, an electric sander will pick much more dust from the floor than it does in the operator's hands, because the air vents are close to the layer of grit and dust that the operation has just deposited there. This dust contains bits of metal and sanding grit, both electrical conductors that, if allowed to accumulate in the motor, will cause short-circuiting.

Sanding Discs

Sanding discs used in sheet metal repair work consist of a stiff fiber disc coated on one side with abrasive grit. The grit used almost universally is aluminum oxide.

Several manufacturers of abrasive discs offer their products to the automobile repair trade. These products vary somewhat in special features, but all manufacturers have standardized disc sizes and the method of identifying grit size by number.

Disc size refers to the diameter of the fiber disc. Two sizes are in common use: 7 inch, and 9⅛ inch. Discs of smaller diameter also are used for special purposes, but they usually are obtained by cutting a larger disc down to the size needed. This is much more practical than purchasing smaller sizes, because they can be cut from the unworn center area of the larger size. Smaller diameter discs are available, however, when they are needed in sufficiently large quantities to justify their purchase.

The sanding disc is held in place by means of a special, wide-flanged nut that passes through the center hole and threads either to the hub of the pad or the spindle. Most disc sanders require a ⅞-inch center hole, although some have been made which require a ½-inch hole. Discs are available having either size of center hole, or a special nut can be obtained that will center the larger-size center hole on the smaller spindle.

Grit size of the abrasive material used to coat sanding discs, and many other coated abrasives, is specified by number, such as 16, 24, 36, 50, and so on. This number refers to the size of screen this grit will pass through. Screen size is determined by the number of mesh per linear inch. Thus, a 16-grit would pass through a screen having 16 mesh per linear inch but not through the next smaller size, 24.

The coarsest grit, 16, is intended primarily for paint removal and coarse cutting. It is not recommended for metal-finishing panels because of the extremely coarse swirl marks left by the large grit. However, most paint can be removed by a 24-grit disc, and whenever possible it should be used. The 24 grit also can be used for

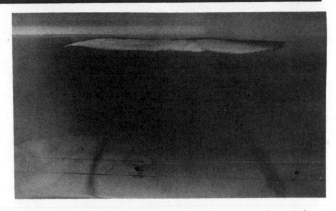

3-49 First stroke with the disc sander, moving from left to right. Swirl marks show up low spots because they follow the flattest crown of the panel.

metal-finishing, but the panel will be left in much better condition if it is finished with a 36 grit. Buffing can be done with a worn 36 grit, but it will be better if a 50 or 60 is used.

Finishing Metal With the Disc Sander

The disc sander has two basic uses in metal-finishing: the first is as a partial substitute for the body file, the second to buff the filed surface to remove deep scratches. Each requires a different stroke of the sander to produce the required results.

To use the sander as a substitute for filing, it is important that the disc be applied to the surface in such a way that it will leave a pattern of grit swirl marks that bridge across low spots. This can be done best by stroking the machine back and forth on the panel, following the direction which is nearest to flat, just as in filing. The pad should be pushed against the metal with enough pressure to cause it to flex, but not enough to cause the machine to slow down. As the disc moves back and forth across the surface, the spindle should be tilted away from the direction of travel just enough to throw the cutting action to the following edge. At the end of the stroke, a fraction of a second is required to stop and start the back stroke in the opposite direction. During this time, the spindle should be tilted to the opposite direction so that the cutting action will switch to the opposite edge, which will become the following edge. The swirl marks this will produce should be in a definite pattern, as explained below.

The swirl marks shown in Figure 3-49 were made by stroking the sander from the left to the right. In Figure 3-50, several back-and-forth strokes have been made. Note that the grit swirl marks show a definite crosscut action because of the tilt of the sander on each stroke. Also note that several dark spots show up. These are low spots that the disc has bridged over.

In Figure 3-51, the low spots have been picked up and resanded over the complete area. This surface is smooth enough to be buffed and painted without further work. However, if there had been considerable rough metal, it would have been desirable to file the sanded

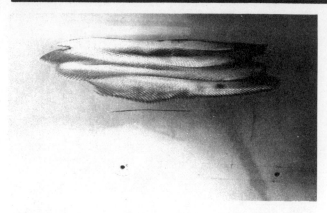

3-50 Appearance of several back-and-forth strokes criss-crossed over low area. Low metal shows up as dark spots.

3-51 Appearance of the sanded area after the low spots have been picked up and resanded. This surface should be buffed for the final finish.

area lightly and inspect for minor low areas before buffing.

The position for holding the sander conveniently so that it may be stroked back and forth easily is shown in Figure 3-52. Note that the body of the machine is at a right angle to the direction of travel, but it is not always possible to assume such a position when using the sander on various parts of the automobile. The beginner should start to gain his experience with the sander on a job that will permit him to assume an easy position. As he gains more skill, it will be easy to adapt to the various positions in which the sander must be held without upsetting the pattern of stroking.

Buffing With the Disc Sander

Buffing with the disc sander differs from the finishing operation in the direction of the stroke and the contact of the disc. The stroke should be at a right angle to the finishing stroke so that it follows the direction of great-

est crown instead of the flattest. The machine should be held so that the spindle is straight instead of tilted to one side. This position permits the maximum area of the pad to lie on the panel surface. Figure 3-53 shows the machine being held and stroked in the proper manner. Figure 3-54 shows the finished job.

Best results will be obtained if most of the work is done on the downstroke, relaxing the pressure on the machine as it is raised into position to make the next downstroke.

In many cases where a large area of metal has been sanded to remove the paint and partly to finish the surface before filing, it will save filing to buff the area also. The reason is that the finishing stroke tends to leave ridges between strokes. Buffing off the ridges is just a means of cutting metal with the power tool instead of doing the work by hand with the file.

Use of Star-Shaped Discs

It is difficult to use a round sanding disc in a sharp reverse crown, because the edge cuts a sharp groove in the surface. This can be avoided by cutting the edge of the disc into points, resulting in what is commonly

3-52 Proper position for easy stroking with the disc sander used in metal finishing.

3-53 Proper position for easy stroking with the disc sander when used for buffing. The direction of the stroke and the position of the machine are both at a right angle to the direction and position used in metal finishing.

3-54 Appearance of the buffed surface, ready for painting.

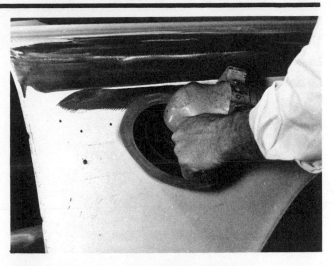

3-55 Disc sanding with a star-shaped disc.

called a star disc. The number of points can vary from six to eight or nine. The sharper the radius of the reverse crown, the more points the disc should have.

The action of the star disc is to break the smooth outer edge of the disc so that it does not form the groove. Instead, the outer edge advances and recedes as each point passes a particular spot on the panel surface. The result is a smooth, polished effect that can be repainted easily. Figure 3-55 shows the finished job and the position of the pad. Note that it is being pushed into the work so that the disc is flexed to fit the curve of the panel. This disc will tend to slap the panel if it is not held firmly against it.

The operator never should use a star-shaped disc without full protection for his eyes and face. This disc tends to throw more grit than the round one. Also, it is particularly dangerous to allow the star disc to turn against an edge, because the points can catch and tear off. A flying chunk of a sanding disc can blind an eye or cause a severe facial cut.

Safety Measures with the Disc Sander

The disc sander never should be used without proper eye protection. It throws off particles of grit and metal cuttings at tremendous speeds. The outer edge of a 9-inch (approximately 23 cm) disc driven by a high-speed sander will travel at speeds faster than 1½ miles per miles per minute. Grit thrown at such speeds will injure and can cause the loss of an eye, thus the need for adequate eye protection—either goggles or one of the many available types of transparent plastic face shields.

There is also serious risk of injury if any portion of the flesh comes into contact with the disc while it is in motion. The edge of a new disc will cut a deep gash in the flesh almost as rapidly as a power saw. Such cuts are slow to heal, because the action of the disc removes the flesh instead of making a clean cut. For this reason, the sander should be started or stopped only when it is in the proper working position. It is best to stop the motor before removing the sander from the job. Never under any circumstances lay the sander on the floor or hand it to another person while it is running.

Shrinking Metal

Shrinking sheet metal is simply a matter of making an upset where it is needed. The exact opposite of stretching, it may be required on any panel spot where it is necessary to reduce surface area to restore the proper contour. However, not all upsetting should be considered as shrinking. The shrinking is restricted by common usage in the body shop to mean only an operation in which heat is used to soften the metal to permit making the desired upset.

The shrinking operation is performed by heating a spot or an area, working it to shape with the hammer and dolly block, and cooling it. When this is done properly, gouges or raised areas will be brought back close enough to exact contour to be metal-finished. The operation seems simple and easy to someone observing a skilled repairman, but it can be quite difficult for a beginner, particularly if he has not mastered the fundamentals.

The wide use of plastic body fillers has caused many repairmen to avoid shrinking metal as much as possible and, when they do shrink, to do it to a much lower standard than described in the preceding paragraph. They limit the operation to bringing high spots down enough to fall below the level of the filler material and, if done conscientiously, to bring up low areas enough to avoid excessive depth of filler. This type of shrinking, referred to here as *partial* shrinking, is often done in a careless or slipshod manner because, once covered over, it is difficult to detect when the job is first completed. However, it often shows up later as cracks or lifting in areas where the filler has been applied too thickly.

It is recommended that the beginner make every effort to develop reasonable skill in *precision* shrinking. The skill required to restore a gouge or otherwise stretched area to the precise limits required for metal finishing will show up as better and faster technique in less exact straightening operations where shrinking is not involved.

In the following discussion, precision shrinking is intended, unless partial shrinking is stated. To master the shrinking operation easily, the beginner should learn the fundamentals first then develop skill through practice. The fundamentals consist of:

1. Recognition of the types of damage that require shrinking.
2. An understanding of the basic shrinking operation.
3. An understanding of how heat may be used to obtain the required softening and stiffening effect.
4. An understanding of how controlling the rate of cooling by quenching can add to or reduce the amount of shrinking obtained with the individual operation.

In addition, it is essential already to have developed sufficient skill with the hammer and dolly block to be able to use them with precision. The work is done on metal that has been softened by heating. A misdirected hammer blow that would be of no consequence on unheated metal can do serious damage on metal at high temperature.

TYPES OF DAMAGE THAT REQUIRE SHRINKING

Shrinking may be required on almost any area of the sheet metal of an automobile damaged in a collision. The appearance of such areas may vary as widely as their location. However, when shrinking is done as part of any straightening operation, it is to reduce a stretched condition or to blend a condition of false stretch into the surrounding contour. Both of these conditions were discussed briefly in Chapter 2, but a more detailed discussion is required to explain the application of basic shrinking procedure.

It should be noted that the same procedure for shrinking damaged metal can be used in forming metal parts by hand. Although extensive hand-forming operations are outside the scope of this book, the repairman who has leaned the proper use of the hammer and dolly block will find that it is easy to hand-form simple parts needed in rust repair. Shrinking is particularly important in such operations becaue it provides a method of eliminating excess surface area easily.

STRETCHED METAL

Sheet metal is considered stretched when the dimensions that make up its surface area have been changed. The determining factor is whether either length or width has been increased. Usually there will be a proportional decrease of the other dimension of area, length or width.

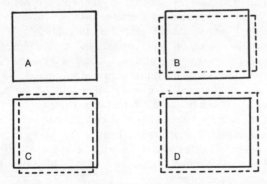

4-1 Typical stretched conditions. A represents an area within a panel of any size. In B and C, the dotted lines show the effect of either lengthwise or crosswise tension; D shows the effect of both lengthwise and crosswise tension. Any combination of these is considered to be stretched metal.

Figure 4-1 illustrates the varying conditions of stretched metal. A represents a small section of a panel surface. This section could be almost any size, from much smaller than shown to several times larger. If such a section could be laid out on the panel before the damage that caused the stretching, the result could be

measured afterward. In most instances, the result would be similar to the conditions in B or C, depending on the direction from which the force acted in causing the stretch. If force did act on the section from both sides, the result would be similar to the condition D.

This figure shows that stretched metal may be found in a wide variety of conditions. In many instances there will be some combination of the two conditions represented by B and C; however, it will be the exceptional condition that is exactly uniform, as represented by the dotted lines. Also, these illustrations are simply flat, rectangular drawings on a piece of paper. Stretched metal will be found on the surface of a panel in almost any conceivable shape. Some stretched areas will be driven below the surface level, whereas others will be driven above.

FALSE STRETCH

False stretch is the term used to identify a condition often confused with a true stretched condition, stemming from the similarity of appearance. False stretch may vary from a simple *oil can* condition to a large, raised hump that appears to be stretched. The key to the identification of false stretch is that it will always be a smooth, unworked surface, which pops in and out easily, adjoining an area that has been upset. The raised area is caused by the gathering effect of the upset.

The most common cause of false stretch is failure to relieve all of the upset in a rolled buckle of the reinforced edge of such panels as doors, deck lids, or hoods; however, it can be found in any panel when the conditions are right. Many times, it is difficult to avoid causing a little false stretch, but it is often the result of improper use of tools. Attempting to beat out stiff, unyielding buckles that should be straightened under tension is probably the most usual reason.

A simple demonstration of a condition similar to false stretch can be made by folding a pleat in the edge of a sheet of paper. When the fold is held in place, the center area of the sheet will be raised into a sharp bulge, and when the fold is released, the bulged area will drop back into place.

The ideal method of dealing with false stretch is to avoid it; plan the rough-out procedure to avoid making upsets. Emphasis on such procedures will be found in later sections of the book dealing with the roughing out of actual damage. However, sometimes it is almost impossible to avoid creating some false stretch. In these instances, shrinking is the practical answer.

Shrinking false stretch is a blending operation. When it is done properly, the effect of the upset will be spread over enough area to relieve the appearance of bulging caused by the abrupt change of dimensions. The shrinking effect must not extend into the upset area, but it must blend invisibly with the adjoining metal. This presents a real problem, because in any shrinking operation there is a tendency to overshrink. Unless very close control is maintained, overshrinking will occur, and the upset will be carried farther ino the unaffected metal. This is the condition sometimes described by repairmen as "chasing a stretch across a panel." However, the man who has learned to recognize the difference between stretched metal and false stretch rarely will find himself in this predicament. The actual procedure for shrinking false stretch is described in detail in a later section.

THE BASIC SHRINKING OPERATION

The basic shrinking operation uses the compressive effect of a blow on a crowned surface to make an upset. This is illustrated by the cross section in Figure 4-2. As the hammer blow strikes the crown, it will tend to drive it down to the position of the straight dotted lines. As the crown flattens, it will tend to push outward against points A and B. The compressive effect produced is the result of resistance to outward movement of points A and B.

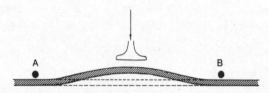

4-2 Showing the compressive effect of a hammer blow on a high crown. Flattening the crown causes outward pressure on points A and B.

If an upset is to be made, the resistance to outward movement must be greater than the resistance to upsetting of the crowned area. The softening effect of heat is required, because without it the crown usually offers much greater resistance than points A and B. The proper application of heat to the crown section will reverse the condition so that it will upset readily. It also will stiffen the resistance to outward movement of the A and B points by expanding the surrounding metal. Thus, heat tends to increase both conditions necessary for shrinking.

The effect of heat is shown in Figure 4-3. In this particular illustration, the temperature range is from 1,400° F. (760° C.) or cherry red at the center of the heated area to normal at, or close to, the A and B points. The expansion resulting from that temperature will raise the crown from the position of the solid line to the approximate position of the dotted line. The result is a low, cone-shaped hump stiffer around the outer edges and softer in the center than the original crown. This new shape offers much greater resistance to the hammer blow around the outer edges, points A and B, and much less resistance to upsetting in the center. Thus, hammer blows on the center area will cause considerable upset because the conditions are right.

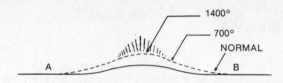

4-3 The softening effect of heat. A hammer blow on the heated spot will cause upsetting, instead of forcing points A and B outward.

Because cooling starts the instant the torch flame is removed from the work, the effect of heating is only temporary. Cooling is rapid enough to require that any work done with the hammer be done as quickly as possible. The smaller the spot heated, the more important it is that no time be lost, if the work is to be effective. This explanation of basic shrinking procedure has been limited to the effect on a single cross section taken through the center of an area of metal raised above the proper surface level. In the simplest stretched condition that would require shrinking, another cross section taken at a right angle to this line would be approximately the same. The four basic steps of shrinking such a spot are shown in Figure 4-4. A represents a cross section of the original spot to be shrunk. Since it is uniform, this may be considered the same as any other cross section taken at any other angle. B shows the application of heat from the welding torch flame to a temperature of about 1,400° F. (760° C.).

The exact temperature and size of the heated area will vary with the conditions of the area to be shrunk. No exact rules can be laid down, except that the temperature should not exceed bright cherry red in normal light and that the area heated should be in proportion to the area of severe distortion. Metal outside the stretched area should not be subjected to high temperature—above the range where discoloration starts—unless the intent is to blend an unstretched area of false stretch into an unavoidable upset. Metal heated to the point of discoloration will be softened enough to upset under the effect of a hammer blow. In fact, many minor shrinking jobs can be done with temperatures well below the red heat range. Many repairmen refer to this as shrinking with "black heat." Temperature variations and the spread of heat are discussed in a later section.

The actual shrinking operation is shown in C of Figure 4-4. The hammer has been used to drive the hot, expanded surface down to a much lower level. Although the hammer is shown in only one position, it would be necessary to strike several hammer blows over the heated surface to flatten the crown to this level. It should be noted especially that the surface is shown with some crown. It would be wrong to drive the surface down so that it is perfectly flat while it is heated, because cooling will cause it to contract and be overshrunk. This slight crown will be reduced as cooling is completed.

The last two steps are shown together in D. The hammer and dolly block are being used to finish straightening the shrunk surface, and the wet sponge is in position

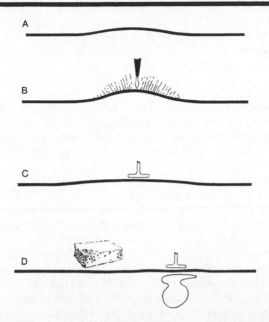

4-4 The basic shrinking operation: A, Cross section of spot to be shrunk; B, the same area expanded and softened by heat; C, the hammer being used to drive down the softened high spot; D, the hammer and dolly block being used to straighten the shrunk area. The wet sponge is used as needed to quench the hot metal.

to quench the hot metal as needed. The hammer is shown on-dolly, which is often necessary to relieve any overshrinking. The hammer also would be used off-dolly to finish straightening any noticeable waves. In this case, the use of the hammer and dolly is not different from that in any other straightening job, except that lighter blows and more care are required, because the heated metal will yield much more readily than unheated metal.

The sponge is not always needed. If the surface has been lowered enough, the rest of the crown will drop into the proper level as the surface cools. If, however, the surface has not been driven down as far as necessary, quenching it with a wet sponge or rag will lower it much more than if it is allowed to cool slowly. Overquenching will cause overshrinking. The problems of quenching are discussed in much greater detail in a later section.

SHRINKING GOUGES

The procedure for shrinking a gouge is similar to that for shrinking an area of raised metal. In both operations the upset is obtained by softening the area with heat and applying force to flatten it. It differs in two respects, however: (1) the gouged area extends below the surface instead of above it, and (2) gouges tend to be stretched more severely than raised areas.

The dolly block plays a much more important part in shrinking the gouge, because force to accomplish the upset must be applied from the underside while the metal is hot. The more severe the stretched condition,

the more important it is that this be done. A very minor gouge can be driven up without heating and then shrunk as if it were a raised area instead. This procedure is recommended for large, lightly stretched areas that have been driven below the surface. However, it is not practical on any but the most minor damage, because it tends to spread the effect over a much wider area. It is a much better practice to use the hammer and dolly block as shown in Figure 4-5.

A represents a cross section through a gouge, with the proper surface level indicated by the dotted lines. In this case, the depressed area is shown as being smooth. Under actual conditions, however, this may be any shape. Quite often the bottom of a gouge shows the imprint of a sharp object. Regardless of the shape, however, the procedure would be the same.

The effect of heat application is shown in B. Expansion has deepened the gouge by causing the metal on the surrounding edges to bulge inward. This is essentially the same as the effect obtained by heating a raised area, except that expansion forces the surface downward instead of upward. Here the temperature required would be relatively high, at least dull red heat and maybe hotter; the more severe the stretched condition, the higher the temperature should be, but *never above bright cherry red*.

The first application of force is shown in C. One or more blows have been struck with the dolly block on the underside of the deepest part of the gouge. This has driven the edges of the gouge above the level of the surrounding metal. On a small, single-point gouge, this high metal will form a ring around the low spot. On a long gouge, several dolly blows should be struck along the

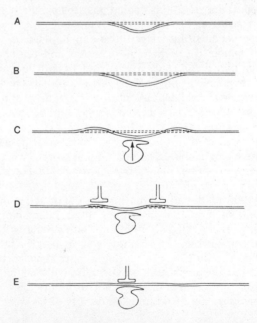

4-5 Basic procedure for shrinking a gouge: A, a cross section through a typical gouge; B, the same cross section expanded and softened by heat; C, the heated area driven up by a blow of the dolly block; D, using the hammer and dolly block to level the high and low spots; E, using the hammer-on-dolly to relieve overshrinking.

heated area so that this high metal will form two lines on each side of the low spot.

The use of the hammer and dolly is shown in D. The dolly block should be pushed hard against the underside of the gouge as the hammer is used to drive the high metal down to level. Usually these two operations will be repeated, often several times. Each time they are repeated, the gouge and the surrounding high metal should be made smaller. Too many variable conditions are involved, however, to attempt to establish the exact number of repetitions. The beginner is advised to try to obtain as much shrink effect as possible from his efforts. It is simply a matter of learning to use the hammer-on-dolly on metal softened by heat.

The last operation is shown in E, with the hammer on-dolly to stretch metal. Sometimes the beginner has difficulty understanding why metal should be stretched immediately after it has been shrunk. The reason is that a line gouge will tend to shrink more lengthwise than across. Covering the area with on-dolly hammer blows will tend to relieve the effect. If allowed to cool without relieving this tendency, the shrunk area will have a drawstring effect on the adjoining surface area, causing large, flappy buckles. This operation is referred to in later sections as *stretching back*.

Probably the most important part of the procedure of shrinking a gouge is in the use of the hammer and dolly block to stretch back as the surface cools. The experienced repairman watches the surface closely and uses his hammer and dolly to relieve buckles caused by too much tension as soon as they begin to form.

Quenching is rarely needed on a gouge, except for final cooling to keep the surface from being too hot to touch. Water should never be applied to the heated metal until the metal has cooled past the point at which steam rises from it.

The procedure described here can be used for any type of gouge, if the heat application and use of the hammer and dolly block are varied to suit the conditions. Shrinking a single spot is the easiest, because only a single spot of heat is required in the deepest part. Shrinking a long, crease type of gouge, such as shown in Figure 4-9, requires that heat be applied along the length, instead of in a single spot. Whenever possible, the entire length should be heated and worked with the hammer and dolly block, but heat should never be applied to more metal than can be handled.

The skill of the individual is the deciding factor in determining how long a section of a gouge can be shrunk with one heat application. The beginner will do well to content himself with fairly short lengths, otherwise he may find that he is doing more damage than good. As he develops skill, however, he will find that he can work longer sections without difficulty. This will improve both the speed and the quality of his work.

THE PROPER USE OF HEAT IN SHRINKING METAL

One of the most important steps in any shrinking opera-

tion is the application of heat. This is true whether the job is relatively simple or quite complicated; however, the more complicated the job, the more important it is that heat be applied properly.

Proper application of heat means that the proper temperature is applied to an area of the proper size. The problem is to apply just enough heat to do the job and no more. If not enough is applied, the metal will not be softened enough to permit the required upset. In this event, the stretched condition will not be relieved, and the surface will be left rough or wavy.

To a limited extent, extra work with the hammer can offset the effect of insufficient heat. Beyond this limit, extra work with the hammer will tend only to spread the crown instead of shrinking it. For example, in Figure 4-2, the tendency would be to push points A and B farther apart instead of making an upset between them.

The effect of too-high temperature is shown in Figure 4-6. This shows the result of heating red hot a small spot in the center of a large, slightly stretched raised area. Instead of shrinking uniformly all over, the hot spot collapses, forming a depression under the hammer. A lower temperature spread over the entire area would have produced a uniform upset and a smooth surface.

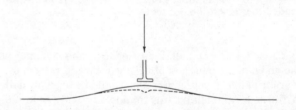

4-6 Effect of overheating a small spot where a much wider area should be heated to lower temperature. The dip in the dotted line represents a collapse on the overheated spot instead of upset.

A common mistake made in shrinking metal is to heat every spot to red heat. No doubt this stems from the influence of the blacksmith. In the early days of the automobile industry, the first repairmen were blacksmiths. An important rule of the blacksmith was that metal never should be forged at any temperature below red heat. This idea was carried over into any work done on automobile sheet metal, and it still persists, even among men who have little or no knowledge of the blacksmith's trade.

Steel such as used in automobile sheet metal begins to soften at the temperature at which the first color forms. The rate of softening increases progressively as the temperature is raised until the dark-blue color temperature range is reached. Past this point, the softening effect is directly proportional to the temperature increase until practically all mechanical strength is lost at bright red heat, close to 1,600°F. (871°C.).

The softening that results from heating to the blue color range is enough to permit considerable upsetting. On large areas that are not severely stretched, heating to the blue range or just slightly beyond will provide enough softening effect to permit the required upsetting as the surface is driven down with the hammer. Figure 4-7 shows an application of heat in the blue temperature range over a wide area. This area could be any size from 1 or 2 inches (25 or 50 mm) in length and width to 5 or 6 inches (125 or 150 mm). Hammer blows spaced over this area will cause uniform upsetting instead of the condition shown in Figure 4-6.

Low-temperature, or "black heat," shrinking, which includes any operation when heat is used below the red range, is not practical if the spot has any degree of work hardening. Severe work hardening requires heat up to the bright-red range to soften it completely. However, such areas also are stretched severely; otherwise, they would not be work hardened. In heating work hardened areas, the high temperature should be confined as much as possible to the areas that are stretched severely, as indicated by Figure 4-8. In a gouge having a cross section similar to this shape, most of the stretched metal, which also is work hardened, would be in the area between the two arrows. Red heat never should extend beyond this area.

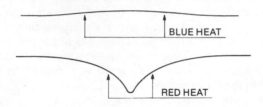

4-7 *(Top)* Showing the approximate spread of low temperature heat over a minor stretched condition.

4-8 *(Bottom)* Showing the approximate spread of high temperature heat over a severe stretched condition.

QUENCHING

Quenching is a means of controlling the rate of cooling. The primary reason for quenching is to retain a greater amount of the upset than would be possible if the spot were allowed to cool slowly after the shrinking with the hammer. After the work with the hammer and dolly has been completed, the sooner the metal can be quenched, the more shrink effect will be obtained.

Quenching adds to the amount of shrinkage by stopping the yield of the heated area to the tension that results from contraction as the metal cools. Quenching is much more effective if the work with the hammer and dolly can be completed before the temperature has dropped below the color range. But it still will have some effect if done while the temperature is above the point at which water will form steam on contact with the hot metal, particularly on relatively large areas. Below that point it is simply a matter of cooling.

Knowing when to quench is largely a matter of experience. The experienced repairman soon learns to judge visually when the surface will cool to the proper contour without quenching. If he sees that it will not, he will pass a wet sponge or cloth across the surface as he

watches the effect. When the proper surface condition has been obtained, quenching should be stopped. Many times, quenching will show up minor buckles that can be straightened with the hammer and dolly block; then the surface can be quenched again. This must be done with the minimum loss of time, however. When reaching for the wet sponge, do not lay down the hammer or dolly where it will be difficult to pick up again. The best method is to hold both tools in one hand while the quenching is done with the other; this will avoid fumbling for tools if further straightening is needed.

Only rarely should a repairman quench a shrink spot all the way without looking at what is happening. It is better to move the wet sponge back and forth across the hot spot. The surface action can be watched between passes and the quenching action speeded up or slowed down as needed.

OVERSHRINKING

Overshrinking is the result of shrinking of the temporarily expanded metal in addition to that which was stretched. When this occurs, it will have a drawing or puckering effect on the metal surface surrounding the overshrunk area.

A demonstration showing an effect similar to overshrinking can be made with a piece of cloth such as a handkerchief. With the cloth lying flat on a table top, gather a section in the center of it between the fingers. As long as this section is held, it will be impossible to smooth the surrounding surface so that it will lie flat.

Overshrinking is more likely to occur when shrinking gouges than when shrinking a stretched condition that has been raised above the surface level. It can occur in either situation, however. A slight amount often is desirable, because it will be relieved by the normal picking and hammer and dolly block work that will be done when the spot is metal-finished. If it is too great, however, it will have a gathering effect on the adjoining surface, resulting in the formation of long wavy buckles in the surface. These can be relieved by using the hammer-on-dolly to restretch the shrunk area and, sometimes, some of the area immediately adjoining. When this is done, care should be taken to space the hammer blows over the affected area uniformly and to avoid pressing too hard against the dolly block. The desired effect is the spreading action of the hammer blow against the dolly. The rebound action caused by pressing the dolly hard against the inner surface is not needed. If the surface is low, it should be lifted by striking the underside of the metal with the working face of the dolly.

SHRINKING PROCEDURES ON THE JOB

A typical example of the use of shrinking is provided by the procedure followed in straightening the gouged dent

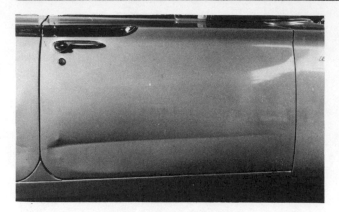

4-9 Crease in a front door lower panel. The rear end of this crease will require shrinking.

4-11 Using the hammer-off-dolly to straighten the unstretched part of the crease. Most of the work was done off-dolly.

in the door lower panel shown in Figure 4-9. Although the emphasis is on the shrinking procedure, all the straightening operations are explained so that the proper relationship of shrinking to the other procedures can be shown.

This damage probably resulted when this automobile struck a glancing impact against a rigid, sharp object, probably a projection on the bumper of another automobile. However, the same damage could have been caused by another automobile striking this one while it was standing still. Whatever it was, the impact object approached from the front at a very sharp angle, contacting the front door almost at the front edge. As the impact object moved farther back, it dug deeper into the panel. Note that a sharp bend has formed along the lower edge from the center to the rear. The reinforced edges caused the impact object to bounce off the front door and strike the rear, causing another gouge before coming to rest.

The inside of the front door is shown in Figure 4-10, which shows the inside of the outer panel, partly covered with undercoating, and the loading hole. Note that easy access for hand tools is provided by this hole.

Figure 4-11 shows the first operation. The metal was dented and scratched up to the point where the hammer is shown, but not stretched. The dent has been straightened up to this point, using the hammer and dolly, so the area to be shrunk can blend to the correct contour.

Part of the next step is shown in Figure 4-12. Before the wire brush was used to remove the paint, the surface was scorched with a strongly oxidizing flame. The flame was held almost on the surface of the panel and kept moving rapidly to avoid overheating the metal. By this method, paint can be burned very rapidly so that the brush will remove it easily.

The paint should always be burned on any surface where metal is to be shrunk. It enables the repairman to judge the temperature by color and leaves the surface smooth so that the level can be judged visually much more accurately. Also, if the paint is not removed, the torch flame will burn it, leaving a gummy residue. Particles of this residue will be picked up on the hammer face, making it rough. If the hammer is used in this condition, it will make rough, choppy marks in the hot metal.

The first heat application for shrinking is shown in Figure 4-13. This picture was shot slightly late as the flame was being removed from contact with the surface. The flame first was played back and forth over the general area to spread enough heat to avoid a sharp break-line between hot and cold metal. This was done

4-10 Inside view of a front door, showing loading holes and part of the inner surface of the outer panel.

4-12 Using a hand wire brush to remove paint after scorching it with an oxidizing flame.

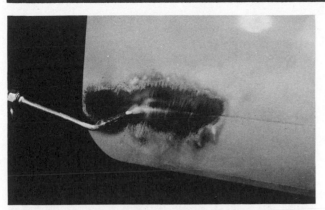

4-13 Heating the gouge before shrinking. A temperature variation from faint color to bright blue was made by changing the speed of the moving torch from fast to slow.

with the tip of the inner cone about 1 inch (25 mm) from the surface. It was then lowered to about ½ inch (12.5 mm) above the gouge at the right end of the burned-off spot and moved steadily to the left to the point where it is shown. Because the stretched condition increases from the right to left, the torch was moved fairly rapidly at the start on the right, but slowed progressively as it moved to the left. This permitted a gradual increase in temperature from right to left. As an indication of the temperature, no actual color appeared in the first inch at the right end, but it had increased to slightly above bright blue at the left.

Shrinking this heated spot was done by using the hammer and dolly in the same manner they were used to straighten the forward section of the gouge where shrinking was not needed (Figure 4-4). As explained earlier in this chapter, only enough heat was applied to permit the required amount of upsetting. In this instance, however, the work had to be done rapidly, because the spot was too small to remain hot long.

The remaining length of the buckle received one more heat application. Because the amount of stretch increased to the left, the temperature was allowed to rise further, up to cherry red in the deepest part. The heating method was the same, however, except that the flame was kept in place longer.

A body spoon and a spoon dolly were needed as the work approached the edge, because the shape of the

facing prevented easy access with the dolly block. These tools and the others used on this job are shown in Figure 4-14. The small screwdriver was used as a pry tool through the drain holes in the lower rear corner.

The end of the shrinking operation is shown in Figure 4-15. This spot has been reheated and is being hammered down again because after the first operation it was left slightly high.

Two steps in the metal-finishing operation are shown in Figures 4-16 and 4-17. In Figure 4-16, a heavy-duty disc sander equipped with a sharp, 36-grit disc has been passed across the straightened and shrunk surface. Paint shows up in the low spots where it has not been burned off, and dark metal appears in the shrunk area. Note that there are few low spots. In Figure 4-17, the low spots have been pried up and filed smooth. After buffing, the surface will be ready to repaint.

PARTIAL SHRINKING

The gouged panel in Figure 4-9 was easy to shrink because the underside was accessible. There are many other areas on doors, quarter panels, fenders, roofs, and so on that can be shrunk and metal-finished similarly. Other, less accessible areas must be worked by other means, usually pry rods or the metal screw-type panel puller. Weld-on pull tabs can be used, but they often break off when used on heated metal. Whatever is used, only partial shrinking will be practical.

Figure 4-18 illustrates the heating procedure for partly shrinking a gouge by lifting with a screw-type dent puller. The notes point out that the screw should be driven in tight to the retainer. This is to protect the hardened threads from the heat as much as possible. In heating, the flame should be directed down the channel of the gouge but away from the thread. The position of the torch should be changed from side to side once or twice so that the heating will be even. As the metal reaches red heat, the flame can be backed up toward the puller, but it is not necessary to have red-hot metal at the screw hole. A means of quick disposal of the torch should be provided so that the hammer can be operated and the metal quenched.

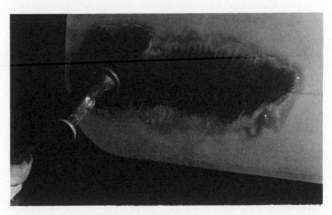

4-15 The final shrinking opertion on a high spot after the gouge has been shrunk to level.

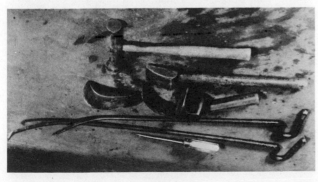

4-14 Tools used in shrinking and metal-finishing the gouge.

4-16 Appearance of the straightened surface after disc sanding lightly with a sharp, 36-grit disc.

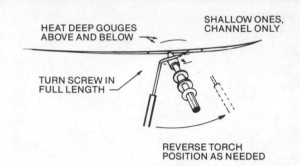

HEAT DEEP GOUGES ABOVE AND BELOW

SHALLOW ONES, CHANNEL ONLY

TURN SCREW IN FULL LENGTH

REVERSE TORCH POSITION AS NEEDED

4-18 Heating procedure when lifting a gouge with a dent puller for partial shrinking. Turn screw in all of the way to protect threads and direct flame to both sides away from it. Heat above and below the screw only on extra deep gouges.

As the work progresses from the shallow to the deeper part of the gouge, it may be necessary to heat the sides of the gouge as well as the main channel. This can be done as the torch changes position by playing the flame on the surface well above or below the screw, instead of lifting it off the surface.

A hammer is not shown because, if needed at all, it should be used sparingly and well away from the high-temperature area. Sometimes a light hammer blow above or below the puller will help raise an area, but it must be struck on a part of the surface that is not hot enough to shrink under the impact. Any shrinkage in the outer edges will cause a shallow buckle to radiate outward into the smooth panel area, adding damage to damage.

A deep, point gouge can be shrunk similarly, but the torch flame should be applied in a circular path around the end of the puller. A small tip, adjusted to a small flame, should be used and directed toward the midpoint of the side of the gouge and kept off the end of the puller as much as possible. It is not always necessary to reach red heat. A steady pull should be maintained on the puller as the gouge is heated. The hammer slide may not be needed, but if it is, it should be used carefully.

Pry rods can be used instead of the slide hammer, as shown in Figure 4-19, but a direct lift under red-hot metal should be avoided; instead of lifting an area, it

will simply punch a hole. The rod shown in use has the outer end bent to approximately a 70-degree angle. It is being used upside down so that the curved surface will contact the metal instead of the point. In general, it is better to make several lifts around an area instead of attempting to bring it up with one.

The procedure with weld-on tabs would be much the same as with the metal screw, but the heat must be kept from the weld. If it is too hot, it will break off, leaving a high spot that often has a hole in it.

Partial shrinking is not a precision operation. The purpose is to reduce the depth of fill by folding excess surface, caused by stretching, back into its proper area. It is important to avoid over-upsetting across the gouge. If this occurs, large, shallow waves will be drawn in the adjoining smooth surface when the upset areas cool, adding needless work to a relatively simple job.

SHRINKING THIN SHEET STEELS

Very thin sheet steel requires some adjustment of the procedure used on conventional thicknesses, but it can be shrunk in the same general manner. The difference stems from the way a reduction of thickness of the same grade of steel affects its resistance to bending. As thick-

4-17 The finished panel, ready for buffing. The low spots have been pried or picked up and filed smooth.

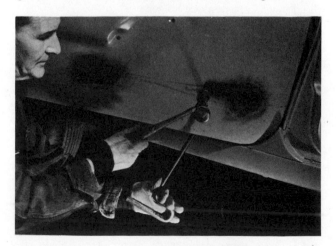

4-19 Using a pry rod to partly shrink a gouge.

ness is reduced, bending resistance drops off to a greater degree. The opposite is true, also: an increase of thickness causes a greater increase in bending resistance. (For the benefit of technically minded readers, bending resistance, technically load-bearing strength, varies as the square of thickness, assuming that length and width are the same. Reducing thickness to one half will reduce load-bearing strength to one quarter. In-between reductions can be calculated from the ratio of the square of one thickness to the other. The formula is $\frac{R_1}{R_2} = \frac{T_1^2}{T_2^2}$, in which R = rigidity and T = thickness.)

The raised area caused by spot heat application bends the metal around the outer edges in two ways: (1) up, to permit the heated area to rise and (2) warp, because the surrounding cooler metal must resist the expansion of the heated area. This action is present in metal of any thickness, but is not a serious problem when heating the thickness for which normal shrinking procedures were developed. It becomes a problem when the thickness is reduced. The problem is affected to some degree by the fact that the thinner steels are usually stiffer, but not enough to make a major difference.

The first adjustment is to reduce the upper limit of temperature. Heat to dull red where bright red would have been used on thicker metal, or, if dull red would have been used, keep the temperature in the black range.

The second adjustment is to avoid concentrating high temperature in a small area. Where it would be safe on thicker metal to heat a very small spot to bright red, it is better to spiral the flame inward over a larger area, making the hottest spot in the center. The result will be a spread of the bending and warping effect over a much wider area.

The third adjustment is that less force can be used with the hammer. The dolly block should be used mostly in the off-dolly positions. Stretching back, to compensate for the extra lengthwise shrinkage along a gouge, should be done largely by slapping the working face of the dolly against the underside. Any hammer-on-dolly blows should be light and the dolly held with a relaxed grip.

The fourth adjustment is the hardest. The thinner metal cools more rapidly, leaving less time to do the work. Safety requires that the flame be shut off or that the torch be handed to another person. Most repairmen learn to regulate the torch valves with the thumb or a finger of the hand holding the torch; this can be done as it is being laid down. The tools should be held ready in the other hand, so that minimum time will be lost. A wet sponge or rag should be in a convenient position, but should be used sparingly.

After that, it is simply a matter of working fast without error. Many experienced repairmen consider shrinking the thinner metal impractical. The time factor adds some validity to the argument, but thin metal can be shrunk by any skilled worker who has recognized the nature of the problems involved and has developed the essential skill.

SHRINKING ALUMINUM

Sheet aluminum can be shrunk in much the same manner as sheet steel, but the procedure is complicated by three factors: (1) it must be done in a much lower temperture range; thus, color is no indicator of temperature, (2) aluminum conducts heat much more rapidly than steel, leaving less time to work the hot metal, and (3) the hammer and dolly block must be used much more carefully, because the already soft aluminum is further softened by heating, so that errors which would be minor on steel will be major on aluminum. It is recommended that shrinking aluminum not be tried until a reasonable degree of skill has been developed on steel.

Heat should be applied with a small tip adjusted to a slightly carburizing flame and held well back from the surface. The size of the area heated should be less than the size of the stretched area, because the heat spreads rapidly by conduction. In general, it is better to underheat and try again than to overheat and burn a hole. The torch flame should be kept moving at all times it is on the metal.

Preparation should be made to dispose of the torch with minimum lost time, so that work with the hammer can be started. Hammer blows should be spaced around the heat-bulged area instead of straight down on the center. As the hammer moves to a new position, the angle should change so that the metal is forced toward the center. The dolly block should be used only to buck up the outer edges. Never strike an on-dolly blow on hot aluminum; it is too soft.

Aluminum requires more care in quenching than steel, because its expansion and contraction rate is greater. A circular pass with the wet sponge or rag should be made around the hot spot, to prevent heat flowing too far into unaffected metal, then quick passes made across it while watching the action carefully. Stop quenching when the surface looks as though it has dropped enough. Overquenching will cause overshrinking. When this occurs, allow the metal to cool and correct it by driving the area up with the dolly block while using the hammer with light off-dolly blows around the edge.

The operation can be repeated if the stretched area has not been completely shrunk. On the second operation there should be little difference in procedure from the first, other than reducing the amount of heat and hammer work to allow for the shrinking already accomplished.

A stretched area of aluminum that has been shrunk properly can be metal-finished the same as a similar area of steel. However, many repairmen will be satisfied to get the high spot shrunk down and complete the finishing by filling. Unless the proper skill has been developed, this may be the safest course, but it is not a substitute for skill.

Welding

In its broadest definition, welding includes most of the processes of joining metal by the use of heat, including soldering. These processes vary widely in method and equipment. The original and the simplest method is that of the blacksmith, who heated the pieces to be joined in the forge until they were plastic and then hammered them together on the anvil. Many modern industrial methods make use of the heat of the electric arc or heat caused by electrical resistance; even heat resulting from friction is used for some special applications. In newer methods, wide use is made of mechanical, electrical, and electronic control systems to make the process completely automatic. Manual methods, such as the oxyacetylene torch and hand-operated electric arc, are still used industrially; however, as progress is made in the development of more efficient mechanized methods, non-automatic welding is becoming more and more restricted to repair and maintenance work.

Welding processes may be classified by whether the metal welded is heated to the melting point, so that it will flow together; heated close to the melting point and joined by the application of force; or heated and joined by diffusion of a molten filler metal into the surfaces of the parts to be joined. The first usually is called fusion welding, because the metal fuses and flows together; it includes both the oxyacetylene and the electric arc processes. The second usually is called pressure welding, because of the pressure applied to make the joint; it includes the electrical resistance and forge welding processes. The most common of the electrical resist-

ance processes is resistance spot welding, used for almost all factory sheet metal welding because of its economy and the fact that it causes practically no heat distortion. The third is called either soldering or brazing, depending on the type and melting temperature of the filler metal used.

The nature of the welding required in sheet metal repair is such that a large part of it is best suited to the oxyacetylene torch processes. These include both the fusion welding of steel and brazing. In fusion welding of steel, the metal being welded is heated to the melting point, and usually a filler rod of similar metal is melted and added to the joint. In brazing steel, the metal is heated only to the temperature at which the brazing rod melts so that it can be deposited on the joint; the brazing material, usually a copper base alloy, flows onto the steel, making a strong joint for most purposes. Brazing requires the use of flux to clean the steel surfaces, but no flux is required for fusion welding mild steel with the oxyacetylene torch. It is essential for the beginner to learn to do both types of oxyacetylene welding in any position, flat, vertical, or overhead.

Some of the welding operations on body and frame repair work can be done better with one of the electric welding processes, arc or resistance. In arc welding, an electric arc provides heat required for fusion and, in two of the three methods, a means of depositing the filler metal in the weld. In resistance welding, heat is generated by flowing an electric current through the metal to be welded, but the weld is made by mechanical pressure applied to the metal when it reaches the correct temperature.

Both basic systems are described in more detail in the following section, but more emphasis is placed on the electric resistance method. It is the basic method used in factory assembly of almost all sheet metal products, particularly automobiles, and has distinct advantages for many body repair operations. The arc welding coverage in the following sections is restricted to the equipment and procedures suitable to the relatively thin steels that the body repairman is required to weld in the normal day-to-day body shop operation.

It is common body shop practice to use the term welding when referring to the oxyacetylene welding of steel with a steel filler rod, because it is the method used most frequently. Other processes are referred to by name, such as brazing, arc welding, and resistance spot welding.

OXYACETYLENE WELDING EQUIPMENT

Although there are several different manufacturers of oxyacetylene welding equipment, all such equipment operates on one basic principle: The flame is produced by mixing the acetylene and oxygen in the proper proportions in the torch mixing chamber and passing them through the orifice in the torch tip, where they are ignited. A steady flame is maintained by adjusting the pressure of both the oxygen and acetylene so that the mixture escapes from the torch tip at the proper speed.

Gas welding equipment consists of the following units:

1. Oxygen cylinder
2. Acetylene cylinder
3. Oxygen regulator
4. Acetylene regulator
5. Hoses
6. Torch, including handle, mixing chamber, and tip
7. Eye protection for the operator, usually goggles or a face shield
8. Spark lighter
9. Hand truck for cylinders

A typical welding outfit, without hand truck, is shown in Figure 5-1.

GAS CYLINDERS

The gas cylinders, sometimes called tanks or bottles, normally are supplied by the company that manufactures the gas. Except in operations where only limited quantities of gas are used, the cylinders are provided without charge for thirty days, after which a demurrage charge is made. Cylinders are also available for limited quantity users on various purchase or long-term lease plans. The exact nature of these plans varies from one manufacturer to another, but in general, the user pays for the cylinders plus the normal maintenance they will require. The user is guaranteed also that full cylinders will be available on an exchange basis when he presents his empties to the dealer. The price for the gas under this plan is slightly higher than for the large-volume user.

Safety precautions require that the cylinders be attached to something that will prevent them from being knocked over. The common practice is to mount them on a specially designed portable hand truck. When portability is not required, they may be chained to something rigid, such as a wall or bench. The use of the hand truck is more desirable, however, because it simplifies the problem of removal in case of fire.

THE OXYGEN CYLINDER

The oxygen cylinder is simply a high-strength steel tank with a specially designed bronze shut-off valve and a safety device to release the pressure under emergency conditions. The standard-size cylinder, shown in Figure 5-2, has a capacity of 244 cubic feet at 2,200 pounds pressure per square inch (psi) at 70°F. (6.9 m³ at 15,158 kPa at 21°C.). Smaller cylinders are also available. One common size holds 122 cubic feet (3.45 m³); similar cylinders of approximately the same size are available from the various manufacturers.

The pressure in an oxygen cylinder varies according to the temperature. A fully charged cylinder will show a pressure of only about 1,780 psi (12,264 kPa) if it is kept outdoors in zero temperature. After it has warmed to

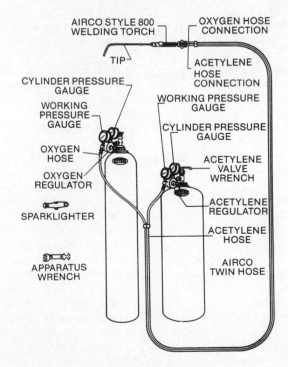

5-1 Oxyacetylene welding outfit.

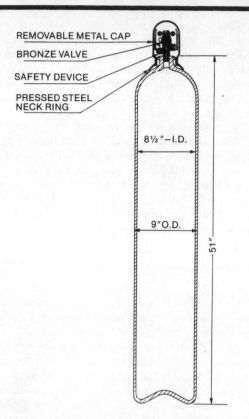

5-2 Oxygen cylinder. Oxygen capacity 244 cu. ft. at 2,200 psi pressure at 70°F. (6.9 m³ at 15,158 kPa at 21°C.).

70°F. (21°C.), the pressure will increase to 2,200 psi (15,158 kPa), and if the temperature is raised to 120°F. (49°C.), the pressure will increase to 2,500 psi (17,225 kPa).

The high-pressure gauge on most oxygen regulators is calibrated to indicate the number of cubic feet of oxygen in the cylinder at 70°F. (21°C.). If the temperature varies from this figure, an allowance must be made to determine the amount left in the cylinder. Although all such calibrations are approximate, they are close enough for ordinary use.

The oxygen cylinder is equipped with a safety cap that protects the valve. This cap should be kept in place at all times when the cylinder, whether full or empty, is not connected to the welding outfit.

Oxygen cylnders are subject to the U.S. Interstate Commerce Commission rules governing containers used for transporting compressed gases. Other countries have similar regulations. These rules are intended to ensure that such containers are safe. The very nature of a container of gas compressed to the pressure normally found in an oxygen cylinder makes it absolutely essential for the user to follow every possible safety precaution. These cylinders should never be stored near heat or highly flammable materials. The National Board of Fire Underwriters has rules for the storage of oxygen cylinders. In many communities, there are also local regulations. These should be followed.

A particular hazard is created when oil and grease are exposed to high-pressure oxygen. A small drop of grease in an oxygen valve can be the cause of a fire and an explosion. Under no circumstances should such material be allowed to get on cylinders or any other gas welding equipment. Other highly oxidizable materials may be equally hazardous. Greasy clothing or gloves should not be used around gas welding equipment.

Oxygen cylinders should never be used to support another object or as rollers to move something heavy. An electric arc should never be struck on the cylinder, because it may cause the cylinder to rupture. The sudden release of oxygen under high pressure would cause tremendous damage; it would probably injure and possibly kill the operator and any other persons in the vicinity.

THE ACETYLENE CYLINDER

The acetylene cylinder differs in construction from the oxygen cylinder, because it is dangerous to store acetylene gas at high pressure in open-space containers. Either heat or shock can cause it to separate into its more simple constituents, releasing tremendous amounts of heat. The fire and explosion hazards under such circumstances are so great that laws and regulations have been established governing the construction of acetylene cylinders.

The problem of storage of acetylene compressed to high pressure was solved by the discovery that it can be dissolved readily into liquid acetone, which can dissolve many times its own volume of acetylene gas. This knowledge led to the development of various porous filling

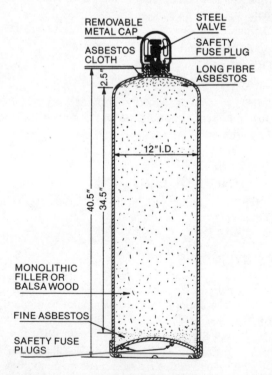

5-3 Acetylene cylinder. Acetylene capacity approx. 275 cu. ft. at 250 psi pressure at 70°F. (7.78 m³ at 1,723 kPa at 21°C.).

materials for the cylinder, serving to absorb the acetone and prevent the formation of open cavities. Thus, all of the acetylene pumped into the cyliner must be dissolved into the acetone. A cross-sectional view of such a cylinder is shown in Figure 5-3.

An acetylene cylinder 12 inches (30 cm) in diameter and 40.5 inches (103 cm) high can store approximately 275 cubic feet (7.78 m³) of acetylene at a pressure of 250 psi (1,723 kPa). Acetylene dissolved in acetone at this pressure in cylinders filled with suitable porous material can be handled with safety. Only a small fraction of this amount of acetylene could be stored safely in an open-space container. For this reason, no attempt ever should be made to transfer acetylene from the proper cylinder to another container.

Safety fuse plugs that melt at 220°F. (104.4°C.) are provided at the top and bottom of the acetylene cylinder. If the temperature of the area in which the cylinder is stored reaches this point, the acetylene will be released into the surrounding air, and the possibility of an explosion will be avoided.

The extreme fire hazard of acetylene dictates rigid safety precautions. The acetylene cylinders should never be used to prop something up or as rollers. Being filled with liquid acetone, they always should be stored and used in an upright position. If a cylinder has been laid on its side, before it is used again it should be allowed to stand upright for at least a half hour to permit the acetone to flow back away from the valve. If not, acetone may be discharged into the welding outfit, causing a void in the cylinder and damage to the equipment.

Pressure variations due to temperature changes are greater for acetylene than for oxygen. Furthermore, because the gas is dissolved in acetone, gauge pressure is not an exact indicator of the amount of gas in a cylinder. The only true indication is weight. 14.74 cu. ft. (0.42 m³) of acetylene gas weighs one pound (0.45 kg). When necessary to determine the exact amount of gas in a cylinder, weigh the cylinder and subtract the tare (empty) weight to determine the weight of the gas. The cubic feet can be calculated by multiplying by 14.74; cubic feet can be converted to cubic meters by multiplying by 0.0283. The tare weight will be found stamped on the cylinder.

THE OXYACETYLENE WELDING OUTFIT

Welding equipment consists of the two regulators for oxygen and acetylene, the hose, and the torch with an assortment of various-sized tips. Goggles or other eye protection, a sparklighter, and a wrench having openings for all of the threaded connections are essential accessories. Most manufacturers offer kits with all these items in one package. The gas cylinders are not considered part of this package because, as mentioned earlier, they usually belong to the company that manufactures the gas. A hand truck for the cylinders is also an essential item, but it usually is sold separately.

The Regulators

The regulators for both gases operate on the same principle, but they are intentionally made not interchangeable, for reasons of safety. The connections to the cylinders are of different sizes, and left-hand threads are used on the connections to the acetylene hose; left-hand threads also are used on the hose connection to the torch handle. This arrangement completely eliminates the possibiity of making a wrong connection anywhere in the system.

A cross-sectional view of a single-stage regulator is shown in Figure 5-4. The important part of the regulator is the valve that controls the flow of gas as it is needed. This is done by the adjusting spring and the compensating spring. In use, the adjusting screw is turned in against the adjusting spring until the desired pressure shows on the low-pressure gauge. This action releases gas to the low-pressure chamber of the regulator, from which it flows through the hose to the torch. As long as the torch valve is open, the flow of gas will continue. Closing the torch valve causes a pressure increase in the low-pressure chamber, which overcomes the pressure of the adjusting spring and closes the valve.

The operation of a two-stage regulator is similar to that of a single-stage regulator, except that the pressure is stepped down in two stages instead of one. The first stage reduces the pressure to a predetermined level, and the second reduces it to whatever figure the adjusting screw is set. The two-stage regulator may be expected to provide more exact control of pressure and to last longer than a single-stage regulator.

The Hose

The hose used in gas welding is made especially for the purpose. It must be flexible, nonporous, and have sufficient strength to withstand the pressure of the gases. Under no circumstances should an air hose or hoses intended for oil be substituted for welding hose, because of the danger of explosion.

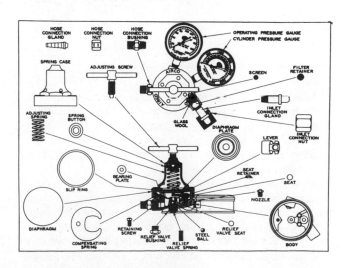

5-4 Single-stage regulator parts.

Separate hoses may be used for acetylene and oxygen, but it is the general practice to use twin, or coupled, hoses because they are easier to handle. Both hoses are of the same size, but they differ in color and the threaded connections with which they are fitted. The acetylene hose is usually red and always is fitted with left-hand threaded connections. The left-hand thread may be identified easily by a groove around the outside of the brass end fitting. The oxygen hose may be either green or black and is fitted with right-hand threaded connections. In replacing these fittings, which is sometimes necessary, it is important to make certain that the correct fitting is used.

Ten feet is about the minimum length of hose practical for work on an automobile. Much less movement of the outfit will be required if a longer hose is used. However, a hose that is to long creates both a housekeeping problem and a safety hazard. In determining the length of hose required, the connections under which it will be used should be considered.

The Torch

Perhaps the most important part of the welding outfit, the torch mixes the acetylene and oxygen in the proper proportions, burns the mixture at the end of the tip, and serves as a means of directing the flame onto the work. To perform these functions, the torch requires connections for the hoses, valves, gas passages, mixing head, and various sizes of tips. The complete unit must be assembled so that a suitable handle is provided for holding the torch as it is manipulated on the work. A torch of the type commonly used in body shops is shown in Figure 5-5.

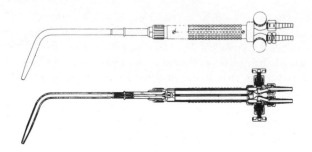

5-5 Oxyacetylene torch assembly.

Most manufacturers of welding equipment design their torches so that they consist of three basic units: the torch handle, the mixing head, and the interchangeable tips. But some torches are designed so that they consist of only two units: the handle and a mixing head combined with each separate tip.

The torch handle includes the hose connections, valves, and gas passages and is threaded on the front end so that the mixing chamber can be attached. Internal and external seats are provided on the handle and mixing head so that a tight connection is made for each gas passage when the mixing head is installed properly.

Most heavy-duty torch handles are designed with the

valves at the rear end, and many light-duty torches are designed with the valves at the front end. Not all manufacturers of welding equipment follow this practice, however. Some light-duty torches are made with valves at the rear end, and some of the early heavy-duty torches were made with front-end valves.

The use of a single mixing head with all sizes of tips is an economy measure. For most work it is satisfactory and saves on the original investment. The use of separate mixers for each tip is desirable, if the volume of work will justify the extra investment.

In addition to opening and shutting off the flow of gases, the valves provide a means of making fine adjustment of the flame. The adjustment of one valve is dependent on the other, because the flow of gases must be kept in proportion regardless of the size of the flame.

Common-sense care and a few simple precautions are all that is needed for trouble-free operation from any good torch. Rough handling should be avoided. The torch should never be used as a lever or bar to push metal into place for welding. When not in use, it should be hung up or put in a safe place to avoid accidental damage. Probably the worst abuse that a torch is exposed to in a body shop is laying it on the floor when working on the lower part of the body; it may be damaged either by being stepped on or by heavy tools being dropped on it. Such abuse can bend the valve stems or tip or even do worse damage.

In changing tips, care should be taken to avoid nicking or scratching the mating surfaces of the connection of the mixing chamber to the handle. Mixing chambers not in use, particularly on torches that have them combined with separate tips, often are damaged by not being cared for properly. They should have a storage place where they will be protected. When mixing chambers are being attached to the handle, they should be inspected to see that there is no dirt on the mating surfaces of the connection.

Torch valves should never be tightened so that they are difficult to loosen. To do so will damage the seat. After the seat becomes damaged, it may not be possible to shut off the gas completely even though the valve is turned too tight. The same rule applies to the sleeve nut that holds the mixing chamber in place.

SETTING UP THE OXYACETYLENE WELDING OUTFIT

To ensure safe operation and avoid troubles such as leaks or plugged orifices, a definite sequence should be followed in setting up a new outfit and putting it into operation. Essentially the same steps should be followed in returning an outfit to use after it has been disconnected for some time, or if there is the possibility that dust or dirt could have entered the passages. The sequence is:

1. Place the oxygen and acetylene cylinders on the truck and chain them securely. Or, if a stationary installation is to be used, be sure that the cylinders are fastened in an upright position.

2. Remove the safety caps and put them where they will be available when needed.

3. Inspect the end of the inlet gland on each regulator and the seats in the outlets of both cylinder valves. If any foreign material is found, wipe it off. The eraser on a lead pencil makes an excellent tool for wiping out the seat in the cylinder valve.

4. Open and close both cylinder valves to blow out any dirt or dust that may have entered the valve passage. Close the valves as quickly as possible to prevent the escape of an excessive amount of gas.

5. Connect both regulators. Do not attach hoses.

6. Be sure that the adjusting screws are released, then open the cylinder valves, note the pressure on the high-pressure gauge, and close the valves.

7. Check for leaks by watching the gauge for pressure drop. If time permits, the gauge should be left under pressure for several minutes. If pressure holds steady, ignore Step 8.

8. If pressure drops, it will be caused by one of the following conditions: (a) leaking connection, (b) creeping regulator valve, or (c) a leak in the regulator. Retightening the cylinder connection may stop the leak; otherwise the regulator should be serviced by a competent repairman before being used.

9. Blow out the regulator by turning the adjusting screw in far enough to release a small quantity of gas, then release the adjusting screw.

10. Attach the hoses to the regulators. Do not attach to the torch.

11. Blow out the hoses by releasing enough gas to carry any dust or dirt to the other end.

12. Attach the torch handle without the mixing head.

13. Blow out the torch handle. Open each valve separately to avoid possible fire hazard.

14. Check the hoses and connections for leaks by adjusting both regulators to maximum working pressures (acetylene, 15 psi [103 kPa]; oxygen, 15 to 30 psi [103 to 207 kPa]), then close both the torch and the cylinder valves and watch the gauges for pressure drop. This should also be left under pressure for several minutes. Retighten the connections if the pressure drops.

15. Attach the mixing head; if separate tip is used, leave it off.

16. Blow out the mixing head, using maximum oxygen pressure. Check both gases for smooth flow.

17. Attach separate tip, if used.

18. Light the torch.

This procedure normally would be followed only once, when the outfit is new. It will not take very long, unless trouble is encountered with leaks. If leaks are present, however, they must be eliminated. With a leak, there is more involved than just the loss of the gas—there is the danger of fire or explosion.

When an outfit has been laid aside for some time and is being put back into use again, the need for blowing it out in the sequence listed above is greater than with a new outfit. This is particularly important if there is any doubt as to how it has been cared for. Even though the hoses have not been disconnected from the regulators and the torch, the complete outfit should be disconnected and each piece blown out separately. This will ensure that dirt in the regulator will not be blown through the hoses into the valves and mixing head.

Each time a full cylinder is installed in the outfit, the cylinder valve should be blown out and the mating surface of the gland inspected for foreign material, particularly oil or grease. After the regulator is installed, the adjusting screw should be checked to see that it is loose, then the cylinder valve should be opened and closed to check for leaks. If the high pressure drops without affecting the low-pressure gauge, it is probably because the connection to the cylinder is leaking. If so, it is best to remove the regulator and recheck the mating surfaces of the connection before applying excessive force to pull the connection tight with a big wrench. Most often, the trouble will be surface dirt that has escaped detection. To leave it there and pull the connection tighter may not stop the leak, but it probably will damage the outfit.

In changing the cylinder, it is important to be careful with the regulator so that it will not be knocked around or dropped. It is especially important that the mating surfaces do not come into contact with any material that will contaminate them. Such precautions are only a matter of common sense and awareness of the problem.

LIGHTING AND ADJUSTING THE TORCH

Lighting and adjusting the torch flame is a matter of making a series of adjustments in the proper sequence. Most of the sheet metal welding operations require the flame to be adjusted so that equal parts of acetylene and oxygen are being burned. Starting with an outfit that previously has been shut off and bled, the procedure for opening it up, lighting and adjusting the flame properly is as follows:

1. Check both regulator adjusting screws to see that they are released.

2. Open the oxygen cylinder valve; keep turning the hand wheel until the open seat position is reached. Several turns will be required.

3. Open the acetylene cylinder valve one-half turn.

4. Open the oxygen valve on the torch about one-quarter turn.

5. Turn the oxygen regulator adjusting screw inward until the required pressure is indicated on the low-pressure gauge.

6. Close the oxygen valve.

7. Open the acetylene valve on the torch about one-quarter turn.

8. Turn the acetylene regulator adjusting screw inward until the low-pressure gauge reads the same as the oxygen.

9. Use the sparklighter to light the escaping acetylene.

10. Adjust the acetylene valve until the yellow flame begins to push away from the tip (see Fig. 5-6).

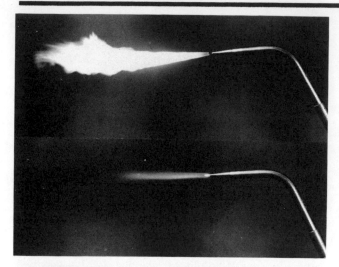

5-6 Adjustment of the acetylene flame before the oxygen valve is opened.

5-7 The neutral flame.

11. Open and adjust the oxygen valve until all but a slight trace of the long, feathery flame disappears, leaving a clearly defined, intense-blue cone of neutral flame burning on the end of the tip (see Fig. 5-7).

The exact pressures to which the oxygen and acetylene regulators should be adjusted are determined by tip size. The reading on the gauge always will be at least equal to the number of the tip, and with some makes of equipment it may be higher. Many welders use approximately 5 pounds of pressure (34.5 kPa) for the tips up to number 5, and increase the pressure to the tip number when larger tips are used. Higher pressures, unless excessive, will do no harm, except to make it more difficult to adjust the torch flame.

The size of the neutral flame produced with any tip can be varied to some degree by adjusting the amount of gases released. The variation in size that can be obtained in this manner is not as great as the difference in size of flame produced by the next larger or smaller tips. For any one tip size, changing the flame size can be done only by changing the speed of the gas flowing through the orifice. If the gas flows too fast, it will blow the flame out, because the gas will be moving faster than the flame can consume it; if it flows too slowly, there will be backfiring, making it difficult to weld.

Some tendency to backfiring is always present in a gas welding operation because of the molten particles of metal that fly from the puddle. When one of these flies into the tip orifice, it extinguishes the flame momentarily by blocking the flow of gas. In most instances, the blocking action is only momentary, because the particle is cooling and shrinking, and gas pressure is building up against it. As the flow starts again, the gas is re-ignited by the molten metal in the puddle. The result will be a minor explosion having sufficient force to blow molten metal out of the puddle; it will make a sound much like a rifle shot. All of this action takes place within a fraction of a second. Occa-

sionally, backfiring will be repeated with almost machine-gun rapidity.

Slowing the gas too much also can permit the flame to enter the tip orifice and follow the passage into the mixing head, making an angry, buzzing sound. When this occurs, the valves should be shut off immediately. It is best to shut the acetylene off first, because the fire cannot burn without fuel. Before relighting, the tip should be inspected for partly blocked orifices and both valves opened separately to be sure that the gas flows freely. The flame should be adjusted so that it is large enough to prevent the condition from recurring, or, if a smaller flame is needed, a smaller tip should be installed.

Adjusting the flame for paddle soldering and some other heating operations is simply a matter of using less oxygen so that a long, feathery flame is produced. The flame may be used at any adjustment that is desired, but it is best to avoid using a yellow flame, because it will tend to deposit soot on the surface being heated.

Acetylene burning alone will give off a large quantity of sooty, black smoke, unless it is forced out of the tip orifice fast enough to mix with the air. The soot will rise into the air and later settle, making a very undesirable mess. This condition may be avoided by opening the valve wide enough to cause the gas to mix with the air and burn clean as soon as it is lighted. It is not uncommon for the beginner to leave the torch smoking while he tries to decide which adjustment to make next. He should be trained to open the valve past the point of heavy smoking as soon as he strikes the light. Proper flame adjustment cannot be made until the acetylene valve is opened to this position, so it is simply a matter of doing it without hesitation to avoid the unnecessary soot.

THE OXYACETYLENE FLAME

The primary characteristic of the oxyacetylene flame that makes it suitable for welding is its intense, high temperature—about 5,850° F. (3,232° C.) when adjusted properly for welding. Temperatures up to 6,300° F. (3,482° C.) can be developed by adjusting the flame to an excess of oxygen; this higher temperature is not suitable for welding steel, however, because of the ill effects it has on molten steel.

The oxyacetylene flame actually consists of two flames: the intense-blue inner cone and the sheath flame. The highest temperature is produced in the blue inner cone. The temperature of the sheath flame, which extends several inches beyond the inner cone, is much lower. The high temperature of the inner cone is used for practically all torch operations.

Three basic torch flames, which may be considered flame types, are made by adjusting the torch valves to vary the ratio of oxygen and acetylene being used: (1) neutral flame, (2) carburizing flame, and (3) oxidizing flame.

The neutral flame is used for practically all welding operations on mild steel. In most instances, either the carburizing or the oxidizing flame will be harmful to steel. Only a very slight resetting of either valve will change the flame from one type to the other. For this reason, it is essential for the beginner to be familiar with the characteristics of all three.

The Neutral Flame

The term neutral flame indicates a flame that has been adjusted so it does not throw off either carbon (from the acetylene) or oxygen to contaminate the molten metal. When the flame is neutral, the torch valves have been adjusted so the volume of acetylene and oxygen entering the mixing chamber is in the exact ratio needed to produce complete combustion. When adjusting the flame setting, this condition can be recognized by the disappearance of the feathery streamers, leaving a sharply defined, intense-blue inner cone.

The neutral flame will produce a clear, clean-appearing puddle that flows easily because the surrounding sheath flame has nothing in it to affect the molten metal. The sheath flame then serves as a protective mantle to prevent burning of the molten metal by oxygen in the surrounding air.

The temperature of the neutral flame, approximately 5,850° F. (3,232° C.) at the tip of the cone, drops rapidly in a very short distance; the midsection of the sheath flame will be about 3,800° F. (2,093° C.) and the outer end will be about 2,300° F. (1,260° C.). Thus, it is obvious that the inner cone should be held quite close to the puddle to obtain rapid melting.

The Carburizing Flame

The term carburizing flame indicates a flame that has been adjusted so it throws off unburned carbon into the sheath flame. The pressure of this condition can be recognized easily by the feathery streamers extending from the tip of the inner cone.

The carburizing flame, by the addition of carbon to the molten metal from the flame, will cause the molten metal to boil and lose the clear appearance it had under the neutral flame. A weld made with a carburizing flame will be brittle when cold.

An experiment to demonstrate the effect of the carburizing flame can be made very easily. Adjust the flame so the feathery streamers extend at least ½ inch (12.5 mm) beyond the inner cone. Then, play this flame on one corner of a piece of sheet metal, keeping it in the position for the neutral flame, so the feathery streamers actually strike the heated surface. While the piece is at bright red temperature, plunge it into cold water. A file test will prove that the metal is much harder because carbon has been added. This experiment can be varied by keeping the carburizing flame on the hot metal for different lengths of time. If the flame is kept on long enough before quenching the metal in the water, the heated spot will become so hard it will snap like a piece of glass.

A slight amount of carburizing may not be particularly injurious to a weld in mild steel, but it is not desirable; if there is excessive carburizing, the weld definitely will be weakened. On some of the nonferrous metals, such as nickel and Monel metal, the carburizing flame sometimes is used without ill results.

Using a carburizing flame to heat metal for the shrinking operation can cause considerable trouble, because hard spots will result. When the file strikes these spots, it will chatter instead of cut and be damaged in the process.

The Oxidizing Flame

An oxidizing flame throws off excess oxygen into the sheath flame. There are no visible streamers, but the flame may be recognized easily by the harsh hissing sound it makes, and the excessive foaming and sparking it causes in the puddle. It can be recognized also as the flame is being adjusted by a shrinking of the inner cone and a purplish color.

The oxidizing flame has no use in welding steel. Excess oxygen will cause the molten metal to burn. Therefore, the slightest trace of excess oxygen should be avoided, because the weld will be weakened proportionally.

The oxidizing flame sometimes is used for heating heavy parts to temperatures below the bright red heat range. It develops temperatures up to approximately 6,300° F. (3,482° C.), which is slightly more than the 5,850° F. (3,232° C.) of the neutral flame.

OXYACETYLENE FUSION WELDING PROCEDURE

The oxyacetylene fusion weld is made by manipulating the torch flame so that a puddle of molten metal is started and carried along the seam. Normally, a bead is built up by depositing molten metal from a filler rod as the puddle moves along. A filler rod is not always necessary, however, if there is enough metal on the edges to be welded so they will flow together and make a bead of sufficient strength without it.

Making a good weld is a matter of manipulating the flame properly and depositing the filler metal in the proper position at the proper time. To do this, the following conditions must be kept under control by the operator: (1) distance of the end of the flame from the work, (2) angle of flame to the line of the seam, (3) rate of travel, (4) side motion (weaving) of the torch, and (5) position of the filler rod end in relation to the puddle and flame.

Each of these conditions is discussed separately in the following sections.

Flame Distance

The distance of the flame end from the work can vary for different welds. In most instances it should be quite close, but it should never touch the molten metal. The approximate distance is shown in Figure 5-8.

The actual distance is determined by the temperature and the spread of heat. The closer the flame is to the work, the higher the temperature will be, and the more it will be concentrated on a very small spot. If the flame is moved back from the work, the drop in temperature is quite rapid. For example, the temperature of the inner cone of the neutral flame is 5,850° F. (3,232° C.), but the temperature at the end of the sheath flame is only 2,300° F. (1,260° C.). When a small tip suitable for welding sheet metal is used, this drop occurs in a distance of 2 or 3 inches (5 to 8 cm).

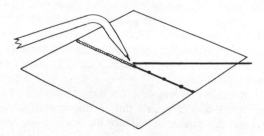

5-8 Angle of the flame to, and its distance from, the work.

In welding sheet metal, it is desirable to raise the temperature of the puddle to the melting point as quickly as possible and also to prevent the spread of heat into the surrounding metal as much as possible. This would seem to indicate that the flame should be held so the inner cone almost touches the metal. However, it is quite difficult to hold the flame in that position without actually touching it to the molten metal occasionally. There is the additional problem of the blast of the hot sheath flame gases that blow against the molten metal in the puddle. A much safer practice is to hold the inner cone away from the puddle just slightly less than its length; thus, a smaller flame would be held closer to the puddle than a larger one. At this distance, the blast effect of the flame is slowed down, and the possibility of accidentally touching the hot puddle is avoided.

Distance affects penetration to some extent. Even on light sheet metal, time is required for heat to flow through from one surface to the other. On heavier metal, time is even more important. By holding the distance about equal to the length of the inner cone, this needed time is provided. If it is held much closer, it may be difficult to obtain full penetration—only the upper surface will be melted.

Greater distance may be required when welding light metal to heavy metal. In such instances, the flame must be directed so that the heavy metal is brought up to the melting point without overheating the light so it melts away. However, other factors as well as distance must be considered when such welding problems are encountered.

Flame Angle

The angle of the flame to the work will vary accord-ing to the job. Actually, two angles must be considered: (1) the angle of the flame to the surface and (2) the angle of the flame to the line of the seam.

In making a simple butt weld on relatively flat stock, the angle of the flame to the puddle (shown in Fig. 5-8) should be somewhere between 30 and 45 degrees and pointed directly down the line of the seam. If increased penetration is needed, the angle should be increased; if less penetration is needed, the angle should be reduced.

Pointing the flame directly down the seam line on a butt weld will preheat both sides evenly. If the torch is turned to either side, that side will be heated more than the other. This will cause unequal expansion and tend to separate the edges even though they are tack-welded together.

On lap welds or when welding light metal to heavy, a different condition will be found. If the torch is pointed down the line of a lap weld seam, the flame will tend to melt the exposed edge of the upper piece faster than it melts the metal it covers. The answer to this problem is to hold the flame so it is turned slightly away from the edge, and to hold the filler rod so it acts as a shield for the exposed edge. This position of flame and filler rod is shown in Figure 5-9. Note that the operator has bent the filler rod so that his hand will be away from the heat of the hot blast from the torch.

In welding light to heavy metal, it always will be necessary to hold the flame so it points toward the heavy piece. The greater the difference in thickness, the more the flame should be pointed toward the heavy piece. It is a matter of experimenting to find the angle and distance from the puddle that will bring both edges to the melting point at the same time.

Rate of Travel

The rate of travel governs the width of the puddle and, to some degree, the depth of the penetration. Holding the flame on one spot without moving it will cause the puddle to grow larger until it melts through; moving it along the seam too fast will not heat the metal fast enough to make a puddle. Obviously, the proper speed is somewhere between these two extremes.

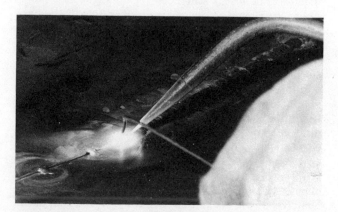

5-9 Position of the flame and filler rod in welding a butt joint. Bending the rod permits the operator to keep his hand away from the heat.

With the torch held at the proper angle and distance, the rate of travel can be adjusted easily by watching the width of the puddle. If it becomes too narrow, travel should slow down; if it spreads too wide, the forward movement should be speeded up.

Lack of confidence many times prevents a beginner from determining the proper rate of travel. Just as soon as the puddle grows a little too large, the novice will pull the flame completely away from the puddle, disrupting everything. All that is needed is to move along the seam a little faster.

Weaving the Flame

Weaving the flame from side to side will spread the heat over a wider path and slow the forward travel. The result will be deeper penetration and more time to add filler metal if a heavy bead is desired.

The weaving motion may be either a straight back-and-forth motion that, when combined with the forward motion, creates a zigzag effect, or it may be a spiral motion. In either case, the result is essentially the same.

When welding the light gauge metal that is found in body panels, it is largely a matter of operator's choice whether the flame should weave or follow a straight line. Mostly, it is necessary only to keep the flame steady and move forward just fast enough to permit the puddle to spread to the desired width. This spreads the heat into the adjoining metal less than weaving will. The result will be slightly faster travel and less heat distortion.

Many welders weave the flame whether it is necessary or not, because they find that they hold it more steadily that way. If so, it is better to weave than to attempt to hold the torch in a straight line.

When welding heavy metal, such as that found in some of the brackets and structural members, weaving is necessary to obtain the required penetration.

Filler Rod Position

The position of the filler rod in relation to both the puddle and the flame varies according to the type of weld being made. In making a simple butt weld, the rod need only be in such a position that the end of it may be melted and deposited in the puddle. Best results occur when the rod is held at a 45 degree angle to the surface and in line with the seam. The end should be kept quite close to the puddle so that as molten drops form on the rod, they may be deposited with a slight downward motion. As the weld progresses along the seam, the rod will describe a continuous up-and-down motion that should never raise the rod above the flame so that the end cools. If the rod melts too fast, it should be held slightly farther from the flame.

The use of the filler rod as a shield to prevent melting away of the exposed edge of a lap weld was mentioned briefly in the discussion on the torch angle. This practice is necessary in many cases where the edge of one piece is exposed more than the other. In making many such welds, the end of the rod will have to be kept in contact with the edge instead of raising it. In such cases, the filler will be fed into the puddle continuously instead of by a series of drops deposited by raising and lowering the rod.

BUTT WELDING

In learning to make a butt weld, one of the problems is to manipulate the torch and filler rod as described in the preceding sections. It is also necessary to position the pieces to be welded so that the edges are in the proper alignment and spacing, and to tack weld them so they will stay in alignment while the welding operation is in progress. When these steps have been performed properly, making the weld becomes a simple matter of making the weld bead.

Although neither the alignment of the edges nor the tack welding of the seam presents any difficult problems, each is important enough to justify separate discussion. Failure to perform either one properly can result in a very difficult welding problem.

Small pieces of metal have been used in the illustrations in the following section dealing with these subjects, because they they make satisfactory practice material for the beginner.

Alignment of the Edges

Alignment of the edges to be welded means that they should be spaced properly. With sheet metal of the thickness used in body panels, proper spacing is primarily a matter of making certain that the pieces are not separated too widely. Full penetration of such metal is not difficult to obtain when the edges are butted together tightly. Some space between the edges will make very little difference; however, a gap wider than the thickness of the filler rod is difficult to fill because of the tendency to melt back the edges. Extra-wide gaps will result in extra-heavy beads that overheat and warp the surface, plus requiring excessive time.

When welding butt joints in heavier metal, it will be necessary to provide some space between the edges to get full penetration. A good rule is that for metal 1/16 inch (1.6 mm) thick or thicker, the space between the edges should be about the same as the thickness.

The importance of having the edges positioned so that the surfaces are flush is much greater on thin metal, such as body panels, than it is on heavier material. If one edge is much higher than the other, it will be exposed to much more heat. Unless the flame is diverted to heat the lower, less-exposed edge, it will melt the exposed edge away, leaving a hole that will be difficult to fill. Diverting the flame will change the angle so that more heat will be directed to the piece that was low, overheating and expanding it more than the other. The result will be uneven heat distortion that will leave the finished job in a much worse warped condition than if the edges had been heated properly.

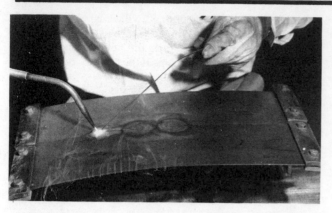

5-10 Tack welding. The flame should be directed toward the tack welds made previously. The smoke is caused by oil on the panel.

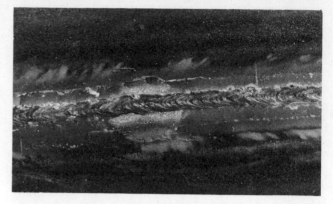

5-12 Rippled appearance of the weld being made in Fig. 5-11.

Tack Welding

Tack welding is necessary for any seam that is more than an inch (25 mm) long. Without tack welding, the preheating effect of the flame ahead of the puddle will cause the edges of the pieces being welded to expand and be forced out of alignment. Depending on the circumstances, the misalignment may be either a wide separation of the edges or an overlap. In either case, the result will not be an acceptable job.

The torch manipulation in making a tack weld is essentially the same as for making a seam weld, except that the torch angle should be more nearly vertical. Tack welding always should be started and carried out so that it causes the least possible heat distortion. In the operation shown in Figure 5-10, the first weld was made in the approximate center, and the third one is in the process of being made. Note that the flame is being pointed so that most of the preheating effect is directed toward the welds that have been made. These welds hold the pieces together so they cannot separate. If the torch were turned in the opposite direction, the warpage ahead of the flame would be much more, because the edges are not held.

Tacking of the other end of this seam will require the angle of the flame to be in the opposite direction. If these pieces had not been held securely in the practice

fixture, it would have been necessary to have tacked the ends first. When tacking an end, the flame always should be directed off the edge, heating the surfaces as little as possible.

The size of the tack weld should be kept as small as possible in order to cause the least possible amount of heat distortion. This is particularly important if the final weld will be finished to a smooth surface. Heat distortion that has been avoided does not have to be corrected.

Controlling heat distortion can be done best with the hammer and dolly block, which were not used in Figure 5-10. They never should be used on a tack until it has cooled well below red heat. Often it is better to wait until the metal has cooled to nearly normal temperature. It is difficult to establish rules to avoid trouble, however, because so much depends on experience. If the tack weld is worked while it is too hot, it will tend to shrink too much; if it is not worked hot enough, it may leave some distortion in the panel. The beginner must learn to judge the conditions for himself.

Welding the Seam

Welding the seam after tack-welding simply involves running a bead to overlap the edges of both pieces. This should be just a matter of maintaining the torch at the proper angle, distance, and rate of travel as the rod is fed into the puddle. No weaving motion of the torch was necessary in making the seam shown in Figure 5-11. Weaving on a seam such as this would only slow the forward motion and heat the adjoining metal more, creating more heat distortion than necessary.

The seam shown being welded in Figure 5-11 was made without stopping. Note that the area of the puddle has bulged upward sharply, and the area at the start of the seam already has started to draw out of shape. This will be warped badly after it finally cools. The warpage could have been reduced considerably by welding only a short distance and stopping so that the metal could cool. The idea would be to avoid excessive heat in the panel by allowing it to escape into the air.

Use of the dolly and hammer to work the area as it

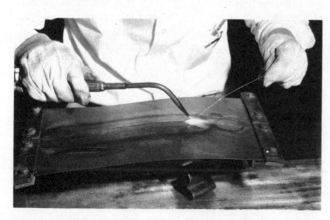

5-11 Welding the tacked seam. Warpage is due to heat.

5-13 Underside of the weld shown in Fig. 5-11. The scale is heavier because this side does not have the protection of the flame.

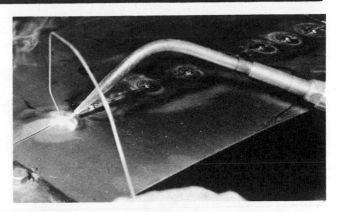

5-14 Using the filler rod to protect the upper edge of a lapped seam being tack welded.

was being welded could have prevented most of the drawing action in this weld. The operation is partly one of straightening and partly a matter of stretching the upset effect of the hot metal. Both are necessary on a weld such as this, if it is to be left in a smooth condition.

Figure 5-12 shows a close-up view of a short length of the upper side of the weld in Figure 5-11, and Figure 5-13 shows the underside of the same section. Note that the ripple action is relatively uniform and raised very little above the level of the surfaces on each side. The cracks showing on each side are in the weld scale; such cracks will be found adjoining any weld. Also note in Figure 5-13 that the weld scale is heavier and more cracked and blistered than that on the upper surface. This condition, also found on any weld, is due to the lack of a sheath flame on the underside to protect it from the oxygen in the air.

The weld bead shown here is a good example of the type the beginner should try to make. Many authorities have recommended that the weld bead should be built up above the surface level as a guarantee against breakage. Such a bead is a disadvantage for a weld that must be finished smooth, even though the final finishing will be done by filling to cover the weld. The experience of most welders is that breaks occur in the metal beside the weld rather than in the bead. For these reasons, it is recommended that the weld beads used on sheet metal be made as nearly flush with the surface as possible. They will be made faster, will hold, and will be easier to finish.

MAKING A LAP WELD

A lap weld is similar to a butt weld in that it requires tacking and a bead to be laid down on the joint. It requires more care and skill to make, however, because tacking must be done more carefully and the upper edge must be protected throughout the operation.

The tacking requires more care because of the over-lapped position of the pieces. In a properly aligned butt joint, inward movement of one piece is blocked by the other; in the lap joint, there is nothing to block move-

ment of either piece. The result is that there will be enough movement to change the alignment before the puddle forms. Unless care is taken with the subsequent tacks, this movement will increase with each one.

This tacking problem is so severe that on a long body panel lap weld it is necessary to hold the metal by means of rivets or metal screws before starting to tack weld. If this is not done, it will be very difficult to prevent movement that will affect the shape of the panel. Screws 2 or 3 inches (5–8 cm) apart usually will be sufficient.

The tack welds shown in Figure 5-14 were made without metal screws, but this job is not representative of the problem on a body panel, because the pieces are free on the ends and relatively narrow. This tack-welding operation was done in the same sequence as the tack welding shown on the butt weld (see Fig. 5-10). The only difference is in the flame angle and the filler rod position. Note that the flame is turned toward the exposed edge of the upper piece in Figure 5-14, instead of pointing down the line of the joint, as in Figure 5-10. This flame angle requires the filler rod to be kept between the flame tip and the exposed edge of the upper piece to serve as a shield. If the flame is not held at this angle and the filler rod held in this position, either the puddle will be too far from the edge of the upper piece, or the edge of the upper piece will melt back faster than the puddle can be started in the lower piece. In either case, too much filler rod will be required to make the tack. The result will be a rough weld and excessive heat distortion, because the flame will be kept on the work too long.

In welding the joint in Figure 5-14, the rod is kept in the same position as for tack welding, because the exposed edge of the upper piece must be shielded from the flame continuously. The flame should be turned more nearly down the line of the seam so the puddle will be kept moving forward. most of the time, it will be better not to raise and lower the rod into the puddle, as is commonly done in welding a butt joint. Instead, the rod is fed into the puddle as it melts away. If the rod is raised only momentarily, the exposed upper edge may melt away faster than the gap can be filled.

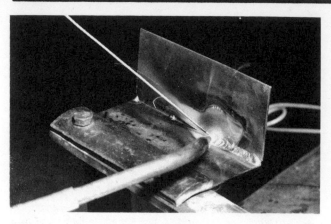

5-15 Torch and filler rod position for welding an inside corner.

Sometimes it may be desirable to weave the flame slightly in making a lap weld, but usually it will be best to keep it steady as it moves forward.

MAKING AN OUTSIDE CORNER WELD

The outside corner weld is the easiest of all welding operations to make with the oxyacetylene torch, because the angle of the surfaces prevents excessive pickup of heat from the sheath flame. To practice, simply prop two pieces of metal together to form the corner and fuse them together. Tacking will be required on long pieces, but short lengths, up to 3 inches, can be welded without it.

Unless it is desired to build up the bead to keep a square corner, the filler rod is usually not necessary in making a corner weld. The edges will fuse and run together easily, leaving a rounded corner without filler.

The flame should be directed down the line of the seam so that the preheating effect is divided evenly on both pieces. Turning it to either side will cause that side to expand more than the other and separate the edges, making the welding operation much more difficult.

MAKING AN INSIDE CORNER WELD

The inside corner weld is the most difficult to make, because the corner restricts the flow of hot gases from the torch, causing overheating. Unless extra care is taken, the tendency will be to burn through the surfaces on one or both sides of the joint before the puddle can be made and filled in the corner. Because of this condition, it is recommended that the beginner wait to start practicing on this joint until he has developed a fair degree of skill in making the more simple welds.

In most instances, the inside corner will be made with one piece in the flat, or horizontal, position, and the other vertical. It will be much easier to make a smooth, even weld if the torch tip is held at an angle much closer to the horizontal piece, and the end of the rod is held above the end of the flame, as shown in Figure 5-15.

Tacking and welding should be done in approximately the same positions.

Care should be taken to avoid undercutting the upper edge of the bead. The metal at the edge of the puddle will tend to thin if it is too hot. If the thinned section is not filled with molten metal from the rod, it will be left weak. Undercutting does not present a problem on the lower edge of the bead, because the hot metal will flow down and fill any thin spots.

Holding the tip of the flame as close to the puddle as possible without actually touching it will simplify the problem slightly, because the heat will be concentrated where it is needed, deep in the corner. It also will be desirable to use a smaller tip than required for welding metal of the same thickness in a lap or butt joint.

MAKING A "BUTTONHOLE" WELD

A "buttonhole" weld, shown in Figure 5-16, is made by melting a hole in the upper piece of a lapped joint, starting a puddle in the lower piece, and adding filler metal to refill the hole. It requires careful manipulation of both the torch flame and the filler rod. However, the beginner who has learned to make a lap weld should not have particular difficulty in making the "buttonhole."

The problem in making a weld of this type is in preventing the hole from enlarging too much as the puddle is started in the lower surface and the hole is being refilled. Enlargement can be kept to a minimum by using as small a flame as possible and keeping it almost vertical to the surface. The rod should be kept close to the flame as the hole is being melted so that filler material can be melted into the hole instantly when needed. As the hole is being filled, the filler rod should be shifted to shield the edge of the hole at any point where the metal begins to melt away too fast.

Figure 5-17 shows the underside of the welds shown in Figure 5-16. Note that there is considerably less evidence of the puddle than on the upper side. This is the way it should look. If too much metal is added to the puddle, it will only sink through below the surface, where it will do no good.

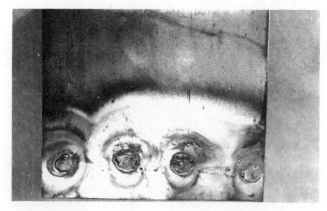

5-16 Buttonhole welds.

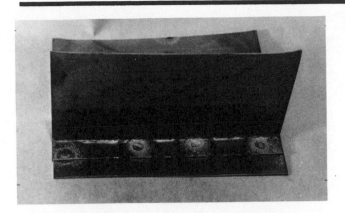

5-17 Underside of the buttonhole welds shown in Fig. 5-16.

BRAZING

Brazing is any metal joining process in which a nonferrous filler material is used to join other metals that have a higher melting point. Brazing and soldering are similar processes but fall into different temperature ranges. Processes using metals that melt at temperatures below 800° F. (427° C.) are called soldering; processes using metals that melt above that temperature are called brazing. The term brazing came into use because the original brazing materials were copper-based alloys, bronze or brass, which were used to join iron and steel. The welding industry has extended its meaning to include a process in which a metal in the brazing temperature range is used to join another metal with a higher melting point. For example, aluminum alloys are produced with a range of melting points wide enough to permit one to melt and flow onto another in the same manner that copper-based metals flow onto steel. This is called aluminum brazing, although there is no brass or bronze involved. Other metals, particularly silver, can be used in the same manner.

In the following discussion the term brazing is used in reference to the use of conventional, copper-based brazing material to join sheet steel.

Braze welding is a term used by the welding industry in reference to a welding operation in which the brazing material is used to fill a prepared open joint or build up a surface. It has little use in body repair operations, but a poorly prepared brazed joint may be simply a braze weld because penetration is not obtained.

PRINCIPLES OF BRAZING

Brazing is made possible by the property of many of the nonferrous metals that allows them to diffuse or penetrate into other metals when the proper temperature and surface conditions are available. The proper temperature conditions are that the copper-based filler material must be melted but not heated above the melting point, and the metal to which it is applied must be heated to approximately the same temperature. Brazing

is done only on metals that have a higher melting point than the brazing material; the metal being welded is never heated to the melting point.

To obtain the proper surface conditions, simply clean to remove foreign material, and use flux to clean the surface chemically and exclude atmospheric oxygen while the molten metal is being deposited. Cleaning to remove paint, rust, or other foreign material may be done mechanically by grinding, scraping, wire brushing, or similar means, but it also can be done by means of a strong flux. Usually, such cleaning is done mechanically, because of the problem of neutralizing the chemicals in the flux residue after they have been used. After the surface has been cleaned mechanically, it can be brazed with fluxes that will not cause corrosion after use.

When brazing is done properly, the molten brazing material wets and penetrates into the surface to which it is applied. This penetration is sometimes called diffusion, because the two metals intermix to cause an alloying action at their interface. The alloy thus formed is often stronger than either single metal. Figure 5-18 represents a cross section of a deposit of brazing material on a piece of sheet metal. Arrow 1 indicates the metal; 2, the brazing material; and 3, the alloy at the interface.

The strongest brazed joints are made by reducing the space between the surfaces so that the alloy layers join. The space necessary for this action when brazing steel is from 0.003 to 0.005 inch (0.07 to 0.13 mm). To understand how joints of this type can be made, it is essential to know the action of the flux and capillary action that draws the molten material into the joint.

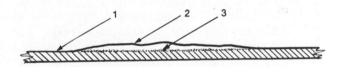

5-18 Cross-sectional sketch of a deposit of brazing material on sheet metal: arrow 1 indicates the sheet metal; 2, the deposit of brazing material; 3, the interface.

BRAZING FLUX

The original brazing flux was prepared in either powder or paste form. The powdered form was used much more than the paste except for very fine work, as in silver brazing. The operator dipped the heated end of the brazing rod into the powder so that a coating of flux would melt and adhere to it. As the filler rod was used to add molten metal to the puddle of brazing material, the flux would melt and run ahead.

Powdered flux has been almost completely replaced by flux-coated filler rod, eliminating the need for constant dipping into the powder can. The quality of the flux used for coating filler rods can vary, but much of it seems to produce better results than was obtained from the powdered type.

Flux can be added directly to the acetylene gas for industrial operations where the torch in in full-time use, but this is not practical for body shop where the torch is used for other welding more than for brazing.

Capillary Action

Caused by the attraction of any surface for any liquid that will wet it, capillary action can be seen in the everyday example of a glass tumbler partly filled with water; a thin film will rise on the sides of the glass about 1/32 of an inch (0.8 mm) above the level of the rest of the water. This film of water rises against gravity because the surface of the glass attracts it. It rises only a short distance, however, because the attraction of the single surface is limited. A similar attraction will be found on the surface of other liquids in other containers. Molten brazing material will have a similar action in a steel container if the surface is clean and fluxed properly.

Two glass tumblers can be used for an experiment to show how proper spacing of surfaces can be used to fill a weld joint with molten brazing material. The tumblers may be either cylindrical or tapered, but the sides must be straight, and one should be small enough to fit into the other. Put a little water in the bottom of the larger glass and lower the smaller one into it until the bottom just touches the water. Capillary action will draw water on it above the surface level just as it has on the side of the larger one. This is the same action described in the preceding paragraph. Now, press the outside of the smaller glass against the inside of the larger one; a film of water will rise to the top of the smaller glass instantly in the narrow space between the surfaces of the glasses. This occurs because the combined attraction of both surfaces is so much greater than gravity. The action of molten brazing material will be similar in a properly spaced clean joint heated to the proper temperature.

In making this experiment, the effect of different spaces between the two tumblers should be noted. Moving the smaller one away from contact 1/16 inch (1.6 mm) will permit the water to drop almost to its original level. As the space is closed, however, a point will be found that permits the water to rise almost instantly. This point will be only a few thousandths of an inch away from contact.

A similar result is obtained when brazing is done under ideal circumstances. Figure 5-19 represents a cross section through an ideal brazed joint. The surfaces have been very close together, but not actually touching—0.003 to 0.005 inch (0.07 to 0.13 mm) would be ideal. At this distance, the molten brazing material will flow into the joint just as water can be made to rise between the glass surfaces in the experiment just described.

Figure 5-20 represents the effect on capillary action of wide spacing and uneven heating. Note that this is the same as the joint in Figure 5-19, except for space between the surfaces. The brazing material has been drawn only part of the way into the joint and has fol-

lowed farther on the upper piece than on the lower. This is to be expected when brazing a seam that can be heated from one side only—usually the case with body seams that can be brazed satisfactorily. In many instances, there will be practically no penetration of the seam. This should not be accepted as unavoidable, however, because a good welder will learn to manipulate his flame and filler rod so that he obtains enough penetration to make the joint much stronger.

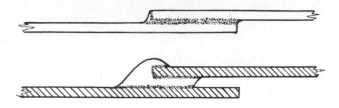

5-19 *(Top)* Cross-sectional view of an ideal brazed joint.

5-20 *(Bottom)* Cross-sectional view through a widely spaced brazed joint, showing the effect of reduced capillary action.

USES AND ADVANTAGES OF BRAZING

The primary use of brazing is in panel replacement to reweld joints originally electric spot welded when assembled in the factory. The advantage is that brazing causes less heat distortion than fusion welding, because the melting temperature of the copper-base alloys used as filler metal is much lower than the melting temperature of steel. Many such welds are located in low crown sections where the extreme heat of fusion welding with a torch flame will cause severe distortion. Most often, more work will be involved in relieving the heat distortion than in making the welds. Brazing sometimes will offer a means of preventing serious heat distortion and save the extra time required to relieve it.

There may be no advantage in brazing on a relatively high crown section that will not distort so readily. Also, it may be better to use proper electric welding equipment, if available, than to use brazing.

Another advantage of brazing is that it can eliminate the need for sealing, if the joint is brazed full length.

Brazing on automobile sheet metal repair should be restricted to overlapped seams. Some materials and methods may be used to make good butt joints, but they are not satisfactory or practical for repairing automobile bodies.

Four joint types suitable for brazing are shown in Figure 5-21. Joints similar to these will be found throughout the body structure of any automobile. A is a true lapped joint, and C is actually a variation of A. Similarly, B and D are variations of the same basic joint in which the flanges extend away from the surface.

To braze joints such as these so that the entire overlapped area is filled is often impractical when using the welding torch. In most instances, the repairman has to be satisfied with a partly filled joint and some build-up

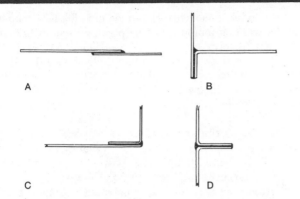

5-21 Four common variations of the lapped joint. Joints A and C are essentially the same, as are joints B and D.

of brazing material on the surface. The problem is to heat both sides of the joint uniformly so that the filler metal will flow by capillary action. If two torches are available, and there is reason to devote the extra effort to the operation, it can be done. Usually, though, only partial penetration into the joint will do.

A brazed joint of the type usually made on sheet metal panels is shown in Figure 5-22. This joint is over-lapped about ½ inch (12.5 mm). It was tested for penetration by cutting narrow strips across the joint and pulling them apart. The penetration was approximately one half of the overlap, or ¼ inch (6.3 mm). This amount of penetration would be adequate for any body joint welded satisfactorily by brazing.

The built-up bead over this joint makes the operation a combination of brazing and braze welding. The irregular deposit on the surface of the bead is flux. Although it will do no harm to leave it in place, this may be chipped off if it is on a surface where it is undesirable.

STRENGTH OF THE BRAZED JOINT

Care in fitting up the joint and in manipulating the flame is very important in making a satisfactory brazed joint. Before the pieces of metal are put together, they should be clean, so that flux and molten brazing material can penetrate. It is useless to expect penetration if the joint is filled with sealer, rust, or other material that would prevent tinning.

If everything else is equal, the joint in which the pieces are spaced just wide enough to permit the brazing material to be drawn in by capillary action will be stronger than one in which the pieces are much farther apart. This is illustrated in Figures 5-19 and 5-20. Note in Figure 5-19 that the bond between the surfaces is made by the alloy formed on the interface. This material is much stronger than the pure brazing material that fills the wider space between the surfaces in Figure 5-20.

Proper torch flame manipulation is a matter of watching to see that the temperature is just right to allow the tinning action to be continuous. When it is right, the molten brazing material will flow or spread at

the leading edge of the puddle. If the temperature is not high enough, the molten material will run over the metal much as drops of water will roll over an oily surface. This also will occur if the surface is contaminated, making the flux ineffective, or if no flux is used. If the surface is too hot, the brazing material will be damaged by burning the tin, which is a part of the composition of the copper-base alloys used for brazing.

Appearances are sometimes deceptive, but a good and a poor brazed joint usually can be determined by inspection. The good joint should be smooth and bright, and the edges should blend into the surface of the metal on which it is applied. In contrast to this, a pitted or blistery surface, or an edge that appears to stand on top of the metal, usually is evidence of an unsatisfactory brazing job. An excessive amount of fine, white, powdery material on both sides of the joint indicates overheating; sometimes there will be a considerable amount of such powder, even though the joint does not look as though it were badly burned. This is always evidence of a rather poor job.

EMBRITTLEMENT

One disadvantage of brazing is that the joint, once made, should not be remelted or subjected to melting temperature longer than necessary. Prolonged heating will cause the molten brazing material to penetrate deep enough into the steel to make it brittle. This is not a problem in a normal brazing operation, because the brazing material is molten for a very short time, but long periods should be avoided.

Repairmen often braze a piece of scrap metal to a body panel or frame to make a connection for pulling equipment. When this is done, the piece should not be removed by simply melting it off. Preferably, it should be chiseled off and the excess ground off. When that is not practical, the piece can be removed by taking advantage of the fact that brazing material loses much of its strength when it reaches a temperature well below its

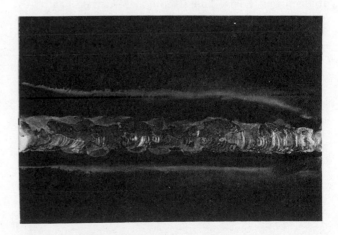

5-22 A typical brazed joint with a low bead built up over the overlap. Testing showed penetration to one half of the depth of the overlap.

melting point. The torch flame should be concentrated on the piece to be removed to heat the entire joint. It will reach a temperature when it can be knocked off with a sharp hammer blow or, if it is thin metal, pulled off with a pair of pliers.

Excessive penetration can be demonstrated by depositing a drop of brazing material on a piece of clean, bright sheet metal and holding it at melting temperature much longer than it would be in a normal brazing operation. If it is held long enough, a faint copperish tint will be seen on the other side. The spot will crack if bent or hit with a hammer. Vibration will cause steel in this condition to crack in normal operation.

RESISTANCE SPOT WELDING

Resistance spot welding is primarily a factory production method of assembling sheet metal parts, but it also serves a useful purpose in the body repair shop. The feature of greatest value to the body shop is the ability to weld long, flat sections of sheet metal with little or no heat distortion. The saving is in time that does not have to be spent in either working out or filling large heat-distorted areas that were undamaged before the welding operation. This welding method is in no way a substitute for oxyacetylene welding, but it is important enough that any competent metal man should understand its uses and limitations and know how to adjust and maintain the equipment. This is essentially a matter of technical knowledge; very little manual skill is involved.

The emphasis of this section is on the use and limitations of resistance spot welding equipment adapted to body repair use. The repair shop has much different problems in replacing a body panel from those of the factory in assembling them on a production basis, even though the equipment used by both operates on the same basic principle. Instead of specialized equipment to do one job repeatedly, the body shop needs equipment with enough flexibility to do a variety of jobs on an intermittent basis. The situation is further limited by economics; the equipment must pay for itself within reasonable time, and it must operate on the power supply that is adequate for other shop equipment.

This discussion is limited to problems of welding sheet steel. Resistance spot welding is used extensively in fabrication of sheet aluminum, but requires special equipment with sufficient power to weld in extremely short periods of time. If such equipment was available for body repair use, the cost would be far out of proportion to the need, so it is not considered further here.

THE BASIC PRINCIPLE OF RESISTANCE SPOT WELDING

Electric resistance spot welding is possible because the resistance of a conductor to an electric current is in direct proportion to the amount of current flowing in it.

A spot on two pieces of overlapped metal can be heated to the welding temperature by placing them in the circuit of an electric current having sufficient amperage to overload their capacity to conduct electricity. The current is applied by electrodes held in contact with the metal surface by mechanical pressure, so that the heat-softened metal will be forced together to form a weld when the correct temperature is reached.

This basic principle is illustrated in very simple form in Figure 5-23. This consists of (1) a step-down transformer, connected to an utility power line, (2) two conductors, large enough to carry the low-voltage, high-amperage current to the electrodes, (3) two blunt pointed electrodes that contact an area of metal considerably smaller than the cross-sectional area of the conductors, and (4) a source of mechanical pressure to force the heated metal together. Two switches are shown: one in the power line to ready the machine for operation and a trigger switch that the operator presses to activate the timer that starts the weld cycle.

This figure emphasizes the difference in the cross-sectional area of the conductors and the spot to be welded. The conductors must be large enough to carry the high-amperage, low-voltage current required to develop welding heat. Power lost by resistance in the conductors reduces the capacity of the machine.

The current must flow only long enough to generate welding temperature in the overlapped surfaces of the joint. The steel in the joint has higher resistance than the conductors, but the point of highest resistance, called the *interface*, is in the contact between the sheets. Heat starts to generate at the interface and spreads to the outer surface very rapidly. When welding temperature is reached, the current is shut off and pressure on the electrodes forces the hot metal together to form the weld. The spot of metal joined is referred to as the *nugget*.

The length of the welding cycle varies to some degree, but it is completed in a fraction of a second. The timer (Figure 5-23) is required for consistent operation, but some relatively low-powered welders operate without one.

A source of pressure is required to force the hot metal together, as indicated by the large arrows. Although pressure must be held slightly longer than the current flow to permit solidification of the nugget, pressure regulation is not as critical as current flow. The

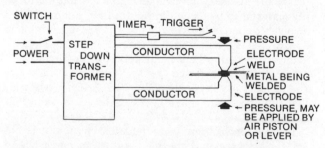

5-23 Basic layout of resistance spot welder using opposed electrodes.

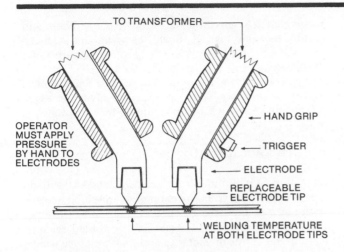

5-24 Hand-held electrodes, used on one side to make two simultaneous welds.

type welder decribed in the next section, designed for body shop use, requires the operator to apply pressure manually.

BODY REPAIR SPOT WELDING

A spot welder equipped with an electrode setup similar to that shown in Figure 5-23 has some body repair use but is impractical for man cause access to the inside surface of many seams is either difficult or impossible. Those that can be reached are usually coated with paint and thick layers of sealer. The problem can be

simplified considerably by a variation in resistance welding technique, using both electrodes hand held on the outside, as shown in Figure 5-24. The machines shown in Figures 5-25 and 5-26 are equipped with flexible cable conductors leading to this type of electrode. This system is easy to use and does not require any change in electrode setup for different jobs. The operator turns the machine on, presses the two electrodes against the seam while pulling the trigger, and maintains the pressure on the electrodes briefly after the timer shuts the current flow off. As shown in Figure 5-24, each operation makes two welds.

The machines in Figure 5-25 and 5-26 are equipped with an automatic timer, and one has a power control. The operator must familiarize himself with the proper settings on these, but, once they have been established, they need changing only to take care of different metal thicknesses. The operator soon learns how much pressure to apply, but he must be consistent in applying approximately the same amoung on every weld.

In this system the sheet metal between the electrodes is made a part of the welding circuit. Some of it passes through the high resistance point of the interface and generates enough heat to weld. In a properly made joint, there should be no difference in the welds made at each electrode, if the timer and power setting are correct and the right amount of pressure is applied. How-

5-25 Electric resistance spot welder equipped with timer and hand-held electrodes.

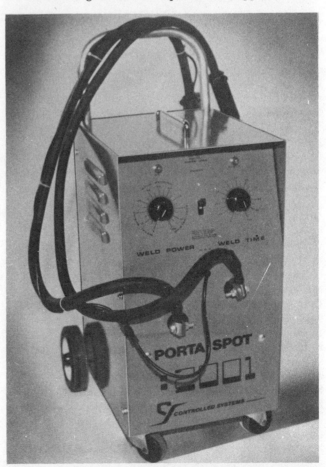

5-26 Electric resistance spot welder equipped with timer, power control, and hand-held electrodes.

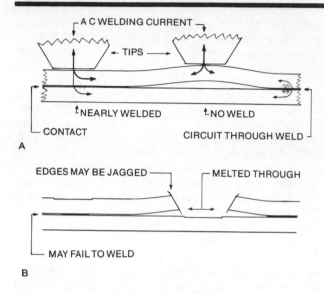

5-27 Cross-sectional effect of attempting to weld without good interface contact.

ever, unless the joint has been prepared properly, it will be impossible to obtain a good weld with these or any other electric resistance spot welder.

WELD JOINT PREPARATION

The joint surfaces must be clean and fit together without buckles of excessive springiness. A welder set up to use opposed electrodes, as shown in Figure 5-23, requires clean metal on both sides of both pieces. The hand-held electrodes in Figure 5-24 eliminate the need to clean the back surface, which is usually the most difficult, but the interface and exterior must be clean and fit together without requiring excessive pressure on the electrodes. This is particularly important on the relatively low-power welders suitable for body repair use.

The effect of attempting to weld with no interface contact is illustrated in Figure 5-27. At A, current flow is indicated by the curved lines extending out of the electrode tips. (Arrows are shown at both ends because the current is alternating.) Some of the current concentrated at the left electrode passes through the interface resistance, but some by-passes through various paths provided by previously made welds, back to the right electrode, as indicated by the curved arrow on the extreme right. All of the current flowing through the right electrode is concentrated in the upper piece, which almost instantly heats to the melting point and allows the electrode to punch through to the lower. Some of the overheated metal is deposited on the lower, but most of it flies out in white hot globs that may travel across the shop, creating a fire and eye hazard. (Never operate a spot welder without eye protection.)

The result of this condition is illustrated in B. The left electrode may make a good weld if there are enough other welds in the area of the right to complete the circuit through the lower piece; the right electrode will

simply punch a hole through the upper piece. There will usually be some crusty "flash" between the surfaces that will extend up around the edges in a jagged, razor sharp fringe.

Opposed electrodes, as in Figure 5-23, will punch a hole in the same way if there are previously made welds or enough other contacts to complete the circuit.

ELECTRICAL CONTACT

The equipment manufacturer's recommended tip diameter is calculated from the ratio of available amperage to the size of the area of contact. The end of the tip, which is in contact with the metal to be welded, must be maintained at this diameter to make satisfactory welds. If it gets too large, the amperage will be spread over a larger area and fail to generate temperature high enough to weld. Figure 5-28 illustrates the result of trying to weld when the contact area is partly covered with any material that does not conduct electricity. Paint is indicated here, but any other material that blocks the flow of current will have the same bad effect.

Figure 5-28 is drawn in direct proportion to the dimensions of a ⅛ inch (3.175 mm) electrode tip contact area being used to weld two pieces of sheet steel 0.035 inch (0.89 mm) thick. The arrow points to paint blocking approximately half of the contact area, so that only a small portion of the tip surface can contact the steel. The entire amperage will be concentrated on this very small area, creating temperatures far beyond the melting point of the steel. The overheated molten metal expands so fast that it actually explodes with enough force to throw out blobs of molten metal that can cause serious burns or ignite flammable material; they will damage paint or window glass on an automobile in an adjoining stall.

The metal thrown out leaves a void in the weld, as shown. A weld in this condition is ruined. Foreign material built up on the electrode tip will often have a worse effect on it than on the metal being welded. Problems of this type are avoidable for the operator who understands the need to clean the metal surfaces properly and to keep the electrode tips in good condition.

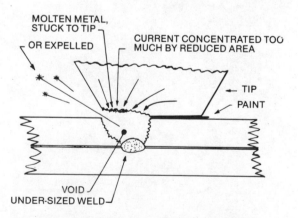

5-28 Effect of attempting to weld with contact area partially covered with foreign material.

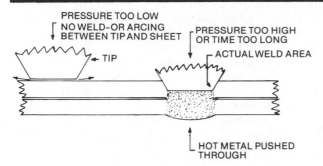

5-29 Effect of attempting to weld with electrode pressure too low *(left side)* and too high *(right side)*.

Electrode Tip Maintenance

Electrode tips tend to spread as well as accumulate non-conductive material on the end. Maintenance is merely a matter of filing or grinding off any foreign material and keeping the end dressed to the manufacturer's specification. A mill file or very fine grit sanding disc is preferable for dressing the contact face, particularly on the relatively small tips normally used in body repair work; coarse scratches limit the contact and will cause premature tip failure and additional maintenance.

ELECTRODE PRESSURE

The effect of too low and too high pressure on the electrodes is illustrated by the cross-sectional Figure 5-29. Not enough pressure, on the left, will make little or no impression on the outer surface in contact with the electrode and, probably, not discolor the lower surface at all. The tip will still complete the circuit (probably by arcing across the gap) so that too much pressure on the other (the right) will penetrate too deep into the surface. This situation is worse when extra-long timer settings are used, because the metal stays hot longer.

The right side shows the electrode tip nearly through the upper piece, leaving only a very thin section of it to weld to the lower. The result is a very weak weld that will break under a very light strain. It is possible to push the electrode all the way through the upper piece, making no weld at all.

This operation involves a degree of skill, but it is simple, compared to many other of the repairman's skills. Any competent worker who recognizes the problems involved and is willing to train himself can learn easily to maintain even pressure.

Electrode pressure is one of the factors of spot weld quality discussed in more detail in the section on Spot Weld Testing.

SPOT WELDING LIGHT TO HEAVY METAL

The capacity of most spot welders practical for body repair use is limited to welding two pieces of sheet metal of the thickness normally used for exterior panels. An attempt to weld thicker metal or one piece of normal thickness to another much thicker will be a total failure if the usual procedure is followed. The technique illustrated in Figure 5-30 will extend the capacity of this type of welder enough to make dependable welds on joints such as the flanges of a quarter panel to the heavier metal of a lock pillar or the seams of a rocker panel. Special preparation is required, but the advantages of spot welding can be retained. The technique is to use a center punch to make small, conical projections on the interface surface of the light piece for every weld. The electrode tips should be oversize when placed against the exterior surface of these projections, where, as shown in A, they serve only as conductors. Each projection becomes an electrode tip for one-time use.

This technique works because the welding current is concentrated on a smaller area than covered by the electrode tip and produces a higher temperature. Higher pressure is required because, as shown in A, the flange must bend slightly as the weld forms. Oversize electrodes are needed to apply pressure over a larger area. There is little risk of punching a hole because the larger tip covers more area than the acutal weld. Also, the heavier metal absorbs the heat faster than does metal of normal thickness.

This technique works best when welding to a heavy piece supported rigidly to withstand the extra pressure. When rigidity is lacking, pop rivets should be installed at 3–4-inch (7.5–10-cm) intervals; otherwise, the joint will slip, and the projection will be expelled. The rivet heads can be hidden by making a weld directly on them. Some rivet heads will leave a center hole, which can be filled by placing a narrow strip of metal between the electrode tip and the rivet and using extra pressure, so that a small piece will be forced into the rivet when the weld is made. A rivet disguised in this manner should not be considered a weld, as it will have no holding power.

Welds made with this projection technique are relatively small, so it is necessary to make at least twice as many as were found on the original seam. After the punch marks are made, the flange should be checked to make sure that the surfaces fit together, as shown in A. After welding it may be necessary to use light hammer blows to drive the outer edge of the flange down between the welds.

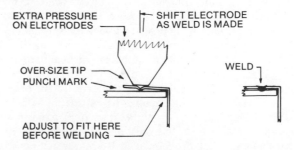

5-30 Technique for welding sheet metal to other metal that is beyond the normal capacity of the machine.

The joint should be prepared carefully when this method is to be used. It is particularly important to avoid blowing holes if it is on a visible surface, such as a lock pillar. If a weld fails but the surface is left solid, the method explained in the next section can be used, but the appearance may not be as good as that of the weld made with the projection.

REWELDING BROKEN SPOT WELDS

A method of rewelding broken spot welds illustrated by Figure 5-31 can be used easily on any joint that has good electrical conduction through the interface. As shown,

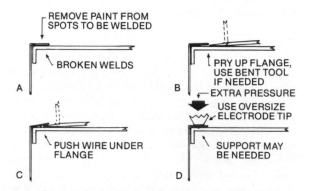

5-31 Technique for repairing broken spot welds. Other electrode, not shown, should be grounded to the under piece.

the edge of the flange is pried up to permit a small piece of wire to be pushed into place. The wire serves the same purpose as the punch marks described in the preceding section. A ⅛-inch (3.175 mm) piece cut from a common paper clip is very satisfactory; the steel in the paper clip is similar to body sheet steel.

If the interface is rusted, it must be pried open far enough to permit removing the rust and driven back down again. The flanges should be close together enough to grip the wire. The spring action of the flange is needed to add to the welding pressure.

Some of the weld-through sealers used in factory production may cause trouble after aging. Any trouble can be determined by testing. Some of the sealers remain conductive indefinitely; others are conductive only when wet and *perhaps* will be reactivated by rewetting with water; still others may simply become nonconductive with time. If the seam is difficult to make conductive, it may be necessary to use another method.

The desirability of rewelding broken seams justifies a trial, particularly on seams such as door hem flanges or lock pillars that are quite visible. This method can be used close to trim parts or body sealer to repair broken welds that are causing squeaks or rattles.

Two welds should be made at a time when using hand-held electrodes, but only one is shown in Figure 5-31, because the procedure is the same for both. A welder having opposed electrodes, as represented in Figure 5-23, can be used for this purpose on joints with

both sides exposed, as on a door hem flange, but considerable ingenuity may be required to use it on other joints.

The procedure is explained by the notes on the figures and is not discussed further here except to emphasize that a great deal of pressure should be used on an over-sized electrode. The electrode serves only as a conductor; the piece of wire is the electrode.

SPOT WELD SEALER

Any spot-welded seam on a surface exposed to the weather should be sealed. Conductive sealers are available, so that a weld can be made through them. The material is applied in a continuous bead to one of the interface surfaces before the joint is assembled, and welding pressure spreads the sealer so that the joint space is completely filled except for the area of the weld nugget.

Weld-through sealer is used on all exposed welds in factory production, and some are further sealed with a bead of heat-curing sealer applied to the outer surface. This sealer cures as the body goes through the paint ovens. It is the tough, rubbery material found on door hem flanges and similar seams.

Electric resistance spot welding has not been used widely by body shops, and many body men and body shop managers are not aware that a spot-wleded seam can be sealed. Some seams are easier to seal than others. Those assembled by laying one piece on the other are simple, but a door hem flange presents problems if it must be hemmed with a hammer and dolly block. The hammer blows drive most of the sealer out of the hem. Tools have been made that roll the flange, but they are not used widely.

When a weld-through sealer is not available, an exposed body seam should be sealed on the exposed edge with a high-grade material. If the joint is to last, the moisture must be kept out.

WELD TESTING

Any repairman starting to use a resistance spot welder he is not familiar with should make several welds on scrap metal and test them for strength before using the machine on actual repair work. Whether or not he has had previous experience with other spot welders, he should familiarize himself with the operating characteristics of *that* machine before using it. The reason for this precaution is that, unlike the fusion welding processes, a spot weld is made between two pieces of metal where it is hidden from view. The operator goes through the motions, but he has to learn from testing when he has struck the right combination of time, pressure, and power, if the machine has a power adjustment, to be sure that he is welding. Weld failure can be both costly and embarrassing.

A simple method of testing spot welds is shown in Figure 5-32. For this test the two strips were welded

5-32 Simple spot weld test. A good weld should tear a button out of one piece, leaving it securely attached to the other.

together, using a machine equipped with hand-held electrodes, and the edges were separated to provide a surface to be gripped by the vise and the pliers. Downward pressure on the end of the pliers will provide enough leverage to tear any spot weld apart in metal of this thickness.

A good weld should require enough force to tear a "button" out of one piece. The rim of the button should be nearly as wide as the metal thickness and should have a fresh, grainy surface where it was torn. A button that snaps out easily and has heat discoloration on the rim is an indication that the electrode has penetrated too deep, as illustrated in Figure 5-29, probably because it has been too hot and may have had too much pressure. A weld that separates cleanly on the interface is an indication that either it was not hot enough or not enough pressure was applied. In either case, it is not a weld.

In starting to make a series of test welds the timer—and the power control, if the machine is so equipped—should be set according to the manufacturer's directions. Each weld, or pair of welds, should be tested when made and studied to determine what variations of time, power, or pressure are needed before making another. The metal used for the test should be of the same thickness as that the machine will normally weld.

If the welder is to be used on extra-thin metal, a series of tests should be made on it also.

ATTACHING WELD-ON PULL TABS

Attaching the weld-on pull tabs, mentioned in Chapter 3 and shown in Figure 3-24, is simply a spot welding operation performed with adapters attached to the electrode holders, as shown in Figure 5-33. The adapter shown on the right serves as a ground while the one on the left does the actual welding. The attaching adapter should be installed on the electrode holder having the trigger so that, after one tab has been welded on, the ground can be hung on it as shown and left until the job is completed.

Before starting to install tabs, the repairman should adjust the machine properly. Machines having a power control should be reduced to about one third of the power range; machines having only a time control should have the time reduced proportionally. Welding the first tab to the panel requires a bare spot for the ground adapter. The back of the curved section should be pressed against the bare spot in the same manner it is shown supported by the bracket in Figure 5-33. If a new tab or one that has been reground is being used, welding contact can be made through the paint by twisting the electrode holder. Press the trigger, and the tab is welded on. The ground adapter can then be hung on the tab and others welded on without further concern for grounding.

These tabs are a low-cost, expendable item. They are easily removed after use by twisting, preferably by using a pair of vise grip pliers, but the tip widens with each use. They can be ground down to the correct size point several times before they are too short for further use. If they are not resharpened when ground, it will be necessary to remove the paint before rewelding them.

These tabs can be used individually with a slide hammer equipped with a single hook, or a gang hook-up can

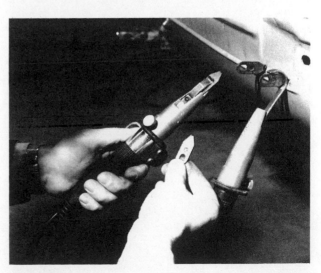

5-33 Electrode holders with adapters to attach weld-on type pull tabs.

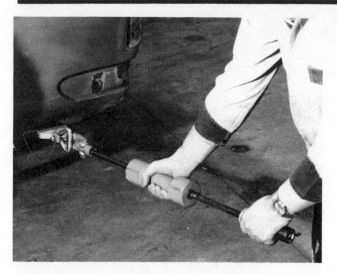

5-34 Weld-on gang hookup with adapter to permit pulling with either a slide hammer or a body machine.

be made, as in Figure 5-34. A slide hammer is shown in use here, but a chain can be connected in the same manner to pull with any type of body machine.

SAFETY RULES FOR SPOT WELDING

Carelessness with any electrical equipment is inexcusable and particularly so when the equipment operates on 230-volt power supply and is portable. Fortunately, the high voltage is confined to the input side of the spot welder; the output is low, usually from 3 to 8 volts. Unless the primary circuit becomes short-circuited to the secondary, there is little electrical hazard to the operator. The following common-sense rules should be followed to reduce electrical accidents to the minimum:

1. The plug-in connection should be removed from its receptacle and the power cord coiled on the machine when not in use.
2. The power switch should be turned off when a delay occurs in the welding operation.
3. The power cord should never be placed where automobiles will run over it.
4. When any damage to the power cord is noted, the machine should be disconnected and taken out of use until repaired.

There is additional risk of personal injury or fire caused by flying sparks. The following rules should be observed to reduce the risk to the minimum:

1. All persons using the machine should wear adequate eye protection.
2. Bystanders should be kept at a distance.
3. The operator should wear gloves and full sleeves.
4. Before starting to weld, the operator should check the area and remove any flammable materials, particularly gasoline, paint materials, or paint-coated masking paper.

ELECTRIC ARC WELDING

The electric arc is used as the source of heat in arc welding. The basis of the method is that an electric current flow can be maintained across an open space after it has been started under the proper current and voltge conditions. Temperatures well above the level required for welding result because of the high resistance of the open space. All arc welding systems make use of this characteristic of the electric arc.

In the original method of arc welding, a carbon electrode was used to maintain the arc, and the filler rod was fed into the puddle in much the same way it is fed into the oxyacetylene puddle. There is still the occasional application of the carbon arc, but is has been completely replaced by other, more efficient methods.

A later development of arc welding was the consumable electrode. In this method, the filler rod is used as the electrode by feeding it into the puddle as it melts off. Bare steel wires have been used for this purpose, but they have been replaced almost entirely by the coated electrode. The coating burns off, creating an inert atmosphere over the puddle area to shield the molten metal from attack by oxygen in the air. The result is a better weld that is much easier to make than with the use of a bare wire electrode. This method is in wide general use for most manual arc welding, particularly repair work. In the following sections, this method of arc welding is referred to as *conventional* arc welding.

A still later development in arc welding has been the use of a shielding gas, which is released through a nozzle in the electrode holder to exclude air from the puddle area. Two methods are in common use, MIG and TIG, with the MIG method much more widely accepted for body and frame repair than TIG.

MIG is an acronym for Metallic Inert Gas, meaning that a metallic electrode is used with an inert gas. The term originated when the only gases used were inert, usually helium or argon. Helium and argon are used in welding many of the nonferrous metals, but carbon dioxide, which is really not inert, is used for welding most steels.

TIG is an acronym for Tungsten Inert Gas, meaning that a tungsten electrode is used with an inert gas. In this system, the tungsten electrode is used in much the same manner as the oxyacetylene torch, and the filler rod is fed into the puddle by hand. Tungsten is used because it does not burn away.

In all arc welding systems, the metal to be welded is made a part of the electric circuit. The arc is produced by contacting the electrode to the work, or *striking the arc*, to complete the circuit and then held slightly off the surface to maintain the arc. The manual skill in arc welding is in learning to maintain and manipulate the arc so that the filler metal is deposited where it is needed and the proper penetration is obtained.

In the following discussion of arc welding, the emphasis is on the conventional system. It is the most widely used in body and frame repair, and the skills required for it are much the same as for the other systems.

CONVENTIONAL ARC WELDING EQUIPMENT

Two basic types of arc welding equipment are in general use: the alternating-current transformer type and the direct-current generator type. Each has its advantages and disadvantages.

The advantages of the alternating-current, or AC, machine are that it is a relatively simple device, costs less, will last a long time, and is adequate for most simple welding jobs. For these reasons, it is the machine most commonly used in automobile repair shops, particularly body shops.

The chief disadvantage of the AC welder is that there are many welding operations for which it is unsuited— for instance, those jobs requiring the use of direct current so that the polarity of the electrode will be either positive or negative. Such jobs cannot be done satisfactorily with an AC machine. However, most such jobs are on alloys or nonferrous metals that the automobile repairman usually is not required to weld. The alternating current of the AC welder is slightly more difficult to weld with in a vertical or overhead position as compared to the direct-current generator type. This is due to the change of polarity of alternating current, which occurs 60 times per second. However, this is not such a drawback to the repairman as it might seem, because he can learn to operate the AC machine in either position with a little practice. Most of his welding will not require work in a difficult position, anyway. A practical AC arc welder is shown in Figure 5-35.

5-35 Alternating-current arc welder.

The advantage of the direct-current generator type welder, or the DC machine, is in its greater versatility, as compared to the AC machine. With few exceptions, the DC welder will do any job that can be done with the AC machine, plus those that either cannot be done or are difficult to do without direct current.

The DC welder normally is driven by an electric motor drawing current from a utility power line. However, it may be driven by any type motor having sufficient power and flexibility to carry the load. Except in rare instances, when other motors are used, they are either gasoline or diesel. The operating costs and maintenance problems of using either motor are much greater than with electric drive, so they are used rarely, except where portability is needed. However, when it is necessary to take the welder to a job where an electric power line either is not available or connection to it would be difficult, the gasoline engine-driven welder provides a satisfactory and efficient means of doing the work. There is no difference in the quality of the work done with either the electric or other type drive.

MIG AND TIG WELDING SYSTEMS

MIG and TIG welding systems are similar, in that they both use gas to shield the puddle, but both the machines and the methods of operation are different. It is possible to adapt a conventional welder to operate on the TIG system because the machine used for both maintains the welding current at a constant amperage level. However, more efficient operation will be obtained from a machine designed especially for TIG welding.

The MIG machine maintains the welding current at a constant voltage level. This difference makes it impractical to adapt a conventional welder to MIG operation. MIG welding is a useful system that has been adopted for many industrial uses, including the body shop industry. When equipped with a timer, it makes a very practical spot welder. A typical maching is shown in Figure 5-36.

The MIG welding gun, shown across the machine, is operated in much the same manner as the electrode holder used in conventional welding, the primary difference being that the filler metal is a fine wire, fed automatically through the gun nozzle, instead of a coated rod that must be hand loaded into the holder.

The operator who has learned conventional welding should be able to adapt to MIG welding with very little trouble. As with any new technique, it is necessary to become familiar with the system, particularly the adjustment of the machine and some other differences, but these do not pose difficult problems.

The TIG system can be used on practically all metals that are considered weldable. The equipment can be adapted to a wide range of thicknesses from thinner than body sheet metal to the maximum that can be welded by ordinary processes. However, it has had limited acceptance by the body shop industry and is not illustrated here.

5-36 MIG welder.

The original shielding gas used with both MIG and TIG systems was helium or argon, hence the I in both names. However, when MIG is used on steel, it is common practice to use either carbon dioxide or a mixture of carbon dioxide with a small percentage of argon. Use of carbon dioxide, which is not an inert gas, makes the term MIG a misnomer, but it is in common use. People in the welding industry prefer to call the MIG system Gas Metallic Arc Welding (abbreviated GMAW) and the TIG system as Gas Tungsten Arc Welding (abbreviated GTAW).

A sample MIG (GMAW) butt weld is shown in Figure 5-37 and a sample spot weld in Figure 5-38. MIG welding is shown being used to assemble the heavy duty truck cab in Figure 5-39. Although this is a manufacturing scene, it is a good example of how MIG welding can be used in rebuilding any sheet metal structure. This same work on a high-production body would be done with resistance spot welding.

AC ARC WELDING GUN

An arc welding gun and special AC transformer is shown in Figure 5-40. When used with the proper electrodes, this outfit makes an arc-spot weld in much the same manner as a MIG spot, but depends on feeding an exact length of the electrode into the puddle instead of being shut off by a timer.

The advantage of this unit is that the equipment is less costly than either resistance or the MIG unit, and it causes less heat distortion than the oxyacetylene torch. It can be used in any position without difficulty, but should never be used without eye protection from flying sparks; if it is used overhead, full face protection should be worn. Colored lenses are not necessary, because the weld is made within the end nozzle.

The transformer produces a lower voltage current than a conventional AC welder, which limits the length of the arc it will maintain. The electrode coating contains iron powder, which aids in starting the arc on contact. The gun is designed to permit a predetermined length of electrode to be fed into the weld puddle. When the feed stops, the arc is extinguished automatically. When the feed length is adjusted properly and the operator learns to push the gun down at the correct speed, these machines will make satisfactory welds with much less heat distortion than can be expected with the oxyacetylene torch. The worst disadvantage is that a much rougher weld is made than by either the resistance or

5-37 Sample MIG butt weld. (Made in a trade school.)

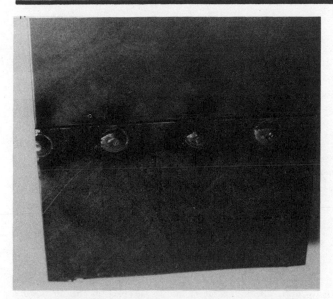

5-38 Sample MIG spot weld. (Made in a trade school.)

5-39 MIG welding being used to assemble truck cabs.

MIG spot methods and that considerable skill is required to avoid burning holes. The metal to be welded must be in close contact.

USE OF ARC WELDING IN BODY REPAIR

The two types of joints in body repair work on which arc welding (by either conventional MIG or TIG systems) is preferable to the torch are (1) joining the heavier metal used in frame members and some body reinforcements and (2) as a substitute for resistance spot welding on long, overlapped seams. In addition to these, other special uses arise from time to time, often enough that the qualified repairman should develop the skill to use the arc correctly on jobs where it should be used. This is simply a matter of practice, preferably under the supervision of a qualified instructor who understands the basic problems of arc welding in body repair. The skills required for body repair work are but a small part of those involved in the overall arc welding field, particularly in heavy industry or building construction.

ARC WELDING PROCEDURE

The process of learning to arc weld starts with learning to strike and maintain the arc to make a uniform weld bead. It is then necessary to learn to make good weld beads on butt and overlapped joints in various positions. Welding straight down on a flat surface is relatively easy, because both gravity and surface tension tend to keep the molten metal in place until it solidifies; greater skill is required to weld on vertical or overhead positions, because gravity works against surface tension, tending to make the molten metal flow out of position before it solidifies. The repairman should learn to

weld in all positions, as many of the joints that should be arc welded are on either vertical or overhead surfaces. The type of machine used and the electrode selected are factors affecting the skill required for many welding opertions, particularly those in the vertical or overhead positions. In general, the AC transformer-type machine requires slightly greater skill than the DC motor-generator. However, transformer-type machines are more widely used in body shops, because they are less expensive, and a good one is adequate for the need when it is operated properly.

Electrodes are made in a wide range of sizes and types, some intended for general-purpose use on mild steel and others for restricted use on certain alloys only. They vary also for different types of joints. Some general-purpose electrodes can be used on any position, others are intended for use only on flat surfaces, and still others will weld in any position but work particu-

5-40 Arc-spot welding gun.

larly well in the vertical and overhead positions. The beginner should start using a good general-purpose electrode for practice in the flat position, but when he comes to vertical and overhead joints, the extra expense for electrodes designed to work in those positions may be more than repaid in faster skill development.

The machine used by the beginner should be adjusted properly for his first practice, but it is as important to learn to adjust the machine as it is to use it. The beginner working alone to learn arc welding has no alternative but to study all available technical information and depend on his own interpretation of it. The advice of an experienced welder can be very valuable in such circumstances.

In the following discussion of arc welding procedure for the beginner, it is assumed that he will be dressed properly, for protection against arc light burns, and is wearing suitable gloves, flash goggles, and helmet. The flash goggles should be worn at all times to provide eye protection against an accidental flash while the helmet is raised. The helmet must be in the down position at all times the arc is in operation. Also, the beginner should be aware of his responsibility to avoid exposing other persons in the vicinity without warning.

PRACTICE MATERIAL

The beginner should practice arc welding on steel of the thickness that will be welded on the job, starting with metal no thicker than ⅛ inch (3.175 mm), and should learn to weld seams in all positions. As his skill increases, the practice should be on thinner metal. Long butt or lap seams with a continuous bead are rarely arc welded on body panels. There are many jobs on which arc tacking will serve as a practical substitute for resistance spot welding. The skill level required to make good tack welds is the same as that required for seams.

The pieces used to learn the arc and run beads may be almost any size. The pieces used to learn to weld butt and overlapped joints need be no larger than 2 by 6 inches (5 × 15 cm); larger pieces will often be a waste of metal. When usable metal is difficult to obtain, pieces used for seam practice by one class can be saved for practicing striking the arc and running beads by a following group.

STRIKING THE ARC

To start striking the arc, a piece of the ⅛ inch (3.175 mm) stock should be placed on the bench in a convenient position for the hand, right or left, that the student normally uses. If small, it should be clamped down, and the ground clamp attached if the bench top is not grounded. Before starting the machine, the movements of striking the arc and running a bead should be visualized, and a convenient position to assume should be determined. Then start the machine, load an electrode into the holder, hold the tip of the electrode poised about

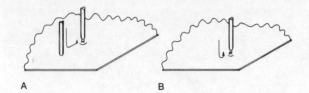

5-41 Striking the arc: A, scratch method; B, touch and lift, the preferred method.

1 inch (25 mm) above a predetermined spot and slanted approximately 20 degrees away from the direction of weld travel, lower the helmet, touch the tip to the surface, and lift it slightly. There will be a flash, which will continue and become the arc if the operation is performed smoothly. If not, either the electrode will stick or the arc will go out.

The correct motion for striking the arc may require a little practice, but it is easily developed. Some beginners find it easier to use a scratching motion at first, as illustrated in A, Figure 5-41. However, the touch-and-lift motion, illustrated in B, is more accurate and should be adopted after a little practice.

With the arc started, close attention will be required to keep it going. Arc length should be held firmly for a moment, to start a puddle of molten metal, then carried forward at a rate that will keep the puddle at a uniform width and build a bead of deposited metal behind it. This can be confusing at first. The electrode must be lowered at the same rate it is consumed by the arc, and at the same time it must be kept in forward motion without changing the angle to the work. Control of the combined motions requires practice but soon becomes a reflex instead of a conscious action.

The beginner is often confused by the answers received to questions about the arc length. Specifications varying from ⅛ to ¼ inch (3.175–6.35 mm) are often given, followed by reference to long and short arcs. Instead of a specification, the arc should be considered as having a range within which it can be varied to control heat. The longer the arc, the higher the temperature. As it gets too long, the color darkens from intense blue to a purple tint, the sound changes from a smooth hiss to a harsh crackle, and blobs of molten metal will form on the tip of the electrode. Past that point it goes out.

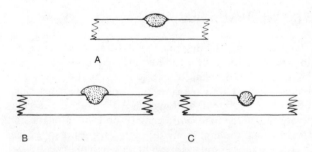

5-42 Cross sections of practice weld beads: A, good; B, weld metal overlaps surface, not acceptable; C, undercut, not acceptable.

If the arc gets too short, it will stick, short-circuiting the entire output of the machine. It should be broken loose or released from the holder before it gets red hot.

The beginner should continue practicing striking the arc and running beads until he can start a predetermined point and make a continuous bead with uniform width and build up, as illustrated in cross section A in Figure 5-42. It is not acceptable to leave an overlay, as shown in B, or excessive undercutting, as illustrated in C. After the slag is chipped off, the bead should have a rippled appearance, much the same as a weld made with an oxyacetylene torch.

BUTT WELDS

A butt joint is simply two pieces of steel joined by a weld bead, but it requires more careful manipulation of the electrode than when making a bead on solid metal. The added factor is penetration. The exposed edges absorb heat faster than a solid surface, increasing the tendency to burn holes.

A good butt weld should penetrate the full depth of the joint, so that the small bead is formed on the lower surface and a much larger one on the upper; the bead should blend smoothly into the adjoining surface. On metal ⅛ inch (3.175 mm) thick, or less, some welders, particularly beginners, feel that they can weld better by weaving the electrode back and forth along the length of the joint or in a circular pattern. Either method will make a larger weld bead than required for the thickness. The beginner may find it necessary to use one or the other of these motions at first, but he should make slight changes in the electrode angle, arc length, and rate of travel to find a combination that will enable him to weld without extra electrode movement.

Four cross sections of common weld conditions are shown in Figure 5-43. The beginner's attempt to avoid burning holes usually leads to piling up too much on the upper surface and not enough penetration, as shown in A. A weld showing traces of the original edges is definitely not acceptable. B represents full penetration with a slight bead on the lower surface and a full bead blended into the upper. C represents the beginning of

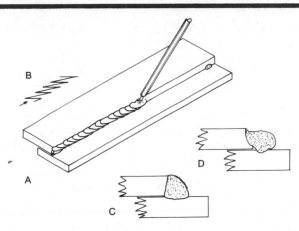

5-44 Lap joint: A, joint layout and electrode position; B, weave pattern; C, cross section of good weld; D, cross section of poor weld, showing excessive undercut, insufficient penetration, and overlap, not acceptable.

undercutting due to overpenetration and failure to fill the puddle completely. The strength of the weld is reduced in direct proportion to the depth of the undercut. Even greater undercutting is represented in D. In any industrial setting where welding is judged by established standards, undercutting is not acceptable. Although strict standards are not enforced in automobile repair work, undercutting should be no more acceptable for it than for any other industrial situation.

The beginner should chip the slag off each practice weld and inspect both sides for improvement. At first, many welds may show all of the various conditions represented by Figure 5-43. However, after reasonable practice, definite improvement should come. Practice should be continued until acceptable welds can be made.

LAP WELDS

Lapped joints can be practiced by using narrow strips, overlapped as shown in Figure 5-44. Strips can be added to either the upper or lower surfaces for additional welds.

A good weld, as represented by the cross section at C, should have full penetration without melt-back of the upper edge or overlay. Unacceptable conditions are shown in D. Here, the upper edge has melted back, thinning the cross section; the inner corner is not fused, thinning the joint more; and molten metal has run out over the surface of the lower piece to form an overlay. A weld with no better fusion than this would break easily if tested, as described in the following paragraphs.

Most beginners will find it necessary to weave the electrode in a diagonal pattern, as suggested by B, to avoid melting too much of the exposed upper edge. Weaving creates a long, narrow puddle instead of a round one. The purpose is to allow the molten metal at one end to solidify partly before adding more. Whatever weave pattern is used, the arc must return to all points before any one cools too much. The pattern in B is only a

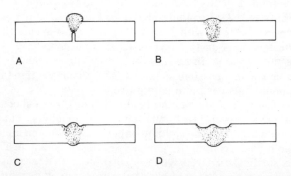

5-43 Cross sections of four common weld conditions: A, not enough penetration; B, full penetration with slight bead on under surface, acceptable; C, undercutting and unfilled gap, not acceptable; D, excessive undercutting and underfilling, not acceptable.

suggestion; each welder must find a pattern that works for him.

Visual inspection is not enough to judge the quality of a lap weld, because the depth of penetration into the inner corner is hidden. Working with small pieces, it is easy to grip one piece in a vise and twist the other around it lengthwise. Almost any lap weld can be broken in this manner by repeated bending, but a good one should stand considerable bending before failing. When the beginner can make welds that seem to pass the bend test, he should saw some of them apart crossways. No traces of the lower corner of the upper piece should be left.

ARC WELDING SAFETY

The problems of safety in arc welding fall into two classifications: protection for the operator and avoidance of fire hazards. Both of these should be considered when doing arc welding.

The operator needs protection from the ultraviolet light given off by the electric arc, against burns from the hot metal, and against the possibility of injurious electric shock. The brilliant light given off by the arc will cause burning, similar to sunburn, on any exposed area of skin if the exposure lasts for more than a few minutes. It will cause serious eye injury in much less time. The eye never should be exposed to the arc for even a fraction of a second.

Protection for the eyes and exposed parts of the face and neck should be provided by a face mask, shown on the left in Figure 5-35, large enough to cover the entire face and neck. It is fitted with a special glass that filters out untraviolet light. If broken, this glass never should be replaced with any other glass without the same filtering characteristics. The shade of the glass is no indication that it is suitable. Many glasses of the same size are available for use in oxyacetylene welding helmets. Use of such a glass is dangerous, even for a short time.

The glass filter in the welding helmet is covered with a piece of clear glass to protect the expensive filter glass. This protection is necessary because the operator must get close enough to the welding operation to see what he is doing. Flying sparks of white-hot metal will strike his helmet and the cover glass, ruining the filter glass very rapidly, if exposed. Replacement of the clear glass with any piece of glass satisfactory for good vision is permissible. However, glass with flaws that tend to distort vision should be avoided.

Protective clothing and gloves always should be worn by the operator. Bare forearms, open shirt collars, or bare hands are an invitation to severe burns. Burning can take place through lightweight clothing if it is exposed to the arc for any length of time. In making a two-minute weld, there is no problem. There is danger, however, if the operation continues for a half-hour or more.

Although the operator receives the greatest amount of exposure because he is closest to the work, protection for a helper or another person working in the area is important. Many times another person will help the operator by holding a piece in alignment. There is usually more risk of injury to the helper's eyes than to the operator's because the helper rarely wears a helmet. Instead, he will usually depend on turning his head or closing his eyes as the operator strikes the arc. It is much better for the helper also to wear a helmet. Better yet, the work should be set up so that the services of a helper are not required.

If arc welding is done in a special area, some kind of screen should be set up so that other persons in or passing through the area will not be forced to look at the light of the arc. This is particularly important in an area where persons not familiar with welding will be exposed to it.

There is little risk of arc burn on the skin for persons who are not actually doing the welding. Under most conditions, such exposure is too short to be of any particular consequence.

There is always a certain element of fire hazard with any welding operation. In general, the risk is about the same for arc and oxyacetylene welding when highly flammable materials are in the area. Under such conditions, welding should be delayed until the materials can be removed or the welding job taken to a safer area. However, around less flammable materials, particularly wood, there is much less fire hazard with arc welding, because it does not release the blast of hot gases characteristic of the torch flame. But it will throw sparks for considerable distance and may set fires the operator does not see because he is blinded by the helmet.

Probably the greatest risk of fire with the arc is in welding a frame in the area of the gasoline tank or the lines. An arc striking a gasoline tank, full or empty, is an almost positive guarantee of a distastrous fire and explosion. Striking a gasoline line with the arc may seem less hazardous than on the tank, but it can be as bad. A small quantity of gasoline burning on the shop floor can heat the tank, causing the gasoline to expand and spew out of the ruptured line to add fuel to the existing flame.

There should be an absolute rule that the gasoline tank must be removed before any welding, by any method, is done on any part of the body or frame where there is risk of welding heat's striking it. Another person standing by with a fire extinguisher is not sufficient protection. Human reaction is not fast enough to stop some gasoline fires. The only safe precaution is to remove the possible cause. When removed, the tank should be stored in a safe place.

The risk of serious injury through electrical shock is always present with any electrical machine, but is much less from the welding cables than from the higher voltage current in the power lead to the machine. This is particularly true when a portable machine is used with a long, plug-in cable. Worn or damaged insulation can expose the conductors; if they come into contact with the metal being welded or even a damp floor, the operator can be injured seriously. Damaged cables should be repaired or replaced immediately.

Filling

Filling has always been an important part of automobile body repair procedure. The original filling material was solder, often referred to as "lead," because of its high lead content, 70 to 80 percent instead of the 50 to 60 percent in solders used for most other purposes. In recent years plastic filler materials have almost completely replaced solder for several reasons, the most important being cost and the relative ease of application. In the following discussion of fillers, plastics have been considered the primary materials and have been used in the various repair jobs explained. The directions for applying solder are given because it still has a place in high-quality body repair work, particularly on high-priced sports cars and antique restoration. Many serious students of the body repair trade are interested in reaching the skill level required for such work. They should at least understand how solder should be applied.

Filling is a part of the straightening operation, but it must be emphasized that it is not a substitute for the whole process; it will save considerable time on many jobs, but there are many others that can be done faster, with much less filling than is often used, if the straightening is done correctly. There is a further disadvantage that excessive dependence on filling tends to stop progress in skill development.

TYPES OF FILLERS

Two types of fillers are used in body repair work: poly-ester and epoxy resin base materials. The epoxy resins make a better bond to steel or aluminum, but have three disadvantages that have limited their general acceptance by the body repair trade: they are more costly, more difficult to use, and more toxic. Even though the polyester base materials do not bond quite so securely, the bond is good enough to justify their use as a general-purpose filler; many shops use them exclusively.

Hardening

Both polyester and epoxy resins harden by chemical action started by adding a catalyst, usually called a *hardener*, just prior to application. Hardening will be speeded or retarded by high or low temperatures. The manufacturer's directions for the amount of hardener to add are based on use at 70° F. (21° C.). Most brands of polyester fillers can be worked within fifteen minutes, if mixed according to directions. No general statement can be made about the hardening time for epoxy fillers, because different manufacturers formulate their material to different specifications.

Regardless of the temperature of the materials when mixed, heat is generated by the chemical action. Polyester filler applied at normal temperature will grow quite warm to touch in a few minutes. It should be allowed to cool a few more minutes before it is filed or planed. The same action takes place with epoxy fillers, but not necessarily at the same rate.

Shrinkage

Both epoxy and polyester base materials shrink in the process of hardening, polyester more than epoxy. An experiment that can be performed by anyone is shown in Figures 6-1–6-3. For this, two batches of lightweight polyester filler were mixed separately, the left one first, using material from the same container. Six drops of the manufacturer's liquid hardener were added to the left one and twelve to the right. The photograph in Figure 6-1 was taken immediately after the right batch had been deposited on the aluminum foil. The foil is the ordinary kitchen type available from any grocery store.

The photograph in Figure 6-2 was taken when the first signs of buckling began to appear around the right batch, approximately four minutes after it was put in place. The left side is buckled much more, but it has had about three minutes more time to harden.

The photograph in Figure 6-3, taken sixteen hours later, shows very definite buckling around both batches but a little more on the right than on the left. There was *almost* as much buckling a half-hour after the photograph in Figure 6-2 was taken, but a photograph of it was not included, because there was only a slight difference between it then and later. This shows that most of the shrinkage occurs as the material hardens.

The under surfaces of these samples were rounded by the drawing effect as the material shrank. The soft aluminum, 0.001 inch (0.025 mm) thick, was used because it has little resistance to the drawing effect of shrinkage. The sheet steel or aluminum in a body panel has far greater stiffness than the foil; however, the drawing effect is always there. It is enough to pull a large, nearly flat, thin steel panel out of shape when a large section is filled. It can be kept to a minimum by following the manufacturer's directions to build up a deep fill in successive coats, allowing each coat to harden before applying the next. However, if the panel is flat and thin enough, excessive filler will be required to make up for the collapse of the slight crown caused by shrinkage of the filler.

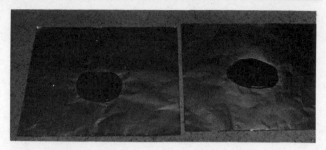

6-2 Photo of batches taken 4 minutes later. Aluminum foil has started to buckle on left batch, but it has had 3 more minutes to harden.

POLYESTER FILLERS

The following sections deal with polyester fillers. The procedures for surface preparation, mixing, applying, and finishing any type of filler are enough alike that, if one is understood, there should be no problem with others. However, when using any new brand or type of filler for the first time, it is only common sense to take time to read whatever instructions the manufacturer provides.

There are many brands of polyester fillers, but only a few manufacturers of the base materials. All contain the fluid resin and a solid to provide the necessary working properties. The two most commonly used solids are talc and tiny glass beads. Glass fiber, flake aluminum, and some other solids are used to some extent, but not nearly as much as the talc and glass beads.

Talc-type fillers are generally cheaper, but they tend to become excessively hard if not finished soon after curing. Talc is moisture absorbent also. The glass bead-type fillers, usually referred to as *lightweight*, will remain workable hours or even days after curing. The glass beads, obviously, will not absorb anything. However, after being painted, the exterior surface is sealed well enough that moisture absorption is not a problem. Any holes in the panel under the fill should be sealed by either brazing or soldering, if the inner surface is exposed to moisture in any way. This statement is contrary to the claims of some filler manufacturers, but it is based on experience.

The type of solid used does not affect the mixing and application procedure.

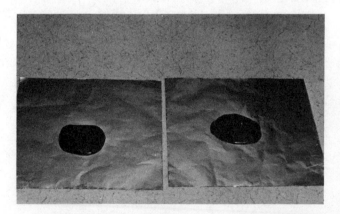

6-1 Shrinkage test of polyester filler. Batch on left was mixed with 6 drops of liquid hardener. Batch on right was mixed with 12 drops approximately 3 minutes later. Photo was taken immediately.

6-3 Photo taken 16 hours later. Right batch, which has had the most hardener, has buckled the aluminum foil the most.

APPLICATION

Applying body filler does not require a high degree of skill, but it should be done properly to obtain a satisfactory fill and to avoid waste. The tools required are (1) stirring paddle, (2) mixing board, (3) wide-blade spreading tool, and (4) disposable wiping cloths.

When first opened, a new container often has liquid resin that has separated from the solids and come to the top. This should be stirred back in to restore the proper balance of resin and solids; *never* pour this off. The stirring paddle can be used to dip out material as needed from the container, but it should not be used for mixing—it may carry hardener back into the container.

Hardener should be added to the batch according to the manufacturer's instructions. However, the exact amount used is not critical to the point that it should be measured. Some allowance must be made for temperature, particularly extremely hot weather. The user soon learns from experience how much variation will be required for different conditions.

Mixing the hardener into the filler should be done with the spreading tool. There is no exact procedure to follow, but good results will be obtained by first scooping material up around the edges and piling it in the center, then working across the pile from side to side with a kneading action. Repeating this several times from different angles should ensure that all of the batch gets mixed uniformly. Mixing is shown in Figure 6-4.

The mixing board may be almost anything with a smooth surface. Molded plastic boards are well liked, because the filler does not bond to them strongly. Pieces of plywood or heavy paper box board are used, but must be cleaned carefully after every use.

Plastic spreaders are inexpensive and easily kept clean. Some repairmen prefer to use a wide-bladed putty knife and accept the extra effort required to keep them clean. The practice of keeping the spreaders or putty knives in a can of scrap thinner should be discouraged, however, because of the fire hazard.

To apply the first coat, the spreader should be held at

6-5 Applying the first coat of plastic filler. The knife is pressed hard against the surface to ensure that no air pockets are left under the material.

a low angle and pressed hard against the panel (Fig. 6-5) to force filler into the depth of the disc sander scratches. These scratches are essential to the bond but, if not filled completely, each one may serve as a tiny, elongated air pocket and pathway for moisture under the fill.

The importance of applying filler in thin coats was emphasized in the preceding section and is repeated here, particularly for the first coat. If the surface is rough, it is best to put on just enough to fill the hollows and allow it to harden before applying more. Hardening, as the term is used in reference to preparation for following coats or final finishing, means that the material has cured enough that it can be filed or planed without gumming up the tools or tearing strips out of the filler. If the first coat has been applied properly, it should be smooth enough to allow application of the second coat as soon as it is hardened, without any finishing; however, any rough, high spots should be planed off first.

The second coat should be applied with firm pressure, but it should be finished with a light touch, holding the spreader at a higher angle, so that the surface can be smoothed without dragging it out of shape. It should then be allowed to harden so that it can be finished.

Sometimes filler will begin to harden before the shaping operation is complete. When this occurs, it is useless to attempt to work it further. Instead of just getting stiffer, it will begin to form into separate large lumps that will roll up on edge, leaving open spaces deep in the fill. This will occur any time that the material is worked too long after mixing, but it will happen more often when the hardening time is reduced by use of extra hardener or because of high temperature. Whatever the cause, it should be allowed to harden completely, then be planed down and refilled.

FINISHING

The tools commonly used to finish body filler are (1) "cheese grater"-type plane, referred to here as the

6-4 Mixing plastic filler with hardener. Kneading motion with the broad-bladed knife mixes in less air than a stirring motion.

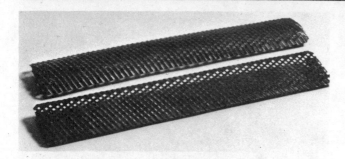

6-6   Flat and half-round plane blades.

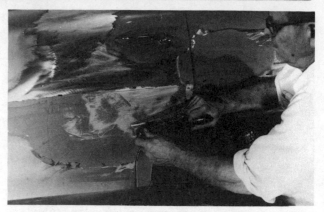

6-8   The start of the rough finishing operation, using a "cheese grater" plane.

plane, (2) air-powered board-type sander, (3) hand board sander, and (4) body file. Rotary sanders are used to some extent, but they make a lot of dust, and it is difficult to control the depth of cut.

The plane consists of a holder and detachable cutting blades, which are available in both flat and half-round shapes (Fig. 6-6). Some prefer to use the half-round blade without the holder for all surfaces, grasping it by the edges, as shown in Figure 6-7. With or without the holder, it should be stroked in a criss-cross pattern similar to the method recommended for use of a body file. The plane is intended for use only when the filler first sets up and is still quite soft. Talc-type fillers will be too hard to plane within an hour or two, depending on temperature and the amount of hardener used; the lightweight, glass bubble-type fillers can be planed much longer, usually after standing overnight.

The plane is a "speed" tool when used to rough-cut the still soft filler, as shown in Figure 6-8. Care must be exercised to avoid cutting too much, particularly when working around the edges of large low spots that will require additional filler. The surface around the low spot should be planed to contour, but care must be taken to avoid cutting it too low, as illustrated in Figure 6-9. This mistake is easy to make, because the toe of the plane tends to drop as it passes over the edge of the low

spot, cutting down the first edge, and the heel drops as it approaches the opposite edge, cutting it down. The result is that the low spot is made to appear smaller when actually it has been made wider than it was at first by cutting away needed material. Large low spots should be refilled, as shown in Figure 6-10.

When a filled area has been planed properly, it should be possible to finish it by sanding down the coarse marks left by the plane.

Either the air-powered or the hand sanding board may be used for the final sanding. The air-powered tool is shown in use in Figure 6-11, being pushed back and forth sideways across the job because its stroke provides the forward motion to do the cutting. The hand board is used in the same manner as a body file on a steel panel. The rough sanding should be done with 36- or 40-grit sandpaper, and then should be final-finished with 80- or 100-grit paper.

The primary use of the body file is on areas too narrow or otherwise obstructed to permit use of the sanding tools. It can serve for the entire job, eliminating all other equipment except fine sandpaper, but is rarely the only tool, because it is too slow and the filler dulls the file blade rapidly.

The job that was filled, planed, and sanded is shown in Figure 6-12. It has been refinished in Figure 6-13.

PROPERTIES OF BODY SOLDER

All lead-base solders differ from almost all other metals in that they melt over a wide range of temperature, instead of changing from solid to liquid at a fixed point.

6-7   Using a half-round blade held by the edges.

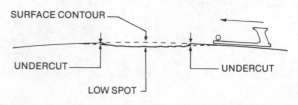

6-9   Undercutting of edges of low spots, caused by careless planing of partly filled area.

6-10 The final coat of plastic, applied after the first coat was roughed planed. This coat refilled the low spots showing in Fig. 6-8.

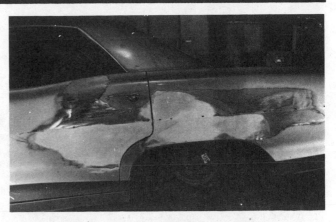

6-12 The finished surface, ready for repainting.

Other alloys of nonferrous metals have this property, but not to the degree found in solders composed of lead and tin. All of the lead-tin solders in common use begin to soften when heated slightly above 360° F. (184° C.), but the final melting point varies with the lead content. Those with approximately 70 percent lead liquefy at close to 500°F. (260° C.). By applying the torch flame properly, a batch of body solder can be kept within the part of this temperature range between solid and liquid, in which it has the consistency of motar. This permits it to be worked into the desired shape, using an oiled hardwood paddle.

Solder Paddles

The best solder paddles are made of bird's eye maple that has been treated with boiled linseed oil. The decline in the use of solder has made paddles difficult to obtain. If one is made up, it should be soaked at least overnight in boiled linseed oil. A second, but less desirable, choice would be outboard motor oil. If another wood must be used, it should be one of the varieties of hardwood having a very close grain; resinous or open-pored wood is almost useless for the purpose.

BODY SOLDER APPLICATION

There are four basic steps in applying body solder: (1) cleaning, (2) tinning, (3) filling and shaping, and (4) metal-finishing.

The procedure for applying solder is essentially the same for any surface condition for which it is a suitable means of repair. The greatest problem for the beginner is to learn to use the torch flame on relatively flat metal, so that heat distortion is avoided. For that reason, it is best for him to practice on higher-crowned surfaces until he has developed some skill before he attempts to apply solder on the more difficult areas.

Cleaning

Any material that will prevent the solder from adhering to the surface to which it is to be applied must be removed. The materials that, under normal conditions, will be on the surface to be soldered are (1) paint, (2) weld scale, and (3) rust.

Occasionally, body sealers, cements, or other foreign matter that has found its way onto the surface by accident also must be cleaned off. The same cleaning methods will be satisfactory for the removal of all types of material.

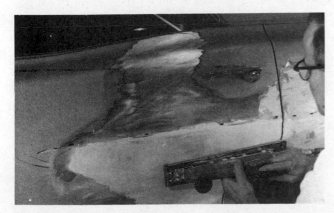

6-11 Final-finishing the plastic, using a straight-line sander.

6-13 The finished job, ready for delivery.

6-14 Removing paint with the disc sander.

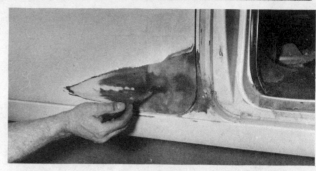

6-16 Brushing flux on hot metal; steam indicates proper temperature.

The clean, bright metal surface left by the disc sander is ideal for solder application (see Fig. 6-14). Wherever possible, use the sander to remove paint, rust, or weld scale. However, body solder is used as a finishing material over surfaces that are entirely too rough to be cleaned with the sanding disc; rough welds are an excellent example. Cleaning a panel with a saucer-shaped wire brush mounted on a disc sander is shown in Figure 6-15. Although not satisfactory for removing large areas of paint, the wire brush will clean out either paint or weld scale from sharp depressions very rapidly and without contamination. It is best, however, to avoid its use on any surface where cements or sealers are present, because it will smear such materials instead of removing them. Such materials may be removed much more easily by heating them and scraping.

Acids should not be used.

TINNING

Tinning is the operation of coating with melted solder the surface to be soldered. Flux is required; either liquid or the flux contained in cored solder may be used. With liquid flux, the metal surface should be heated enough to form steam when the flux is brushed on, as shown in Figure 6-16. A small quantity of solder is then rubbed on the hot surface (Fig. 6-17). The flame should

then be played over as large an area as possible without causing heat warpage to bring it to the melting point of solder, so that the applied material can be wiped across it. When done properly, the result is, in effect, a surface painted with melted solder. The wiping cloth, shown in use in Figure 6-18, should be handled as though it was a paint brush; used with a scrubbing action, it will simply rub the hot solder off.

When using flux-cored solder for tinning, the surface should be heated as for liquid flux and the end of wire solder rubbed over it enough to leave patches of melted solder and flux over approximately one fourth of the area. Wiping is the same for either type of flux.

The Torch Flame

Assuming that the work will be done with an oxyacetylene torch, the tip should be selected for the size of the spot to be filled. A No. 3 would be satisfactory for the spot shown. When lighting, the acetylene valve should be opened slightly past the point where it stops giving off black smoke. The oxygen should be opened just enough to remove all traces of yellow. The result will be a soft, blue flame, which should be held 3 to 6 inches away from the surface and kept in constant motion when directed at the surface. When it is lifted away, to permit the tinning and application operations, the operator should be careful to hold it in a position where it will not cause damage or set a fire.

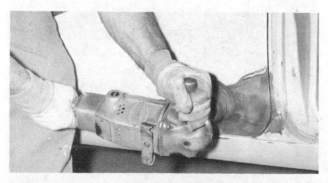

6-15 Using the saucer-shaped wire brush on the disc sander to clean paint out of a deep gouge.

6-17 Applying small quantity of solder for tinning. Note torch flame adjustment and distance from panel.

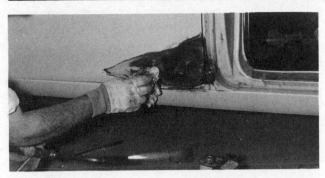

6-18 Wiping melted solder over the surface to complete the tinning operation.

6-20 Paddling the solder into shape.

Adding Solder

Solder is shown being added in Figure 6-19. The operator has held the flame well back from the panel, but directed toward the tinned surface, while holding the end of the bar of solder much closer as about 1 inch (2.5 cm) of the end softened. When the end of the bar began to sag, it was pushed against the preheated surface with a twisting motion, leaving the softened solder joined to the tinning coat applied previously. Note that the flame is directed under the automobile, where it will do no harm as the solder is applied to the panel.

Shaping

The shaping operation is shown in Figure 6-20. The flame has been played back and forth over the entire area to bring the deposited solder to the proper temperature to work. The paddle is being used to push the hot solder into place. It should never be turned on edge, just pressed down as the paddle slides toward the point where solder is needed.

Oil

The paddle was wiped on a freshly oiled rag before the operation was started and was rewiped after every three or four strokes. When solder was in general use,

several good lubricants were available for application on the paddle, but many repairmen used motor oil. Outboard motor oil is the best modern substitute, with automatic transmission fluid second choice. The oil tends to prevent solder sticking to the wood, but it will be necessary to sand the surface occasionally and re-oil it.

Quenching

A container of water and a sponge or rag should be at hand so that water can be dashed on the hot surface as soon as paddling is finished, as shown in Figure 6-21. If the surface is not quenched, some of the swelling caused by expansion may remain as heat distortion in the finished job. Quenching is particularly important on a flat surface, such as this door panel, but should be done on any solder fill job.

Metal-Finishing

The metal-finishing operation is shown in Figure 6-22. The best practice is to blend in the edges before finishing the center. The beginner is usually inclined to file solder too much. It cuts rapidly and tends to clog the file teeth. A sharp rap on the back or edge of the file will usually clean the teeth, but sometimes it is necessary to pick the solder out. A new, sharp file will clog more than one that is duller, because it tends to bury the teeth into the soft solder instead of shearing it off. It is better to use a slightly dull one.

6-19 Applying solder for filling. The torch flame has been used to soften the bar and keep the tinned surface in the plastic temperature range.

6-21 Quenching the hot solder.

6-22 Finishing the lower edge. The center area will be filed to blend it into the finished outer edges.

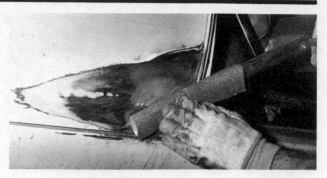

6-23 Smoothing the surface with sandpaper wrapped around the file.

Sanding

The finished surface is being sanded for the final finish in Figure 6-23, using a sheet of 80-grit production paper wrapped around the body file. If the surface is not sanded, it will be difficult to hide the file marks when the panel is painted. Sanding should be done with full strokes, criss-crossed as in metal-finishing, and not overdone; sanding too much will tend to cut too much solder out at the blend area, leaving a "river bank" effect. At this point the panel is ready for repainting.

Both door panels, ready for repainting, are shown in Figure 6-24.

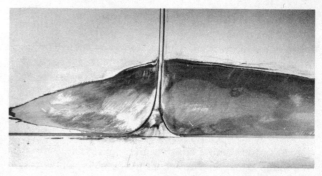

6-24 Both door panels, metal finished and ready for repainting.

Basic Straightening Procedures and Equipment

In the preceding chapters, the repairman's job was broken down for the purpose of study into separate components dealing with fundamental information and basic operations. The next step is to weave these separate elements into a flexible pattern that the beginner can apply to actual repair jobs as he enters the second phase of his training and begins to do actual repair work. It is recognized that the dividing line between the first and second phase is not clearly defined, but, it is assumed that it has been crossed at this point. This part of the text deals with methods of applying force to various types of damaged panels so that the straightening will be accomplished efficiently and with the least possible distortion. This includes a discussion of the essential equipment and its direct application to the types of repair work for which it is intended. Major repair jobs have not been included.

The discussion in parts of this chapter are about the repair procedure for specific damage panels selected to represent typical repair problems. However, most of it is general rather than specific. At any stage in the progress from rank beginner to fully qualified tradesman, the problem is always how to do the job now at hand. A specific duplicate of a job explained in a textbook may never be encountered in the individual's work experience. General information is all that is obtainable from a lengthy explanation of one repair job. For that reason, most of this chapter is devoted to the type of general information that the repairman must rely on in deciding how to do the various repair jobs encountered daily.

THE PHASES OF STRAIGHTENING

The repair operations on all but the most simple damages can be separated into three groups, or phases: (1) roughing, (2) bumping, or smoothing, and (3) finishing. On major jobs the first phase usually involves *aligning* as well as roughing. Aligning refers to the operations required to shift the reinforcing members back into position to restore the proper fit to door, body glass, and rear lid openings, and it can involve the fit of hoods and fenders. The conditions of the individual job determine whether aligning should be done before roughing or after it, or whether the two operations should be combined. Physical damage appraisers and insurance adjustors usually make a separate entry on the estimate form as a means of evaluating the time required for aligning beyond that required for individual panels.

ROUGHING AND ALIGNING

The terms roughing, aligning, panel, and structural members are defined as they are used here: (1) roughing refers to the operations required to bring a damaged panel from the shape in which the impact left it to an approximation of its correct shape, (2) aligning refers to the operations required to readjust the position of structural members of the body, (3) panel refers to the exterior surface metal only, and (4) structural members refers to the reinforced parts, usually box sections, that make up the body openings and serve as the framework of the body; floor pans can be considered as structural members, because they are primarily reinforcements and appearance is not as critical as for the other surface panels.

The definitions of panel and structural member should not be confused because some surface panels and a part of a structural member are made in one piece. Some quarter panels that have the lock pillar and the deck lid gutter are examples; although made of the same piece, these parts serve separate purposes. On other panels these parts may be stamped separately and welded to the exterior panel. However, these definitions do not apply to part names, as they are listed in the factory part book. Sometimes similar parts are called by different names by different manufacturers.

The estimator and repairman should recognize four types of misaligned conditions: (1) those that should be corrected before the adjoining panels should be either repaired or replaced, (2) those that, when corrected, will relieve a strain on an adjoining panel and allow it either to pop out or to be roughed out with very little additional effort, (3) those that require the adjoining panels to be roughed out carefully as the aligning progresses, and (4) those that will be completely eliminated when the damaged areas are cut out to permit replacement with new parts. These conditions determine the repair procedure and must be considered in the estimator's time allowances.

There is divided opinion among various estimators about whether to make a separate entry on the estimate form for aligning time or to divide it among the various affected parts. In general, both insurance companies that require their adjustors to prepare their own estimates and automobile damage appraisal agencies prefer to itemize alignment separately, because it conveys a better concept of the condition of the damage to interested persons who may never see the automobile. It is of less concern to the shop estimator, but is desirable because it requires closer attention to detail.

ROUGHING

Roughing, sometimes called *roughing out*, is the application of force so that it will undo the effect of the force that caused the damage. This subject is dealt with very briefly in Chapter 3 in the explanation of proper use of the dolly block and hammer. On some minor jobs the simple operations shown there may be adequate, but much more is usually involved when the damage is more severe than in that example.

Skill in roughing out damaged panels is in knowing how to apply force so that it does not create additional damage. A fender or other sheet metal panel can suffer severe damage from force applied in the wrong way or in the wrong place by a well-intentioned repairman. Even though the force that he can apply may be much less than the force involved in a collision, if he is making a mistake, he is likely to concentrate it on a small but vulnerable area where it will cause serious damage that will be added to the original.

There are three basic methods of applying force to rough out damaged panels:

1. Drive the metal back into place, using a dolly block, heavy hammer, or other striking tool. The tool used should not mark or mutilate the metal surface any more than absolutely necessary.
2. Push the metal back into place, using a pry bar, jack, or other means of applying steady force without impact.
3. Pull the metal back into place, using a jack as the power source and some means of attachment to apply tension lengthwise of the member or the panel surface.

Each of these methods has both advantages and disadvantages for certain types of damage conditions; all but the most simple damages will require a combination of two or all three. For the purpose of study, it is desirable to identify the types that are best suited to each method. The importance of being able to recognize the correct roughing-out procedure cannot be overemphasized. A minor mistake makes it necessary to finish the job under a handicap; a major mistake often must be buried under a replica of the panel carved out of filler.

BUMPING

Bumping is a less definite term than roughing because it consists of the hand tool work necessary to prepare the roughed out surface for metal finishing. Highly skilled metal men tend to combine bumping with the roughing operation; this was done in the roughing procedure on the fender repair illustrated in Figs. 7-5 to 7-11. Some others tend to omit the bumping phase entirely and fill areas which should be either straightened and metal finished, or straightened enough that less filling would be required.

Simple Dents

A simple dent in either a high crown area or an area where a combination high and low crown blend should be driven out without use of other means. A good example of this type of dent is shown in Figure 3-41 on the fender pictured to show correct use of the hammer and dolly block. These conditions are illustrated by A and B in Figure 7-1. The important factor is that all of the affected area is free to flex as the sharp buckle is driven out. When the proper conditions exist, roughing out a simple dent should leave only minor surface

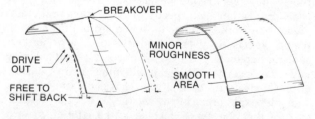

7-1 The type of dent that should be driven out. A, the original condition; B, the condition after roughing out.

roughness in the area of the break-over path, and much of the displaced metal in the low-crowned area should either snap back or require very little effort to bring it back, as suggested by B. Damages of this type, often called *soft* dents, are found in the blend area between a low crown and a combination crowned surface.

The two parts in Figure 7-1 represent the before and after conditions of a rolled buckle in a sheet of curved metal. The dotted lines on the lower sides represent the original positions of the edges before the rolling action caused them to shift to new positions. Roughing out the valley of the rolled buckle properly would permit these edges to shift back and most of the surface not in the break-over path to snap out into almost perfect shape.

The example just given can be considered ideal, in that it is about as simple to rough out as can be found. However, this method is not restricted to use on simple damages. Most damaged panels have two or more rolled buckles extending outward from an area of displaced metal that should be roughed out in this manner. When this condition is found, it should be examined closely to determine on which buckle the roughing operation should start. Sometimes it will make no difference, but quite often one will be holding the displaced metal under a strain that will prevent free movement of the others. When this condition exists, working the wrong buckle first may cause additional buckling of as yet undamaged but displaced metal. Finding the right buckle to start on may be a problem for the beginner. It is a sure sign that the work has been started in the wrong place when new buckles begin to form in areas that have been smooth.

When the start has been made on the correct buckle, it is almost always best to work it only partway before going to the other—or others, if there are more than one. It may be possible to rough it all of the way, but the work should not be carried past the point that new buckles begin to form in the smooth areas. When this happens, *stop and rethink the procedure.*

The best possible sequence to follow in the rough-out procedure would be suggested if it was possible to see a reversed slow-motion picture of the panel or assembly as it yielded under the impact. Even though the motion picture is not available, study of the damage will enable

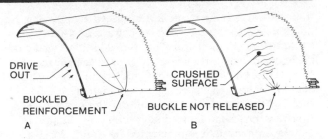

7-3 The error of roughing out buckles caused by a bent or buckled reinforced member. A is the original condition, and B is the effect.

the repairman to visualize the scene well enough to see the sequence in which the various parts should move. It is not practical for one man to work several points at once, as the reversed film idea suggests, but the elasticity of the metal will permit each one to be worked partway before working another. The correct procedure will permit as much as possible of the displaced area to return to normal position without further buckling. The basic idea of reversed motion is discussed in much greater detail in a later section.

The limit of conditions that can be roughed by driving buckles out is reached when the impact of the driving tool batters or crushes the surface it contacts, but causes little or no movement of the surrounding area. Three of the most common causes of this condition are (1) the buckle is folded over so far that it presents a narrow V-shaped ridge to the impact tool, (2) the impact area has been forced into a "knotted" condition that is too rigid to unroll in this manner, and (3) the buckle has been caused by a shift of a stiffer part of the body structure that holds it out of place. This third condition, often called *secondary* or *indirect* damage, must be roughed out along with the straightening of the condition that caused the shift. It is discussed in more detail in the section Jacking Out Dents and Factors Governing the Use of Tension. However, after the condition is roughed out, it would be worked in much the same manner as a rolled buckle caused by a direct impact.

The six cross sections in Figure 7-2 illustrate the difference in the problems of roughing out a shallow and a deep rolled buckle. A represents the forming of the shallow dent at the point where the roughing out would start. The arrows indicate the inward movement as the center is drawn down. Rough-out force reverses the flow of forces, causing the sides to push outward as suggested by the arrows on B. The outward push is most effective when the opposite sides of the buckle meet at the widest angle and have the least curvature. The condition represented here should be straightened with a little more hammer and dolly work to produce the slightly wavy but full-length condition shown in C, which could be finished easily.

When the dent is much deeper (D), the sides will have been drawn in much farther and meet at a much sharper angle. Force applied by a dolly block to metal in this shape (E) meets greater resistance than in the example in A and provides much less outward push. Instead, it tends to spread and upset the area contacted by the face of the dolly and lift the sides above the

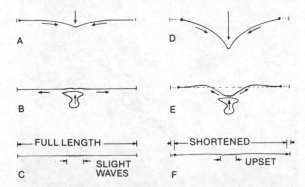

7-2 Cross sections illustrating the effect of driving out shallow and deep valleys of rolled buckles. In A, B, and C the length has been fully restored; in D, E, and F the valley is upset, shortening the length.

proper level, as shown in E. Continued hammering on the ridge will cause further upsetting and batter the contact area out of shape. The final condition would be more like E, upset in buckled area and too short, if the area could be finished, but would probably be filled instead. Being too short, it would distort the overall shape of the panel. The error of driving out a buckled area that has been caused by a bend or collapse in a heavy reinforcement is illustrated by A and B in Figure 7-3. A buckled box member is shown in A with a buckled section of welded-on panel extending above. B illustrates how any rough-out work on the buckle will simply crush the surface if the buckled reinforcement is not relieved first. This would add damage to existing damage. A welded-on box member is shown, but any type of reinforcement that is much stiffer than the buckled metal will have the same effect.

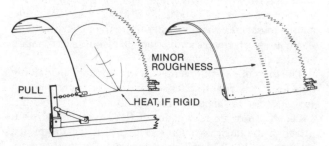

7-4 The effect on a buckled panel when a buckled reinforcement is straightened properly. The method of anchoring the portable machine is not shown, but it would have to bear against some rigid part of the structure.

A and B in Figure 7-4 illustrate how relieving the condition in the reinforcement will relieve the buckled panel so that roughing what remains of the buckle in the panel is a simple operation. A portable body and frame machine is shown in use, but an operation of this type could be done in many different ways on various parts of the body. Portable machines are discussed in more detail in later sections.

When working out a damage that is more than just a simple dent, the procedure must be planned to avoid creating the "horrible" examples, actually a false-stretch condition, represented by D, E, and F in Figure 7-2. One mistake of this type, involving a very small portion of the surface area, will have a drawstring effect on the surrounding metal, sometimes drawing the entire surface slightly but noticeably out of shape. Although it is not always possible to avoid some false stretch, the wrong procedure can make a major problem out of a relatively simple dent. Most often, it is the cause of excessive use of filler on jobs that could have been done faster with less filler by a repairman who knew how to straighten metal.

The repairman must "read" the conditions of each damage he works to determine (1) the sequence in which each buckle should be worked and (2) whether each buckle should be driven out or a jack set up at a right angle to the main valley to reduce the angle at which the sides of the valley meet. Referring to A and D in Figure 7-2, the sides of A offer considerably less resistance to a lifting force than the sides of D.

DRIVING OUT SEVERE DAMAGE

The dented fender skirt area in Figure 7-5 is a much more complicated straightening problem than the rolled buckles discussed in the preceding section. It was picked from a body shop's scrap and repaired, off the car, by the author to illustrate this section. This is typical damage of the type the beginner should practice on as soon as he has learned to straighten simple rolled buckles.

This fender had been damaged by the glancing blow of a small hard impact object, possibly a projecting bolt end on a bumper. The first impact point is indicated by the arrow on the beaded edge of the wheel opening, and

7-6 The effect of the first rough out. A tinner's hammer was used on the inside surface of the bead.

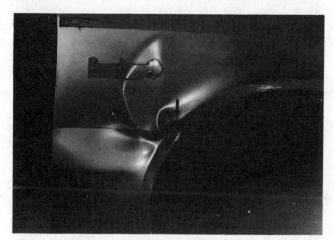

7-5 Damaged fender, obtained from scrap pile. Arrow indicates the first impact point.

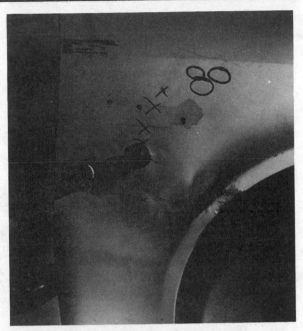

7-8 Relieving the upper ridge with the hammer. O's indicate areas lifted by striking the under side with the dolly. X's indicate hammer blows, working from the upper section down, but without the dolly block.

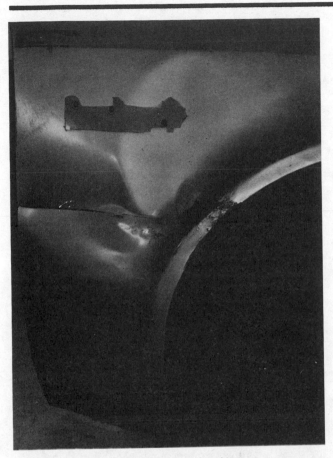

7-7 The effect of a few hammer blows on the sharp ridges adjoining the bea. A radius hammer was used.

a rebound impact has made a minor line gouge across the rear edge. Rebound, or second, impacts are quite common, because both the panel and the impact object tend to bounce off and come back. This one has come back on an area already displaced by the first impact. If there had been no rebound, either there would have been no gouge at all, or the panel would have ripped across its full width.

The displaced metal above and beside the impact area is rolled buckles that have spread from the impact and driven the edge of the fender inward. However, they differ from the simple rolled buckles discussed in the preceding section in that they are held by the knotted condition of the impact area instead of a break-over path at the outer edge. Starting the rough-out procedure at the outer edges would add damage to existing damage. However, straightening the minor buckles in the displaced areas will be simple after the knotted impact area has been *untied*.

The roughing and bumping phases are combined in the repair procedure used on this fender.

The result of the first rough-out operation is shown in Figure 7-6. Three or four solid hammer blows, using a tinner's hammer with a chisel-shaped end, have been struck on the inside of the impact area of the bead, bringing it more than halfway back to position, far enough to make considerable change in the surrounding buckles. Before this, the impact area had tied up elastic strains in the outer area. Now, most of these strains

have been freed, and further movement of the impact area is being resisted by the remaining strains.

The next step, Figure 7-7, was to strike a few hammer blows on the small, semicircular buckle, using the radius-faced hammer and smoothing the bead with the hammer and the lip of the dolly block. This was followed by the operation shown in Figure 7-8. The three circles indicate the lowest part of the upper rolled buckle. The underside of this area was lifted by two or three light blows, using the flattest part of the working face of a general-purpose dolly block. Next, the dolly was held with firm pressure against the lowest point of this area

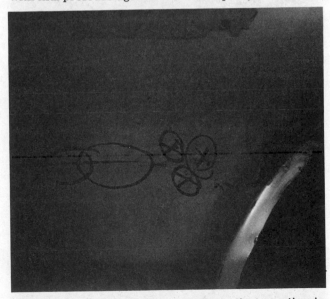

7-9 The lower area marked to indicate the operation in progress. O's enclosing X's indicate use of the hammer-on-dolly. Open O's indicate areas to be driven up with the dolly block.

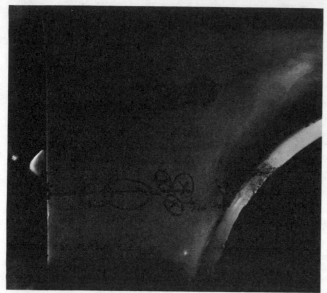

7-10 Rolling out a low area by striking an angling hammer blow under the edge. The hammer and dolly work of the adjoining surfaces has been completed.

while a series of hammer blows were made down the row of X's to the position shown in the photograph. Both the low point and the beginning of the ridge were located by shifting the eye position to see the ripples in the light reflected from the surface. Work with the hammer began at the start of the ridge, and the hammer blows were placed carefully to bring the surface down to level without marking it. In effect, the rolling action

has been reversed to the point where the hammer is shown.

In Figure 7-9 the impact area has been lifted further and smoothed with the hammer and dolly, and the adjoining reverse crown area has been smoothed with the radius-faced hammer and dolly. The open-circled areas have been lifted, using the dolly; some hammer and dolly smoothing has been done in the area with the circle-enclosed X's.

In Figure 7-10 most of the hammer and dolly work has been completed, and the hammer is shown in position to "roll" the rear edge where it had been depressed by the second impact. (This operation should have been included with the preceding photograph.) The low point was first driven out with the hammer striking almost at a right angle. This was followed by two or three blows above and below the point with the hammer held at 45 degrees or less to the surface. Blows coming from this angle will lift the surface forward of the edge where it had been tilted down by the impact. This operation must be performed carefully. Striking too hard or trying to raise a low spot that is too deep will drive the edge forward, leaving an ugly wide spot in the door edge gap.

Normally, if this fender was repaired, the work would be done without removing it from the automobile. Done in that position, a light-duty body jack would be used instead of the hammer for the roughing-out operation. However, when panels of this type are obtained for practice material, the work must be done as it was here or using whatever equipment is available to hold it. Working panels off the car should not be considered a handicap because, to become a qualified repairman, one must learn to straighten metal in whatever position one finds it.

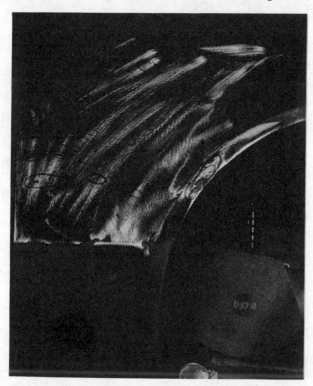

7-11 The result of the first dics sanding operation, using the six-pointed disc shown. The largest low spots were picked up and resanded before this photo was taken. Circles enclose small low spots.

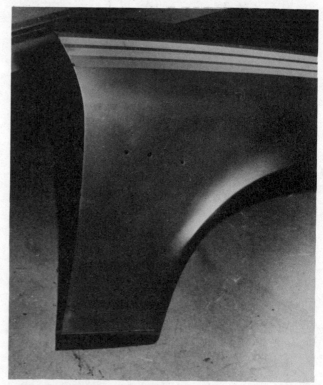

7-12 The painted fender.

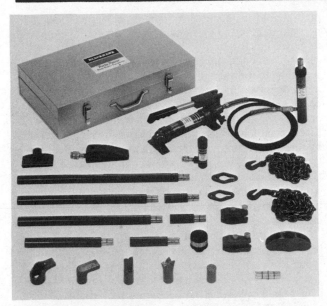

7-13 Four-ton body jack.

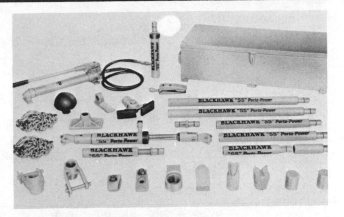

7-14 Ten-ton body jack.

If this work had been done with the fender on the automobile, a slide hammer equipped with a wide hood would have been used on the edge, and part of the rear edge would have been pried up instead of doing most of the work with the hammer and dolly block.

The result of the first disc-sanding operation is shown in Figure 7-11, using the six-sided disc shown on the sander. No picking to raise low spots has been done at this point, but circles and loops have been drawn around spots that need it. These were picked, using the edge of the bumping hammer, because it is more blunt than a pick hammer, and resanded. Enough filling was done to check for undetected low spots, and the surface was buffed with a fine-grit disc for the final operation.

The repainted fender is shown in Figure 7-12.

BODY JACKS

Complete four- and ten-ton-capacity body jack sets are shown in Figures 7-13 and 7-14, typical of most body jacks available in that they are hydraulically operated by separate pump units connected by high-pressure hoses. The pumps shown are hand operated, but air-operated ones can be substituted easily by means of a quick-disconnect coupler. Various types of mechanically operated jacks are and have been available but have never been as popular as the hydraulic, because they are not as easy to operate. This coupler makes it easy to change the pump from one ram to another. However, simultaneous operation of two jacks requires two pumps.

Use and Care of Body Jacks

The manufacturers of body jacks build their equipment to withstand considerable abuse, because of the nature of the work they are required to do. However, the most rugged jack possible to build can be damaged by careless use and neglected maintenance. The useful life of a body jack can be extended for years by following a few common-sense rules:

1. Offset loads should be avoided as much as possible. When necessary, the jack should be set up as shown in A, Figure 7-15 and kept below its maximum output, if possible.

2. Do not use a light-duty jack on a job that is beyond its capacity.

3. Fittings, whether of the slip-on type or threaded, should never be used in direct contact with a steel surface; protective caps are a part of the equipment and should be used.

JACKING OUT DENTS

Using a jack to push out dents is similar to driving them out but has three advantages: (1) the relatively slow movement of the jack eliminates the impact of the driving tool on the inner panel surface, (2) a buckle can be jacked out partway and held under pressure while other buckles are worked, and (3) a jack or a spreader, which is just another type of jack, can be used in enclosed spaces where there is no room to swing a hammer or a dolly block. It is important to recognize that the emphasis is on the versatility of the jack rather than on its full capacity to push. Applying too much force with a jack can be as damaging as driving too hard with the dolly block, illustrated by D, E, and F in Figure 7-2.

The jack is most effective as a rough-out tool on large panels that have been dented deeply enough to cause two or more severe rolled buckles but little or no misalignment of the body structure. Good examples of this are often found on roof panels that have been crushed in a soft roll-over on flat ground, spreading the impact over a large part of the panel surface. It is not uncommon to find a crushed roof with little or no evidence of a direct impact but two or more severe rolled buckles extending into the corners over the windshield or rear window. The more severe these buckles are, the more important it is to use the controlled movement of a jack to rough them out. The rough-out procedure should start

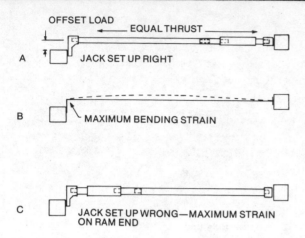

7-15 The right and wrong offset jack setups.

close to the outer end of the break-over path, as explained earlier.

Skill in the use of a body jack is more a matter of knowledge than of manual dexterity. Fortunately, most of the knowledge required is of the common-sense type rather than technical. Some common beginner's problems with the use of a body jack are (1) not providing enough temporary support for the base end, (2) pushing too hard, (3) failure to relieve buckles as an area is jacked out, and (4) failure to allow for the angle effect.

The jack exerts equal pressure, or thrust, at both ends. In almost every use, the jack must be based against an undamaged area to push out damage in another area. There are only a few areas of the entire automobile where the jack can be based directly on body or frame steel without risk of damage. An example would be the underside of fenders where the jack can be based on frame metal. In almost every other place, the safest procedure is to place one or more blocks of wood in position to spread the load over a much larger surface area. This is particularly important on the newer down-sized automobiles that are much lighter in construction than those of the past.

The importance of not pushing too hard may be better understood after studying the discussion of Reversed Motion later in this chapter. The essential part is that any movement of the jack should cause the metal to reverse the movement caused by the impact. When the jack is extended and this reversed movement is not obtained, the setup should be re-examined. *It may be wrong.* Further pushing could add damage to existing damage.

The effect of angle can be ignored in many jack setups, but not all. Jack pressure simply pushes whatever it bears against in the direction in which it offers the least resistance. This is illustrated in Figure 7-16. In A the jack is shown at an angle of approximately 45 degrees between body members. The base could be a rocker panel, and the working end could be a roof rail, but other parts would react in the same manner. Both parts will tend to move in line with the jack, but the stiffer one will force the other to yield. Normally, this type setup would be needed on a roof rail, so the repair-

man should be careful to provide enough blocking to prevent damage to the rocker; it would not be expected to move, but it could be crushed, if not protected with suitable wooden blocks. The effect on the roof rail would be to follow the angle of the jack, which is a combination of both upward and outward. However, the construction of the area affected may offer more resistance to movement in one direction than the other. If lifted too much, welded-on flanges on the underside will be torn loose, as illustrated in B. Or, if forced too hard, the rail might simply be crushed, as illustrated in C.

When damages of this type occur, it is the fault of the operator. The beginner must be aware that a body jack is an indispensable tool, but it must be used with common sense.

The worst possible abuse of a body jack is overloading on an offset load, as shown in Figure 7-15. When set up as shown in cross-sectional illustration A, its precision parts are as far as possible from the point of maximum strain, as indicated by B. In effect, the full length of the jack becomes a lever working against the relatively short L-shaped fitting on the end. When the jack is set up as shown in C, the end of the ram and cylinder are subjected to the maximum leverage. Forethought is all that is needed to avoid this equipment-damaging situation.

It is almost equally destructive to force a jack to the absolute limit of its capacity. There are some straightening operations in heavy truck repair that will require more than the practical output of a 10-ton jack. Very few operations on automobiles will require more than half of that capacity, although some may be beyond the capacity of a light-duty jack. When excessive force is required, the setup should be re-examined; it is probably wrong and should be changed.

REVERSED MOTION

The repair of any sheet metal damage is simply a matter of making the various parts move back where they belong. The idea of a slow-motion picture of a panel

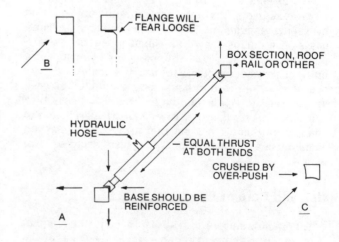

7-16 The effect of too much force.

being damaged, suggested earlier in this chapter to explain the use of a body jack in the rough-out procedure, is expanded here as a very good means of determining the procedure to follow in aligning and roughing out much more complicated damaged assemblies.

This idea is based on two assumptions: (1) that almost everyone has seen a motion picture run in reverse, making broken glass fly back together or a fly ball come from the far outfield, bounce off the bat as it spins the batter in a reverse swing, and bounce back to the pitcher and put him in a reverse windup and (2) that almost all should be equally aware that a slow-motion picture can spread almost instantaneous action over a much longer period to permit time to study it.

Automobile companies and other interested agencies use slow-motion pictures to study the action of staged automobile collisions. These pictures will make a damaged panel seem to drift slowly inward as the effect spreads. However, the spread will be in steps rather than in one continuous movement as pressure or tension builds up on the various points until they collapse and allow the pressure to flow on to the next. At the point of final penetration the motion will stop and spring back to the point where the estimator and repairman find it. Running the picture backward would reverse the motion and bring it back toward the impact point, dropping off sections of undamaged metal until, finally, a fully restored automobile would be seen.

The automobile collision repair industry would not exist as it does if the repair of collision damage was as simple as a reverse showing of a slow-motion picture would make it seem. As the damaging force spreads from the impact area, it sets up new conditions in every bit of metal that it strains past the elastic limit. The repairman's problem is to relieve these conditions methodically so that the reversed action can be kept moving progressively back to the start. The ideal sequence would be suggested by viewing a reversed showing of a slow-motion picture of the damage as it was formed by the impact. However, that is both impossible and unnecessary; the repairman trained to "think backwards" should be able to visualize the reverse sequence, and he will have a better plan than by relying on a set of rules that must be general rather than specific. Visualizing may be slow at first, but will become easy with practice.

Figure 7-17 shows the flow of force from an impact area on a two-door-model quarter panel through the lock pillar into the roof rail and roof panel. The heavy arrow indicates the direction of the impact. The light arrows beside the pillar and pointing toward the impact indicate the pull effect the pillar has had on the floor and the roof. For this discussion it is assumed that the floor has resisted the force, but the roof and roof rail have yielded. As shown, the roof and roof rail would be pulled down approximately 1 inch (2.5 cm) and the same amount inward. That amount of movement would tend to draw the fore and aft sections of the roof rail toward the pillar and affect the door and windshield alignment. Further movement would cause misalignment of both, but probably not affect the rear compartment lid alignment.

A slow-motion picture should not be needed to realize that a lighter impact would damage the quarter panel without affecting the roof or that a much heavier impact would cause damage to spread farther into the quarter panel, roof assembly, and floor.

A slow-motion picture of the damage suggested by Figure 7-17 would show the action start by depressing the impact area of the quarter panel surface, pulling the surrounding metal with it. A few moments later, the shape of the pillar would yield, drawing the quarter panel outer and inner surfaces with it. As the pillar continued in motion, it would pull down and in on the roof structure, roof and roof rail, and pull up and in on the floor and rocker panel. Both would be seen flexing under the strain but retaining shape for a surprisingly long time and at considerable distance from the original position. Assuming that the first yield would be in the roof, a slight ripple would appear in the sharply curved metal just above the drip molding. This would grow rapidly into a severe rolled buckle as the pillar moved downward and the fore and aft section of the roof side moved into the buckle. At this point most of the resistance to further movement of the roof would be concentrated on the very small area of metal in the break-over path; as it went through the rolling upset the paint would fly off, leaving flaky edges. If enough force continued coming, the door and windshield opening would be pulled out of alignment as the fore and aft sections of the roof were drawn together.

The important fact to be learned from the slow-motion picture example is that, even though an accident seems instantaneous, damage spreads in a *series of steps*. Showing the picture in reverse would reverse the steps. The correct repair procedure sequence will follow the steps in reverse order. Correct, as the term is used here, means procedure that is established by the conditions of the specific damage, not a dogmatic set of rules.

Manual skill enters the scene as the repairman begins the process of straightening the damage. The skill with which he releases the various buckles and upsets needed to keep the reverse action moving is as important as the sequence in which they are worked. A few horrible examples, as represented by D, E, and F in Figure 7-2, can ensure that (1) the final result will never

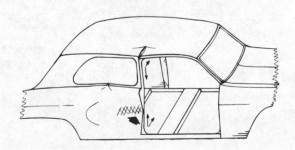

7-17 The flow of force from an inpact area on a quarter panel into the roof.

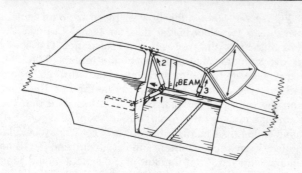

7-18 Typical jack setups to reverse the effect of the flow of force illustrated in Fig. 7-17.

be quite right and (2) more time and material will be used than should have been required.

Figure 7-18 shows some of the typical jack setups that could be used to straighten a damage similar to that shown in Figure 7-17. A wooden beam is shown across the opposite door opening to provide a safe base for the jacks. This may not be needed on every body, but some will crush if not protected in some manner. The safest procedure is to protect the sheet metal with enough wood to prevent unwanted damage.

Jack 1, pushing against the inner surface of the impact area, should be considered the lead. The first step must be to obtain enough reverse motion here to begin releasing the strains that have carried into the roof and floor. However, this is not just a simple matter of setting the jack in place and pushing. The pillar section has been crushed, and the inner panel may block access to the underside of the impact area, depending on the location of whatever holes the manufacturer has provided. It may be necessary to make several different jack setups or to use external pulling equipment to rough the panel out enough to begin relieving its effect on the roof. If external equipment is used, a piece of sheet metal may be brazed or welded to the door opening edge so that a clamp can be attached to it. If the quarter panel is to be repaired, the various areas of the panel should be straightened with hand tools as the work proceeds. If the panel is to be replaced, less care will be required, but the strains should be relieved enough to permit the other areas to be worked.

Jack 2 bears against a piece of wood placed just above the pillar-to-roof joint. As explained in the Use and Care of Body Jacks section, it is both lifting and pushing outward in this position. Both effects will be needed on most damages of this type. Unfortunately, the lift may be more effective than the outward push, particularly if the edge of the roof is buckled severely and the rolled buckle has considerable upset. It was pointed out in the preceding section that the fore and aft portions of the roof tend to move toward each other; the upset metal in the rolled buckle serves as a tie to hold the buckles formed by this movement. If these conditions are not too severe, the use of the jack may be enough to free these buckles. As a general rule, it is best to heat the rolled buckle before the jack is operated so that the metal will be as free as possible to move. As

with any heating operation, the paint should be scorched and wire-brushed off first. Using a small tip adjusted to a neutral flame, heating should start at the tip of the break-over path and kept on it while the jack is extended. Spoons and hammers should be within easy reach so that the buckled metal in the edge of the roof can be worked without delay while the metal is still hot.

These operations will almost always leave some high metal at the tip of the break-over path. A minor amount of this can be relieved by shrinking. However, this is false stretch; shrinking will blend it into the surrounding area to some degree, but the spot will always be high unless the full length is restored to the upset metal in the break-over path by applying tension lengthwise of the roof while heating the upset area. One practical method of doing this is explained in the next section.

Jack 3 is shown in position to shift the windshield opening, which would not be required if the glass was not broken, but is essential if it has been broken by a shift of the pillars. This operation would alternate with the work shown at Jack 2 position. It would not be necessary to use a third jack. The final check on the opening is the fit of the glass; the edges of the pillars should be parallel to the edges of the glass, and the glass should make contact with the metal all around the outer edges.

When alignment has been fully restored, the sequence of further straightening and metal-finishing operations is not important, unless a panel is to be replaced. Then it is best to delay the metal-finishing operations until the panel is welded in place, because unexpected jacking operations may affect an already finished panel.

TENSION

The use of tension offers many advantages over either driving or pushing dents, particularly in panels that may be classified as low crowned. The main advantage is that the tendency toward upsetting is avoided, because force is transmitted through the panel surface

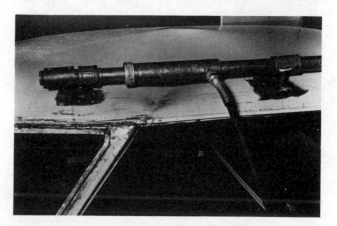

7-19 A typical setup in which a jack and tension plates are used to pull a dent out of a roof panel.

in tension instead of pressure. It is a matter of lifting a dent out by either pulling on each side of it, or by pulling on one side when the opposite side is rigid enough to provide the resistance needed, instead of pushing or striking it on the underside. A typical pulling setup is shown in Figure 7-19.

The trend toward low-crowned, nearly flat panels has tremendously increased the importance of tension in roughing out major damages. As pointed out earlier, the effect of an impact on a low-crowned panel is to pull inward the metal adjoining the impact area. If the impact is strong enough, adjoining reinforcements will be drawn inward, also. The use of tension to pull such damaged metal back to place simply means that force is applied to the already damaged metal in such a way that the least additional damage will be made by the repair procedure.

The difference in the effect of force acting through the surface of a piece of sheet metal in tension and under pressure was discussed in Chapter 2. It was shown that the length of a flat piece of metal makes no difference in the resistance to tension, but it can make a tremendous difference in the resistance to pressure. The limit of tension that can be used is the force required to cause the metal actually to yield. When tension is used properly, however, the yield point never is reached. Almost all damages can be pulled into place with far less force than is necessary to cause yielding, because tension strains the entire area uniformly. The only qualification is that the point of attachment used to apply the tension must be wide enough, at least 2 inches or more, to avoid stretching the metal. Another error to avoid is the tendency toward too much tension.

Tension also can be a great advantage where heat is used to reduce the yield point. This will be discussed in more detail in the descriptions of actual jobs.

In comparison to tension, pushing or driving a dent out tends to concentrate force on relatively small areas, which upset easily. The panel never can be restored to proper contour unless these upsets are relieved. In addition to being a fast method, tension avoids these upsets.

The basic principle of the use of tension, the tendency to produce a straight line, is illustrated in Figure 7-20. The lower line represents a cross section through a typical dent, the upper line the same cross section after it has been pulled out. Note particularly that some of the original bend, which in most cases would be the valley section of a rolled buckle, remains in the upper line. Even though pulling will restore the contour of a dented

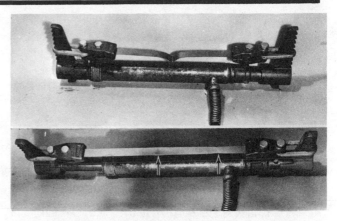

7-21 *(Top)* Jack and clamp setup on bent metal strip to show the limits of straightening by tension alone.

7-22 *(Bottom)* Jack and clamp setup after stretching strip almost to the breaking point. Center arrow points to trace of the original buckle remaining in strip. Arrow at right points to narrow section that is breaking.

flat panel to the roughed-out state better than any other method, it is necessary to do some straightening on sharp bends. Pulling will reduce sharp bends so that they are much easier to straighten, but it will never straighten them completely.

The need for some straightening is illustrated in Figures 7-21 and 7-22. In Figure 7-21, a strip of metal with a sharp bend in it is shown set up so that it can be pulled by means of a jack and two parallel jaw clamps. The bend was made by folding the metal over double and then opening it enough by hand to reach the clamp jaws. In this condition it represents a typical cross section through a typical dent that should be straightened under tension.

In Figure 7-22, the strip has been stretched almost to the breaking point. Note the narrow spot in the right end. Also note that the bent area has retained almost its original width, but the rest of the strip has narrowed enough to make this wide point noticeable. Work hardening, resulting from the bending, has strengthened this bent area enough to cause almost all of the yielding to take place elsewhere. Also, a slight trace of the original bend remains. If the intention had been to straighten this strip, instead of using it as an example of what not to do, it should only have been pulled tight and the buckle worked with the hammer and dolly block.

FACTORS GOVERNING THE USE OF TENSION

The procedure for straightening any damaged panel must be determined by examining the conditions existing on it. Such an examination will determine whether the damaged area should be driven, pushed, or pulled out. On panels where the use of tension is indicated, it is necessary to determine the exact points of attachment for applying tension, how hard to pull, and to form a

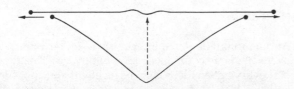

7-20 Basic principle of the use of tension to straighten dents. The lower line represents a cross section of a panel being pulled; the upper line represents the result.

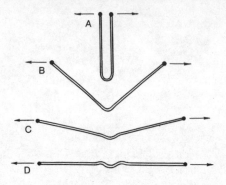

7-23 (A) First of four illustrations showing the loss of leverage as a bend is straightened. A full 180° has the maximum leverage.

7-24 (B) Loss of leverage as a bend is straightened.

7-25 (C) Progressive loss of leverage as a bend is straightened. Note the indications of outward bends beside the original inward bend.

7-26 (D) Loss of leverage as a bend is straightened. Slight buckles remain, but all leverage has been lost.

general idea of the step-by-step procedure. This problem is not as complicated as it may seem at first, if the factors governing the use of tension are understood. Such an examination then becomes an intelligent analysis that will result in a practical answer to the problem.

Of the basic factors that must be considered in using tension to pull dents out of low-crowned panels, the most important are (1) leverage angle, (2) lift reaction, (3) work hardening of the buckled area, (4) variations of surface crown, and (5) alignment with the crown of the panel.

These factors are discussed and explained separately.

Leverage Angle

The leverage angle is the most important factor in determining the effectiveness of any pull on any panel. This is illustrated in Figures 7-23–7-27. In these four illustrations, the metal on each side of the sharp buckle is considered as two levers. When tension is applied to them, they open in much the same manner as the handles of a pair of tongs. The leverage angle is the angle made by two lines connecting the two points of tension application to the lowest part of the dent. The lines that form this angle will become a straight line when the panel has been straightened.

In Figure 7-23, the two lines forming the leverage angle are in a 180-degree fold. It is rare in any panel repair that a full bend such as this is encountered. However, such a bend will provide the maximum leverage angle.

In Figure 7-24, the outward movement of the two surfaces has started to open the bend and draw it closer to a straight line. As the angle between the two surfaces becomes wider, the leverage they can exert against the stiffened bend decreases proportionally. A leverage

angle as small as this, however, is larger than is commonly encountered in most repair work.

In Figure 7-25, the outward movement of the two surfaces has increased the angle and made a further decrease in the leverage as the depth of the dent has been reduced. Note that typical outward bends are shown on each side of the original inward bend. These outward bends usually form because the original bend is stiffer, due to work hardening, than the adjoining metal. If the dent were being driven out from the underside, these bends would form in exactly the same manner, except that they would be sharper because of the resistance to movement of the adjoining metal.

The position shown in Figure 7-25 is more nearly typical of a cross section through a dent suitable for straightening under tension than the conditions shown in the other illustrations. The remaining leverage is much less than with a smaller angle, but there is still enough left to be very effective.

In Figure 7-26, the metal on each side of the original bend has been drawn almost to a straight line. Note that some of the original bend is seen, as are some of the outward bends formed in straightening. Further tension will not pull these out, because there is no leverage on them, and they are the strongest metal between the two points of tension application. Whatever remains of the original bend will require straightening with hand tools.

In the discussion of leverage angle so far, no consideration has been given to the size of the dent and the overall length of the panel. It is not uncommon to have a condition such as represented by the cross-sectional illustration in Figure 7-27, which represents a small, fairly sharp dent in a relatively long panel. The dotted lines connecting points AA and BB represent the leverage angles that could be used. Pulling from points BB would provide a more effective angle than pulling from points AA, because the angle is sharper. The sharper angle provides greater leverage.

7-27 Different leverages to be obtained by pulling from points close to or at a distance from a shallow dent in a long panel.

Another factor, lift reaction, must be considered before deciding whether the attachment to pull out a dent should be made close to the damage (points BB) in Figure 7-27, or at the extreme ends.

Lift Reaction

An understanding of the term lift reaction requires knowledge of one of the basic laws of physics. This rule is: For every action there must be an equal and opposite reaction. This can be demonstrated in many ways. If explained in terms of lifting an object off the ground, it means that when enough force is applied to lift it up, there also will be an equal amount of force exerted against the ground. If explained in terms of applying force to straighten a panel, it means that when enough force is applied to raise the dent, there also must be an equal amount of force applied in the opposite direction somewhere on the panel surface to support the lift.

Sometimes a person who has not made a study of the basic sciences has difficulty in understanding this law, because he is accustomed to thinking of a force application as involving motion. This is not necessarily true; force can be applied without motion. A table standing on a floor is exerting a downward force, and, likewise, the floor is exerting an upward force. The fact that there is no motion simply indicates that the forces are in balance, so the objects involved, the table and the floor, remain at rest. However, if enough weight is added to the table, its downward force may be increased until it is greater than the floor can resist. In that case, the table would push its way into the floor, bending or breaking it.

Applying this reasoning to the problem of lifting a dent is simple if the directions of force application are recognized. An upward force under the dent is required to raise it. It is still an upward force, whether it is applied directly to the underside or indirectly, by pulling on the metal on opposite sides of the dent. For this force to act, an equal force must be acting in the opposite direction. If the dent is being pushed out, the opposite force would act on whatever supports the panel. If the dent is being pulled out, it will act on the points to which tension is applied. This is the lift reaction.

The points to which tension is being applied are referred to hereafter as the attaching points. In the following discussions, lift reaction on the attaching points is considered as a downward force, because it is the opposite of the lifting action.

Lift reaction is illustrated in Figure 7-28. Arrows pointing outward at each end of the curved line indicate tension being applied to lift the dent. The arrow pointing upward in the center indicates the lifting action on the dent. The arrows pointing downward at each end indicate the lift reaction. The combined lift reaction on both attaching points must always be equal to the force required to lift the dent.

This illustration and the discussion accompanying it should make it clear that the force exerted outward to pull, or lift, the dent is not the same as the force exerted downward by lift reaction. When the dent has been pulled up to the proper level, lift reaction will drop to nothing. However, any amount of force, even enough to tear the panel, could continue to be applied in tension on the already lifted surface.

The importance of lift reaction is that it must be con-

sidered in selecting the points of attachment to which the tension will be applied. If these points are not rigid enough to resist the reaction to the lift, they will collapse instead of lifting the dent.

Thus in repairing any panel, attaching points should be selected that are rigid enough to support the load. Many times there is no problem. For example, in pulling a dent in a door panel, simply attach clamps to the edges. The edges, being rigidly supported by the facings, provide far more support than is needed to lift the load. In other instances, there is a real problem, because one or both of the desirable attaching points will not provide sufficient support to lift the dent. It then is necessary to do one of two things: (1) compromise by shifting to a more rigid though less desirable point, or (2) provide extra temporary support for the point.

It would be impossible to detail all of the conditions under which each of these alternate methods would be employed. Common sense will dictate when they should be applied.

An example of shifting to a stronger though less desirable attaching point will be found in most damaged door panels on which the dented area is close to one edge. On many such panels, a large part of the surface will not be forced out of position by the damage. The ideal attaching points would be one edge, using a clamp, and the center area of the panel, using a tension plate. However, the practical methods would be to use two clamps, one attached to each edge of the panel. This would increase the length of the pull and leverage angle, and slightly decrease the effective leverage, but the loss would be offset by the simpler hookup and the much greater support under the edges.

Temporary support should be provided only when the problem cannot be solved by shifting to a stronger point. Usually such conditions will be found on deep dents in long panels, such as roofs and quarters. One means of temporary support is to set a jack under the attaching point; this works particularly well with roof panels because the underside usually is open. Another method suited to quarter panels is to extend the jack tube to some rigid point and block up under it.

The important point is to prevent the collapse of the attaching point, because this only complicates the damage. There will be no difficulty if the basic law of physics is understood and applied to the job at hand.

Effective Angle

The effective angle should be considered on some large area panels but may be ignored on heavy box members. Usually the area to be pulled is approximately 1 foot (30 cm) wide. Tension should be applied on a line that will cross that area. However, tension applied to a wide, nearly flat surface spreads into the area instead of being concentrated in a straight line, as illustrated in Figure 7-29. Applied tension will be much more effective at point B than at point A. The force lost reduces the reaction of the area being pulled and, if the distance is great enough, will cancel it completely, caus-

7-28 Lift reaction. End points will be subjected to down thrust equal to the resistance to lifting offered by low point in center.

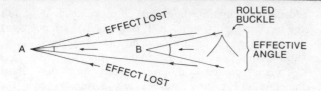

7-29 Loss of effectiveness of tension as point of application moves away from buckle.

ing the entire area to move instead of unfolding the buckle.

It is not always possible to apply tension from a point close enough to a buckle to provide the most effective angle, but when compromises must be made, the application point should be as close as possible to the buckle.

Work Hardened Metal

Work hardened metal in the buckled area is the direct result of the working that occurred as the panel unfolded under impact. Such hardening cannot occur without some changes in the dimensions of the affected area. Most such changes are upsets instead of stretches. The repair problem is to rework this metal back to the original dimensions. Except when heat will be used, reworking will add to the already slightly hardened condition. This is normal; if it does not prevent the panel from being restored to original contour, there is no reason to be concerned if an area of metal is slightly harder than the adjoining metal.

The need to rework the hardened metal to proper shape accounts for most of the work of final smoothing and metal-finishing of a damaged area after it has been pulled. It is the repairman's problem to determine how to do this so that the dimensions are restored. When they are restored, the panel surface will be restored, also. If there is access to the underside so that the dolly block can be used, the hammer and dolly block will be the best means of working the area. When they cannot be used, it is necessary to resort to spoons, pry tools, or any other means available.

Regardless of the method used to rework an upset area in a panel that has been pulled, as much of the area as possible should be reworked before the tension is released. The reason for this is simple: the work done on any upset area should tend to stretch it back to full length. If it is under tension while this work is being done, the tendency to return to full length will be much greater. This is illustrated in Figure 7-30. The arrows at each end indicate that tension is acting on the metal represented by the line. The wavy section of the line in the center represents the remaining part of the original bend, which in most cases would have been a rolled buckle. The rougher this wavy part of the surface, the more it will tend to shorten the panel, causing loose, springy bulges in the adjoining surface that often are mistaken for stretched metal. By holding the entire area under tension, whatever length is lost in the curved sections will be regained when they are straightened.

Holding tension on the panel during as much of the

final straightening operation as possible also removes any spring-back tendency caused by adjoining reinforcements. A common example of this often is found on a door panel that has been pushed in so far that the facing has been pulled far out of line. Pulling the panel back to shape also will pull the facing with it; but when the tension is released, the facing will tend to spring back toward its position when bent. This spring-back action is illustrated in Figure 7-31. Note the arrows at each end pointing inward. Pressure acting inward on a section of metal that is not finally straightened will tend to resist the flattening action when hand tools are used on the remaining buckles. Such an area will tend to rise in a bulge instead of blending with the level of the adjoining metal. Sometimes the springy action of such an area will be enough to be noticed by an experienced repairman.

In considering work hardened metal as a factor in determining the procedure in the use of tension, it must be recognized that each individual job differs. On some it will be so minor that it may be ignored; there is no problem with work hardened metal on a panel that pops back into shape when about half pulled. On others, it is a major problem, and, if ignored, may require excessive labor to work it out.

Sometimes the metal may be work hardened so severely that heat is needed to relieve it. Examples of this are given in the repair procedure section. Heat is used when the work hardened area has been upset so much that it is causing a serious bulge in the adjoining surface. The heat softens the metal so that it can be stretched back to, or close to, the original length.

As with the other factors, good judgment will determine whether allowances must be made for the effect of work hardened metal. Releasing the tension before the panel has been restored to final smoothness may cause a spring-back action that will make final straightening very difficult on some panels, whereas on others it may not.

Variations of Surface Crown

The surface crown must be considered when analyzing any damaged panel to determine where tension should be applied. The crown of almost every automobile panel varies from all others to some degree. Many of them vary from a relatively flat crown over a large part of the surface area to combination high and low or

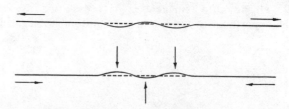

7-30 *(Top)* The desirability of straightening the remaining buckles under tension.

7-31 *(Bottom)* How pressure from adjoining area can resist straightening of remaining buckles.

reverse crowns along the edges; others may include every possible kind of crown on the various areas of the surface.

The variations in the details of the damage that can be found on different panels are almost without limit. Regardless of the details, however, all damage can be reduced to five basic conditions: (1) simple displacement, (2) simple bends, (3) rolled buckles, (4) stretches, and (5) upsets.

These basic conditions were covered in detail in Chapter 3, so they will not be discussed here except to point out that they will be relieved when damage is repaired properly. To repair any panel, force must be applied so that it does the most good. This means relieving the bends and rolled buckles so that the simple displacements can snap back into place and the upsets and stretches can be worked out with minimum effort.

The best results will be obtained from tension when it is applied where it has the greatest effect, and that is on conditions that tend to shorten flat crowns. These include practically all rolled buckles and any other damage in which adjoining areas tend to be drawn together. An excellent example of the latter condition is the folded-over door lower edge shown in Figure 7-32; this is similar to a rolled buckle, even though it is actually only a combination of simple bends in the outer panel and the facing.

Rolled buckles are found most frequently extending into a combination high and low crown area adjoining a relatively flat area. The severity of the rolled buckle is determined by the amount of break-over path that it has formed. When break-over paths have been formed, they usually will extend well into the high crown area. The more severe the break-over path, the more important it is that tension be applied close enough to it that it will be subjected to as much of the pulling force as possible. This, then, is the first rule: If there are severe upsets in the high crown area, tension should be applied to it as close as possible.

The ideal approach to unrolling many rolled buckles would be to make the first pull just below the highest point. As the high point rolled down to the line of tension, the attaching points would be dropped and

another pull made. In this way, it would be necessary to make several attachments to unroll a single buckle. This is the ideal procedure, but a more practical solution usually demands compromise; a single pull made at the point where the high and low crowns blend is often almost as effective as though several pulls had been made by starting much farther into the high crown and working progressively back to this position.

When working a damaged area such as the folded-over door edge shown in Figure 7-32 tension should be applied directly to the edge. Here this would mean applying the greatest amount of force to the strongest part of the damage. The flanged door edge welded to the facing is much stronger than the panel adjoining it. Furthermore, if upsets are left in the door edge, they will have a gathering effect on the adjoining flat metal. In many cases such as this, it is desirable to use heat on the buckles while they are under tension to restore full length. Only a few thousandths an inch of upset in this edge will cause severe gathering of the adjoining metal; this would be the condition called false stretch in Chapter 3.

Alignment with the crown of the panel must be correct if the desired results are to be obtained from the use of tension. The problem of determining proper alignment of the pulling setup with the crown of the panel is simple; the answer is based on the fact that tension tends to produce a straight line. Therefore, the tension setup must be aligned with the flattest surface line of the panel. If this rule is followed, no problems should arise due to improper alignment of the pulling force with the panel surface.

Many beginners have not been taught the importance of this rule and are often tempted to use a diagonal pull on a panel that has considerable crown in one direction. However, a diagonal line across the surface of such a panel would describe a curve instead of a straight line. Applying tension diagonally across such a panel would flatten or distort it by tending to make a flat surface where it should be crowned.

There are exceptions to this basic rule, but they apply only where a limited amount of force is needed. An example is minor damage of the pop-out type that probably would not be severe enough to warrant the use of tension.

TENSION ALIGNMENT

Tension alignment must be considered when making a heavy pull using any type of equipment, portable or fixed installations. Figure 7-33 illustrates the tendency of tension to produce a straight line between the two points from which the force is applied. The straight line includes the chains or any other linkage between the anchor and pull points of the machine in use. As shown, there is always a tendency either to lift the machine or to cause the body to drop if there is any difference in the heights of the anchor and pull points *unless* the chains or other linkages are hooked up on this line.

This tendency can be neglected on light pulls, but

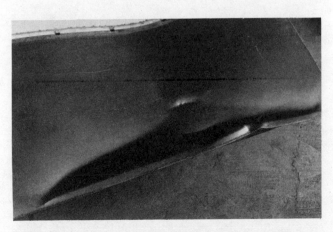

7-32 Folded-over door edge that should be straightened under tension and heated to relieve the upset.

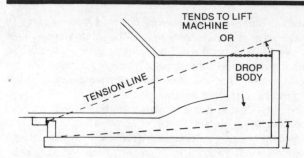

7-33 Tension will cause either the machine to rise or the body to drop, to form a straight line through the body from the anchor to the point of attachment to the machine.

heavier ones may require extra tie-downs or blocking to obtain the effect desired. Several examples are shown in Part 2 of the next chapter.

This same line is formed when pulling and anchoring from points on the same level but is not a problem, because the hookup is on or very close to the tension line.

SHOP EQUIPMENT

PORTABLE BODY AND FRAME MACHINES

One typical portable body and frame machine with accessories is shown in Figure 7-34. The accessories consist of: (1) two pairs of special support stands with tubular crossbars, shown behind the machine, (2) a crossbeam, which can be clamped to the main beam for twist setups, (3) chains, shown coiled beside the hydraulic pump, (4) a bolt-on plate, to attach to frame horns for chain connections, (5) anchor clamps, shown on each side of one chain in the lower left, (6) a self-contained

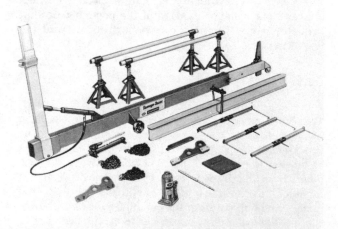

7-34 Typical portable body and frame machine.

hydraulic jack, in the left front, and (7) a set of self-centering gauges, in the right front.

Other manufacturers make similar equipment that operates on the same general principle but may vary widely in construction details and special features. Equipment of this type is adequate for most of the needs of the average small body shop, particularly for work on conventional frame construction, but it is limited to a single pull when used alone. This reduces its utility to some extent, because of the obvious trend toward smaller automobiles of unitized construction that tends to require more multiple hookups. However, enough operations still can be performed with the portable to make it essential equipment, particularly as it can be used anywhere in the shop. Its utility can be expanded greatly by the addition of one of the many systems of anchoring and pulling from floor *anchor pots*.

The basic use of portable equipment, with and without extra anchoring systems, is explained in Chapter 8, Part 2.

MULTIPLE HOOKUP EQUIPMENT

Equipment manufacturers have recognized the need for machines that have the capability of anchoring and pulling from more than one point at the same time, and many designs have been made available.

The manufacturer has two basic choices in the essential design of the machine. One is to take advantage of the rigidity of the concrete floor, which all shops have, and the other is to build an entirely self-contained machine, usually referred to as a drive-on machine. Both have advantages and disadvantages. The big advantage of in-the-floor equipment is less expense and that, when not in use, the space can be used for other activities. This partly is offset by the fact that some jobs will require more time than necessary for the self-contained unit. The big advantage of the drive-on unit is versatility. However, when installed, the space it occupies cannot be used for other activities. The later is not a disadvantage if the shop has sufficient volume to keep the machine busy.

In-the-Floor Equipment

Two systems of in-the-floor equipment are used: anchor pots, often called tie-down or floor pots, and a steel frame set in the floor.

The anchor pots have the advantages of being relatively inexpensive and that they can be installed in an existing floor or can be preset in new construction. Installing a few, to be used in conjunction with a portable machine, will extend the shop's capability to handle major wreck work. However, a complete installation, including one or more power units designed for the purpose, is a more productive setup. It is quite practical to install a few in each working stall in the most advantageous positions and a complete setup in one stall. This will enable the shop crew to handle most of the work in

7-35 Body and frame equipment designed for use with anchor pots, set up to align rear door opening. Anchors are out of view on opposite side.

7-37 The machine shown in Fig. 7-36 setup on van body.

the individual stalls and route only the big jobs to the fully equipped one.

The system shown in Figure 7-35 features a large number of anchor pots and two compact power units. In the setup shown, pulls are being made on the center and rear lock pillars. Both operations would be required before the door could be fitted into the opening. It is not possible to show the anchors in a photograph taken from the position of this one, but an experienced repairman would know that they would be on the opposite side, preferably two, one at each end of the midsection and attached to the frame.

The system shown in Figure 7-36 uses anchor pots also, but has two special features, the built-in floor jack and the extra height. The jack is a convenient feature for setting an automobile on safety stands, but is not intended to support it while making a pull. The extra height is very desirable for work on the upper parts of vans and recreational vehicles, as illustrated in Figure 7-37.

Steel beams set in the floor, as in Figure 7-38, provide almost unlimited versatility to pull or push from any angle and at any level. An anchor or power unit can be set in the exact position it is needed and, if necessary, changed slightly with very little lost time. Equipment of this type has the capacity to handle heavier work than normal automobile body and frame straightening.

Drive-On Equipment

Many different types of drive-on equipment have a wide variety of special features. However, all of them

7-36 Body and frame equipment designed for use with anchor pots, featuring built-in floor jack and extra height.

7-38 Body and frame equipment featuring in-the-floor steel beams.

7-39 Drive-on type body and frame machine, featuring four swinging power heads; only two heads show.

consist of a heavy steel frame, or base, large enough to surround the automobile and provide a runway for it to stand on. Added to this is a means of anchoring and various types of power heads to pull, and sometimes to push, from various angles. The machine shown in Figure 7-39 features four swinging power heads, one equipped for vertical lifting, and a winch to pull incapacitated automobiles onto the runway.

Evaluating Equipment

The equipment in this chapter is shown without recommendation. Each has its special advantages and disadvantages. Also, each shop has its special problems, such as volume of business, space, skill level, and many others. Equipment that would be highly desirable for one shop might be inadequate for another and beyond the needs of a third.

The human factor must be considered along with equipment when evaluating any system. The equipment has the capacity to do the work if it is used in an intelligent manner, but it is only a means of putting the operator's skill to work. It is not uncommon to find a competent repairman doing high-quality work with inadequate equipment while another, using the best equipment available, fails to satisfy his customers.

FRAME-CHECKING EQUIPMENT

The final checking of a straightened frame or the corresponding parts of a unitized body should be done with a frame tram or a set of centerline gauges, sometimes both. Preliminary checks before straightening are rarely required, because there is almost always other visual evidence on the automobile to indicate a frame condition requiring straightening. Door and front-end sheet metal alignment and the condition of bumpers or other parts of the body and suspension systems are reliable indicators of frame damage serious enough to require repair.

Frame tram gauges are used to make diagonal measurements across sections of the frame of the type represented by the diagonal lines on A in Figure 7-40. They are sometimes used to make three-point checks for raises or sags and are essential when it is necessary to check track and wheel base.

Frame Tram Gauges

A frame tram is simply a long bar that has at least two, and should have three, parallel pointers extending

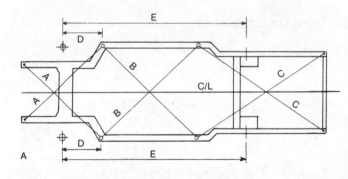

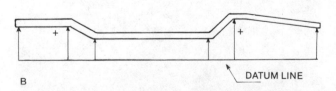

7-40 Typical frame layout. A, diagonal lines represent pattern of cross-checking. B, typical datum line specifications available from shop manuals or independent sources.

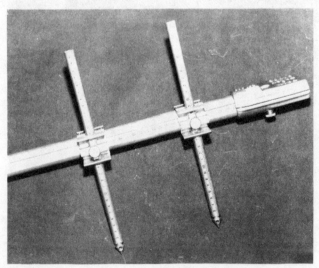

7-41 Tram gauge with attached tape. Extra pointers and bar not shown.

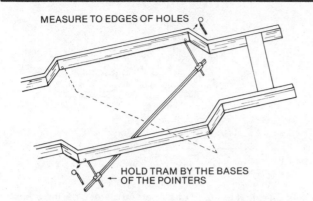

MEASURE TO EDGES OF HOLES

HOLD TRAM BY THE BASES
OF THE POINTERS

7-42 The two positions for making a cross-check. The tram must be held in the same manner in both positions for accurate measurements.

at a right angle and attached so that they can be moved to any position along its length. Preferably, the pointers should be designed so that the distance they extend above the bar is adjustable, and at least one should be removable. A close-up view of one end of a tram gauge is shown in Figure 7-41. The bar consists of sections that snap together, so that it can be set up to the desired length, and is equipped with an extension tape, enclosed in the handle; the pointers are calibrated in inches. The extra bars and third pointer are not shown. The third pointer is used only for three-point checks.

Careful handling of any tram is required to obtain accurate measurements, particularly when measuring over long spans. It should be held at opposite ends by two persons, preferably at the base of the pointers, as indicated in Figure 7-42, except when making very short measurements. When changing to the opposite measurement, each person should change over to the corresponding reference point and take a position that will permit viewing it from the same angle; never change reference points. One should hold his pointer on the reference point while the other makes the adjustment.

When making a three-point check, the pointers should be set to make contact on the undamaged side. The accuracy of the settings can be checked by holding

one end in contact while the other end is raised slowly into position. If the adjustment is correct, the center contact will be felt at the same time as the end touches. On a long span the center pointer may bump two or three times as the bar vibrates up and down. On the other side one person places his pointer in contact, and the other raises his pointer until the first contact can be felt. If all three pointers contact at the same time without flexing the tram bar, there is no raise or sag. However, if there is a gap at either the end or center, it is necessary to determine from the available evidence which point is too high or too low.

Figure 7-43 shows the setup position above and the checking position below on a typical frame without the body. In this case, a gap is shown at the outer end, assuming that the body was there. If the door above the center pointer fitted properly, it would suggest that the outer end of the frame rail was too high. If the door dropped appreciably when opened or was jammed shut so that it would not open, it would suggest that the rail was sagged under the cowl.

The frame tram can be used to check *track* and *wheelbase* when there is reason to suspect that they are not correct and that the normally used reference points may be damaged. Track refers to the alignment of the rear axle to the front wheels and suspension. When it is correct, the center line of the rear axle will be on and at an exact right angle to the overall centerline of the automobile. The rear wheels will then follow the front ones in the same tracks. A track check is illustrated in A of Figure 7-44. No attempt has been made to show the persons holding, but two are required, one at each end. For uniformity when changing from side to side, they should not change ends.

In making a track check, the tram is used to project a line from the rear wheels to the end of front wheel spin-

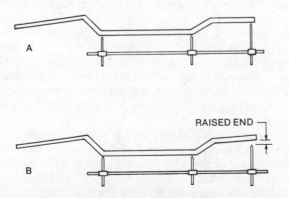

A

B
RAISED END

7-43 Making a three-point check for raises or sags. A, setting up on one side with all three pointers in contact. B, comparing the first setting to the opposite side. Tram must be held without strain.

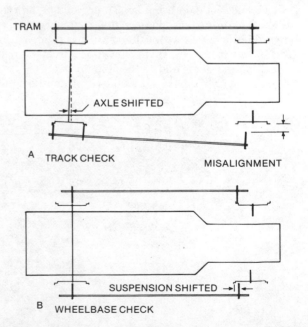

TRAM

AXLE SHIFTED

A TRACK CHECK   MISALIGNMENT

SUSPENSION SHIFTED

B WHEELBASE CHECK

7-44 A, Track check. B, Wheelbase check. Rear axle must be known to be in alignment for this check to be accurate.

dle. When it is correct, the tram set to the two points on the rear wheel and the one on the spindle should fit the corresponding points on the opposite side exactly. When it is not correct, the difference will show up in the gap between the end of the pointer and the spindle, as indicated at the lower right (Figure 7-44).

Making a track check requires some preparation. The front suspension system must be in good condition and the steering wheel turned to the straight-ahead position. Both rear wheels must be checked for lateral runout (wobble) and, if any is found, the point of maximum runout must be turned to either the top or the bottom. There should be no dents or bends in the narrow flat surface of the rim the two pointers will contact. The tram should be held in contact with these two points while the third is adjusted to the end of the front spindle. When moved to the opposite side, pointers will fit the same if the rear axle is in alignment, or track. However, if there is a gap at the front pointer, it indicates that the rear axle or frame is out of alignment. The actual misalignment will be one half of the gap, because the front pointer had to be set back an amount equal to the misalignment on the opposite side. If the first gap shows up at the front pointer on the rear wheel, the tram should be reset on that side and the reading taken on the other.

A wheelbase check is illustrated by B, Figure 7-44. This check will reveal whether the suspension is holding the front wheel in position, as indicated at the lower right, but not why. That must be interpreted by the persons taking the check after considering all the other available information.

A wheelbase check cannot be accurate unless the rear axle is in correct alignment and the front suspension is fully assembled and has no obvious bends. Before taking it, the front wheels should be set in the straight-ahead position as accurately as possible. The check should be taken from the center point of the rear axle shaft to the nearest point on the front wheel rim, as shown. The fore and aft positions of this point will be affected much less by slight variations from straight ahead than the outer end of the spindle.

A track or wheelbase check is rarely needed, but

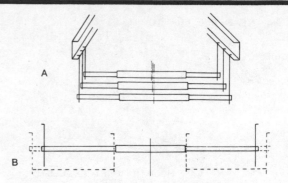

7-46 Typical features of centerline gauges having adjustable horizontal bars. A, checking accuracy of the gauges by hanging them close together between parallel supports. B, showing the approximate range of extension of most gauges of this type.

both the repairman and estimator should understand them. They are a last-resort check when an automobile has been rebuilt after serious frame and suspension damage and there is reason to doubt the reliability of the reference points used to check alignment. Sometimes an automobile that has been damaged previously and rebuilt improperly will be in such condition that the dependability of the normal reference points is questionable. Confronted with this situation, the repair shop can be sure that the automobile will operate properly if the other front-end alignment adjustments are correct and track and wheelbase check out properly. If they are off to an appreciable degree, particularly track, trouble can be expected, because the automobile will tend to run in a circle, requiring the driver to turn the steering wheel to one side to go straight ahead.

CENTER LINE GAUGES

There are two types of center line gauges. The type shown in Figure 7-45 consists of a center unit hung in the frame by chains. The other, illustrated in Figure 7-46 and with Figure 7-34, consists of an adjustable base with upright arms on each end. These arms on most gauges are adjustable for height so that the gauge can be set to datum line specifications when necessary. Both types of gauges have an upright center pin to indicate the center line of the automobile at the point in which the gauge is located. The chain type is centered by using equal lengths of chain on both sides. The adjustable-base types have a mechanism to maintain the pin in center position as the opposite sides move closer together or farther apart. Either type is a practical tool when used properly.

Center line gauges are used in sets of three or sometimes four units. A minimum of three is required. They can be used to check both center line and sags or raises. In use, one gauge is set up in the end of the frame being checked, two more are set up at the opposite end, if it is used. Checking is simply a matter of sighting the alignment of the center pins for center line and the level of the crossbars for raises or sags.

7-45 Centerline gauge set with chain attachment.

To check center line, the eye should be moved back and forth so that the pins can be seen from both sides. If correct, the clearance between the pins will appear the same from both angles. To check for raises or sags, the eye should be raised or lowered to a position from which the alignment of crossbars can be seen. If correct, they will appear parallel. Any out-of-parallel area will be indicated by a wedge-shaped space between the edges. Assuming that the automobile has been damaged on the end being viewed, if the near and far gauges are parallel and the center one low, a sag is indicated at the center position; or if the center and far gagues are parallel and the near one high or low, the near end of the frame is high or low.

The primary value of the center line gauges is that they provide a quick, one-man check for most of the common frame problems. They are much easier than a tram check but are not a complete substitute for the tram, because they do not do everything. They are intended primarily as a final check on the finished job, rather than a preliminary check to determine if repair is needed.

Any set of center line gauges should be checked for accuracy occasionally, as shown in A, Figure 7-46, by hanging them close together on parallel supports. This will make any misaligned condition of any of the gauges obvious. B shows the usual range of adjustment of the horizontal bars of that type of gauge.

Repair Procedures

PART ONE

This chapter is divided into two parts. The first deals with the three-step approach to planning and performing the repair procedure for specific jobs. However, that is pursued only far enough to demonstrate the importance of making and following a plan for every job. The emphasis is on job analysis rather than hammer-blow-by-hammer-blow directions. The second part moves from that aspect to a broader viewpoint in which the general types of damage are related to the construction involved and the general repair procedures that may be used. This is actually a step into the future, as the beginner learning his trade will earn his living on repair jobs that do not exist yet. In fact, if he spends a lifetime at his trade, most of the automobiles he can expect to work on will be built after he has become a skilled repairman.

THE THREE-STEP APPROACH

All of the procedures on actual damage in the following sections have been organized in a three-step approach:

1. Inspect the damage area to determine the type of damaged conditions present and the basic repair procedures suited to them.

2. Determine the general repair sequence to be followed. This is an application of the idea explained in detail in the Reversed Motion section of the preceding chapter.

3. Do the job, following the sequence decided on but watching for situations where trouble will develop, particularly on complicated jobs.

The available equipment must be considered in both the second and third steps. Ideally, everything needed should be available; actually, this is not possible. Also, the planned procedure must be flexible. Even the most experienced repairmen find it necessary to alter the planned procedure at times. Minor changes are to be expected, but when major ones are needed, the job has not been analyzed properly.

DETERMINING REPAIR PROCEDURE

After the inspection has been completed, the next logical step is to determine how to proceed to straighten the damage. In some instances, this may be such a simple process that practically no thought at all is required; in others it may be so complicated that it is difficult to decide where to start. In either event, the only information to guide the repairman in applying his skill is what he reads from the panel surface. His problem is to visualize the folding action that took place as the damaging force was applied and to find the best way, or ways, to apply force to accomplish the opposite effect.

One of the worst possible mistakes is to start the job

without any particular plan. This is even worse than to have analyzed the damage incorrectly and started with the wrong plan, because, with the wrong plan, it will soon be seen that the desired results are not being obtained. With no special plan, there is also no pattern of results to be expected.

An excellent way to plan the repair procedure is to find the answers to such questions as the following:

1. Where should the start be made?
2. Should it be made by driving, pushing, or pulling?
3. What will the shape of the damaged area be as the result of the first step?
4. If there is more than one impact area and related damage, should one be completed before the other, or should both or all be worked together?
5. Where should the next step be taken after the starting and each of the following steps be completed?
6. What methods should be used as the work progresses through the various steps?

General questions such as these can be applied to any damaged panel. The answers, of course, will vary widely from one panel to another, because the damages vary. The value in finding the answers is that intelligent thought is applied to the problem before starting to work. The ideal result of such thinking would be to change the repair of any damaged panel from a problem to a series of simple steps to be carried out in predetermined sequence.

DOING THE JOB

Doing the job is putting the planned procedure to work. If perfection could be obtained, this stage would be no more than just a specified amount of labor. This is rarely the case, however, because the almost infinite number of variables make it necessary to be on the alert for undesired results. This means that the repairman should be constantly inspecting and analyzing the results of his various steps so he can modify his procedure as required.

1. Inspect the damaged area to determine the types of damage conditions present and the basic repair procedures suited to the conditions.
2. Determine the exact repair procedure to be followed.
3. Do the job.

This approach is recommended for any job and to any worker, beginner or experienced. The amount of time spent in the first two steps no doubt will vary widely for the beginner and the experienced man, because the beginner may be forced to study to learn facts about a job that the experienced man can see at a glance. However, the amount of time spent in deciding how to do the job is not in itself an indication that the job will or will not be done properly. It is much more important that the correct procedure be followed than it is to get started in a hurry. A few more minutes spent in getting all of the facts so that the job is started properly may avoid mistakes that will require hours to correct.

INSPECTION

In making the inspection, certain specific information must be learned about the damaged panel. This can be done best by forming the habit of following a definite pattern or sequence of examination. It is also essential to know what to look for. The following list of inspection steps, arranged in the sequence to be followed, includes the information needed:

1. Location of the point, or points, of impact.
2. If two or more impacts are invovled, determine:
   a. Are they equal, or should one be considered as the major and the others as of minor importance?
   b. The exact areas of secondary damage related to each one.
   c. Will the repair of the damage from one impact be related to the repair of the others, or are they independent?
   d. If they are related, which one should be started first so that it will reduce the severity of conditions in the other, or others?
3. The exact nature of the various damage conditions—upsets, stretches, rolled buckles, hinge buckles, displaced metal, and so on—that make up the total damage and determine which are the most severe.
4. Relate each of the damage conditions to the repair method best suited for roughing it out.

An inspection of the damage on an automobile will reveal many facts about the collision that caused it. The information that is of particular interest to the repairman has to do with the nature of the other object involved and the action that took place. Speed, size, rigidity, and direction of motion of the impact object all leave telltale marks that serve to reveal the exact nature of the damage.

Failure to observe that the desired results are not being obtained accounts for more wasted effort and substandard jobs than any other cause. The reason for this is easy to understand. The use of force is required in every step, and the forces must be enough to bend, upset, or stretch the affected metal in some way in each step. If the wrong results are being obtained and the repairman continues to work, the damage will be compounded.

The three-step approach outlined here is nothing more than the thought processes of a skilled professional put into words. Such thinking is essential to analyze any job before it is started. As skill is developed, much of the thinking becomes automatic. Automatically or painfully slowly, however, the repairman must know what he is going to do before starting to do it.

DENTED FENDER

The fender dent shown in Figure 8-1 is relatively minor damage. It has been selected for discussion because it is a typical example of a dent that can be straightened easily and quickly by proper use of the hand tools, even though access to the underside is partly blocked.

8-1 Minor dent in the side of a fender. Note that there are no severe distortions.

The question arises as to whether or not a job such as this should be filled. In this case, it is possible to use a dolly block and a pry rod on the underside of the metal, even though the access is limited. It would not be possible to finish the job with filling alone, because of the high ridges above and below the impact point of the molding. These ridges must be lowered before the shape can be restored by filling. Just a little more care in the use of the hand tools in doing this necessary straightening will leave no place to fill. The extra time to do this straightening is minor, less than would be required to apply and finish the filler.

This same dent farther forward on the fender would probably require filling, unless a lot of extra time was used on it, because it would be much more difficult to reach the underside. In that case, the procedure would be considerably different from that discussed in the following pages. It would then be a matter of prying it out to rough shape and filling the rest.

Inspection

Inspection of this damage reveals the following information:

1. There are no severe distortions.
2. Most of the dented area is under only an elastic strain and should pop out when the buckles in the ridges are relieved, leaving only minor roughness.
3. Limited access to the underside is provided by the construction of the fender and cowl. In Figure 8-2, it may be seen that the underside can be reached for limited use of the hammer and dolly block, and all of the area can be reached with a pry rod.
4. The curved buckle above the molding is the most severe. Less severe buckles are at the lower edge, following the line of rub marks, and vertically at the rear edge where the metal has bent over the inner reinforcement.
5. A minor concave buckle can be expected under the crushed molding. In the undamaged condition, the upper edge of this molding follows a convex crease stamped in the side of the fender. This crease line will have to be restored as a part of the straightening procedure.

Repair Plan

The repair of this damage should be planned to take maximum advantage of the elastic condition in the center area. The more nearly it can be made to pop out to shape, the less additional work will be required to finish the job. The upper ridge and the concave buckle under the molding are holding the area out of shape more so than the lower buckle. For that reason, the lower buckle will be left until the upper area has been worked out.

If space under the fender permitted, the concave buckle under the molding could be driven out by striking with the dolly block. As this is not practical, the dolly can be held against the underside and stiff pressure exerted against it while the ridge is worked out with the hammer. Reaction to the hammer blows will cause the dolly to drive out much of the low metal.

Additional work with the dinging spoon and the hammer and dolly should smooth the area so that it can be metal-finished.

Repair Procedure

The first repair operation is shown in Figure 8-3. The repairman is reaching through the door opening to the underside of the fender to hold the lip of a general-purpose dolly block against the crushed crease line, indicated by the line of elongated oval marks. Stiff hand pressure is being applied to the dolly block while the hammer is used on the upper ridge, here indicated by a long line with short crossmarks. This operation reduced most of the ridge and allowed much of the displaced metal to snap back to shape.

After most of the ridge had been removed with the hammer, the dinging spoon was used as shown in Figure 8-4. This would not have been practical for the first operation for two reasons: (1), the original ridge was too sharply formed to work with the dinging spoon; and (2), the reaction of the dolly block on the underside would have been lost. After this operation was completed, additional work on the crease line was done with the hammer and dolly block.

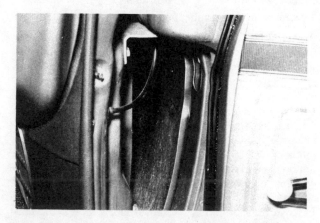

8-2 View of the underside of the fender from the rear end with the door open.

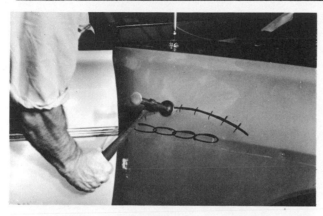

8-3 Working out the dent with the hammer and dolly block. The lip of the dolly is being held under the area of the elongated oval marks and pushed outward with as much pressure as possible.

8-5 Using the small head of the bumping hammer on the vertical ridge. The small head is more effective on springy metal than the large one.

In Figure 8-5, the small head of the hammer is shown being used on the vertical crease. It was used also on the lower ridge. The small head was used because both these ridges are in areas that are springy, making it desirable to reduce the area of hammer contact as much as possible. Using the large head or the dinging spoon will not work in areas such as these as well as the small head.

The worked-out area, shown in Figure 8-6, is relatively smooth, and most of the original crease line above the molding has been restored.

The result of the first sanding operation is shown in Figure 8-7. The sander has been stroked over the area in the back-and-forth motion used for finishing metal. Note that a few low spots are indicated by the black primer remaining in them, but the overall surface is in good condition. An overlay of dust from the sanding operation can be seen on the paint above and to the right of the area that has been sanded. This is normal.

The sanded area has been filed, showing up the remaining low spots in greater detail, in Figure 8-8. The file strokes are parallel to the flattest crown of the fender, except at the lower edge where it was necessary to slant them downward to avoid interference with

the reverse crown on the edge of the fender. No picking has been done on the filed area, but enough filing has been done to show sharp outlines of the low spots. This is the method of filing discussed in Chapter 3. In effect, it is in part a smoothing operation and in part an inspection operation. The overall area was near enough to final smoothness before the finishing operation was started so that the larger areas of smooth filed metal can be considered finished. All that remains to do is lift the low spots slightly so that they can be filed to blend into the adjoining areas.

The repairman is in the process of prying up low spots in Figure 8-9. The upper hinge is being used as a fulcrum for the pry rod as the point is shifted from one low spot to another. Note that he is pointing with one finger toward the spot being lifted. This is not necessary, but many repairmen find that it helps them to locate the spot they wish to pry. The principal caution to observe on an operation such as this is not to pry too hard. It is better to pry the same spot several times than to pry it once too hard.

The filed-off panel, ready for final sanding, is shown in Figure 8-10. The time for this filing operation was very short, only a few minutes—less time than would have been required to fill and finish the surface.

The result of the final sanding operation is shown in

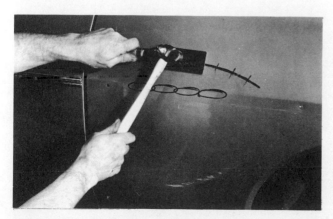

8-4 Using the flat spoon on what remains of the high ridge.

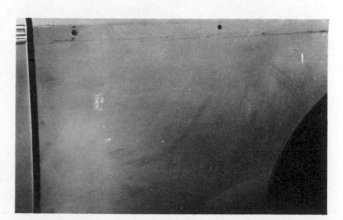

8-6 The straightened area, ready to start metal-finishing.

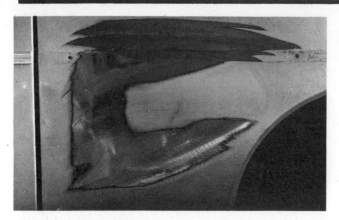

8-7 The result of the first sanding operation. A little paint remains in the low spots.

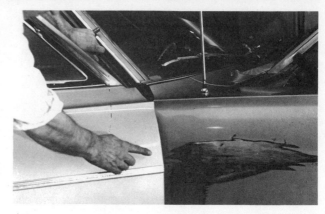

8-9 Using a pry rod on the low spots through the rear end of the fender. Some doors do not swing out of the opening to permit this operation.

Figure 8-11. This sanding was done with a buffing stroke, as described in Chapter 3. For this buffing operation, the sander pad was held so that the swirl marks run as near as possible to the lengthwise direction of the panel, and the machine was stroked up and down instead of back and forth. A worn 36-grit disc was used, and the pressure on it was very light because the intention was to buff, not cut.

Note that a little less attention was paid to the metal that would be covered by the molding than to that in the other areas. A slight low spot, which will be covered by a molding, will not be a problem, because it cannot be seen after the automobile is reassembled.

The final, repainted fender is shown in Figure 8-12. It is in excellent shape, and it was done very quickly. The repairman took advantage of the construction features of the automobile and the nature of the damage and made them work for him. Not all makes and models are so designed that easy access at the rear end of the fender is provided. On some automobiles, different procedures would be necessary. The important point is that the construction features of the automobile must be considered when planning the repair procedure and the maximum advantage taken of those that simplify the job.

UNITIZED FRONT-END REBUILD

The damaged front end on the small automobile in Figure 8-13 has been selected for discussion because it represents some of the types of problems that repairmen can expect in the future. Although not new, it conforms to the trend to obtain maximum stiffness with minimum weight. It differs from many current models by having the fenders and front panel welded instead of bolted in place. Regardless of design differences, some of the repair problems of the future will be on much lighter construction than the body repair industry has dealt with in the past.

Inspection

This front end appears much worse than it actually is because of the condition of the fender and front-end panel. Apparently it has collided with a small, rigid object that approached from an angle of 35 to 40 degrees. Whatever it struck, or struck it, has driven the fender and side panel back against the forward edge of the cowl (see Fig. 8-18), ripped the welds joining the

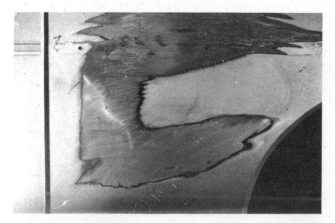

8-8 The result of the first filing operation, showing the remaining low spots in much greater detail than they appeared in the ground surface.

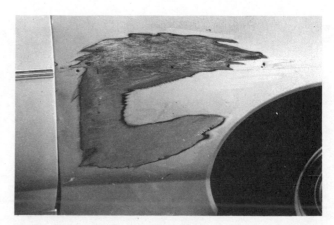

8-10 The surface after filing off the pried-up spots. Low spot in molding line will be covered after molding is replaced.

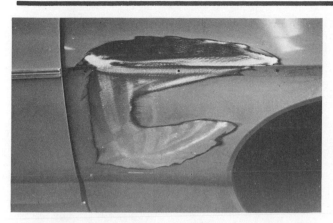

8-11 The finished surface, after buffing, ready for repainting.

8-13 Front-end sheet metal damage on unitized construction automobile.

front end of the fender and front panel, bent the bumper bracket, crushed the right corner of the hood, and pushed the entire front end sheet metal assembly to the left. Additional parts damaged include the headlight assembly, side marker light (folded out of sight), right parking light, and grille. Under the hood the right side panel is buckled and pushed back, the heater assembly is crushed between the fender and the engine, and some of the flexible ducts are broken. There is no serious mechanical damage. The frame structure and right suspension seem intact, but the right wheel alignment should be checked.

The amount of side shift of the front-end sheet metal is indicated by arrows on the rear end of the fender and hood in Figure 8-14. The fender has twisted enough to cause a small buckle at the upper rear end, indicated by the large solid arrow, and broken the welds that join it to the cowl at the position of the two opposed small arrows. The rear end of the hood is bent down between the two open arrows. This bend can be seen from the inside in Figure 8-15, which shows a sharp buckle in the inner diagonal brace as well as the outer panel. The right hood hinge was bent as the hood shifted, but it is not shown in detail, because it is only a simple straightening job.

The back thrust on the cowl has tipped the hinge pillar slightly, allowing the door to drop at the lock pillar,

but not enough to prevent opening and closing. This would not be expected on most past model unitized construction bodies, but should not be ruled out for future models.

Repair Plan

Four essential steps should be completed before pulling the right side panel back to position: (1) remove the damaged right fender, (2) pull the twist out of the left side of the front-end panel, (3) realign the left fender and reweld it to the cowl, and (4) rough out and fit the hood to the realigned fender and cowl. With these steps completed, the side panel can be pulled into position and fitted to the hood and the replacement fender fitted to both it and the cowl.

A parts problem developed after the job was started and complicated the repair plan slightly. The owner (the author did this job, but is not the owner) had purchased

8-14 Left side view of the automobile shown previously. Large solid arrow indicates buckle. Opposed solid arrows indicate broken weld and open fender to cowl joint.

8-12 The finished job.

8-15 Setup to pull twist out of grille opening.

8-17 Straightening left rear corner of hood, using improvised tool.

this automobile from a salvage dealer and was rebuilding it for his own use. A salvage fender and front-end panel were part of the deal. Normally, salvage parts would simplify the parts replacement, because the fender and front panel are already welded together and could be replaced as a unit. After starting, it developed that the parts were for a past model that had a different bracket in the lower part of the front panel for the bumper bracket attachment. As new parts would be additional expense for the owner, the brackets were stripped out of both panels so that the replacement could be fitted to the original. Otherwise, the parts could be made to fit and match in appearance after shrinking out a pressed-in depression in the lower section below the headlight. The shrunken spot can be seen in Figure 8-24.

Repair Procedure

Pulling the twist out of the front panel is shown in

Figure 8-15. A heavy duty C-clamp was used as a hook in the right corner of the grille opening. No attempt was made to protect the panel, because this part is to be cut away later. This was a diagonal pull, but most of the effect was to the side instead of forward, because there was less resistance to movement in that direction. The machine is anchored by the chain to an opening in a bracket on the frame that supports the lower control arm. The same anchor was used for the next operation, but, as both were light pulls, there was no risk of front end misalignment.

The fender has been removed, and a strap is being used to pull the fender into position in Figure 8-16. A light force was applied to swing the fender to the right just far enough to make a uniform gap between the rear edge and the cowl. The fender was then welded to the cowl edge by brazing. Before brazing, the joint was cleaned by scorching the paint with a oxidizing flame and wire-brushing it bright. This simplified the problem of making the brass flow down into the joint, leaving the upper edge with normal appearance.

The operation on the front of the fender is not shown,

8-16 Strap setup to pull left fender back into alignment with the body.

8-18 Close-up view of dent in cowl top panel.

8-19 Using dent puller on cowl dent.

8-21 Anchor setup for lengthwise pull.

but the clamp used was left in place. The fender flange had been pushed in slightly by the hood. This was given a light pull while the machine was in place.

The straightening operation of the rear corner of the hood panel is shown in Figure 8-17. Two holes were drilled in the corner reinforcement and a heavy metal screw threaded into them for the slot in the pry bar (an old spring leaf). The diagonal bracket was heated and the buckle lifted out while it was in the red heat range. The locking pliers held the pry bar from twisting to the side. No measurements were taken, because an experienced eye can judge when a part such as this is in shape. This is a good example of the situation in which the repairman must improvise with what is at hand.

A close-up view of the dent in the cowl top panel is shown in Figure 8-18. This was made as the cowl and fender were driven back by the impact. A scrap of the fender is still attached to the cowl, but it has been completely removed from the side panel; note the circular spot-weld cutter marks.

In Figure 8-19, the side panel has been pulled for-

ward, and a dent puller is being used on the cowl dent. This area is completely boxed in so that it is impractical to drive it out from the inside, leaving the dent puller as the only practical method to use.

A hookup to pull the upper part of the side panel is shown in Figure 8-20, using a special clamp intended to be attached by bolting through holes in the panel. The chain is attached to the piece that is hidden by the panel. The fender bracket, just forward of the clamp, made it necessary to install the chain piece inside, but it is effective either way. One bolt was put through an existing hole, and a new hole was drilled for the other.

The method of anchoring for the lengthwise pulls is shown in Figure 8-21. The clevis is attached to a shipping bracket, put on by the factory to tie the automobile

8-20 Pulling upper edge of side panel.

8-22 Pulling lower part of side panel.

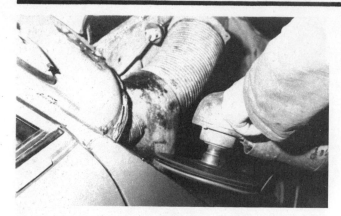

8-23 Grinding pinch weld flange.

down in transport. It was fortunate that this was in place, because the automobile has very little under-construction rigid enough to withstand a hard pull.

The setup for the main lengthwise pull is shown in Figure 8-22. The clamp is attached to a reinforcement where there is little chance that a piece will pull out instead of moving the panel. At this point, the machine is under slight tension, but most of the pulling remains to be done; note the buckle next to the reinforcement. The panel will be pulled and shaped to fit to the hood, which has been installed.

Most of the damaged section of the front panel has been cut away. The upper bar of the grille opening has been measured and trimmed to length; the lower part at this time has been rough-cut with the torch. The replacement piece will be laid over the lower section and clamped in temporary position so that the length of the grille opening can be measured carefully. The old section will then be marked and trimmed to fit to the replacement piece. Trimming can be done here with a pair of aviation-type tin snips.

The operation is not shown, but a light-duty body jack was set up inside the door to aid in realigning the opening. Wood blocks were placed against the wheel housing

and the working end of the jack placed against the cowl hinge bracket. This may not have been necessary because the pull in Figure 8-20 should have tipped the cowl forward. However, doubts about the rigidity of the anchor made it seem desirable to limit the force applied. Setting up the jack required far less time than would have been needed to repair the damage if the anchor did pull loose.

The old flange had to be ground off the pinch-weld that joins the rear edge of the fender to body side panel, as shown in Figure 8-23. Unlike most spot-welded seams, the welds in this one are very close together, almost overlapped, making an almost continuous weld. The only practical way to separate it is to cut the old fender as close to the flange as possible and grind the rest away. The replacement panel required the same operation, because it was salvage. However, this was not a major operation, because the seams are short.

In Figure 8-24, the replacement panel has been clamped in place and tack-welded at the upper and lower edges of the grille opening. Unfortunately, the torch hose almost totally hides the lower weld. This should have been noticed when the photo was taken, but was missed. The space between the front ends of the fenders was held by the tack-welds in the upper bar of the front panel, but the straps and turn buckle were needed to draw the rear end tight to the cowl top panel. The clamps on the pinch weld hold the fore-and-aft position.

It was mentioned in the repair plan that a depression in the lower section of the front panel was shrunk out.

8-24 Replacement fender tack welded, clamped, and strapped in place.

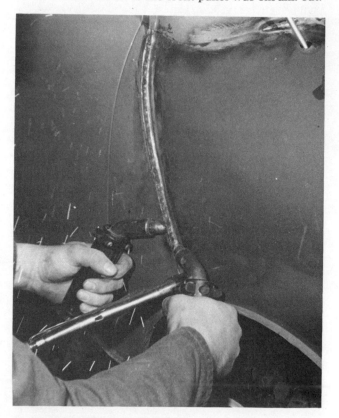

8-25 Spot-welding hem flange. Short white lines are sparks, thrown off by left electrode.

8-26 "Buttonhole" welds in fender flange.

8-28 the finished job, ready for reassembly and repainting.

This is the blackened spot directly below the head light opening.

Spot-welding the pinch-weld flanges is shown in Figure 8-25. The short, white lines in the lower left are sparks thrown off by the left electrode. This was a two-step operation. In the first step, welds were made about 2 inches (5 cm) apart from the top to the lower end. In the second stop, closely spaced welds were made along the full length of the seam.

Note that the electrodes are held apart instead of directly opposite. This has two advantages: it speeds the operation because the machine has the capacity to make two welds, and it eliminates the possibility that variations of pressure could cause the electrodes to penetrate the surfaces and come into direct contact. The second advantage is particularly important on this seam, because the previous welding and grinding may have left thin spots. However, hand-held electrodes should be used in this manner on any seam that can be welded from both sides.

The inner surface of the fender flange would have required excessive grinding to prepare it for spot welding, so it was torch welded, as shown in Figure 8-26. These are "buttonhole" welds. Many shops use brazing for this type of joint. Either is satifactory.

The right front and left rear corners of the hood were filled, because inner construction prevented access for hand tools. A hand-held half-round plane blade is shown being used to finish the fill in Figure 8-27. This same photo is shown in Figure 6-7.

The panels have been finished, ready for repainting, in Figure 8-28. Note the paper over the right side of the windshield. This was to prevent flying grit from marking the windshield glass when the disc sander was used on the fender.

The refinished automobile is shown in Figure 8-29.

8-27 Finishing filler on hood, using hand-held half-round plane blade.

8-29 The completed job.

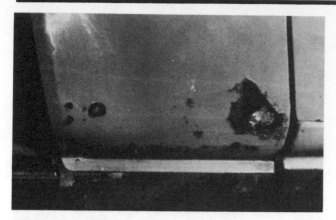

8-30 Typical fender rust damage.

RUST REPAIR

Rust repair may be done by welding in metal or by several non-metal methods, and to various standards of quality. All of the non-metal methods use some form of resin to provide adhesion and stiffen a fibrous material. It should be obvious to anyone interested that the larger the hole in the panel, the more it is important to repair it by welding in metal to restore physical strength.

Rust repair by any method cannot be expected to restore an automobile to new condition. It is not economically practical to disassemble welded sheet metal assemblies to clean out every trace of rust and restore the treatment of the inner surfaces applied in the factory prior to painting. The repaired automobile must go back into service under the same conditions that caused the original metal failure, but carrying the handicap of inadequate inner-surface protection. A high-grade undercoating should be applied, but it is not the equivalent of factory pretreatment of the metal. The result is that the life of the automobile will be extended, but will rarely be doubled unless the car is operated in very dry climatic conditions.

The rust that perforates body panels works from the inside. It almost invariably starts in the lower sections of the body where dust will settle and muddy water will accumulate in wet weather. The water dries by evaporation, leaving whatever soil it contained added to the dust. The deposit accumulates and is rewet by wet weather or in washing operations, particularly the commercial installations that flood the automobile with hundreds of gallons of water in a very few minutes. If the vehicle is operated on icy roads treated with salt to provide traction, rusting will be accelerated by the addition of salt to the accumulated deposit.

The rusted area on the inner surface is almost invariably larger than it appears on the outer. This is often hard to explain to some owners who see only a small hole and bring it to the repair shop to be repaired before it gets any larger. The lower section of the fender shown in Figure 8-30 is a good example. This is a four-wheel-drive vehicle operated on all types of roads under very difficult winter driving conditions. It seems to be just one large hole and several smaller ones along the lower edge. When tested with the hammer, light blows made holes out of the dark spots where the hammer is shown and dented the metal easily in the bead section above that point where the paint seems to be good. An uninformed owner would be surprised to find the damage as extensive as it is, as shown in Figure 8-31.

Any rust damage should be tested with the hammer as shown here, preferably in the owner's presence and *with his or her permission*.

Patching this fender is complicated by the rather deep reverse crown at the wheel opening. It could be patched by laying several strips in the reverse crown area, wrapping a flat sheet around the straight part, and welding the whole thing together. Instead, a piece of scrap metal, cut from a salvage hood top panel, was shaped to general contour, welded on, and finished with body filler. No attempt was made to shape the patch perfectly, because the economics of the situation limit the amount of time that can be spent on a job of this type. However, when conditions do justify the extra time, flat metal can be shaped to an exact contour by the general method shown here. An example would be high-quality restoration work on special-interest or antique automobiles, where appearance, inside and out, is more important than cost.

The rough-cut patch is shown clamped to the wheel opening in Figure 8-32. The rear end has been trimmed to fit to the shape of the door opening, but the lower edge still has to be cut to fit to the fender flange, and the

8-31 Hammer test, to determine extent of inner rust damage.

8-32 Fitting the lower patch.

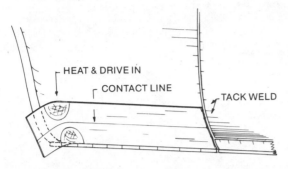

8-33 Method of fitting patch to contour of fender. The flat patch should be bent so that it fits on the contact line in the center. Metal above and below will be heated to permit stretching.

front end is too long. The paint has been removed from both sides by searing, using an oxidizing flame, and wire-brushed off.

Figure 8-33 shows the preparation of the patch for forming to the shape of the fender. The first step was to bend the front end (left side in the photos) to fit to the reverse crown. This should be done carefully so that the center (marked contact line) is in contact with the old metal, or where the old metal should be if it is entirely rusted away.

The next step was to align the rear end of the patch to the door opening and tack-weld it into place. If the intention had been to shape the patch to exact contour, it would have been tack-welded only in two places, approximately 2 inches (5 cm) apart, so that it could be removed for final shaping. This was welded securely, because it was intended to stay in place.

With the panel secured at the rear, the lower edge was tack-welded at the rear end and center. The spots marked on the illustration were heated and driven in, as shown in Figure 8-34, using the handle part of a general-purpose dolly block. A No. 4 torch tip was used to heat a large area so that the effect would spread instead of concentrate on the contact line. The piece tended to twist when struck, but excessive twisting was

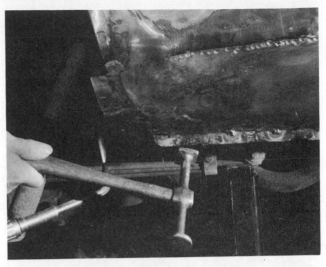

8-35 Use of heat and hammer to finish rough forming. Brazing could have been used to weld the upper and lower, but the spot weld is preferable for the upper.

prevented by the tack-welds, locking pliers, and the hand-held steel bar on the lower edge. The action is shown on the upper, but both upper and lower were worked in the same manner. The process was continued until a reasonably close fit was obtained.

After the general shape was established, it was welded as shown in Figure 8-35 and the final shaping completed with the hammer and torch. This is a shrink-

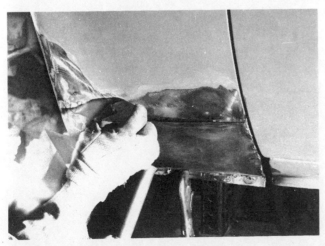

8-34 Driving the heated metal into shape. For precision work, this would be done with a block of hardwood and hammer.

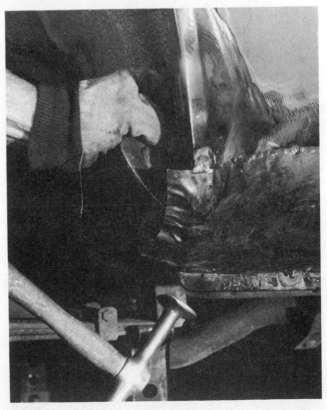

8-36 Forming the flange by shrinking with hammer and long, thin palm dolly.

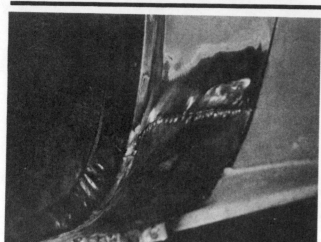

8-37 The finished flange. Welding is complete except at rear edge.

8-39 The patched area, partly filled and rough planed.

ing operation, essentially a shortcut. The exact shape could have been contoured at this point by breaking the spot welds so that the piece could be worked with the hammer and dolly block. Some shrinking would have been required, because it would be quite difficult to avoid some buckling on the contact line. Lighter welds would have been made if removal had been planned.

The flange of the patch was heated and shrunk down to the fender flange, as shown in Figure 8-36. This could have been done to any degree of smoothness. It was shrunk enough to avoid overlaps, as shown in Figure 8-37.

In Figure 8-38 an extension has been added to cover the weakened metal shown up by the hammer test. It

was spot-welded in place and shrunk down in much the same manner as the lower but, obviously, required less effort.

The first filling coat has been applied and rough-planed in Figure 8-39. Filling has been completed and finished in Figure 8-40. The repainted fender, ready for delivery, is shown in Figure 8-41.

A patch of this type can be made to exact contour by varying the procedure, if the conditions justify the much greater time required. The flat piece would be fitted to the contact line, but attached so that it could be removed for hammer and dolly work. Assuming that here is enough good metal left to weld to, which this fender had, the rear end would be pushed against the

8-38 Upper patch, welded in place and partly formed.

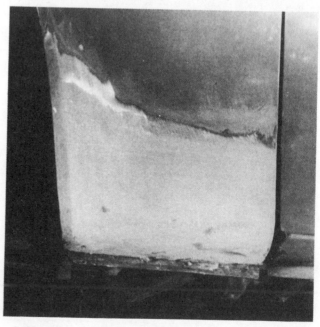

8-40 The completed fill job.

fender enough that two light tack-welds could be made approximatley 1 inch (2.5 cm) above and below the contact line. At the front end, two cuts, approximately ¾ of an inch (19 mm) apart, and centered on the contact line, would be made. These cuts would extend to the start of the reverse curve to make a tab that could be bent around and clamped to the fender flange; sharp corners would be heated for an exact fit.

The patch would be heated and worked in the same manner, except that a piece of hardwood, such as the large end of a broken ball bat, would be used instead of

8-41 The repainted fender, ready for delivery.

the dolly block. It would work better and absorb less heat, although it would smoke and smell. When worked into rough shape, the piece would be removed and clamped to something rigid for final shaping with the hammer and dolly. Some shrinking would be required, because some buckling would be difficult to avoid.

Although beyond the scope of this text, there are many methods of hand-making specially formed patches for use on high-quality automobile restoration projects.

PART TWO

The discussion of repair procedures in this section is from the dual viewpoint of the repairman and the estimator. The dual viewpoint may surprise some repairmen who do not write estimates on the incoming repair work. However, most of them do more estimating than they realize, some from only a critical viewpoint, but many others actually participating in the estimating process, either as advisors or as writers.

The repairman and the estimator have a common interest in repair procedure. The former must read his procedure from the job; the latter must have already read the same procedure from the job and determined essentially the same general procedure to allocate a fair time allowance. If he does not, either the customer is overcharged or the repairman is asked to do more than practical within the time allowed.

The beginner expects the estimating to be done by a more experienced person. Although the estimator's duties vary widely from shop to shop, the alert beginner should see the estimating assignment as a first step into promotion or, if he is interested in starting his own business, as an important step in qualifying himself to become a shop proprietor. Unfortunately, many beginners fail to realize the need for a broad viewpoint until they are well past the point when they can be considered beginners. This is emphasized here in the hope that at least some of the students starting the trade will develop attitudes that will make them promotable, either within their employer's organization or in their own enterprises.

The emphasis in the following sections is on the type of damage in which the alignment of the overall structure is involved. It is arranged in the sequence of frame and frame problems, body shell alignment, and some body panel problems. Body problems include some suggestions that apply to the replacement of complete panels or sections. Only enough has been included to provide general coverage. It would be impossible to make a complete list of all possible damage variations.

General suggestions about the factors that govern the time required for most of the repair problems are included because, as stated previously, this portion of the text is intended for both the repairman and the estimator. Both have, or should have, an interest in the subject. However, there is no way or formula by which specific times can be established. An estimated repair time will reflect the personal opinion of the person who set it.

FRAME TYPES

Three types of frames are used in automobile construction. They are (1) ladder, (2) perimeter, and (3) unitized body and frame. These are broad types; frames built by different manufacturers may be of the same type but vary widely in design detail.

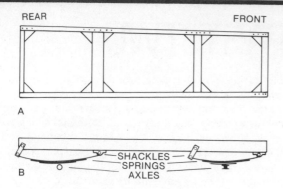

REAR   FRONT

A

SHACKLES
SPRINGS
AXLES

B

8-42 Basic layout of ladder-type frame. A, top view; B, side view, with spring and axle positions shown.

LADDER FRAMES

The ladder frame is so called because of its resemblance to a giant ladder. Its principal features are two lengthwise beams and at least four cross members. (The term rail is used in this text to refer to side parts of all frames. It is common practice throughout the automobile industry to call frame crosspieces *members*.) The ladder-type frame was used in all of the early automobiles and is still in wide use in trucks, including some pickups and four-wheel-drive vehicles. Figure 8-42 represents a simplified ladder design.

The primary disadvantage of the ladder-type frame for automobiles is that the passenger compartment and whatever load-carrying capacity it has must be above the level of the side rails. This is essential for heavy trucks that require a platform to support the load, or other vehicles that require high ground clearance, but a distinct disadvantage where streamlining is desired. It has another disadvantage in that there is little bracing between the side rails, so that an end impact will tend to shift one in relation to the other (called *diamonding*). This is discussed in the section dealing with damage and repair procedures.

PERIMETER FRAMES

The perimeter frame (Fig. 8-43) is actually a ladder frame redesigned to eliminate some of its worst features. The center section is made much wider, so that the passenger compartment floor can extend into the space between them. In effect, the lower part of the body is within the perimeter of the frame instead of on top of it. Lowering the floor permits lowering of the roof line and a lower center of gravity. Both contribute to stability to reducing the tendency to roll over.

The side rails of most perimeter frames are set out far enough to be in line with the front and rear wheels. This requires offset, or compound bends at the corners of the passenger compartment section, because the rails must be higher and closer together in both the front and rear sections. The front section does not require as much height as the rear, but rails must be set

in farther to provide clearance for the wheels to swing in steering. The rear section rises higher to permit up-and-down movement of the axle assembly.

The amount of offset in these bends requires quite rigid construction, because they are subjected to a twisting effect at all times. It also causes a tendency to collapse under an end impact. The needed rigidity is provided by joining two C channel sections for a single box section. Bracing from side to side is provided by one, or sometimes two, heavy front cross members. In most instances the front cross member provides the support for the suspension parts.

The rear offset sections are of similar but lighter construction than the front. They tend to collapse in the straight part over the axle rather than farther forward in the compound curved offset. However, the forward section will collapse under sufficient impact force.

Automobile engineers seem to prefer the perimeter-type frame for larger-sized automobiles. It is relatively flexible, so that it tends to absorb noise and road shock better than earlier designs. However, as the trend toward lighter, more fuel-efficient automobiles continues, it will probably be replaced to a large extent by the unitized design.

UNITIZED FRAME AND BODY

In unitized construction the frame and body are combined in one unit. The term unitized is applied by the automobile industry to any type of construction in which the side structures are stiffened so that they can serve the same purpose as the side rails of the ladder- or perimeter-type frame. The heavy lines around the door openings and front and rear sections in Figure 8-44 represent the stiffened areas. The exact design varies widely from one manufacturer to another, but in all designs the side structure becomes, in effect, a truss resting on the front and rear suspension.

Unitized construction is used for most of the smaller automobiles where light weight and economy are the prime considerations. It has less flexibility than the perimeter-type frame, but this is not a severe disadvantage for an automobile having a relatively short wheel base. However, the rigid construction causes damage

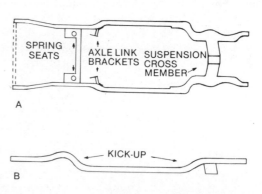

SPRING
SEATS   AXLE LINK   SUSPENSION
         BRACKETS   CROSS
                MEMBER

A

KICK-UP

B

8-43 Basic layout of perimeter-type frame. A, top view; B, side view.

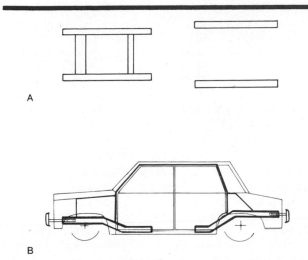

8-44 Basic layout of unitized body. A, position of front and rear frame rails; B, body layout with reinforced areas represented by heavy lines.

patterns that differ from those caused by similar impacts on either a ladder- or perimeter-type frame. The generally lighter parts tend to crush more at the point of impact instead of acting as force paths into the adjoining sections to cause damage there. Another reason is that the lighter the automobile, the less inertia it has to an impact. In any collision, the automobile struck tends to resist movement until it absorbs enough force, by crushing under the impact, until its inertia has been overcome. Once set in motion, it can absorb more of the remaining impact force only by moving faster. It then acts in the same manner as a kicked football; it may strike another object, skid, or roll over and receive further damage in new impact areas, but the damage in the first impact area is complete when the inertia is overcome.

It is difficult to predict future design trends, but it seems reasonable to assume that the use of unitized construction by all manufacturers will continue to increase. The trend toward more fuel-efficient automobiles is fixed by law, but would be an economic necessity even without the legal aspect. It is well suited to front-engine, front-wheel-drive construction, because it permits better use of space in both the engine and passenger compartments. It also seems reasonable that it will go through several evolutionary changes. A relatively high kickup section in both front and rear is shown on the sketch. The adoption of front-wheel drive and independent rear suspension will tend to reduce the front kickup height and could eliminate it altogether in the rear.

TYPICAL FRAME DAMAGES

Frame damages may be classified in several basic types, directly related to the type of accident in which the automobile has been involved. Also, each type of damage can be related to a suitable repair procedure. The time to do the job is simply the accumulated time required for the individual steps required to complete the procedure. The estimator's problem is to visualize these steps and allocate sufficient time to do the work.

In the following discussion of frame damages, the sequence is from relatively simple to more complex conditions. A suitable repair procedure is suggested for each one, but there is no intention to present the suggested procedures as the *correct* procedure. There are many ways in which most frame-straightening jobs can be done; some will be better than others, but which is correct is usually only a matter of opinion of an individual.

Body parts have been omitted in the figures showing repair procedures on separate frame and body construction. Sometimes it is necessary to work the body and frame together, but most frame repair work should be done first to relieve whatever effect it has on body alignment.

SIMPLE BENDS

Most simple bends are found in combinations of at least three in most damaged frames, because movement at one point of the structure requires at least two others to yield. An exception is on a protruding member such as a frame horn, which is a section of the front side rail that extends forward of the suspension cross member to support the bumper assembly and sometimes the front-end sheet metal parts.

Figure 8-45 represents two typical horn damages. The inward bend, A, is probably the most common and the easiest to repair. In estimating this type of horn damage, the estimator should determine whether the repairman can simply place a jack between the indi-

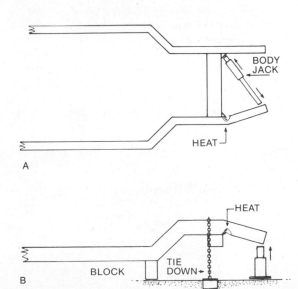

8-45 Simple frame bends. A, jack setup to straighten bent-in frame horn; B, jack with tie-down and block to straighten bent-down frame horn.

cated pressure and anchor points, or if an external setup will be required because other parts block access for the jack. The use of heat is indicated, but in some cases of very minor damage it may not be needed.

A bent-out frame horn is not illustrated, but the same procedures apply except that a pull jack would be substituted for the conventional push jack where construction permits its use. External equipment would be used more often on it than on the bent-in horn.

A down-bend, illustrated by B, occurs less frequently than the in-bend, but is quite common when a heavy impact has caused other damage farther back on the side rail. The setup to straighten this, as suggested by the arrows, could be as simple as a chain across the top of the frame and attached to a ring in the shop floor for the center anchor and blocks at the rear. Usually the use of heat will be required. A down-bend combined with other damage almost always will require an equipment setup to apply fore-and-aft tension.

A minor sag, usually under the cowl section of the body, can be considered a simple bend, if the other parts affected by it are not strained too severely. Figure 8-46 represents this condition. This could be caused by a roll-over in which the automobile has landed hard on its roof. Or the repairman might find the rail still sagged after pulling a collapsed side rail to length. When it is found with no other frame damage, there will almost always be plenty of evidence to suggest that the frame should be checked. A V-shaped gap between the door and fender edges, or a door that drops sharply when opened may be considered such evidence.

A sag under the cowl section tends to twist the suspension cross member of a perimeter-type frame, but usually the twist effect is within the elastic limit. Sometimes it is necessary only to tie it down in two places and jack it up into place. The tie-downs can be as simple as the two pots shown in Figure 8-46, or whatever method is provided by the equipment being used. However, selection of the tie-down points on the frame is important. The front chain should be over the top of the suspension cross member, not out on the end of a projecting horn. The rear should be at the reinforced rear end of the center section. In general, heat should not be used; this means that is will be necessary to push the rail well past the desired level to overcome the tendency to spring back, usually twice the distance actu-

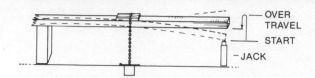

8-47 Approximate amount of over-travel needed to straighten frame or other reinforced member without using heat.

ally gained. The problems of spring-back are explained in more detail in the discussion of twist and illustrated in Figure 8-47.

A sagged rail should not be confused with one that has been raised on the end. Any appreciable lift at the front end will strain the suspension cross member much more than would the same amount of movement in a sag under the cowl. A very minor condition may not cause strains beyond the elastic limits of the cross member and the opposite side rail; such a condition can be straightened with the setup for a sag. It is sometimes difficult to determine whether a frame is sagged under the cowl or if the front end is raised. This will not make a major difference in the time required, but it is essential that the repairman identify the condition properly. If the front end is lifted enough to twist the cross member but he simply jacks up the cowl enough to realign the door, the frame will be left in a twist.

SPRING-BACK

Allowance for spring-back must be made in any cold bending operation because of the elasticity of the metal. Slow-motion moving pictures have been made of automobiles being crashed under various circumstances. The first-time viewer of one of these will be impressed by the extreme deflection the various parts of the automobile go through at the instant of collision. The slow-motion pictures will show that most of the damaged parts have been distorted much more at the moment of impact than they are an instant later.

Spring-back works both for and against the repair operations. It is important to recognize the elastic strains in damaged areas that will spring back in the repair operation when the buckles holding them are released in the repair operations. The repairman also finds many parts of the automobile will withstand considerable flexing before actually yielding to applied pressure; this often uses up a large part of the travel of his body jack ram before getting enough strain on a flexible member, such as a frame side rail, to make it yield. Sometimes enough over-travel is required to cause damage, usually buckles in large smooth areas, before the required mend is made.

Figure 8-47 illustrates the problem of over-travel to offset spring-back. The total travel is shown as about twice the amount of actual gain. This will vary with the shape and construction of the part being worked, but it is common to find at least that much required. A plain

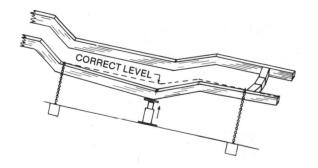

8-46 Jack and tie-down set to straighten frame sag in cowl area.

box member is shown here, but the problem would be similar on almost all cold straightening operations.

A bend that has been heated as it is straightened will spring back much less than one straightened cold. However, when a sharp bend is heated to straighten, the corrective force must be applied at considerable distance from the spot actually heated. All of the metal between the force application points and the heated area will be subjected to elastic strains. When the force is released, the elastic strains will spring back, but the spring-back in the heated area will be relatively little.

SIDE SHIFT

A ladder-type frame is shown in Figure 8-48, because this type is more apt to shift in this manner than the others. However, any type of frame will side shift under the right circumstances.

A side shift is almost always the result of a side impact at the extreme end, front or rear, acting against the inertia of the automobile. The bumper assembly and cross members, if any, serve as force paths to carry the impact to the opposite side member; these members may collapse, adding to the total damage.

A direct impact in the midsection will bend the automobile lengthside, making much more severe damage than a simple side shift. If repairable, the procedure would be much more complicated than the procedures for side shift discussed here. This problem is discussed in a later section.

Some of the common indications of a side shift are (1) door edge spaces, or gaps, too tight on the side to which the frame has shifted and too wide on the impact side, (2) when sighting through windshield and back glass, front or rear end appears out of alignment with center of body, and (3) the known tendency of the particular make of automobile either to side shift easily or to resist shifting. Often, the evidence of shifting is enough that further inspection is needed only to determine that additional damage—crushed members, twists, and so on—are not involved.

An accurate check for the amount of side shift is difficult if either the cross member or the side rail has collapsed. These members should be straightened first.

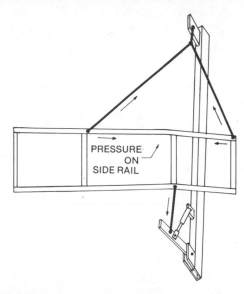

8-49 Basic "bow and arrow" hookup to straighten a side-shifted section. V-shaped anchor connections develop compressive pressure on side rail.

Some minor side shift is almost always involved in any collapsed condition. However, the estimator should determine whether the extra setup will be needed and, if so, allow time for it.

The two anchor points and the place to pull to correct a simple side shift are indicated in Figure 8-48. This is a relatively easy setup to make on any type of straightening equipment that permits multiple hookups, drive-on, or in-the-floor installations. Pulling at the end is suggested in the figure to avoid shifting the other end of the vehicle, but the same effect would be obtained by pulling on the other points.

A portable frame and body machine can be used to straighten a side shift, as shown by Figure 8-49, but it has a distinct disadvantage when compared to the direct action of the multiple hookup type of equipment. This setup requires two pull lines, usually chains, connected to separate points on one side and a third line pulling between them on the opposite side. It is important that the two lines on the one side be long enough to form a narrow angle where they meet to avid excessive pressure on the side rail between the attachment points, as noted in Figure 8-49. This pressure can be enough to collapse a light side rail if the lines are too short. However, a competent operator can use this hookup safely, if he exercises good judgement. All connections should be made where there is a cross member connecting the sides or a temporary connection should be made.

This hookup is often called a *bow and arrow*, the frame being the bow and the machine the arrow. Some operators prefer to use the machine diagonally across the shifted section. This works if all the bends that permitted the shift are within the section being pulled. However, it has little mechanical advantage over any bend effect that extends into the adjoining section.

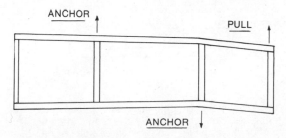

8-48 Appearance of a side-shifted frame section. Arrows indicate where the anchors and a pull should be applied to shift the section back.

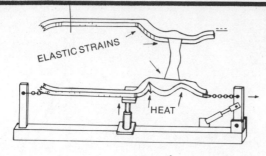

8-50 Portable frame machine set up to pull a minor collapsed side rail on a perimeter-type frame. This arrangement should not be used if center section has been driven back.

COLLAPSED SIDE RAIL

Figures 8-50 and 8-51 represent a minor and a severe collapsed side rail on the right front side of a perimeter-type frame; each includes a practical setup to repair the damage. These are typical damage conditions that any experienced estimator or repairman knows to look for when an automobile having this type frame has been involved in a hard front-end collision concentrated on one side rail. The examples shown would be the result of a straight-on impact. An impact coming at an angle from either side would complicate the damage by adding side shift to the collapsed side rail.

The first concern when inspecting a damage of this type should be to determine whether or not the impact has driven the center section out of square. Referring to Figure 8-51, the diagonal measurement A will almost always be slightly longer than measurement B, because the front section is pressed back against it. This may be only an elastic strain that will be relieved when the front section is straightened. On more severe damage, the center rail may have been forced back far enough to affect the kickup and cross member over the axle. Two telltale signs of this condition are (1) a semicircular rim of freshly exposed surface beside the rear body bolts and (2) cracked road film on the surface or an actual buckle in the offset curve of the opposite front side rail. However, the safe procedure is to cross-check the center section before establishing the time allowance.

It would be impossible for one side of the front section to be driven back far enough to cause buckling back of the suspension cross member without putting a strain on the entire frame. In moving back, the cross member acts as a lever on the opposite side rail. These strains may or may not exceed the elastic limits of the affected parts. When they do not, the result is a rather simple repair job, as represented by the sketch in Figure 8-50, which requires only the use of suitable equipment and careful heat application to pull the buckle back to shape. When done properly, this operation should relieve the elastic strains in the frame and make some improvement in the before and after diagonal measurements in the center section. However, if they are still

out of tolerance, the job has been misjudged, and a hookup similar to that shown in Figure 8-51 will be needed to pull it into alignment.

The hookup in Figure 8-51 places the entire frame under a diagonal stain without pulling diagonally. Equipment permitting multiple hookups is required. Anchor pots are shown here, but other equipment will do the same thing, and some is easier to use. (It would be possible for a skilled operator, using an extra-long, heavy-duty machine, to pull diagonally from the front cross member to the anchor point shown on the opposite side; however, there is risk of damage to the equipment, and it may be difficult to avoid bending the anchor point outward.) With the hookup shown, force will be applied to both sides from the correct angle. The two side anchors prevent the vehicle from swinging into diagonal alignment with the main anchor points. Use of the anchor for the machine eliminates the risk of bending its horizontal beam.

The procedure for both setups (Figs. 8-50 and 8-51) should be to apply enough to put a light load on the deep buckles on the right side. At that point the torch should be applied to the sharp part of the buckles to relieve them. From then on, it is a matter of proper torch manipulation and extending the machine to *maintain* tension on the frame. *The worst possible mistake would be to pull too hard.* The force applied should never exceed the minimum required to keep the buckles unfolding as they are released by the heat. As the job progresses, the force required will increase, because some of the mechanical advantage is lost as the rail straightens, but it should never increase to the total capacity of the machine. (Very few automobiles having this type of frame have ever been built that would require the total output of straightening equipment powered by a 10-ton jack.)

As the work progresses on the main buckle, it is essential to keep close check on the center section diagonal measurements, the length of the collapsed side rail, and the overall center line. A skilled operator can usually bring all three out together. However, when the job appears to be nearly right, it is best to stop, release

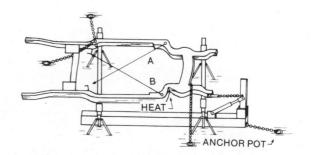

8-51 Portable frame machine and anchor pot setup on a perimeter-type frame to pull a collapsed side rail. This hookup should be used when the center side rail has been pushed back but changed back to the arrangement shown in Fig. 8-50 when the side rail has been moved enough that length A equals length B.

the machine, and check the conditions. Almost always it will be desirable to make some changes in the hookup. An extra jack is shown in place to lift the center in Figure 8-50. This may be needed if the front end is high. Or it may be necessary to tie the center down, shift the jack to the rear, and raise the hookup on the machine to lift the front. If there has been a buckle in the opposite side rail, it may require heating to permit the front to swing into center line. Heat should be applied while the frame is under full tension. Nothing would be gained by heating before the frame was nearly straight, because there would be very little strain on it until then.

The center section should be cross-checked as the work progresses. If it checks correctly before the main buckle in the front side rail has reached full length, the anchor should be changed from the opposite to the buckled side—left to right in the illustration—before making the final pull. When the rail has been pulled to full length, the final checking can be done with the center line gauges.

CREEP

Any large structural area that has been straightened without heating can be expected to *creep* back slightly after the straightening operations are completed. The tendency to creep varies with the construction. Frame members or other long box sections made of relatively heavy metal will creep more than panel assemblies, making it primarily a frame rather than a body problem.

The amount of creeping to be expected on a particular job is hard to predict, but some should be anticipated on the type of job described in the preceding section. Knowing that it will occur, the repairman should carry the straightening operations a little past the point of full correction, so that at least a part of whatever creep that occurs will be an improvement rather than a loss of alignment.

Creeping is due to the fatigue of temporary strains set up in the metal by the straightening operations. A change large enough to affect tolerances may be found in some frames within an hour or two after the last jack has been released. Further but slight change may occur after the automobile is put back into use. However, the total is rarely enough to affect overall alignment if the straightening operations have been carried slightly past

the center point of the tolerances; alignment can be affected if the operations are stopped when the measurements just reach the point of specified minimum tolerance.

DIAMOND SHIFT

Figure 8-52 represents a very simple example of a frame damage condition called *diamond shift*. It was not uncommon with the simple frames used in the early years of the automobile industry, but it is almost unknown on automobiles built in recent years. It can occur on some heavy truck frames, but few beginning body men or estimators will be confronted with this type of damage, unless they get involved with heavy truck repair.

The name diamond grew out of the elongated appearance of the normally square section of the frame, which to some persons suggested the facets of a diamond. Although not a common condition, it is explained here because many repairmen still use the term diamond or diamonded in reference to the condition in which a part of a frame rail has been pushed out of diagonal squareness with the other side. The center section of the frame condition described in the Collapsed Side Rail section is an example. The term is sometimes used in reference to other units, such as core supports, windshield or rear window openings, or door openings.

BOTH FRONT RAILS COLLAPSED

When both side rails are collapsed, two similar hookups are required, essentially doubling the job of repairing one rail. However, the estimator should consider the repairman's problem of making the final check. When the opposite rail is undamaged, he can simply make comparison checks to it, using a tram to measure length and the center line gauges to check height. When both rails are damaged, he may be able to get by with a guess or he may be forced to take time to consult the specifications and work to length and datum line measurements. Such problems should be reflected in the estimator's time allowance.

The estimator should be alert to detect damage that is not severe enough to be readily noticeable, particularly on separate frames. Sometimes badly crushed sheet metal parts will tend to conceal the fact that both frame rails have been pushed back just enough to cause misalignments when the job is rebuilt. It is much better to find such conditions first.

It is desirable to use equipment that permits multiple hookups when straightening both rails. When a portable machine must be used on two badly collapsed rails, it is best to alternate from side to side, pulling each partway. Attempting to pull one side all the way will leave it under a strain from the cross member. When the other side is pulled, the strain is removed and the first side moves farther. By alternating sides, the strain is kept within controllable limits.

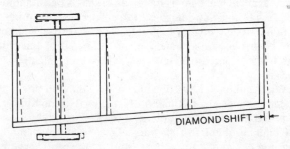

8-52 Basic diamond shift.

TWISTS

The basic condition of twist is illustrated by Figure 8-53, together with the setup to correct it. This is simply a matter of tying down and lifting at opposite corners. Two jacks are shown, because twist must be straightened cold, requiring the assembly to be pushed far past the desired point to allow for spring-back. The full travel of one jack will often be needed to load the assembly so the other one can begin to be effective. It should make no difference which jack is extended first or if they are worked together.

The construction of the automobile involved governs the tendency to twist, but almost any will twist to some degree. Those having the greatest resistance to twisting are usually the hardest to straighten when they *are* twisted.

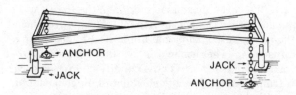

ANCHOR
JACK
JACK
ANCHOR

8-53 Basic twist, with four-point setup to straighten.

Twist is not always the simple, overall condition shown in Figure 8-53. Usually it is combined with localized bending, which makes a more complicated repair problem. One simple example of combined twist and bending is shown in Figure 8-54. A conventional frame will bend in this manner when the automobile is involved in a roll-over and comes down hard on a front corner. The side member is subjected to a direct bending strain at the junction of the front and center sections. As it lifts, it has a twisting effect on the suspension cross member. Depending on the construction and the amount of force involved, the cross member and the opposite rail may be only under an elastic strain or they may be actually twisted; if they were bent to a noticeable degree, it is unlikely that the job would be considered for repair.

If the cross member was only under an elastic strain,

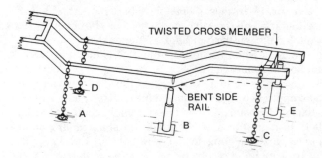

TWISTED CROSS MEMBER
D
BENT SIDE RAIL
A
B
E
C

8-54 Basic setup to straighten up-bend in side member combined with a twisted cross member on a perimeter-type frame.

the two tie-downs, shown at A and C, and the jack shown at B would be all that was needed to straighten the damage. When the center was lifted enough to be back to proper level, a center line gauge check would show no twist.

If the cross member and opposite rail are actually twisted, only straightening the right rail would leave the entire frame in a condition similar to that shown in Figure 8-53. The extra tie-down and jack, shown at D and E, would be required to relieve the twist. This makes a setup similar to the one shown, except that the jack on the right side is at the midpoint of the frame instead of the rear. It should be kept there; otherwise, the buckle straightened by it may come back. Extending the jack at E will release the tension of the chain at A. The chain could be used on the other side, if necessary.

A conventional frame was chosen as an easy example to illustrate this condition, but there are many other parts of both conventional and unitized construction that will have similar damage. It will always occur where a fairly long member has moved as it bent, or buckled, and applied a twisting effect to adjoining construction. It is not uncommon for damage of this type to require enough over-travel in the straightening operation to cause buckling of undamaged panels. It is quite important for the estimator to be alert for this condition, or the probability of it. Sometimes the actual condition is hard to predict, if there has been no previous experience with a new model or a make that the shop rarely repairs. Once the job is accepted, it must be repaired regardless of the extra time required to straighten a previously undamaged panel.

REAR-END DAMAGE—PERIMETER FRAMES

Rear-end damage to perimeter-type frames tends to follow typical patterns, which are enough alike that a few general procedures will apply to almost all straightening operations. Although there is some similarity in the general shape of the front and rear ends, the rear is much lighter and has higher kickups. This, plus the fact that the body absorbs much of the force of almost all rear-end impacts, tends to reduce the severity of rear-end damages; straightening the body will often be a larger operation than straightening the frame.

Figure 8-55 is typical of the rear-end construction of some of the down-sized perimeter frames in current use. In comparison to former designs, the weight of these frames has been reduces as much as possible: the metal is thinner and harder, and some parts have been eliminated entirely; for example, the rear cross member has been eliminated because the rear end of the side rail bolts directly to a relatively heavy cross member in the trunk floor.

When subjected to a direct rear-end impact, this type frame is most apt to buckle at the points indicated on Figure 8-55: (1) the high point of the kickup, (2) between the high point and the rear end, sometimes at the end of the bumper shock absorber, and (3) the front curve of the kickup, where it swings out to join the center sec-

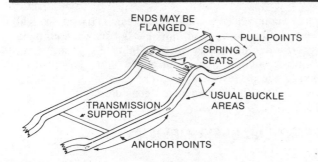

8-55 Perimeter-type frame layout showing areas where a rear-end impact usually causes buckles and the points from which hookups to anchor and pull can be made.

tion. All these areas will be strained under a rear-end impact, but the most leverage is concentrated at the high point, so it often buckles without apparent damage in the other areas. However, all will buckle if the impact force is great enough.

Most rear-end damages on this type of frame can be straightened conveniently with a portable body and frame machine. However, multiple hookup equipment may be needed for the body damage. The estimator should determine whether the body and frame can be pulled together or if separate hookups will be required for each before setting the time allowance. Some minor damage may not affect the body at all, so that it can be ignored. On more severe damage, it is often necessary to make separate connections to both body and frame for both anchoring and pulling. If not anchored securely, the body may slip on the forward hold-down bolts when force is applied, throwing it out of alignment with the fenders and hood. If multiple hookup equipment is used and the body bolts in the damaged section are not pulled out or bent, it is usually best to make separate hookups to the body and frame and pull them together. If the bolts are damaged or pulled out, it is often better to remove them, straighten the frame to proper length and shape, and pull the body to fit to it.

As with any other sharp buckle, heating will be necessary on the buckles in the kickup section. Fire and safety hazards are greater at the rear than at the front, because of the proximity of the gasoline tank and lines, wiring, body sealer, hydraulic brake lines, and body trim. The job should be examined carefully to determine what parts will have to be removed and replaced to permit heating, and, preferably, these should be listed separately on the estimate. If not specifically directed to do so, some repairmen will be tempted to take a chance and not remove parts or take other safety precautions. This is always done at the risk of fire, serious injury, or loss of life.

SIDE DAMAGE—PERIMETER FRAMES

The severity of a side damage in the center section of a perimeter frame can vary widely. Most often, repairing the body will be a bigger problem than repairing the

frame. As shown in the cross-sectional view in Figure 8-56, the side rail is enclosed on three sides by the floor pan and rocker panel, inner and outer. Unless the frame rail is caught by a very low-impact object, the rocker panel and floor must be crushed before the rail is damaged.

When the center section of a side rail has been driven in no more than an inch or two (2.5–5 cm), the repair operation is just a matter of restoring appearance. However, when it has been driven in to a depth of 5 or 6 inches (13–15 cm), the front and rear sections on that side will be drawn together enough to affect both track and wheel base. Checking with center line gauges would show a definite curve instead of a straight center line. This plus the body damage may cause the automobile to be salvaged. However, if it is rebuilt, it is essential that the procedure followed will restore the full length to the side rail. Otherwise, it may be difficult or impossible to restore correct wheel alignment.

The effect on the body will be similar. The door pillars will be drawn and the entire floor pan affected by crushed rocker panels. There will be additional damage in the panel, or panels, which received the direct impact: door, quarter panel, center pillar, and so on.

It will be necessary to remove the damaged outer rocker panel, and often the inner, to get access to the frame. The straightening operations should start on the frame. On minor damage, it may be possible to complete the frame before working the body but, if the damage is severe, it may be necessary to use multiple hookup to straighten both together.

A repair setup to restore full length to the side rail is shown in A, Figure 8-56. Full tension should be maintained on the side rail throughout the operation.

Selecting the wrong anchor and pull points for the lengthwise tension could damage the frame. They are shown connected directly to the ends of the center section; pulling from the outer ends of the frame will not be as effective, because some of the force will be absorbed in the kickups and offsets in the front and rear sections; connecting to the extreme rear end would be particularly bad, because the construction is much lighter.

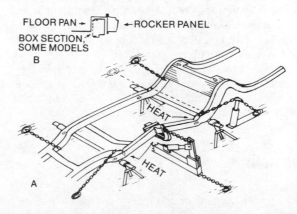

8-56 A, Multiple hookup to straighten side damage in the center section of a perimeter-type frame; B, cross section showing floor pan, rocker panel, and frame construction in the center section.

The anchors for the cross pull are shown connected at the cross members. It may not be practical to connect close to the cross member over the rear kickup on some automobiles. If the connection must be made farther forward, it may be desirable to connect the two side rails by means of a chain and a toggle-type chain tightener. The positions for these connections are shown by the dotted lines on Figure 8-56.

The operation should be started by applying lengthwise tension while watching the movement of the indented rail. It should move freely at first, but resistance to further movement should built up rapidly. Any sharp buckles should be heated to bright red to prevent cracking. Three buckles are shown in the figure, but there may be fewer, or sometimes more. The cross pull should be put in operation as soon as further heating does not cause additional free movement. At this point, both jacks should be operated together to maintain tension on the lengthwise pull as fast as it is relieved by the cross pull.

A steel pad is shown between the hook and the inner surface of the rail. This would be difficult to put in place until after the rail had been moved away from the crushed floor section by the lengthwise pull. If the side rail has been crushed too badly, it might not be completely effective. Another method would be to weld pull tabs to the upper and lower outside corners and not use the hook. Any breaks should be welded securely and the rough spots smoothed as much as possible. It may be necessary to open a "window" in the side or lower surface of the rail, but this should be done only as a last resort.

An open channel side member will require less heating than the box section. The steel pad should be the right width to fit into the channel. Most commercially available hooks have extensions that will reach into the full depth of the channel. If necessary, additional steel can be added to fill the inside. Usually the edges of the flanges must be shrunk, but this should not be done until measurements indicate that the full length has been restored.

The straightening operations on the body will be similar to those required on similar damage to a unitized body but slightly less critical, because wheel alignment is not involved. Some variation of the distance between door pillars can be made up by door adjustment. Doors should be hung in place and fitted before the outer rocker panel is installed. If the floor damage has been severe, it may be necessary to hold the floor pan under lengthwise tension while the rocker panel inner and outer is welded.

FRONT-END IMPACTS

Similar minor impacts on the front ends of conventional and unitized construction bodies can be expected to cause similar damages. Any differences would be caused by the different construction of fenders, hood, front-end panels, and so on. Similar major impacts,

great enough to penetrate to the frame structures, will cause different types of damage, because the unitized construction has much less flexibility. For this reason, the effects of hard impacts on conventional and unitized bodies are discussed separately. The removable exterior sheet metal parts are not considered.

FRONT-END SHEET METAL PARTS

Part for part, the exterior sheet metal parts of conventional and unitized construction automobiles correspond, although they vary in size and design. All hoods, most front fenders, and whatever front parts support the grille are separate units that bolt together. A few front fenders on some unitized models are welded in place, but this is the exception rather than the rule. Whether severely damaged parts are bolted or welded on is an important factor to be considered by the estimator when deciding whether to replace or repair them.

The situation is entirely different with the inner sheet metal parts that support the outer. The primary inner part on conventional construction is the radiator core support that holds the complete front-end sheet metal assembly together on conventional construction. It is a bolt-on part supported on the front end of the frame, but insulated from it by rubber-padded hold-down bolts. The inner sheet metal parts on unitized construction are an important element of the structure that serve as the frame in the front section.

HOODS

Hoods are less exposed to nicks and dents than most body panels because of their high location. When damaged, it is usually a part of the overall damage pattern in which the other front-end sheet metal parts are affected. Hoods that extend to the grille are more exposed than those that close behind a front-end panel. However, damage limited to the front end is usually relatively simple, as compared to that which extends to the center or rear sections of the panel.

Hoods that have been bent out of alignment are often replaced for these reasons: (1) the inner panel, used on most hoods, prevents tool access to the under surface, (2) the metal is quite flat, making it difficult to work, (3) the flat shape makes surface irregularities quite noticeable, and (4) replacement requires only a very few minutes.

When inspecting any hood with structural damage thought repairable, the following conditions should be considered as well as the condition of the outer panel: (1) the metal may be aluminum and more difficult to work than steel, (2) the hinge attaching surfaces may be pulled out of shape, (3) wide separation may exist between the inner and outer panel, indicating that the plastic bonding between them is broken, (4) there may be broken welds, and (5) there may be evidence of previous repair.

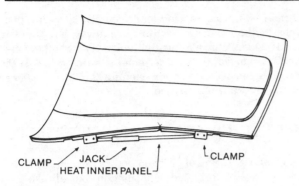

8-57 Jack and clamp setup to straighten buckled hood flange.

A jack and clamp setup to straighten a very common but repairable type of structural damage is illustrated in Figure 8-57. The hood is the type with the inner and outer panel joined with a flange that extends downward. A similar setup can be used on hoods joined with a hem flange, but the clamps would extend outward instead of down.

In the setup shown, heat should be applied only to the inner panel. Softening the inner panel reduces its resistance, allowing most of the tension to work on the outer panel. The hammer, or hammer and flat spoon, should not be used until the buckle has been pulled as far as it will go without excessive force, and then used carefully; the hammer work should start at the beginning of the buckle and work toward the edge. When disc sanded, a fresh, sharp disc should be used to avoid excesive frictional heat that could cause heat distortion. Completed properly, this operation should restore the full length to the outer edge and avoid leaving an area of false-stretched metal in the adjoining area.

A buckle of this type often extends into the adjoining deep rib-type reinforcement pressed into the inner panel to stiffen the side and provide a mounting surface for the hinge. If the buckle is minor, it can be worked with a panel puller while the outer edge is under tension. Or, with the ends supported firmly, it can be heated and hand pressure applied to push it out. A more severe buckle may require a setup to pull it out; if so, it should be done before the outer edge is worked. No setup is shown, but the jack can usually be based against the hinge at the rear. At the front, a solder-on tension plate is ideal, but, lacking that, a piece of scrap metal can be brazed or screwed to the panel for use with a clamp.

A hem-flanged hood should always have the reinforcement straightened before the outer edge.

RADIATOR CORE SUPPORT

Radiator cores vary widely in design, but almost all consist of a rigid frame for the core with side extensions to support the fenders and air baffles. Most modern supports have the radiator section lowered between the frame horns, so that the shape is similar to that in Fig-

ure 8-58. Heavy rubber pads isolate the assembly from metal-to-metal contact with the frame at the hold-down bolts. Oversized holes for the rubber mounting pads provide a wide range of fore-and-aft and side-to-side adjustment. Shims can be added on each side to raise the support, and some are factory-equipped with a shim pack so that the assembly can be raised or lowered by adding or removing.

A major collision may directly damage the core support, but they are more often damaged by forces transferred through the fenders, front bumper, or hood. In addition to any obvious direct impact damage, the support should be examined carefully when the condition of the outer sheet metal suggests the possibility of damage. Conditions to look for are (1) back or side shifts on the frame, (2) diamonding of the core opening, (3) twists, and (4) torn-out and hold-down bolts. Most of this is visual inspection; it may be necessary to use a creeper to look up at the underside of the hold-down bolts for semicircles of bare metal indicating shifts, but the conditions of the core will reveal most of the other conditions.

It is policy in many shops to replace the core support if it has been damaged in any way. This policy is based on the assumption that the hood and fenders cannot be aligned properly if the support is not perfect. But this assertion is open to question for two reasons: (1) minor damage is relatively easy to repair, and (2) the appearance of the core support is not critical, because much of the assembly is hidden from view. Some minor misalignments can be corrected by shifting the position on the frame. A body jack can be set diagonally in the core opening to correct most diamond conditions. It is much better to base the decision, when the decision is to replace or repair, on a comparison of the costs of both.

CONVENTIONAL FRONT-END CONSTRUCTION

Figure 8-59 represents a cowl that has been tipped back in a front-end collision and a practical repair setup to correct it. When inspecting any severe front-end damage, look for three signs of this condition: (1) a door which is either jammed tight against the lock pillar or drops noticeably when opened, (2) a wide gap between the door edge and roof rail at the upper corner of the windshield, and (3) a buckle in the roof over the lock

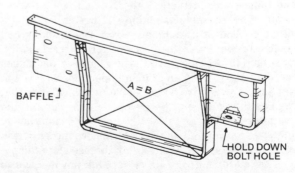

8-58 General features of the radiator core supports used on conventional construction.

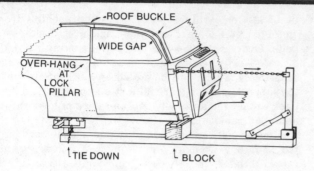

8-59 Typical hookups used to pull tipped cowl side back into alignment. Shown on conventional construction, but sometimes needed on unitized.

pillar. If the door is jammed shut, look for separated hem flange welds on he door hinge facing. There may or may not be additional dents, gouges, or collapsed sections on the cowl top, side, or fire wall and edge damage on the door. These latter conditions vary widely, so no attempt has been made to show them on Figure 8-59.

On older models it was safe to push most tipped cowls back into place with a body jack set either diagonally in the opening or based against the bracing for the rear seat. There is risk of crushing metal at either or both ends of the jack on more present-day bodies by using it in that manner. No doubt the risk will increase with the trend toward lighter construction and thinner metal. It is a much safer procedure to use some type of external pulling equipment, portable or stationary. Any frame straightening should be done first. Allowance should be made for spring-back by slight over-correction, because this is a cold bending operation.

Whatever type of equipment is used, the rear end should be tied down and a block used under the cowl so that the bending strain will be concentrated under the base of the hinge pillar. It is usually safe on most bodies to let the frame rail bear against the block, but a few may require extra support between the lower edge of the rocker panel and the block to prevent floor damage. The operator should watch this point carefully as the work progresses.

The connection to pull is shown on the door pillar at the upper hinge. This position must be well-reinforced on all bodies. A plate can be put under the bolts on bolted-on hinges or welded to weld-on ones. However, some hinges are attached to the pillar crossways instead of fore and aft, making it necessary to use another method of attachment. Usually something can be bolted or welded to the same general area, because it must be reinforced to take the strains from the hinges when the door is open and during operation on a rough road. Some cowls have a forward extending flange that serves as the weld joint between the fire wall and the outer panels. Most of these have a brace (not shown) extending from the hinge pillar to the front edge of the flange, making a safe position for the use of a clamp.

The estimator must be alert to catch any damage to the inner bracing of the cowl. Both upper and lower hingers require rigid bracing to withstand the strains of

normal operation. A front-end collision is more apt to damage the upper braces than the lower, but both can be affected. Some may straighten easily, but others may require removal of the side panel to gain access. If the panel is removed, the door opening should be checked for fit before it is replaced.

UNITIZED INNER FRONT-END CONSTRUCTION

The manufacturers of unitized bodies have many different designs of front-end construction, but all are combined with the body to form a rigid structure. Figure 8-60 shows the general construction features, but does not represent any specific make or model. Shock absorber towers, usually referred to as *towers*, are shown, because they are typical of the MacPherson-type suspension systems used on many unitized automobiles. No attempt has been made to show other suspension parts of the means of attachment, because there are too many variations for any one to be considered typical.

Almost all unitized front-end parts are made up of three major assemblies: two side panels and a front-end panel. The side panels are rigid members, welded securely to the front end of the cowl so that they become extensions of the body side frame. They have a relatively light box member welded to the lower edge, corresponding to the conventional frame side rail, but its primary purpose is to support the bumper assembly and the lower control arm and strut of the front suspension. The side panels are relatively heavy, as compared to body panels, with reinforcements on the upper edge. On some designs, the reinforcement extends full length, whereas on others it extends from the cowl section to the front suspension area.

The front panel is reinforced at both top and bottom, but is not usually as rigid as the side members, because it is subjected to much less strain than the side members.

Front-end repair problems vary too widely on unitized construction to establish a typical damage condition, making it impractical to show a typical repair setup. Instead, the typical problem areas are num-

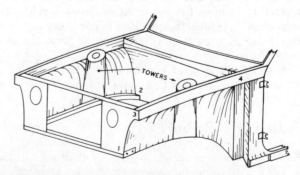

8-60 General features of the front end of unitized construction bodies. Numbers indicate areas most frequently damaged in front-end collisions. Not representative of any specific make or model, but similar to most.

bered, to provide a reference to the discussion of a variety of typical repair problems.

The lower front corner, marked 1, is exposed to more collision damage than the other parts, because the bumper is attached to it. It also provides the mounting points for the lower control arm and strut of the front suspension system. It is important that any collapsed condition in this section be restored to full length. For minor damage this may be as simple as anchoring to the rocker panels and pulling with any type of equipment. The problems of connecting to the front end vary with the construction. On some, it is as simple as bolting a plate onto the bumper attaching point; on others, it may be necessary to use weld on clamps or improvise a special bracket. The harder the pull, the greater this problem becomes, because metal used in this area is relatively light.

Direct impact on the bumper section has less tendency to drive the rail section back into the floor of the cowl (2 on the left side) than a conventional frame has to bend in the same general area for two reasons: (1) the tendency of the forward section to collapse and (2) the rigid bracing in the cowl area. When it does, however, the side panel assembly must be pulled back to position either as part of the repair operation or in preparation for replacement. In either situation, the length must be restored for wheel alignment. Pulling on the old panel is simply a matter of using it as a means of applying force to the damaged section of the cowl. It is also the best assurance that, when the old assembly is removed, the new one will fit. There may be a few exceptions to this general rule, but it will apply to almost all damages affecting the cowl.

Higher impacts, in the top area marked 3, or farther back, do not affect the structure of the shock towers and usually require only a light pull to straighten the side panels. If the front panel is crushed badly enough to require replacement, it is usually best to remove it first to simplify straightening the side panel.

A high impact hard enough to drive the side panel back into the cowl (4) or cause door misalignment is uncommon. However, then this does occur, a variation of the hookup shown in Figure 8-59 should be used. Instead of connecting the pull chain to the hinge section of the door, it should be applied to some part of the side panel assembly, often to the top of the shock tower or the forward edge of the cowl. The anchor clamps should be attached to the rear end of rocker panels to raise the line of tension as high as possible. This is explained in detail in the Tension Alignment section in Chapter 7 and illustrated in Figure 7-33.

Side impacts on the front section have less tendency to cause a side shift than those on conventional frames, because of the lighter construction. The tendency is to collapse the cross members instead, concentrating the effect on the side receiving the impact and crushing the cross members. Whatever the damage condition, it should be pulled back into general position, either as part of the repair operation or in preparation for replacement.

Side pulls are generally more difficult to make than on conventional frames, because the unitized construction provides fewer rigid anchor points and those that are available are usually less rigid. Equipment manufacturers are beginning to make anchor systems in which the rocker panel lower flanges are held rigidly against movement in *all* directions. Lacking such equipment, the repairman is often forced to weld on or improvise special brackets for the purpose, usually spending extra time in the operations.

Center line realignment is more critical on unitized construction than on conventional frames because of its rigidity. The only provision for side-to-side adjustment of fenders is made by oversized holes for the bolts that hold the fender flange to the upper edge of the side panel. Any misalignment great enough to shift the front section off center line beyond this narrow range of adjustment must be corrected. A cross-check across the top should be the final step of any straightening operation and should be used in aligning any new side panel assembly before it is welded in place securely.

When making a preliminary inspection of a severly damaged unitized front end, the estimator and repairman should first look at any undamaged exterior sheet metal parts for evidence of serious misalignment. Doors that open and close properly are evidence that the cowl structure is not affected seriously. The hood, even though damaged, may still be in alignment with the top of the cowl and possibly one fender, indicating that the center line is not affected. The distance between the top of the shock towers should be checked against specifications. When these conditions are correct, the repair job will probably be a matter of straightening the front end of the side panel, or panels, and straightening or replacing the front panel. However, when any of these areas are misaligned, it is probable that a multiple hookup will be required to restore alignment before the straightening or replacement operations can be completed.

When the suspension has had a direct impact, it is particularly important to check the control arm bushings for evidence of twisting or torn metal. This applies also to the anchor bracket that holds the control arm strut. These points should be restored to exact position, as specified by the manufacturer.

UNITIZED BODY REAR-END REPAIR

A in Figure 8-61 represents a typical repair setup on a unitized body that has relatively minor rear-end damage. It is shown with part of the damaged quarter panel, rear-end panel, and floor pan cut away to reveal inner construction. This is not intended to suggest that these parts, when damaged, should always be replaced; the decision to replace them should be based on the condition of individual panels and sometimes on whether removal is necessary to permit access to other panels.

Only general statements can be made about the repair of rear-end damage on unitized bodies, because they vary in construction. However, almost all of them

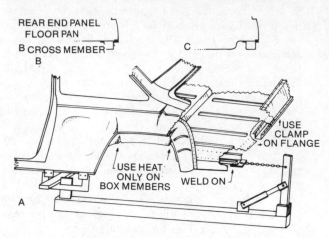

8-61 A, typical repair setup on unitized body having minor rear-end damage; B, typical cross section of rear of floor having no flange convenient for clamp attachment; C, variation of detail B, which further complicates problem of attachment.

have flanged U-shaped channels welded to the underside of the floor pan to serve as frame rails and rear-end cross members. The result is a relatively rigid body, as compared to conventional construction.

When alignment is involved, it is necessary to use some type of pulling equipment on almost all rear-end damages because of the lighter construction of unitized bodies. An attempt to use a jack inside the body will often cause more damage to the base it rests on than it corrects. Minor damages of the type represented by Figure 8-61 can usually be straightened with a portable body and frame machine if the floor pan is not damaged seriously. The condition is different if the floor pan is crushed so that it ought to be pulled from two different angles. There are some exceptions, but it would almost always then be better to pull one setup partway and hold it under tension while pulling the other. Working this way, each setup would tend to relieve the strain on the other; doing this with a portable machine would

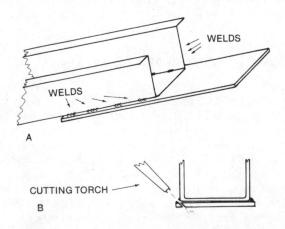

8-62 A, method of welding temporary pull plate to lower surface of upright U-channel frame rail. B, use of cutting torch to remove temporary plate.

require changing the machine and the advantage of holding one hookup under tensions while operating the other would be lost.

Before allocating repair time for a rear-end repair, the estimator should determine what problems will be encountered in making and using the connections to pull and anchor. Connecting can be as simple as attaching a clamp to a convenient flange, as indicated at the rear end of A. Other methods are needed, however, when there is no flange. Some rear-end panels are connected to the floor by a flange that extends inward instead of outward, as shown in B. This construction would make it necessary to remove the rear-end panel before a clamp could be attached to the flanged edge of the cross member and floor pan. The problem is further complicated when the floor pan is depressed below the level of the cross member, as shown in C. With the rear-end panel removed, this could be pulled only enough to straighten the cross member, assuming it is not damaged badly enough to require replacement.

Sometimes a pull connection can be made by bolting to the holes for the bumper attachment, usually at the point of attachment for the bumper shock absorbers, although some bumper shock absorbers are rugged enough to withstand a direct pull on the outer end.

A welded-on connection is shown in A. Sometimes this is the only practical method, but it should be considered as the last resort, because it takes extra time and the welding burns the protective coating off of the metal. The two views in Figure 8-62 illustrate a good method of doing this to the lower surface of an upright U-channel. Welds should be made only along the sides so that they can be cut cleanly with a cutting torch. This method is not satisfactory for U-channels that have the open side facing either outward or inward.

Brazing is not as desirable as welding for frame attachment, because of the risk of embrittlement when the piece is removed. When brazing is used and the piece is removed by heating, the flame should be kept on the attached piece, heating it uniformly until it is close to the red heat range. At the right temperature, it can be knocked off with a sharp hammer blow. The remaining brass should be ground off. Melting if off will guarantee embrittlement, particularly on thin metal.

Anchoring for a rear-end pull can usually be done by attaching a set of anchor clamps to the lower flanges of the rocker panels. However, many anchor clamp sets designed for use on conventional bodies may damage lightweight rocker panels when subjected to a hard pull. As illustrated in Figure 8-63, the clamp assembly tends to rotate around the point of force application; the

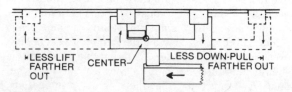

8-63 Extra-long anchor clamps will reduce the risk of damage to rocker panel lower edge.

clamp position forward of this point pushes upward, tending to crush the lower side of the rocker, and the rear clamp position tends either to strip off or tear the flange. These tendencies are greater when the clamp positions are close together. Some equipment manufacturers have designed anchor clamp sets that are much longer and have multiple clamps to spread the load enough to avoid crushing the rocker panel. The trend is toward clamps that grip full length and can be anchored in all directions.

The use of heat is essential in straghtening any sharply buckled metal, particularly the lighter metal used in unitized construction. Otherwise, buckles will break or tear instead of straightening. More care is needed in heating light metal than on the heavier material used in conventional frame construction. The note on Figure 8-61 emphasizes that heat should be applied only to box members. If the member has two or more bends that must yield at the same time, they must be heated at the same time. On complicated jobs, it is often worthwhile to have a second torch and a temporary helper so that some buckles do not cool while others are being heated. This is particularly important on thin metal, which cools relatively rapidly.

UNITIZED BODY SIDE DAMAGE

Figure 8-64 represents a suggested repair procedure for deep impact damage on the side of a unitized body. The seriousness of this type of damage is directly related to the depth of penetration into the side of the body. If deep, it must be repaired properly to restore wheel alignment. Penetration of the impact to an appreciable depth will draw the front and rear sections together, reducing the wheel base on that side and bending the entire automobile lengthwise. A center line check will show a curve instead of a straight line. If this is not fully restored to the straight line condition, the automobile will tend to travel in a long curve instead of straight ahead.

Severe damage of this type is a test of ability for both the estimator and the repairman. The estimator is apt to under-estimate the damage unless he is familiar with the problems involved, and he must know that the shop crew is competent. The repairman who spends most of his time straightening body panels is accustomed to have his work judged primarily on appearance. On this type of job, accuracy is as important as appearance.

The importance of restoring a side-damaged conventional frame is explained in an earlier section. This type of damage presents the repairman with a more difficult problem because, instead of a single, heavy box member, the side of the body is made up of several pieces of light metal that join at right angles. The movement under impact tends to stretch the lengthwise parts, particularly the inner and outer rocker panel, and crush the floor and its reinforcements.

Two important steps must be taken before any attempt is made to pull the damage out with a cross pull: (1) the crushed sections of the rocker panel, and sometimes the whole panel, must be removed, and (2) the lengthwise pull must be set up to exert the maximum tension it is safe to use.

The complete outer rocker panel is shown removed, with the added note to remove the crushed sections. Whether to remove all or only part should be determined by the condition of the floor cross braces at the front and rear. If they are bent or crushed, the panel should be removed. On severe damages, it is usually best to remove the complete panel.

The inner rocker panel is shown still in place. This is not always practical, but is desirable when possible. When removal is necessary, it is best to remove as little as possible. Unless mangled severely, the cut-out section can be straightened and welded back in place as easily as a new piece can be installed. The cut-out section has the advantage of fitting.

Welding in a complete inner rocker panel requires considerable labor, particularly if the oxyacetylene torch must be used. The problems of replacing rocker panels are discussed in the next section.

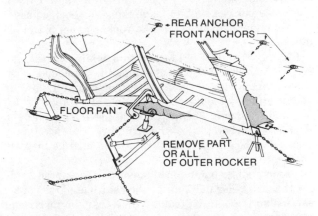

8-64 Multiple hookup on side damage in the center section of unitized bodies. Similar hookup may be needed on conventional bodies.

In operation, the cross pull will relieve the lengthwise tension. It is good practice to operate both jacks together so that the tension is never allowed to slacken. The various buckles in the floor pan should be watched carefully so that elastic strains can be relieved as they form. Bent floor reinforcements must be dealt with, as they come under strain as the work progresses.

The cross pull is shown anchored by two chains so that it can be shifted along the side as needed. The hook would be used as much as possible, but clamps will be needed to connect directly to the edge of the floor pan in areas where the inner rocker panel has to be removed because the welds holding it in place have broken. On severe damage, it may be necessary to reposition the side pull unit several times.

A separate jack is shown in position below the bulged-down floor pan. This would not be needed at the start of the operation, but will be necessary to finish it. The floor will begin to unroll easily as the lengthwise tension and the cross pull are applied, but it will build up resistance until at some point the movement will stop. The lift jack should then be extended enough to apply an elastic strain to the floor. From that point on, it should be gradually extended to maintain the elastic strain, but never forced enough to push the floor up faster than the other operations are pulling it into shape.

Finding suitable points from which to pull and anchor can be a problem on many unitized bodies. This problem has increased with the trend toward small, lightweight automobiles in which much of the steel is thinner and harder. However, it varies from one make to another, so that specific rules cannot be made. In some makes it may be as simple as attaching a clamp to a conveniently placed flange; on others the repairman may be forced to improvise special brackets or resort to welding on.

Two methods of connecting for the lengthwise pull are shown. The direct connections to the inner rocker panel are preferable for the straightening operations when the rocker panel can be used. After these operations have been completed, tension should be released and the side measured for length. Often the floor pan will draw back enough to leave the side short, unless it is held under tension while the rocker panel is welded into place.

Holding the floor under tension while welding the rocker panel may require changing the connections. On some automobiles, it may be practical to pull the rear end by attaching to the rear axle link; other automobiles may not have one. The next best approach is usually to weld on to a rigid part of the structure. Unless a flange is convenient at the front, welding on may be the only choice.

Three anchor points are shown on the opposite side for the crosswise pull, one at the rear end of the center section and two at the front. At the rear the repairman may have no choice other than to weld on. At the front it is usually possible to make a connection to a rigid part of the structure to which the front suspension parts are attached. If so, the forward anchor would be used. If not, a more convenient attachment may be possible at the junction of the front and center sections by either welding or a clamp. A clamp would be anchored to a point farther back.

The importance of wheel alignment on this type of job makes it desirable to recheck the measurements of the entire automobile, front, center, and rear sections, after the rocker panel has been tacked in place enough to hold. When the welding has been completed, a good grade of undercoating should be applied to the inside of the rocker panel and the outside of the floor.

ROCKER PANELS

Rocker panels are long, narrow box members, usually made of heavier metal than the rest of the exterior panels of the body. Both shape and construction limit the repair possibilities to what can be done from the outside or by piercing holes for pry or pulling tools.

Sometimes a crushed section can be pulled out by welding or brazing a piece of metal to an edge for a clamp. However, when damaged severely, the outer rocker panel usually will be removed to permit access to straighten the floor pan.

Because of complicated construction, it is common practice to replace only the damaged section instead of the complete panel. The hinge and center pillars sit on top of the rocker and are welded to it. This causes the upper flange to be sandwiched between inner rocker and the pillars. The problem is further complicated on some two-door models by the quarter panel welded to the outer edge of the top surface; this joint is welded in the factory before the body shell is assembled, but it is almost totally inaccessible on the assembled body.

When the areas under the pillars, and some two-door quarter panels, are undamaged it is common practice to make a straight-across butt joint within the door opening instead of removing the entire panel. This is a simple joint to make if the proper welding procedure is followed, but weld draw will warp the outer surface up or down if the joint is not aligned and tack-welded properly.

The welding procedure is illustrated in four progressive steps in A, Figure 8-65. After the panel has been cut and fitted, the procedure should be (1) weld the upper and lower flange to the inner panel, (2) tack-weld the outer edges and check the alignment, (3) add tack welds as needed in a skip pattern, and (4) complete the seam, welding no more than ½ inch (13 mm) in one place, allowing it to cool slightly and moving to another. A small flame should be used if welding with an oxyacetylene torch. Shielded arc with a cored electrode is a better method, if available.

Two butt joints are required when a section is welded into a door opening. If the piece is less than 1 foot (30 cm) long, the first and second steps should be completed for both joints, but the third and fourth should be completed on one weld at a time. Each completed weld should be allowed to cool before going to the next. If the welds are much closer together, it is better only to clamp the piece to the inner rocker panel, using vise

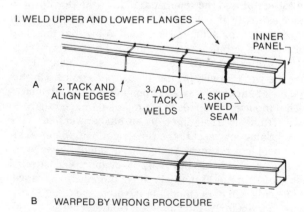

I. WELD UPPER AND LOWER FLANGES

INNER PANEL

A 2. TACK AND ALIGN EDGES   3. ADD TACK WELDS   4. SKIP WELD SEAM

B   WARPED BY WRONG PROCEDURE

8-65 A, the progressive steps to butt weld a rocker without causing warpage. B, warpage caused by improper welding procedure.

grip pliers on both flanges, and complete one weld. Then weld the flanges and complete the other, following the procedure described. This way, weld draw from the first will not affect the second weld.

B in Figure 8-65 illustrates what can happen if the joint is welded without concern for heat control. The outer surface is shown warped down, but it can go either way, depending on how the welding was done.

Extra care is desirable when welding in a new inner rocker panel. The accumulated weld can be enough to shorten the wheel base on one side of unitized construction if the welding is done carelessly. The floor pan should be held under tension, as shown in Figure 8-64, and a skip-weld pattern used to avoid getting any section hotter than necessary.

The time allowance should be based on what actually has to be done. When the entire side of a body has to be replaced, rocker panel replacement is relatively simple. It can be a much greater problem if the rocker is damaged from end to end but the other panels are not. However, putting a section in a door opening is relatively simple. Sometimes a short damaged section can be cut out, straightened, and put back in place to make a satisfactory repair more economically than a new part can be installed.

HINGE PILLAR AND COWL SIDE PANELS

A hinge pillar, cowl side panel, and their reinforcements make up a complex sheet metal structure that is relatively difficult to repair. It is often necessary to remove a damaged hinge pillar to provide access to straighten the inner parts. However, many damaged pillars can be repaired more economically than they can be replaced, leaving much of the original factory welding and sealing intact.

Use of a body jack diagonally across the cowl to push out a damaged pillar is not practical on most automo-

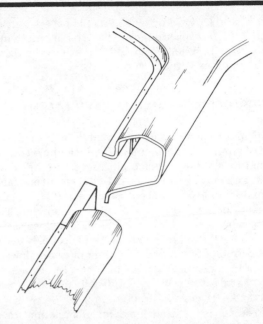

8-67 Offset joint in windshield pillar should be used to avoid continuous butt joint.

biles, because of the risk of damage to the opposite side by the base of the jack. The setup shown in Figure 8-66 is more practical. The method suggested is to drill a hole for an eyebolt in the heavy metal of the pillar; the hole must be welded shut or otherwise plugged later. The plate should have a hole of suitable size so that it can be placed over the bolt on the inside, making a positive connection when the nut is screwed on. The buckle should be heated because it is much stiffer than the rest of the structure. The flame should be kept off the eyebolt as much as possible.

No anchors are shown in this hookup, because method of anchoring will vary widely from one automobile to another. However, the anchor bar of a portable machine should *not* be used against the inside of the opposite rocker panel. This pull will require enough force almost to guarantee damage to the rocker panel. The anchoring problem should be checked before setting the time allowance, particularly on unitized construction.

This hookup can be used at any point, high or low, on the pillar. When used where the pillar is enclosed by a welded-on inner panel, it will be necessary to drill through both the outer and inner. When this is done, the plate should be large enough to cover the flanges of the outer; otherwise, the plate will be pulled into the pillar.

When replacing a hinge pillar that is not damaged in the upper end, it is common and acceptable practice to make the joint in the windshield opening instead. However, an all-around butt joint should be avoided by cutting the inner and outer at different positions, as shown in Figure 8-67. This way, each weld is reinforced by an uncut section of the other piece.

This method has two additional advantages: (1) the flanges can be clamped before welding and the opening adjusted to an exact fit for the glass before any welding

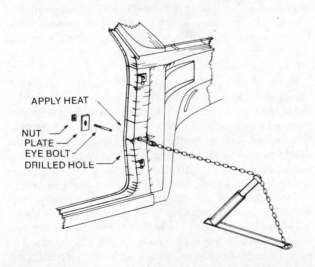

8-66 Use of eyebolt to straighten bent hinge pillar; method of anchoring not shown. Requires hole to be drilled and later filled.

APPLY HEAT

NUT
PLATE
EYE BOLT
DRILLED HOLE

is done, and (2) weld draw will be almost entirely eliminated if the flanges are tacked before the butt joints are made. The butt joints should be skip-welded, never straight across without stopping.

WINDSHIELD OPENING MISALIGNMENT

Windshield opening misalignment is almost always a part of a pattern of roof damage caused by either a side impact or a rollover. Some misalignments are obvious, but others may be missed by both the repairman and the estimator unless checked carefully. If the glass is cracked, broken, or popped out of its rubber channel, the opening is probably misaligned. The glass serves as a brace for the pillars as long as it is properly installed, but the pillars tend to bend at the upper and lower corners of the opening when the bracing of the glass is lost. They rarely bend in the midsection of the opening unless they receive a direct impact.

Three types of windshield misalignments are common: (1) one pillar bent inward without affecting the other, usually causing the header to raise away from the glass, (2) both pillars pushed to one side approximately equal amounts, and (3) the header collapsed, sometimes with part of it too high and part driven down into opening. Most windshield damages have a combination of two and sometimes all three of these conditions.

A jack is shown in Figure 8-68 set up diagonally from the right rocker panel to the left upper pillar. This will push the left pillar outward and draw the roof and right pillar with it. This setup can be made quickly and used for both the first and second condition, but the technique varies for each. For the first condition, the header will almost always be raised above the opening and the header buckled. The procedure is to heat the buckle before extending the jack, causing the buckle to drop instead of pulling the opposite pillar out of alignment—or, if the opposite pillar has shifted outward, not to pull it past the point of correction. The technique is to balance the heating and the jack operation so that the

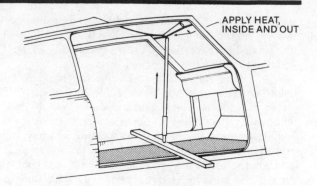

8-69 Jack set up to raise windshield header when collapsed into opening. Buckles, inside or out, should be heated as jack is operated.

header drops into position as the pillar moves outward. Not enough heat will draw the opposite pillar too far inward; too much will allow the heated area to stretch, making a mess out of the header.

It is better to make two or three tries, checking the opening between each, than to carry the operation too far. Diagonal measurements across the opening will provide a rough idea of the alignment, but the final check should be made with the glass set on the flanges. Before use, the glass should be taped around the edges both for safety and to reduce the risk of breakage. It may be found necessary to use a block of wood and a heavy hammer on the pinch weld flange on an area of the header that is hard to make drop into place. However, this should be avoided as much as possible, as it can make more problems than it solves; the block and hammer should *never* be used on the outer edge of the roof and used on the pinch weld *only* when the header is under tension.

When the block and hammer are used for the latter condition, both pillars shifted approximately the same amount, care must be exercised not to allow the header to flatten too much, a tendency always found in any curved member under tension. If the misalignment is minor, this tendency may be ignored. However, when the misalignment is greater, the pillars should be tied together in some manner, usually using clamps and either a pull jack or a turnbuckle.

When the header has been collapsed into the windshield opening, a sharp buckle will always be formed in the outer edge of the roof panel. This buckle will extend well back into the panel and usually form a high ridge in the midsection. Also, there may be a buckle on the inside of the header, caused by a portion of the windshield staying in the opening.

The header should be lifted back into general shape before correcting any sideshift. The jack setup shown in Figure 8-69 and the proper use of heat on the buckle (or buckles, if there are two) should raise the header and relieve most of the roof buckle at the same time. The jack should be equipped with a wide-blade-type fitting, to bear on the underside of the pinch weld before setting it in place with just enough pressure to hold it while the buckles are heated. A small torch tip should be used

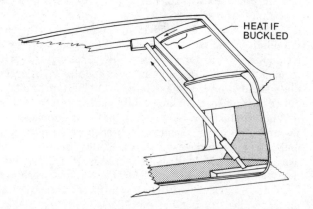

8-68 Jack set up to shift windshield pillars to the side. Header, if buckled upward, should be heated to aid reshaping.

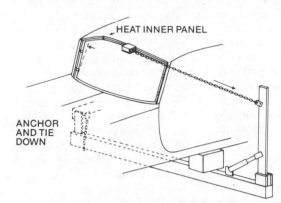

8-70 Portable frame machine set up to shift windshield pillars and straighten header. May be combined with use of jack, as shown in Figs. 8-58 and 8-59.

and the heat concentrated on the sharp creases. When the buckles are red hot, the jack should be extended rapidly so that the heat-softened metal will unfold with the least possible resistance.

In this operation, the roof buckles may usually be ignored until the header is back into position. However, if any valley buckles extend to the sides, it may be desirable to rough them out so that they do not interfere with the free movement of the roof panel.

The outside hookup shown in Figure 8-70 is not normally needed but is well worthwhile when one side of the header has buckled and the other side flattened, causing severe misalignment of the opening. When the proper position is selected on the pinch weld flange, this hookup will tend to draw raised areas down and push low areas up. Jacks can be used with this as needed. When an area has been raised quite high, it may be necessary to set up a jack diagonally to oppose the pulling action and concentrate more force on the buckle on the inner surface of the header.

This hookup is shown using a portable frame machine, but it can be done as well or better with any type of multiple hookup equipment. The body must be supported and anchored as shown, or the pull will simply tip it over. The dotted lines show the machine bearing against the inside of the opposite rocker panel. If this is done, the operator should watch the operation carefully. Most bodies have enough reinforcement in this area to withstand a light strain; the pillars and roof will not offer great resistance. However, another method of anchoring should be found if this area begins to crush. A block of wood of the right size should always be used between the anchor beam and the rocker panel.

CENTER PILLARS

Center pillars are rigidly reinforced by a heavy steel stamping that extends from the base to the midsection of the window. When this reinforcement has been driven out of shape by a direct impact, it is usually best to replace the pillar.

Center pillars are often bent in or out at the belt line without other serious damage. Either condition is relatively easy to straighten. An in-bend can be pushed out with a body jack based against the opposite rocker panel as shown in Figure 8-71 or pulled out with an external setup. Most out-bends can be straightened with a large C-clamp and a piece of wood, preferably 4 × 4 (10 × 10 cm), and the approximate length of the pillar. A smaller piece of wood should be used under the clamp at the belt line to protect the sheet metal. The piece of wood is placed upright against the inner surface of the pillar and the pillar drawn against it with the clamp.

A center pillar will occasionally be bent fore or aft by a door being driven against it or twisted by a rear door that has been struck from the rear while open. A fore or aft bend will usually be part of a damage pattern that will require other fore or aft pulls, with the pillar being pulled at the same time. The estimator can make a quick check for these bends by sighting across to the opposite pillar for an out-of-parallel condition.

Flat-rate time allowances for pillar replacement usually show two operations. One for replacement of the complete pillar, the other for cutting the pillar between the top of the reinforcement and the roof. The latter should be used unless the upper part is actually damaged or the roof is being replaced. The welds in the inner and outer should be staggered, as shown in Figure 8-67. Cutting the pillar in the reinforced section is not considered practical, because the reinforcement is completely covered by sheet metal, blocking access for welding.

8-71 Jack set up to push out bend in center pillar.

QUARTER PANELS

For the purpose of repair, the two-door quarter panel has three sections: (1) front, forward of the wheel opening, (2) center, over the wheel opening, and (3) rear. Each has different repair problems that vary to some degree by make and model, but in all the primary problem is access to the inner surface. Four-door models do not have the front section, but the problems in the center and rear are essentially the same as for the two-door models.

It is common practice to use panel pullers and filling to repair minor dents in all areas of the quarter panel. This is much more acceptable in the front and center sections, but not acceptable in the rear, where most of the inner surface is exposed to view when the trunk is open. Where it is practical to use hand tools or pry rods, they are preferable to the panel puller. Where the puller is used, the holes should be sealed, preferably by brazing. Weld-on pull tabs are acceptable in any area.

Probably the nearest to a typical problem is repairing major damage in the front section is re-establishing alignment of the pillar section to the front door. If door damage is involved, the repaired or replacement door should be installed and fitted to the rest of the opening so that the panel can be roughed out to fit. This is equally important if the panel is to be replaced.

A particular method or roughing out front-section damage cannot be recommended for conditions that vary widely. However, a repairman who understands rough-out procedures should be able to avoid serious problems in this area.

The rear section is exposed to both direct impact and secondary damage caused by frame impact on the rear end that carries through to the floor pan, quarter panel, and often the wheel housing. Repair procedures vary for conventional and unitized types. The greater flexibility of the unitized construction often permits the frame and body to be done separately. The lesser flexibility of the unitized body usually makes it necessary to straighten all of the damage as a single unit. The alternative is to remove the quarter panel, or portions of it, and straighten the rest of the structure so that a new panel can be fitted.

Quarter Panel Replacement

No attempt is made here to establish guidelines to follow in determining whether a damaged quarter panel should be repaired or replaced. However, it is emphasized that, when the panel is obviously repairable, the quality of the repair job may exceed the quality of the replacement when judged in terms of durability. It is desirable to retain as much of the original factory processing as possible. Welding, pre-paint processing, paint priming, paint curing, and sealing operations can be done in the repair shop, but not to the standards of quality obtainable in factory production. When the panel is judged not-repairable, it is still desirable to retain as much of the original factory processing as pos-

sible. For this reason, it is recommended that, when the damage is all within one section, only the portion of the new panel actually needed should be put in.

There is an occasional cost saving when the unused portion of a panel can be used on another job. However, this happens less often than might be expected. The most common saving is obtained when it is possible to replace the rear end of a two-door model with a less costly four-door panel. The rear-end section of some makes are identical in shape on two- and four-door models, but this is not true of all. If not known, this should be checked carefully before ordering parts. When there is a difference, it is usually enough to make alterations impractical.

Quarter Panel Sections

Some of the more common ways that a quarter panel can be sectioned are illustrated in Figure 8-72 by the dashed lines. This is not a copy of any particular panel, but is similar to many. The locations of dashed lines indicating where cuts may be made are intended as suggestions; variations of shape and window design will determine the exact location.

The rear section is the most commonly used. A cut in the general area indicated by line A will require the least labor and mutilation of the original structure. However, the shape of the side panel and the welding method to be used must be considered. Broad, nearly flat surfaces are more difficult to weld and finish smoothly than those with a fairly high crown, particularly if the welding must be done with a torch. Resistance spot welding in an offset joint is preferable. A skip pattern should be used if either arc-spot or brazing is used. A few skilled repairmen can butt weld a joint of this type and peen the weld smooth, using a hammer and dolly block, so that little or no filling is needed except at the ends. Whatever type of joint is used, the ends should be fusion welded.

When only the front section is needed, the panel can be cut in the general area indicated by line B. This requires cutting the window frame, preferably in the general area of the lines marked B, C, and D. Cutting the

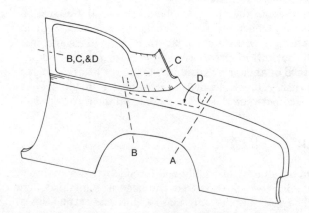

8-72 Various sections of a quarter panel that may be used when the complete panel is not needed.

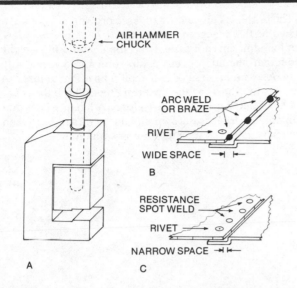

8-73 A, offsetting tool for use wth air hammer; B, spacing of offset seam desirable for either arc welding or brazing; C, close fit of offset seam desirable for resistance spot welding.

panel at either line C or D will permit putting in the complete lower section without disturbing the roof area; at C is preferable if the rear window must be removed for other purposes. If not, it is usually better to drop below into the general area indicated by line D. Line D may be the choice when the roof has a vinyl cover and the rear glass is unbroken. When the glass must be removed for other purposes, it sometimes is better to strip a vinyl roof cover back so that the weld joint will be in a covered area, particularly on a four-door model that does not have a quarter window.

Weld joints in window corners should be avoided, because they require considerably more time and effort to align and finish.

In general, the rest of the quarter and the adjoining panels should be aligned before cutting out the damaged section. However, strains in the damaged section may prevent re-alignment of other areas until cut away. Alignment problems must be solved according to the existing conditions.

Before any cutting is done, the lines to be cut should be laid out on both the damaged and the new panel. When more than one cut is to be made, the layout for the first one should be completed on both panels before going to another. The extra length for overlap seams should be on the new panel so that an air hammer-driven offsetting tool, as shown at A in Figure 8-73, can be used without interference. As shown at B, the gap between the panel edge and the shoulder of the offset should be wide if arc tacking or brazing will be used in welding the joint; this will keep the arc puddle away from the shoulder and permit better penetration of brazing metal between the surfaces. If resistance spot welding is used (C), it is better to leave as small a space as possible so that the weld spots can be staggered instead of kept in a straight line.

Before using the offsetting tool, the sharp crease lines should be notched slightly as shown in Figure 8-74, leaving that section to be butt joined, preferably by fusion welding. The offsetting tool may be used on fairly short radius curves without any problem, but attempting to use it across a sharp crease, as shown in the center section, will cause a high spot that will project above the surface.

The panel should be clamped in place and the alignment checked carefully. A few tack-welds may be required in the door or deck lid opening, but these should be kept to the minimum until *all* of the joints to be welded are in alignment. Removing the panel to correct a previously unnoticed misalignment is simple at this stage, but can be a real problem if extensive welding has been done.

When the alignment is correct, the overlapped seams should be drilled and fastened with pop rivets or metal screws, but not welded until the panel has been welded around the outer edges, making sure that enough spots are fastened securely enough to prevent any shifting due to weld draw. The butt joints at the ends of the overlapped seams should be welded before welding the seam. This is particularly important when the oxyacetylene torch will be used, because these joints will tend to draw the seam slightly. While it is still joined only by rivets or screws, the panel retains some flexibility to permit the surfaces to slip slightly as the butt welds cool and tend to draw them together.

The overlapped seam should always be welded in a skip pattern, if either arc or brazing is used. In quite flat areas, it is desirable to cover the edges of the seam with water-soaked asbestos if brazing is used, but this is not necessary for arc spotting. The important point is never to let any area get hotter than absolutely necessary. As a general rule, it is better not to quench welds, but it may be necessary if heat distortion is allowed to get out of control.

Brazing the full length of the overlapped seam may cause excessive heat distortion in the flat sections. This can be reduced by making short tacks, leaving approximately one half of the length unbrazed. Small spots, approximately ¼ to ⅜ inch (6–10 mm) long, are preferable to longer welds and gaps.

When using resistance spot welding, heat distortion is not a problem, but the seam can be misaligned by the pressure applied with the hand-held electrodes if

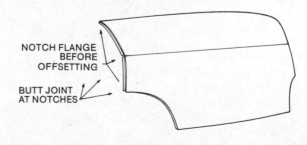

8-74 Notching of crease and sharp break-lines for offset seam.

enough rivets or screws are not used. In flat areas it may be necessary to place these no more than 2 inches (5 cm) apart to prevent slippage.

The finished seam should be checked for high spots before being finished with filler. If the seam is in an exposed area of the trunk, the rivets or screws should be removed. The offset seam should be sprayed with undercoating—normal procedure for any repair operation. Filling and finishing is the same as for any other repair operation.

The problems of welding reverse crowns are not mentioned in the preceding discussions, because very few are found in current styles, and the demand for weight reduction should prevent their return. However, any joint *across* a reverse crown should be offset unless the curve is too short for the upsetting tool. Those that cannot be offset should be butt welded. A lengthwise seam of a shallow reverse crown should be offset, but when the curve is short, a simple lap is satisfactory.

Doors

This discussion is limited to general information about (1) the basic sheet metal construction of passenger compartment doors, (2) weatherstrip sealing of door openings, (3) hinge operation and adjustment, (4) lock operation and lock striker adjustment, (5) door alignment procedures, (6) removing and replacing the door assembly, (7) major damage repair, and (8) outer panel replacement. No attempt is made to explain specific service procedures that vary from one make to another. The best and only reliable source of such information is the manufacturer's shop manual or service bulletins.

Although this discussion is limited to passenger compartment doors, much of the information applies to the other hinged assemblies, hoods, deck lids, hatchback lids, and station wagon tail gates. These other parts differ in detail but, with the exception of the two-way swing station wagon tailgates, service problems on them are less complicated than on doors. The two-way tailgate should present no serious problems to the repairman who understands the basic adjustments of hinges and door lock strikers.

DOOR CONSTRUCTION

Some of the important features of door construction are shown in detail in Figure 9-1, illustrating a front door; rear doors have similar features, except that many have fixed instead of movable glass. The details are representative of doors in general, not intended to show the exact construction of a particular one. The design can vary considerably and still accomplish the same purpose.

A spot welded hem-flange is shown in detail A. Although keyed to a single spot weld, this flange extends the full length of the front, lower, and rear edges of the outer panel and is welded at intervals of 3 or 4 inches. When the panel is stamped, the flange is left standing at a right angle to the surface so that it can be hemmed over in the assembly operation. When an outer panel is replaced in the repair shop, the hemming

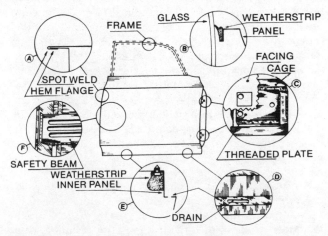

9-1 Typical door construction features.

operation is done with a hammer and dolly block. In factory assembly, the inner panel is placed into the outer and the flange is folded down by a hemming die. It then goes to a welding press that holds the assembly rigidly against another die while all of the welds are made simultaneously.

Welds made in the press join only the hem-flange to the flange of the inner panel facing. This is desirable for both the factory production and the repair shop situations. If they appeared on the other surface, it would be necessary to finish the surface before it could be painted in the factory. In the repair shop, it becomes a relatively simple operation to remove the outer panel by grinding through the edge, using a disc sander held at a right angle to the panel surface. Sometimes additional welds at the upper corners must be cut or broken; often the outer surface can be lifted off after the edge is ground, leaving the edge exposed so that the rest of the hem-flange can be broken off easily. Repaneling is described in more detail in a later section.

The detail of the upper flange and one method of sealing the space between it and the window glass are shown at B. Some flanges have a reinforcing piece welded to the flange, but many are as shown here. The rubber weatherstrip is attached to this flange, sometimes by screws, but more often by clips. This weatherstrip, not to be confused with the weatherstrip that surrounds the door, makes sliding contact with the door glass to seal out most of the weather. Ideally, it should seal out all air or water, but this is difficult to accomplish in practice. Drain holes provided to dispose of water and ventilate the inside are shown in detail D and will be explained later.

A similar weatherstrip is used on the inner surface of the glass. It is usualy attached to the upper edge of the door trim panel. Without it, there would be excessive air flow in or out of the body, depending on wind conditions and the direction of travel into or out of the wind. Other materials have been used for this weatherstrip; whatever is used, it must make sliding contact with the glass without scratching or too much friction, and it must provide good sealing.

The construction that permits the adjustment of bolt-on hinges is shown in detail C. The essential feature is fairly heavy steel plate, drilled and threaded to accept the hinge bolts, and held in place on the underside of the facing by a welded-on cage. The cage is large enough to permit the threaded plate to shift the full range of adjustment permitted by the oversized bolt hole in the facing, usually approximately 5/16 of an inch (8 mm). The usual practice is to shape the hinge so that the attachment to the pillar is at a right angle to the attachment to the door facing. Thus, the door can be shifted fore or aft on the pillar and inboard or outboard on the facing. An up or down adjustment can be made on either attachment.

A growing trend in automobile body design is to weld the hinges in place permanently in factory assembly. This requires very precise holding fixtures; otherwise, the doors would be difficult to align after installation on the body. The only possible adjustment for a welded-on

hinge is that which can be obtained by bending. When the hinge facing of either a door or pillar is damaged in collision, welded hinges complicate the straightening job, because very precise alignment must be restored.

The position on the dramin holes in the lower edge is shown in detail D. Only one hole is shown, but another would be located in the corresponding position at the opposite end, and some have a third hold in the center. These holes are located below and outside the weatherstrip so that water draining from the door goes to the outside. The position of the weatherstrip in relation to the drain hole is shown in the cross section in detail E. The arrow on the bent line leading from D into E indicates the drain hole position.

The weatherstrip in E is shown held in place by a plastic retainer. Holes for these retainers are spaced around the facing at suitable intervals, and matching holes are molded in the weatherstrip so that installation is simply a matter of pushing the retainers through the holes after they have been snapped into the rubber weatherstrip. The sealing action of weatherstrips is explained in a later section and illustrated in Figure 9-3.

The approximate position of the safety beam is shown in detail F. These beams, required by safety regulations in all passenger compartment doors, are made of heavier metal than the inner and outer panel and welded securely to the facings over the lock assembly. Safety regulations require door locks to remain securely attached to the striker and the striker to remain attached to the pillar when subjected to almost any strain caused by collision impact. Prior to the adoption of this type of lock and safety beams, it was not uncommon for a door to be driven through the opening into the passenger compartment by a relatively light impact. This construction has saved many lives and reduced the severity of many bodily injuries. Safety beams are required on the two-door-model quarter panels, but would serve no purpose on deck lids and hoods.

HINGE FACING REINFORCEMENT

The hinge facing is subjected to much more strain in normal operation than any other part of the door. It must be rigid enough to support the full weight of the door assembly and resist the twisting strain applied when the door is forced open as far as it will go. Some method of stopping travel is required on all doors; otherwise it could swing around and damage the adjoining panel. Whether the *stop* is built into the hinge or a separate link is used, it must be only a relatively short distance from the hinge pin. The opposite edge of the door is much farther away and has a proportional mechanical advantage over the much shorter leverage of the stop. The result is that the hinge pillar and the hinge facing of the door are subjected to tremendous forces when the door is pushed open against its stop.

One method of reinforcing the hinge facing is shown in the cross-sectional drawing in Figure 9-2. In this case

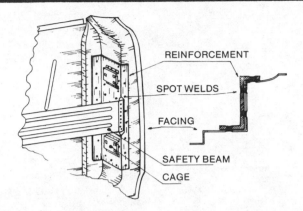

9-2 Inside view of typical door lock facing with reinforcement and safety beam. Cages allow threaded plate to shift up, down, in, and out.

the reinforcement is simply a liner stamped to fit into the inner surface of the inner panel and welded securely in place. The wide flanges and heavier metal provide sufficient rigidity to withstand any normal strain.

Other methods of reinforcement have been used by the various manufacturers. The one shown here is similar to methods in common use, but not representative of any particular make or model. All are rigid enough to withstand normal operating strains, but can be seriously damaged by a severe impact.

WEATHERSTRIPS

The sealing action of a door weatherstrip is shown in the cross-sectional view in Figure 9-3. At A the door is in the off-latch position, so that the weatherstrip is expanded to its full thickness. At B the door is latched. In this position the space between the door facings and body surfaces is less than the thickness of the soft weatherstrip, compressing it between the surfaces. In effect, it becomes a gasket to seal the opening.

The plastic retainer that holds the strip to the door is shown in C. The T-shaped head is installed in a cavity,

molded in the weatherstrip, through a small hole by stretching the rubber over it.

Weatherstrips for doors that have an upper window frame are usually made in one continuous piece. Doors that have the glass edge exposed, however, require a separate upper weatherstrip attached to the body opening instead of the door. The lower section would be unchanged, except for provision to seal the section at the base of the window opening where the upper and lower meet. This usually is done by vulcanizing specially molded pieces of sponge rubber to ends of the lower section.

The weatherstrip shape shown in cross section in this sketch is not intended to represent any particular make or model, but is similar to some in use. Many others are used by the various manufacturers. On many, the shape varies in different sections of the same weatherstrip. However, whatever the shape, they all seal in the same manner—by compressing the soft sponge rubber.

The pressure on a weatherstrip should be uniform, or very nearly so, all around the perimeter of a properly aligned door. Too much pressure at any one point will make the door difficult to latch; too little pressure will cause air and water leaks. In theory, the pressure should be correct when the door outer edges are spaced evenly in the opening and the surface is flush with the adjoining panel. In practice, variations are often found, sometimes due to a faulty panel, but more often due to improper straightening of a sealing surface.

Weatherstrip pressure can be checked by closing the door against a sheet of paper laid across the contact surfaces, as shown in Figure 9-4. The weatherstrip should grip the paper enough to require a definite effort

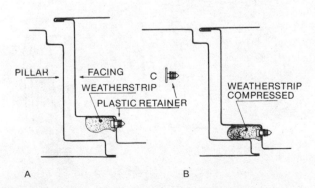

9-3 Weatherstrip attachment and sealing details. A, door open; B, door latched, compressing weatherstrip to seal opening.

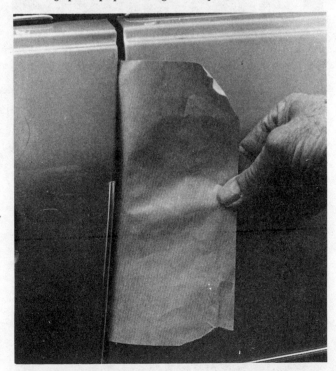

9-4 Checking weatherstrip pressure by withdrawing a sheet of paper with door latched. Pressure should restrict movement, but not enough to cause paper to tear.

to pull it out, but not enough to tear. If the paper is gripped too hard, the cause should be determined and corrected. It may require adjustment of one or both hinges or the striker, or it may be necessary to rework the contact surfaces.

Any weatherstrip will not retain its original shape, as shown in Figure 9-3 at A, after it has been in use for several months. Whether the automobile is in use or parked, the weatherstrips are almost always under pressure, because the doors are kept closed most of the time. The rubber tends to deform into the shape in which it is held. This will not affect sealing under normal circumstances. However, if the door is removed and replaced, the repairman should be careful to put it back in the original position. Even more care is desirable when a used door is removed from one body and placed on another immediately. There is usually enough difference in the two body surfaces to make some difference in sealing. Time will take care of such conditions, unless they are unusually bad, because the rubber will gradually expand to its original shape when the pressure is light.

HINGES

The obvious purpose of the hinges to to provide a pivot to permit the door or other hinged assembly to open, but most manufacturers add devices to limit the distance the door can open and a means of holding it open. How-

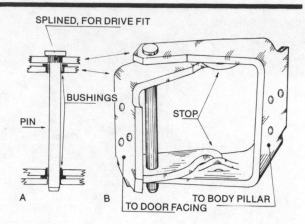

9-6 Mate to hinge shown in Fig. 9-5. A, details of hinge pin and bushing; B, hinge assembly with built-in stop.

ever, a few use separate devices for these purposes, usually a link between the hinge pillar and door facing that serves both purposes.

A photograph of a hinge with a built-in hold-open device is shown in Figure 9-5. A hinge of similar design, except that it has a built-in stop, is shown in more detail in B, Figure 9-6. The construction features of the pin and bushings are shown in A. The pin is splined under the head so that it is a drive fit in the bracket that attaches to the body pillar. The bushings, which are press fitted into the bracket that attaches to the door, provide a good bearing surface for the pin. The bushing material may be either bronze or plastic. If plastic, it is important that the hinge not be subjected to heat, which would melt the plastic.

The view of the hinge in B is from the angle of the passenger with the door open against the stop. Bolt holes are shown, as this one is intended as a mate to the door in Figure 9-5. However, similar hinges can be installed by welding simply by omitting the bolt holes and running a weld bead along the upper and lower corners of both brackets.

Figure 9-7 represents another type hinge used by

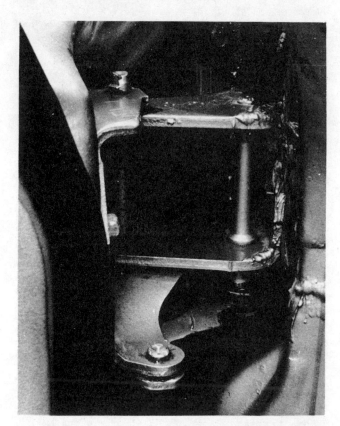

9-5 Typical bolt-on hinge with built-in hold-open device.

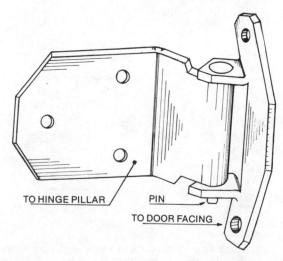

9-7 Hinge similar to some used on compact models.

9-8 A pair of weld-on hinges that have a bolt-on feature in the hinge pillar bracket.

some manufacturers, usually on relatively small automobiles. Bushings, if used, would be installed in the bracket that attaches to the hinge pillar, and the pin would be a drive fit into the bracket that attaches to the door facing. One or both brackets of this hinge can be attached by welding along the edges, but it has mostly been used with bolt-on attachment, as shown.

A photograph of a pair of weld-on hinges of entirely different construction is shown in Figure 9-8. This rather simple and quite practical hinge has a bolted joint in the bracket that attaches to the hinge pillar but requires a separate check link to stop and hold the door open. This door can be removed easily by disconnecting the check link and removing the two bolts in the hinge brackets.

Many other hinge designs are in use by the various automobile manufacturers, and others will come in the future. From the viewpoint of the repairman, the design of the hinge is important only insofar as it affects the problem of re-aligning the door after it has been misaligned either by collision or, sometimes, by normal

wear. Hinges that have a full range of adjustment are easier to adjust than those that are welded on and can be adjusted only by bending. However, an adjustable hinge *must* be re-adjusted every time the door is removed. The separate pieces of welded-on hinges must be located very precisely on the door and pillar facings so they will mesh and the pin can be inserted when the door is installed on the body, in factory assembly. Unless damaged severely, they do not present severe realignment problems. These problems are discussed more fully in the following Door Alignment section.

DOOR ALIGNMENT

Door alignment, or aligning, as the terms are used here refers to whatever operations are required to position a door properly within its opening. Some aligning may be needed as a follow-up to a major straightening operation, particularly if the door has been removed and replaced, the outer panel replaced, or a new assembly used. Each job must be analyzed to determine what is needed. The skill involved is mostly a matter of experience and good judgment; the manual dexterity required is relatively simple.

To be considered in alignment, a door should meet four conditions: (1) it should be centered in its opening so that the spaces between its edges and the adjoining panels are uniform, (2) the surface should be flush with the adjoining panels and continuous lines should match, particularly sharp creases or narrow ledges at the belt line or lower edge of the window opening, (3) all parts of the weatherstrip should seal against the contact surfaces of the adjoining panels, and (4) it should open and close easily without lift or drop as the striker enters the lock.

The space between the door edges and the adjoining panels is referred to in the following discussions as *edge gap*. When the edge gaps are acceptable, weatherstrip pressure and effort required for opening and closing will usually, but not always, be acceptable. When differences are found, they are more often caused by damage to one or both of the weatherstrip contact sur-

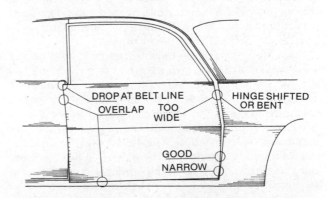

9-9 Effect of bent or shifted hinge. Other hinge serves as a pivot point, so that all points move in direct proportion to the distance they are from it.

faces than by variations in the panel caused by the manufacturing processes. Hard closing will almost always be caused by too much pressure on some part of the weatherstrip at some point.

The effect of a bent or shifted upper hinge is illustrated in Figure 9-9. The typical conditions are: (1) a V-shaped edge gap, narrow at the lower end and too wide at the upper, (2) a drop-off at the belt line on the lock pillar, (3) overlap on the adjoining panel, quarter or rear door, and the rocker panel.

When the position of one hinge is changed, the movement causes the entire door to tend to pivot around the other hinge. Thus, all points on the outer edge of the door move in direct proportion to the distance they are from the pivot point. This pivot action is shown in Figure 9-10. Although the movement is only a fraction of a degree, it should be considered as rotation around the other hinge, in this case the lower. Four radius lines are shown from the lower hinge: to the upper hinge, to the lock pillar belt line, and to both lower corners. Obviously, any movement at the upper hinge will cause much greater movement at the rear belt line and lower rear corner, but much less at the lower front.

The illustration shows the effect of shifting of the upper hinge, but a similar shift of the lower hinge would have an exactly opposite effect. This could be shown by turning Figure 9-10 upside down.

Correcting a misalignment due to a bent or shifted hinge is simply a matter of shifting it back to position. Bolted-on hinges can be loosened and moved, if not already at the limit of the adjustment range. When this occurs, either the attaching surfaces are bent, or the opening is out of alignment. Welded-on hinges can be adjusted only by bending.

INSTALLING AND ADJUSTING BOLT-ON HINGES

The correct procedure will simplify the adjustment of bolt-on hinges, whether they have been completely disassembled or only a slight shift of one hinge is required. One problem is that every time a hinge is loosened, the weight it supports is transferred to the other hinge, causing it to flex slightly and allow the door to drop in the opening. If the hinges are loosened and retightened alternately a few times, the door will drop the lowest part of the vertical adjustment range.

Some trial-and-error adjustments should be expected when replacing a door after the hinges have been completely disassembled. When replacing the door, it whould be set well above the proper vertical position to take advantage of the tendency to drop as the hinges are loosened in making adjustments. This is particularly important when installing a new door that has no hinge marks to aid in positioning the hinges. When reassembling the original hinges on the original door, it is best to position them to hold the door slightly high, because it is easier to lower it than to raise it.

To lower a door in the opening, (1) adjust the door facing bolts so they are snug but not tight, and (2) drive

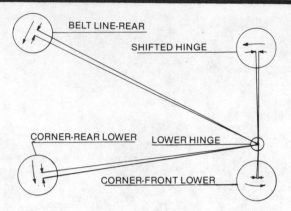

9-10 Movement of various points on door around other hinge, as shown in Fig. 9-9.

each hinge up on the door facing, using a block of wood and light hammer blows. To raise it in the opening, (1) place a support under the lower edge of the door close to the hinge pillar, and (2) drive each hinge down in the same manner. The support should be just high enough to hold the door an inch or two (2.5–5 cm) above its proper level; the support will reverse the strain on the hinges so the weight of the automobile will aid the shift. If the adjustment is made on the pillar instead of the facing, the hinge should be driven in the opposite direction.

After an adjustment has been made, the hinge bolts should be drawn up to the high limit of torque specified by the manufacturer. It is not practical here to give a torque specification that would apply to all hinge bolts, because of the wide variations from one make to another. Manufacturers specify torque for most of the bolts on their products. Their specifications should be followed.

When making a simple fore or aft shift at the upper hinge without changing the height of the door, the hinge bolts should be slacked off and the hinge driven into place. Before retightening the bolts, the hinge should be driven down slightly to pick up at least part of the weight transferred to the other hinge as it moved.

A hammer and a block of wood should be used to drive hinges either fore or aft, or up or down, if possible. However, this is not always practical when a front door hinge must be moved rearward while the fender is still in place. A slide hammer equipped with a hook should be used in such cases.

Hinges should never be driven into a "cocked" position. The upper and lower pins must be on or close to the same center line, or they will bind when the door is opened or closed, and the bushings will wear excessively. Fortunately, the elasticity of the metal will tolerate a reasonable amount of misalignment of the center line, and excessive misalignment can be avoided by use of *common sense*.

SHIFTING WELDED-ON HINGES

Welded-on hinges can be adjusted only by bending.

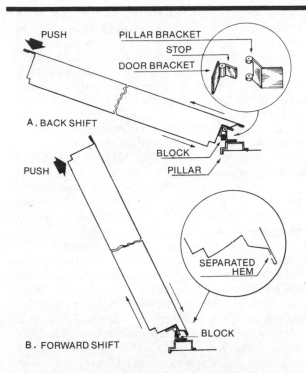

9-11 Cross sections showing blocking hinges to shift weld-on types in opening. A, shifting rearward; hinge detail shown in circle—typical but not a copy of any specific hinge. B, shifting forward; this operation is always done at the risk of separating the hem-flange, as shown in circle.

However, unless damaged, they should stay in alignment. The parts are located very precisely on the pillar and door facing in factory assembly and need very little further adjustment, unless they are bent or dislocated in collision. All doors with hinges of any type can be adjusted rearward (aft), as illustrated in A, Figure 9-11, and most welded-on hinges have a stop designed so that it can be used for a forward shift, as illustrated in B. To shift either way, an obstruction is placed in the hinge and the door forced against it.

This operation must be performed carefully to avoid breaking the hem-flange spot welds. When shifting aft, the outer panel pulls against the hem-flange, as shown by the arrows on A. There is risk of breaking the welds, but the flanges will not separate. When shifting forward, the outer panel pushes against the welds so that, if they break, the flange will separate, as shown in the detail linked to B.

A method of rewelding broken spot welds, using electric resistance spot welding, is explained in Chapter 5. Arc welding or brazing can be used if the resistance welder is not available. The separated flanges can be put back in place by blocking the hinge in the opposite direction. If the edges are fully separated, it is best to pry the hem up first, so there will be no interference. Sometimes the flange can be rewelded without removing the door.

Broken welds left unwelded are almost sure to cause annoying squeaks and will cause the facing to break if left long enough.

When the misalignment is more than just a slight condition, the exact cause should be determined. It may be that the opening is distorted. If so, the opening must be re-aligned before door alignment is attempted. Check the opening by measuring between the hinge and lock pillars on both sides of the car for comparison, at the points shown in Figure 9-12. The measurements can vary slightly, but a difference of more than ⅛ of an inch (3-4 mm) may be necessary to correct the opening before the door can be fitted.

These measurements will often save considerable time when re-aligning a door opening that has been damaged in a front-end collision. The measurement from pillar to pillar at the belt line must be reasonably close before the door is re-installed. This measurement will almost always be too short, because the pillar is often driven back but rarely driven forward.

Assuming that pillar-to-pillar measurement is correct, the measurements between the upper and lower hinges and the lock pillar, as shown, should be quite close to similar measurements taken either on the other door or on another automobile.

Use of a hammer and a block of wood to drive a welded-on hinge forward is shown in Figure 9-13. This is always better procedure than blocking a hinge for a forward shift, because it avoids the risk of breaking the hem-flange welds. However, this should not be done if the measurements shown in Figure 9-12 are correct, which indicates that any misalignment must be in the door facing.

Door facings are often driven inward at the upper hinge by the cowl and hinge pillar when the automobile has been involved in a front-end collision. In such cases the hem-flange welds will be strained and may be broken. If broken, the facing flange will move at least enough to crack the sealer, and it may separate from the hem-flange completely. This is the condition that should be repaired by forcing the door closed against a blocked hinge, as shown in A, Figure 9-11. However, if there is complete separation, the hem-flange should be pried open to permit free movement.

Any broken spot welds should be rewelded, but only after completion of any other alignment operations to be performed on either the door or the opening.

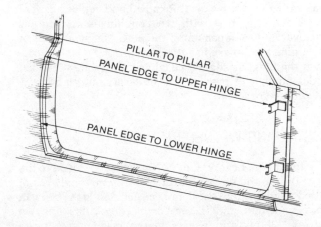

9-12 Measurements to check door opening alignment.

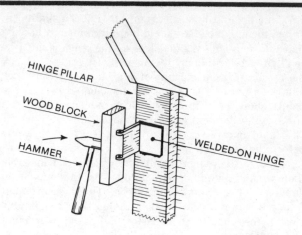

9-13 Driving a welded-on hinge forward. A safer method than blocking, as shown in Fig. 9-11.

A door facing can be pulled outward at the upper hinge by a hard side impact or a crushed roof that forces the hinge pillar forward. This condition can be determined visually, because the hinge will be bulged well above the rest of the facing. If the outer panel is to be replaced, the bulge can be straightened by blocking, as shown in B, Figure 9-11, because the welds will have to be broken anyway. If the door is to be repaired, it is much better procedure to straighten the bulge as shown in Figure 9-14, using a hammer and a block of wood. The rapid impact of the hammer blow is much less apt to break the hem-flange welds than the steady push used when blocking the hinge. The risk of hem-flange separation can be reduced further by welding it first, as shown. Oxyacetylene welding will make it necessary to repair the paint, but there is usually other damage that will require repainting; if not, it may be preferable to risk the separation and omit the welding. If rewelded by the electric resistance method, several welds will be required.

The probability of misalignment of the upper and lower hinge pins is less than with the bolt-on type, but it can happen if the repairman is careless in straightening a hinge pillar or has used too much force in the operation shown in Figure 9-11. Removal and replacement of any door equipped with weld-on hinges is done by removal and replacement of the pins. The small ends of most pins are tapered so that they can be installed easily if the hinge is slightly misaligned. Any misalignment great enough to prevent the pin from entering easily should be corrected.

INSTALLING WELDED-ON HINGES

The two hinge brackets, or *halves*, are assembled to the door facing and hinge pillar in manufacture and are not fitted together until the door is assembled to the body. In that operation, the factory door hanger fits the two halves together and inserts the pin. It is common practice for the upper pin to be inserted from the under side

and the lower from the top. A spring retainer clip may be used.

Although rarely required, when replacement of a welded-on hinge is necessary, it must be aligned exactly with the other hinge. The safest procedure is to drill and bolt the hinge in position on the facing and pillar temporarily so that alignment can be checked before welding. Depending on construction, it may be necessary to make an estimate of position off-the-body but, if possible, the door should be installed on the undamaged hinge and propped in alignment in the open position. If only one half is being replaced, it should be assembled to the other by installing the pin, and then drilled while in position if possible. If not, the position should be marked carefully before the hinge is removed for drilling. The drill used should be the tap size for the bolt that will be used, unless the inner surface can be reached to install a nut. After drilling, the hole in the inner surface should be tapped, and the outer one enlarged with an oversized bit to permit a degree of final adjustment.

Welding should be delayed until the final alignment has been established and the door opens and closes properly. If possible, welding should be done with the door in place, but, if it is necessary to remove the door, extra care must be taken to avoid shifting the only temporarily aligned hinge. Hinge construction varies too widely to specify exact welding procedures, but arc welding is usually best, if available.

In general, the construction of door facings and hinge pillars designed for welded-on hinges is not rigid enough to permit substituting bolts for welding.

It is rarely necessary to replace both hinges, because the door would probably be damaged enough to justify replacement, which would include the two hinge halves.

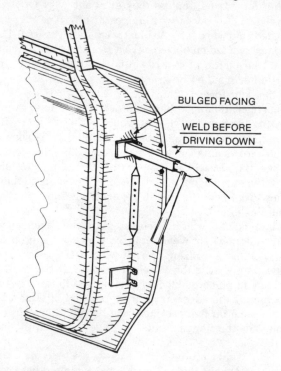

9-14 Straightening a bulged-out door facing with a hammer and block of wood.

However, if both hinges must be replaced, both halves of one hinge and one half of the other should be installed with temporary bolts. The general procedure outlined above would be followed from that point on.

LOCKS

In common usage, any mechanism that holds a hinged assembly in the closed position is called a lock. The locks on passenger compartment doors, deck and hatch lids, and station wagon rear gates serve two purposes: (1) they hold the unit in the closed but unlocked position, and (2) they lock to prevent entry without a key. A better term for the first purpose is *latching*, and that term is used in the following discussion of lock operation, except where the reference is to actual locking.

Any lock system consists of two primary units: the lock assembly and the striker. As stated in an earlier section, any lock and striker combination used on passenger compartment doors must conform to safety regulations: (1) the lock must not unlatch under sudden shock or strain, (2) the striker and lock must not sepa-

rate under tension, and (3) the latching mechanism must have two steps, so that the door will be held securely even though not quite fully closed. In effect, these regulations require that a door, when latched, must stay latched, unless the latching mechanism is literally torn apart. In addition to safety regulations, there are the obvious use requirements that, when latched, (1) the lock and striker should not rattle or cause other undesirable noises and (2) should open and close easily.

Many possible designs can meet the safety and use requirements for locks. One of the most common is the *fork bolt*. (In reference to locks of any type, the term *bolt* refers to whatever secures the striker; it has no reference to a threaded bolt.) In this type lock the striker is engaged by a fork-shaped bolt that holds the striker against a sliding wedge so that there is no movement in any direction. An outside view of one lock of this type is shown in Figure 9-15 in the unlatched position. In this view the ends of the fork bolt are labeled 1A and 1B, the tip of the arrow labeled 2 indicates the pin that serves as the pivot for the fork bolt, and the plastic wedge block is labeled 3. This plastic block is placed so that it will be pushed back against spring pressure as the striker reaches the latched position. The spring action wedges the striker securely between the fork bolt and the plastic block.

In Figure 9-16 the striker has been removed from the pillar and latched in place in the lock. It is held securely so that there is no possibility of movement to cause rattles or wear, whether the door is properly fitted or not. However, it will rattle in the safety position, because the striker will not be far enough into the lock to engage the wedge.

Unlatching is simply a matter of lifting a pawl, hidden

9-15 Typical door lock, as seen from the outside. 1-A and 1-B, ends of the fork bolt; 2, location of the fork bolt pivot; 3, plastic wedge block, with spring on wedge block hidden.

9-16 Striker, removed from pillar and latched in place in lock. One washer is always used; the second serves as a shim, when needed, to align the bolt to the striker assembly.

inside the lock, so that the fork bolt will be free to turn back to the unlatched position. This particular lock has no spring on the fork bolt to return it to the unlatched position, but one is not needed. Weatherstrip pressure will cause slight movement, but the person opening the door will push it away from the lock.

Locks built by other manufacturers operate in much the same manner, but differ in detail. Some have two fork-type bolts, one above and one below the striker. Others have a striker that consists of a loop of metal welded to a plate. No doubt, additional designs will be introduced but, whatever the design, the basic requirements will remain the same.

There are no adjustments on door lock assemblies, and parts are not available. If bent or otherwise damaged past the point of repair, the entire assembly must be replaced. Repairing should be limited to straightening minor bends in the lock frame. If the internal mechanism is damaged, replacement is justified for safety reasons.

An adjustment range of approximately ¼ inch (6 mm) up or down and in or out is provided for the striker by a threaded plate retained loosely be a cage, similar to the cage and plate provided for bolt-on hinges. In theory, the striker should be removed while the hinges are adjusted to hold the door in its proper postion; the striker should then be installed so that it enters the lock without causing the door either to lift or drop and holds the panel surfaces flush. In practice, it is not necessary, except when a major re-adjustment is needed. If the door seems in alignment but either lifts or drops when unlatched, it may be necessary only to re-adjust one of the hinges so that the door will meet the striker properly.

One heavy washer is always used under the base of a striker of type type shown in Figure 9-16 to provide rigidity. Sometimes extra washers are added to shim the head of the striker forward so that it does not make contact with the fork bolt as it enters the lock. The proce-

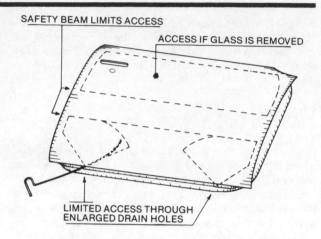

9-18 Areas of door that may be worked easily with pry rods inserted through enlarged drain holes.

dure for striker adjustment is essentially the same for any type of lock.

REMOVING AND REPLACING DOORS

A hydraulically operated door jack, of the type shown in Figure 9-17, will avoid the need for an extra man to help lift a door assembly while removing or replacing it. When a door is strapped in place on this jack (the straps do not show in the photo), it can be wheeled into place and held at the proper height, leaving both hands free to install the bolts or hinge pins. It has the additional advantage of reducing the chance of paint damage during the operation.

DOOR OUTER PANEL DAMAGE

Door panel damages that may be considered repairable can be classified into two broad groups: (1) simple dents, gouges, bent edges, and so on, which can be repaired with hand tools, and (2) major damage that has distorted the shape of the door so that it does not fit the opening. The latter usually requires a setup with pulling equipment to restore shape. Doors damaged more severely will require either repaneling or replacement.

SIMPLE DOOR DAMAGE

Access to the under surface is a problem on almost all doors. Although accessibility varies on different makes and models, it is the reason many repairmen rely—perhaps excessively—on the dent puller for repairing most dented panels.

Accessible dents often can be straightened with hand tools faster and better than with the puller, as shown in Figure 4-5. many late-model rear doors with fixed window glass are more accessible than the one in this

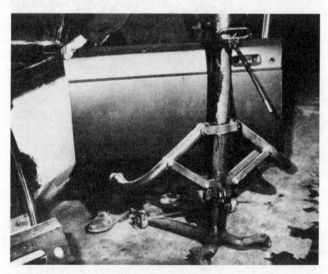

9-17 Hydraulic door jack, holding door in position for installation on the body.

example. Other areas, not accessible for hand tools but within reach of pry rods, can often be straightened as fast or faster without piercing the panel. Areas that can be reached easily are shown in Figure 9-18. If availble, weld-on tabs may be used in almost any area, but they require a resistance spot welder for application.

If quality workmanship is required, any hole pierced in the outer panel should be sealed shut and the entire repaired area undercoated with a good quality material. Moisture will attack the exposed edges of the holes and the underside of the filler material. Some fillers are claimed to be moisture resistant, but it is only common sense to avoid exposing the repaired area many more than necessary.

Holes can be either soldered or brazed shut, with brazing recommended here, because acid in the solder flux is difficult to neutralize. Traces of acid on the surface will cause rusting under the filler coat. There is no apparent problem with brazing done with flux-coated rods. The old-style dip-type brazing flux will leave lumps that should be chipped off. Holes can be brazed with very little heat distortion in most straightened areas, if a small tip is used.

The inner surface should be undercoated, using a high-quality material. Although both closing the holes and undercoating the panel are usually neglected, failure to do so is poor shop practice and is evidence of inferior work. In addition, an unprotected repair may quickly deteriorate, and come back to the shop at the repairman's expense.

MAJOR DOOR DAMAGE

Major door damage, as discussed here, includes conditions too severe to be repaired with hand tools. However, there is no attempt to establish the limit of repairability; that must be decided by the persons involved for the particular door.

Excepting deep, long gouges and torn metal, most major damage will involve crushed facing as well as the outer panel. Facings must be straightened properly to prevent an area of false-stretched metal in the adjoining panel section. An attempt to drive out a deeply crushed facing of the type represented by A and B in Figure 9-19 will upset the hem-flange and adjoining metal in both the outer panel and facing. These problems can be avoided by roughing the dented section out under tension and applying heat to permit the hem area to be pulled back to full length.

A is shown below the area of the safety beam where it would present the least straightening problem. A severely crushed facing in the safety beam area may require removal of the outer panel to permit straightening, creating the choice between repaneling or replacement. The crushed lower edge, shown in B, poses essentially the same problem, but straightening it can be more difficult, because the section is flat. The opposed arrows at the lower left-hand corner of A and B indicate edges drawn in by the crushed area.

Welding the hem-flange is indicated by notes on A, B, and C. There is always a problem of hem-flange separation on this type of damage. Before any straightening is started, the edge of the hem should be welded securely to the facing at the deepest point of the dent; if a long section is affected, additional welds should be made about 2 inches (5 cm) apart. The best results will be obtained by making a short weld bead, using the oxyacetylene torch and a steel rod. Brazing is not satisfactory; the sealer in the hem will probably prevent good penetration, and the metal may become embrittled.

Almost any practical means of applying tension is satisfactory. Clamp positions are shown in A with a double-pointed arrow to indicate that they should be pushed apart. Normally, the facing has some vertical crown, so it is desirable to place the clamps as close together as the conditions of the damage will permit. A body jack can be placed between them; alternatively, clamps that attach directly to the ends of a jack are available.

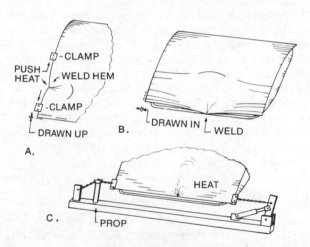

9-19 A, typical crushed door facing; B, typical crushed lower facing; C, tension setup, using portable body and frame machine; prop supports door at convenient height for easy working.

The sharply creased areas of both the outer edge of the panel and the facing should be heated as tension is applied. Hand-tool work may be needed on the facing but *must* be avoided while the metal is hot. The progress of unfolding should be watched carefully and hand-tool work delayed as long as the overall unfolding continues. As various buckles develop resistance to further unfolding, they should be relieved, usually by light hammer work on the outside. During the roughing-out process, there will usually be less need to lift low spots than to work ridges down. When lifting is necessary, careful work with a pry rod is preferable to use of a panel puller. However, not all areas can be reached with pry rods, so some work with the puller may be necessary.

A setup of the type shown in C for the lower edge is preferable to the use of a jack between clamps, as suggested for A. The anchor chain is supported by a piece of jack tubing with a V fitting on the upper end holding the lower edge of the door in level position and at a convenient working height. This would not be needed if an anchor beam with sufficient height was available. No support is shown under the upper part of the door; anything of convenient height is satisfactory, because the door is held rigidly as long as it is under tension.

There are many other ways of applying tension. Any method that will maintain steady, controlled tension to pull the panel and facing into shape is satisfactory. It is particularly important to have the capacity to apply considerable force for the final pull. Sometimes a severe buckle may need an extra setup with a jack and pair of clamps; most of the adjoining area should be relatively smooth, but, if any area of false stretch appears in the panel, it will be due to *unrelieved* upset in the hem area. Heat and tension should relieve the upset. The process should be continued until the bulged area of false stretch disappears.

Do *not* quench an area heated for this purpose, and do *not* release tension on a heated area until it has cooled far below the red heat range.

The effort and time spent in properly roughing out door damages of the type discussed here should be more than regained in the finishing process. Assuming there are no long tears or deep gouges, excessive effort to metal-finish or a deep build-up of filler should not be required.

A good-quality undercoating should be applied to the inner surface of any panel that has been repaired, particularly to areas that have been heated in the process of repair.

DOOR OUTER PANEL REPLACEMENT

Door outer panels, often called "skins," are available for many makes and models. Because the cost for a skin is considerably less than for a door assembly, many shops consider it normal procedure to replace a severely damaged outer panel if the inner and safety beams are either undamaged or easily repairable. Many insurance adjustors insist on using an outer panel in those circumstances. However, there is no uniform practice; some that should be replaced are repaneled, and other that could be repaneled easily are replaced.

There is a valid argument against repaneling doors on nearly new automobiles. The new door assembly has been through the factory processes of weld-through sealing, welding, phosphate coating, and primed with bake-on-type primer. The outer panel has had the same paint pre-preparation and priming, but the repair shop must break the primer to weld it to the inner panel. Also, many shops omit any sealing between the surfaces. Some repairmen further complicate the problem by not turning the hem-flange properly, and then find it necessary to use filler on the outer surface of the new panel to fill rough spots caused by poor workmanship. When done in this manner, the only rust protection for the bare metal in the seam is whatever sealer is applied to the hem-flange. The inner surface is exposed to any

moisture or chemicals, usually salt, that enter through the glass opening.

This argument can be largely offset by applying a bead of good grade sealer to the inner surface of the outer panel, preparing the hem-flange for welding, turning the hem-flange properly, and using good welding technique. When the door is installed properly and the hem-flange is sealed, the quality of a repaneled door is close to that of the original.

Any repair work required on the inner panel or safety beam should be done after removal of the outer panel—with one exception: A bulged-out hinge facing should be straightened by blocking the hinge, as shown in Figure 9-11, while the edge is held by the hem-flange welds. This will be quicker than straightening it afterward. If the hem-flange welds break, it is no real loss, because they are to be broken anyway.

Most doors require complete removal of glass, trim, and weatherstrips for repaneling. However, a few have no welding across the upper edge, making it possible to repanel them without disassembly other than of the weatherstrip. When this is done, the upper edge and flange should be painted and the weatherstrip installed before the panel is put on the door. Lacquer can be used for this if enamel paint is to be used. The color should be close, but a match is not necessary, because any exposed paint will be repainted.

The steps in repaneling are (1) remove outer panel, (2) if it is damaged, straighten facings and safety beam, (3) if facings or safety beam have been straightened, rehang inner panel in opening to check fit, (4) prepare hem-flange surfaces for welding, (5) assemble inner and outer with bead of sealer between surfaces, (6) turn hem-flange, (7) weld, and (8) seal hem-flange.

A disc sander should be used to separate the outer panel from the hem-flange, as shown in Figure 9-20. When held at a right angle to the surface, a sharp disc will cut through the exposed edge rapidly, leaving the hem-flange still attached but easy to remove. Separating it across the upper edge will require breaking any

9-20 Grinding hem-flange through with disc sander.

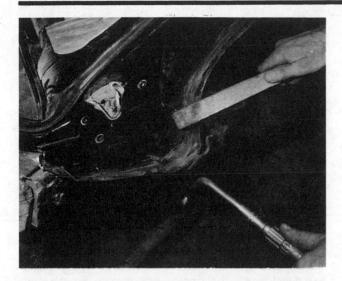

9-21 Wire-brushing sealer after scorching it with an oxidizing flame.

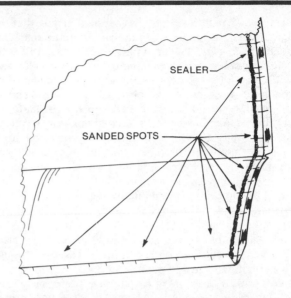

9-22 Preparation of new panel for brazing or spot welding.

welds found. There is too much difference in makes and models to give exact instructions.

Crushed flanges can be straightened much easier with the outer panel removed. Careful work with the hammer and dolly is all that is needed on most, but it is important that the alignment should be checked by hanging the inner panel back in the opening in the latched position. At this point it is very simple to make any needed corrections of the outer flange if it is not flush with the adjoining panels or the edge gap is either too wide or too narrow. Allowance should be made for the thickness of the outer panel in checking both. If the panel is welded on before making any needed corrections, correcting them will be a major operation that could have been avoided.

When the facings or safety beam have not been damaged, or the door twisted, checking is not necessary.

Cleaning the inner-panel flange requires removal of the old hem-flange and sealer. Some of the hem welds will separate by raising the end of the flange and twisting it back and forth; those that do not break readily should be ground off after breaking or cutting most of the flange away. It is best to avoid breaking the weld button out of the flange.

Before grinding the weld buttons, the old sealer should be removed; otherwise it will smear the disc and later interfere with the welding operation. Part will scrape off, but most should be wire-brushed, as shown In Figure 9-21, after scorching with an oxidizing flame. The flame should be kept in rapid motion to avoid overheating.

Brazing requires removal of the primer from the inside of the hem-flange, and electric resistance welding requires it to be removed from both inside and out. Hand sanding is much safer than using a disc on the inner surface; the disc may catch on the narrow flange and hurl broken pieces at high speed in any direction. For brazing, spots should be selected a few inches apart, as indicated in Figure 9-22, sanded clean and

marked on the outside so that they will not be lost when the flange is turned. For resistance spot welding with twin, hand-held electrodes, the spots should be selected in pairs; if preferred, an oscillating sander may be used on the outer surface. A high-speed disc sander may thin the edge unevenly and make it difficult to make a smooth hem joint.

A small bead of good grade sealer should be laid close to the hem-flange along its full length. This is shown in both Figure 9-22 and A in Figure 9-23. Excessive sealer should be avoided, because it will spill out into the hem-flange and interfere with welding if either brazing or arc welding is to be used. However, if resistance spot welding will be used, a small amount of weld-through sealer should be applied. Sharp corners should be notched out.

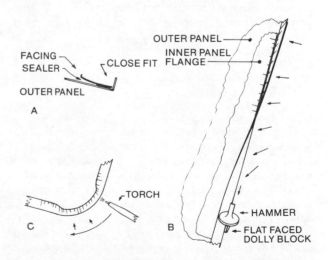

9-23 Assembling the panels. A, cross section showing proper fit; B, turning the flange; C, heating curved flange to avoid wrinkling.

The hem-flange can be turned, or hemmed, so that the edge of the outer panel will require very little finishing, if done properly. The technique (Fig. 9-23, in B) is to avoid stretching the edge of the hem by driving it down a little at a time. The door assembly should be placed on a padded bench, outer panel down, and positioned so that the outer edge can be backed up with a flat-faced dolly block. As shown, the flange should make a long, sweeping turn by using the hammer back and forth along the edge and changing the angle to follow the movement. The arrows along the right side represent a series of progressive hammer blows, each of which should be backed up by the dolly. The flange should be driven down until the three surfaces are in contact, but *no more*.

A piece of heavy-duty jack tubing or a round steel shaft may be used to back up sharp reverse crowns. This is not illustrated, as it would be essentially the same as other areas. It is best to use a hammer with a suitable radius on these crowns, but the high crown part of dolly block may be used as a hammer instead.

When a door has a rounded corner, that should be hemmed last. As shown in C, the adjoining edges should be hemmed as close as possible without causing buckles. Then, the oxyacetylene torch, adjusted to a small flame, should be passed around the corner just fast enough to heat the upper edge red hot. The edge should be driven down in much the same manner as on the straight sections. When heating, the flame should be kept away from the outer panel surface. Reheating may be necessary.

When hemmed, the assembly should be turned over and the edges welded.

WELDING HEM-FLANGES

The hem-flange should be welded to the facing without warping the outer panel and causing an unnecessary repair on a new panel. This is no problem using an electric resistance spot welder, but brazing and arc welding must be done carefully. Brazing is the most commonly used and the most apt to cause warpage.

Brazing

The tip used should be small, preferably No. 1, adjusted to a small, neutral flame, and the rod should be flux coated. The torch and rod positions for the start of the operation are shown in Figure 9-24. The flame is directed on the facing close to the edge of the hem-flange. The end of the filler rod is placed very close to the surface, where it will protect the edge of the flange while it heats. The double arrows on both rod and torch indicate in-and-out motion but no weaving. The rod should be withdrawn if it reaches melting temperature before the facing is hot enough. The torch should be withdrawn if the edge of the hem flange gets too hot before the facing is ready. Weaving to spread the heat

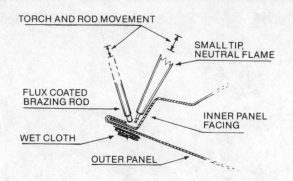

9-24 Correct torch position for brazing the hem-flange.

will only guarantee warping the outer panel. When this is done properly, one drop of molten brazing metal will be deposited next to the edge and will flow into the joint by capillary action. The flame should be removed instantly.

Further build-up of filler rod will add practically no strength to the joint, but the extra metal will hold heat and increase the tendency for warpage. A folded wet cloth is shown on the underside to absorb heat. It can be held in place with a locking welding clamp. Use of a cloth is not as important on the crowned part of the front and rear edges, but it is desirable. It should always be used on the lower.

Arc Welding

Skill and equipment are important factors for welding the hem-flange with the conventional arc method. A skilled welder, using a small electrode and a good machine having fine control in the low power range, can weld a door flange easily and quickly. Only a very small tack-weld is needed to join the edge of the hem-flange to the facing. A larger weld is both unnecessary and an almost sure guarantee of heat distortion in the new panel.

Any build-up of weld metal should be ground off. However, this should not be a problem to a welder having the required skill. No one should try arc welding a door hem-flange without having had enough practice tacking sheet metal, using the same equipment and electrodes, to feel confident of his ability.

MIG and TIG

Both the MIG and TIG methods are well adapted to this type of welding. Assuming that the equipment is available and has the capacity to work in the sheet metal range, either is a very good method on hem flanges. Many MIG machines are equipped with a timer for spot welding; if available, this should provide more consistent results than doing it manually.

Whatever method is used, conventional, MIG, or TIG, if it is done properly, the final sealing will conceal it.

FINISHING THE PANEL EDGE

Some finishing will be required around the outer edges of the new panel, but this should be a relatively simple job, if the flanging and welding have been done correctly. The lower edges should be checked with a straightedge and the high and low spots straightened. This will be simple *if* the edge has not been hammered too much in the flanging operation. All the edges should be examined both visually and by feeling, and straightened as necessary. It should be possible to do most of the finishing with a few passes of a fine-grit disc on a conventional sander.

Sealing and Undercoating

A sealer that can be painted should be applied to the hem-flange between the primer and color coats. It should be smoothed enough to restore the original appearance, which should be no problem if no built-up welds are projecting through it.

The inner surface of the new panel should be sprayed with a good grade of undercoating. It may be necessary to do this after the painting operation is complete, if heat is used to dry the paint; otherwise, the undercoating may run down to the lower part of the door and clog the drain holes.